T0251833

MINING USER GENERATED CONTENT

Chapman & Hall/CRC
Social Media and Social Computing Series

Series Editor
Irwin King

Published titles

Mining User Generated Content
Marie-Francine Moens, Juanzi Li, and Tat-Seng Chua

Chapman & Hall/CRC
Social Media and Social Computing Series

MINING USER GENERATED CONTENT

Edited by

Marie-Francine Moens
Katholieke Universiteit Leuven
Belgium

Juanzi Li
Tsinghua University
China

Tat-Seng Chua
National University of Singapore
Singapore

CRC Press
Taylor & Francis Group
Boca Raton London New York

CRC Press is an imprint of the
Taylor & Francis Group, an **informa** business
A CHAPMAN & HALL BOOK

CRC Press
Taylor & Francis Group
6000 Broken Sound Parkway NW, Suite 300
Boca Raton, FL 33487-2742

© 2014 by Taylor & Francis Group, LLC
CRC Press is an imprint of Taylor & Francis Group, an Informa business

No claim to original U.S. Government works

ISBN 13: 978-1-4665-5740-6 (hbk)

This book contains information obtained from authentic and highly regarded sources. Reasonable efforts have been made to publish reliable data and information, but the author and publisher cannot assume responsibility for the validity of all materials or the consequences of their use. The authors and publishers have attempted to trace the copyright holders of all material reproduced in this publication and apologize to copyright holders if permission to publish in this form has not been obtained. If any copyright material has not been acknowledged please write and let us know so we may rectify in any future reprint.

Except as permitted under U.S. Copyright Law, no part of this book may be reprinted, reproduced, transmitted, or utilized in any form by any electronic, mechanical, or other means, now known or hereafter invented, including photocopying, microfilming, and recording, or in any information storage or retrieval system, without written permission from the publishers.

For permission to photocopy or use material electronically from this work, please access www.copyright.com (http://www.copyright.com/) or contact the Copyright Clearance Center, Inc. (CCC), 222 Rosewood Drive, Danvers, MA 01923, 978-750-8400. CCC is a not-for-profit organization that provides licenses and registration for a variety of users. For organizations that have been granted a photocopy license by the CCC, a separate system of payment has been arranged.

Trademark Notice: Product or corporate names may be trademarks or registered trademarks, and are used only for identification and explanation without intent to infringe.

Visit the Taylor & Francis Web site at
http://www.taylorandfrancis.com

and the CRC Press Web site at
http://www.crcpress.com

Contents

Michal Ptaszynski, Yoshio Momouchi, Jacek Maciejewski, Pawel Dybala, Rafal Rzepka, and Kenji Araki

Chin-Yew Lin

Marie-Francine Moens, Juanzi Li, and Tat-Seng Chua

Foreword

I am delighted to introduce the first book on multimedia data mining. When I came to know about this book project undertaken by three of the most active researchers in the field, I was pleased that it was coming in the early stages of a field that will need it more than most fields do. In most emerging research fields, a book can play a significant role in bringing some maturity to the field. Research fields advance through research papers. In research papers, however, only a limited perspective can be provided about the field, its application potential, and the techniques required and already developed in the field. A book gives such a chance. I liked the idea that there would be a book that would try to unify the field by bringing in disparate topics already available in several papers, which are not easy to find and understand. I was supportive of this book project even before I had seen any material on it. The project was a brilliant and a bold idea by two active researchers. Now that I have it on my screen, it appears to be even a better idea.

Multimedia started gaining recognition as a field in the 1990s. Processing, storage, communication, and capture and display technologies had advanced enough that researchers and technologists started building approaches to combine information in multiple types of signals such as audio, images, video, and text. Multimedia computing and communication techniques recognize correlated information in multiple sources as well as an insufficiency of information in any individual source. By properly selecting sources to provide complementary information, such systems aspire, much like the human perception system, to create a holistic picture of a situation using only partial information from separate sources.

Data mining is a direct outgrowth of progress in data storage and processing speeds. When it became possible to store a large volume of data and run different statistical computations to explore all possible and even unlikely correlations among data, the field of data mining was born. Data mining allowed people to hypothesize relationships among data entities and explore support. This field has been applied in many diverse domains and continues to experience even more applications. In fact, many new fields are a direct outgrowth of data mining and it is likely to become a powerful computational tool.

Irwin King

Preface

In recent years, we have witnessed the convergence of social networks, mobile computing, and cloud computing. These trends have encouraged users to carry out most of their social interactions online on social networks and on the move. Through these social networks, users routinely comment on issues, ask questions, provide answers, tweet or blog about their views, and conduct online purchases. Through their mobile devices, they perform spontaneous check-ins to their favorite venues, and readily share their photos and videos of local situations, and so on. The content accumulated has evolved into a huge unstructured source of timely knowledge on the cloud, which forms a rich part of users' social engagements and communication.

Statistics on Facebook[1] and social networking[2] indicate that over 11% of people worldwide now use Facebook (which amounts to 1.15 billion users) with 680 million mobile Facebook users, while 98% of 18 to 24 year olds in the United States are already social network users. Each day, Facebook users share 2.3 billion pieces of content and upload 250 million photos. Outside Facebook, social network users post 190 million tweets on Twitter, and view over 3.1 billion videos on YouTube. In terms of e-commerce, the percentage of retail sales that are made online in United States is 8%, and the number of online users who have made an Internet purchase is 83%.[3] The statistics are even more tilted toward social networking and mobile computing in China.[4] These overwhelming statistics clearly demonstrate the pervasiveness and influence of social media today.

The social media shared by users, along with the associated metadata, are collectively known as user generated content (or UGC). UGC comes from a myriad of sources, including the social networking sites like Facebook and LinkedIn; live microblog sites like Twitter; mobile sharing sites like 4Square and Instagram; information sharing sites like forums and blogs; image and video sharing sites like Flickr and YouTube; and the various community question-answering sites like Wiki-Answers and Yahoo! Answers; as well as their counterparts in China. The content comes in a variety of languages

---

[1] http://expandedramblings.com/index.php/by-the-numbers-17-amazing-facebook-stats/

[2] Statistic Brain on Social Networking Statistics dated November 2012; http://www.statisticbrain.com/social-networking-statistics/

[3] Statistic Brain on E-Commerce/Online Sale Statistics dated August 2012; http://www.statisticbrain.com/total-online-sales/

[4] http://www.go-globe.com/blog/social-media-china/

such as English and Chinese, and modalities such as text, image, video, and location-based information, and the corresponding metadata. In addition to the multisource, multimodal, and multilingual content, another important element of social media is the users and their relationships. It is noted that the most useful UGC comes mainly from the publicly available data sources that reflect the social interactions of people.

To analyze and fuse these UGCs, we need techniques to deal with the huge amount of real-time multimedia and multilingual data. In addition, we need to tackle the social aspects of these contents, such as user relations and influential users, and so on, with respect to any topics. This offers new challenges that have attracted a lot of active research. Various higher order analytics can be mined and extracted, including structures of UGC with respect to any given topic, live emerging and evolving events/topics; relationships between key users and topics, user communities, and the various events/activities with respect to location, people, and organizations. Key research areas of UGC include: (a) reliable strategies for harvesting representative UGC with respect to any topic; (b) indexing and retrieval of huge media resources arising from these media; (c) organization of unstructured UGC and users on any topic into structured knowledge and user communities; (d) fusion of UGC to generate analytics related to location, people, topic, and organization; and (e) basic research on the analysis and retrieval of text, live discussion streams, images, and videos.

Many large research groups now collect, index, and analyze UGC, with the aim of uncovering social trends and user habits. One example of such an effort is the NExT Research Center jointly hosted at the National University of Singapore and Tsinghua University [141], which focuses on harvesting and mining the huge amount of UGC in real-time and across cultural boundaries. A global effort centering around the idea of the Web Observatory by the Web Science Trust is also taking shape, Web Science Trust: The Web Observatory.[5] The Web Observatory aims to coordinate the common use of social UGC data collected and analytics developed by the various social observatory systems from around the world. Central to the establishment of a Web observatory is the selection of a profile of standards, which each Web observatory node must adopt to facilitate data sharing. This effort is expected to benefit many users and researchers of social media. Given the active range of research and activities on UGC, it is timely to initiate a book that focuses on the mining of UGC and its applications.

This book represents the first concerted effort to compile the state-of-the-art research and future direction on UGC research. The book is divided into four parts. The first part presents the introduction to this new and exciting topic. Part II introduces the mining of UGC of different medium types. Topics discussed include the social annotation of UGC, social network graph construction and community mining, mining of UGC to assist in music

---

[5]http://Webscience.org/Web-observatory/

retrieval, and the popular but difficult topic of UGC sentiment analysis. Part III then discusses the mining and searching of various types of UGC, including knowledge extraction, search techniques for UGC, and a specific study on the analysis and annotation of Japanese blogs. Finally, Part IV presents the applications, in which the use of UGC to support question-answering, information summarization, and recommendation is discussed.

The book should be of interest to students, researchers, and practitioners of this emerging topic.

Marie-Francine Moens, Juanzi Li, and Tat-Seng Chua

Editors

Marie-Francine Moens: Marie-Francine (Sien) Moens is a professor at the Department of Computer Science of the Katholieke Universiteit Leuven, Belgium. She holds an M.Sc. and a Ph.D. degree in computer science from this university. She is head of the Language Intelligence and Information Retrieval (LIIR) research group (http://www.cs.kuleuven.be/groups/~liir/), and is a member of the Human Computer Interaction unit. Her main interests are in the domain of automated content retrieval and extraction from text using a combination of statistical, machine learning, and symbolic techniques, and exploiting insights from linguistic and cognitive theories. Dr. Moens is author of more than 240 international publications among which are two monographs published by Springer. She is coeditor of 15 books or proceedings, coauthor of 40 international journal articles, and 29 book chapters. She is involved in the organization or program committee (as PC chair, area chair, or reviewer) of major conferences on computational linguistics, information retrieval, and machine learning (ACL, COLING, EACL, SIGIR, ECIR, CORIA, CIKM, ECML-PKDD). She teaches courses on text-based information retrieval and natural language processing at KU Leuven. She has given several invited tutorials in summer schools and international conferences (e.g., tutorial "Linking Content in Unstructured Sources" at the 19th International World Wide Web Conference, WWW 2010), and keynotes at international conferences on the topic of information extraction from text. She participates or has participated as a partner or coordinator of numerous European and international projects, which focus on text mining or the development of language technology. In 2011 and 2012, Dr. Moens was appointed as chair of the European Chapter of the Association for Computational Linguistics (EACL) and was a member of the executive board of the Association for Computational Linguistics (EACL). She is a member of the Research Council of the Katholieke Universiteit Leuven. E-mail: marie-francine.moens@cs.kuleuven.be

Juanzi Li: Juanzi Li is a full professor at Tsinghua University. She obtained her Ph.D. degree from Tsinghua University in 2000. She is the principal of the Knowledge Engineering Group at Tsinghua University. Her main research interest is to study semantic technologies by combining natural language processing, semantic Web, and data mining. She is the Vice Director of the Chinese Information Processing Society of the

Chinese Computer Federation in China. She is principal investigator of the key project cloud computing based on large-scale data mining supported by the Natural Science Foundation of China (NSFC), she is also the PI of many national basic science research programs and international cooperation projects. Dr. Li took the important role in defining Chinese News Markup Language (CNML), and developed the CNML specification management system which won the "Wang Xuan" News Science and Technology Award in 2009 and 2011. She has published about 90 papers in many international journals and conferences such as WWW, TKDE, IJCAI, SIGIR, SIGMOD, and SIGKDD. E-mail: lijuanzi2008@gmail.com

Tat-Seng Chua: Tat-Seng Chua is the KITHCT chair professor at the School of Computing, National University of Singapore. He was the acting and founding dean of the school from 1998–2000. Dr. Chua's main research interest is in multimedia information retrieval, question-answering (QA), and live social media analysis. He is the director of a multimillion-dollar joint center between NUS and Tsinghua University in China to develop technologies for live social media searches. The project will gather, mine, search, and organize user generated content within the cities of Beijing and Singapore. Dr. Chua is active in the international research community. He has organized and served as the program committee member of numerous international conferences in the areas of computer graphics, multimedia, and text processing. He was the conference cochair of ACM Multimedia 2005, ACM CIVR 2005, and ACM SIGIR 2008. He serves on the editorial boards of: ACM Transactions of Information Systems (ACM), Foundation and Trends in Information Retrieval (NOW), the Visual Computer (Springer Verlag), and Multimedia Tools and Applications (Kluwer). He is a member of the steering committee of ICMR (International Conference on Multimedia Retrieval) and Multimedia Modeling conference series; and is member of the International Review Panel of two large-scale research projects in Europe. E-mail: chuats@comp.nus.edu.sg

Contributors

Kenji Araki: Kenji Araki received BE, ME, and Ph.D. degrees in electronics engineering from Hokkaido University, Sapporo, Japan, in 1982, 1985, and 1988, respectively. In April 1988, he joined Hokkai-Gakuen University, Sapporo, Japan, where he was a professor. He joined Hokkaido University in 1998 as an associate professor in the Division of Electronics and Information Engineering and became a professor in 2002. Presently, he is a professor in the Division of Media and Network Technologies at Hokkaido University. Dr. Araki's research interests include natural language processing, spoken dialogue processing, machine translation, and language acquisition. He is a member of the AAAI, IEEE, JSAI, IPSJ, IEICE, and JCSS. E-mail: araki@media.eng.hokudai.ac.jp

Manuel Eduardo Ares Brea: M. Eduardo Ares Brea is a Ph.D. candidate and a research and teaching assistant at the IRLab of the University of A Coruña. His main areas of research are semisupervised learning, Web mining, and applications of natural language processing. E-mail: maresb@udc.es

Shenghua Bao: Shenghua Bao is a research staff member at IBM Research–China. He obtained a Ph.D. degree in computer science at Shanghai Jiao Tong University in 2008. His research interests lie primarily in Web search, data mining, machine learning, and related applications. He received an IBM Ph.D. Fellowship in 2007 and was named IBM Master Inventor in 2012. Currently, Dr. Bao serves as an editor of CCF Technews, is a PC member of conferences like WWW, EMNLP, and WSDM, and a reviewer of several journals, including, IEEE TKDE, ACM TALIP, and IPM. E-mail: baoshhua@us.ibm.com

Roi Blanco: Roi Blanco is a senior research scientist at Yahoo! Labs Barcelona, where he has been working since 2009. Dr. Blanco is interested in applications of natural language processing for information retrieval, Web search and mining, and large-scale information access in general, and publishes at international conferences in those areas. He also contributes to Yahoo! products such as Yahoo! Search. Previously, he taught computer science at A Coruña University, where he received his Ph.D. degree (cum laude) in 2008. E-mail: roi@yahoo-inc.com

Kalina Bontcheva: Kalina Bontcheva is a senior research scientist and the holder of an EPSRC career acceleration fellowship, working on text summarization of social media. Dr. Bontcheva received her Ph.D. on the topic of adaptive hypertext generation from the University of Sheffield in 2001. Her main interests are information extraction, opinion mining, natural language generation, text summarization, and software infrastructure for NLP. She has been a leading developer of GATE since 1999. Dr. Bontcheva is also leading the Sheffield NLP research teams in the TrendMiner (http://www.trendminer-project.eu/) and uComp (http://www.ucomp.eu/) research projects, working respectively on mining and summarization of social media streams and crowdsourcing of NLP resources. E-mail: k.bontcheva@dcs.shef.ac.uk

Jia Chen: Jia Chen received double bachelor degrees in mathematics and computer science at Shanghai JiaoTong University in 2008. He is now a Ph.D. candidate in the Department of Computer Science and Engineering in Shanghai JiaoTong University. His research interests are in image annotation, content-based image retrieval, and machine learning. E-mail: chenjia@apex.sjtu.edu.cn

Constantin Comendant: Constantin Comendant holds an M.Sc. degree in media informatics from RWTH Aachen and the Bonn-Aachen IT Center (B-IT) in Germany. In his master thesis, he treated the topic of link prediction in networks. He is currently a Ph.D. student in the group of Jan Ramon, where he works on models for random graphs. E-mail: constantin.comendant@cs.kuleuven.be

Pawel Dybala: Pawel Dybala was born in Ostrow Wielkopolski, Poland in 1981. He received his MA in Japanese studies from the Jagiellonian University in Krakow, Poland in 2006, and a Ph.D. in information science and technology from Hokkaido University, Japan in 2011. Dr. Dybala is a director and general project manager at Kotoken Language Laboratory in Krakow. Currently, he is a JSPS postdoctoral research fellow at the Otaru University of Commerce, Otaru, Japan. His research interests include natural language processing, humor processing, metaphor undestanding, HCI, and information retrieval. E-mail: paweldybala@res.otary-uc.ac.jp

Mostafa Haghir Chehreghani: Mostafa Haghir Chehreghani received his B.Sc. in computer engineering from Iran University of Science and Technology (IUST) in 2004, and his M.Sc. from the University of Tehran in 2007. In January 2010, he joined the Department of Computer Science as a Ph.D. student, Katholieke Universiteit Leuven. His research interests include data mining and network analysis. E-mail: mostafa.haghirchehreghani@cs.kuleuven.be

Xianpei Han: Xianpei Han is an associate professor in the IR Laboratory at the Institute of Software Chinese Academy of Sciences. Prior to joining the IR Laboratory, he received his Ph.D. degree in the NLPR, Institute of Automation, Chinese Academy of Sciences in 2010. His research interests include natural language processing and information extraction. E-mail: xianpei@nfs.iscas.ac.cn

Noam Koenigstein: Noam Koenigstein received a B.Sc. degree in computer science (cum laude) from the Technion–Israel Institute of Technology, Haifa, Israel, in 2007 and an M.Sc. degree in electrical engineering from Tel-Aviv University, Tel-Aviv, Israel, in 2009. Currently, he is working toward a Ph.D. degree in the School of Electrical Engineering, Tel-Aviv University. In 2011, he joined the Xbox Machine Learning research team of Microsoft, where he developed the algorithm for Xbox recommendations serving more than 50 million users worldwide. His research interests include machine learning, information retrieval, and large-scale data mining, with a specific focus on recommender systems. E-mail: noamk@eng.tau.ac.il

Christina Lioma: Christina Lioma is an assistant professor and Freja research fellow in the Department of Computer Science, University of Copenhagen, Denmark. Her research focuses on the computational processing of language, mainly in the areas of information retrieval and computational linguistics. She publishes internationally in these areas, often coauthoring with collaborators from a widespread network of researchers. She is broadly engaged in program committees and reviewing in main journals and conferences within the areas covered by her research interests. E-mail: liomca@gmail.com

Chin-Yew Lin: Chin-Yew Lin is a research manager of the Knowledge Mining group at Microsoft Research Asia. His research interests are knowledge mining, social computing, question-answering, and automatic summarization. Dr. Lin is developing technologies to automatically learn social interaction knowledge from large-scale real-world data and transform unstructured and semistructured Web data into structured data to enable semantic computing. He has developed automatic evaluation technologies for summarization and machine translation. In particular, he created the ROUGE automatic summarization evaluation package. ROUGE was the official automatic evaluation package for Document Understanding Conferences and has become the de facto standard in summarization evaluation. He is a member of the Editorial Board of Computational Linguistics (2013–2015) and an action editor of the Transactions of the Association for Computational Linguistics. He was the program cochair of ACL 2012 and program cochair of AAAI 2011 AI & the Web Special Track. E-mail: cyl@microsoft.com

Kang Liu: Kang Liu received his Ph.D. degree from NLPR, Institute of Automation, Chinese Academy of Sciences in 2010. Before that, he received his M.Sc. and B.Sc. degrees from Xidian University in 2002 and

2005, respectively. Currently, he is working as an assistant professor in NLPR, Institute of Automation, Chinese Academy of Sciences. His current research interests include natural language processing, information extraction, question-answering, opinion mining, and so on. He has authored/coauthored more than 20 papers in leading conferences, including ACL, IJCAI, EMNLP, and CIKM. E-mail: kliu@nlpr.ia.ac.cn

Yang Liu: Yang Liu is a fourth-year Ph.D. candidate in NLPR, Institute of Automation, Chinese Academy of Sciences. He received his bachelor's degree from Harbin Institute of Technology in 2009. His research interest is information extraction. E-mail: liuyang09@nlpr.ia.ac.cn

Claudio Lucchese: Claudio Lucchese (http://hpc.isti.cnr.it/~claudio) received his master's degree in computer science (summa cum laude) from Ca' Foscari University of Venice in October 2003, and Ph.D. in computer science from the same university in 2007. Currently, he is a researcher at the Italian National Research Council (CNR). Dr. Lucchese research activity focuses on large-scale data mining techniques for information retrieval. He has published more than 40 papers on these topics in peer-reviewed international conferences and journals. He has participated in several EU-funded projects, and served as program committee member in numerous data mining and information retrieval conferences. E-mail: claudio.lucchese@isti.cnr.it

Jacek Maciejewski: Jacek Maciejewski studied for an M.Sc. degree in computer science at the University of Adam Mickiewicz, Poznan, Poland. He was awarded a scholarship to Hokkaido University, Japan, for the period 2008–2010. During his scholarship, he participated in research activities at the Graduate School of Information Science and Technology, Hokkaido University. His research interests include software engineering, natural language processing, Web mining, and information retrieval. E-mail: jacek.maciejewski@gmail.com

Yoshio Momouchi: Yoshio Momouchi was born in 1942 in Hokkaido, Japan. He obtained a master's degree and a doctorate in engineering from Hokkaido University. He was a member of the Division of Information Engineering in the Graduate School at Hokkaido University from 1973 to 1988. Since 1988, Dr. Momouchi has been a professor in the Faculty of Engineering at Hokkai-Gakuen University. He fulfilled duties as dean of the Graduate School of Engineering at Hokkai-Gakuen University during the years 2005–2008. He specializes in intelligent information processing, computational linguistics, and machine translation. He is a member of IPSJ, ANLP, ACL, MLSJ, JCSS, and JSAI. E-mail: mouchi@mo/eli.hokkai-su.ac.jp

Cristina Ioana Muntean: Cristina Ioana Muntean graduated in business information systems at Babes-Bolyai University, Cluj-Napoca, where she also received a Ph.D. in cybernetics and statistics in 2012. She is currently a research fellow at HPC Lab, ISTI-CNR, Pisa. Her interests are tourist recommender systems, machine learning, and information retrieval applied to Web and social network data. E-mail: cristina.muntean@econ.ubbcluj.ro

Raffaele Perego: Raffaele Perego (http://hpc.isti.cnr.it/~raffaele) is a senior researcher at ISTI-CNR, where he leads the High Performance Computing Lab (http://hpc.isti.cnr.it/). His main research interests include data mining, Web information retrieval, query log mining, and parallel and distributed computing. He has coauthored more than 100 papers on these topics published in journals and in the proceedings of peer-reviewed international conferences. E-mail: raffaele.perego@isti.cnr.it

Michal Ptaszynski: Michal Ptaszynski was born in Wroclaw, Poland in 1981. He received an MA degree from the University of Adam Mickiewicz, Poznan, Poland, in 2006, and a Ph.D. in information science and technology from Hokkaido University, Japan in 2011. Currently, Dr. Ptaszynski is a JSPS postdoctoral research fellow at the High-Tech Research Center, Hokkai-Gakuen University, Japan. His research interests include natural language processing, dialogue processing, affect analysis, sentiment analysis, HCI, and information retrieval. He is a member of ACL, AAAI, IEEE, HUMAINE, AAR, SOFT, JSAI, and NLP. E-mail: ptaszynski@media.eng.hokudai.ac.jp

Zhenyou Qi: Zhenyou Qi is a last year Ph.D. candidate in NLPR, Institute of Automation, Chinese Academy of Sciences. He received his bachelor's degree from the University of Science and Technology Beijing in 2007. His research interest is information extraction. E-mail: zyqi2013@163.com

Jan Ramon: Jan Ramon obtained his Ph.D. in 2002 from the KU Leuven, Belgium, on clustering and instance-based learning in first-order logic. Currently, he is a senior researcher at KU Leuven. Dr. Ramon's current research interests include statistical and algorithmic aspects of graph mining and machine learning with structured data. He also has a strong interest in applications, among other things in medical domains and computational biology. E-mail: jan.ramon@cs.kuleuven.be

Dominic Rout: Dominic Rout is working toward a Ph.D. in summarization of social media at the University of Sheffield as part of an EPSRC-funded project on this topic. He has been a member of the Natural Language Processing Research Group since 2011, working as part of the GATE team in research and training. He is currently also involved part time in the EC-funded TrendMiner project (http://www.trendminer-project.eu/), where his summarization research is tested with users in the political and financial domains. His other research interests include user interest modeling, user and content geolocation, and content recommendation and ranking.

In addition to his research work, he is passionate about teaching and has been an assistant in a number of courses, as well as developing and teaching outreach classes. E-mail: d.rout@sheffield.ac.uk

Rafal Rzepka: Rafal Rzepka received an MA degree from the University of Adam Mickiewicz, Poznan, Poland, in 1999, and a Ph.D. from Hokkaido University, Japan, in 2004. Currently, he is an assistant professor in the Graduate School of Information Science and Technology at Hokkaido University. His research interests include natural language processing, Web mining, commonsense retrieval, dialogue processing, language acquisition, affect analysis, and sentiment analysis. He is a member of AAAI, ACL, JSAI, IPSJ, IEICE, JCSS, and NLP. E-mail: kabura@media.eng.hokudai.ac.jp

Markus Schedl: Markus Schedl graduated in computer science from the Vienna University of Technology. He earned his Ph.D. in computational perception from the Johannes Kepler University Linz, where he is employed as assistant professor in the Department of Computational Perception. He further studied international business administration at the Vienna University of Economics and Business Administration as well as at the Handelshgskolan of the University of Gothenburg, which led to a master's degree. He has coauthored 80 refereed conference papers and journal articles (among others, published in ACM Multimedia, SIGIR, ECIR, IEEE Visualization, Journal of Machine Learning Research, ACM Transactions on Information Systems, Springer Information Retrieval, IEEE Multimedia). Furthermore, he serves on various program committees and has reviewed submissions to several conferences and journals (among others, ACM Multimedia, ECIR, IJCAI, ICASSP, IEEE Visualization, IEEE Transactions of Multimedia, Elsevier Data & Knowledge Engineering, ACM Transactions on Intelligent Systems and Technology, Springer Multimedia Systems). His main research interests include Web and social media mining, information retrieval, multimedia, music information research, and user interfaces. Since 2007, he has been giving several lectures, for instance, "Music Information Retrieval," "Exploratory Data Analysis," "Multimedia Search and Retrieval," and "Learning from User Generated Data." Dr. Schedl further spent several guest lecturing stays at the Universitat Pompeu Fabra, Barcelona, Spain; the Utrecht University, the Netherlands; the Queen Mary, University of London, UK; and Kungliga Tekniska Hgskolan, Stockholm, Sweden. E-mail: markus.schedl@jku.at

Fabrizio Silvestri: Fabrizio Silvestri (http://pomino.isti.cnr.it/~silvestr) is currently a researcher at ISTI-CNR in Pisa. He received his Ph.D. from the Computer Science Department of the University of Pisa in 2004. His research interests are mainly focused on Web information retrieval with a particular focus on efficiency-related problems such as caching, collection partitioning, and distributed IR, in general. In his professional activities he is a member of the program committee of many of the most important conferences in IR. Dr. Silvestri is author of more than 60 publications in highly relevant venues spanning from distributed and parallel computing to IR and data mining related conferences. E-mail: fabrizio.silvestri@isti.cnr.it

Mohamed Sordo: Mohamed Sordo is a postdoctoral researcher at the Music Technology Group of the Universitat Pompeu Fabra in Barcelona, Spain. He obtained his Ph.D. at the Music Technology Group in 2012, with a thesis entitled "Semantic Annotation of Music Collections: A Computational Approach," mainly devoted to the topic of music automatic tagging. Dr. Sordo's research areas involve music text/Web mining, music information retrieval, and machine learning. He has participated in a number of European-funded projects, including Variazioni, Pharos, and CompMusic. He is currently involved in the latter, developing systems to extract semantically and musically meaningful information from Web data. E-mail: mohamed.sordo@upf.edu

Zhong Su: Zhong Su is a senior technical staff member at IBM Research China (CRL) and senior manager of the Information Analytics Department. He joined CRL after receiving his Ph.D. degree in computer science at Tsinghua University in 2002. Dr. Su has been involved in many projects at CRL including text analytics, NLP, rich media analysis, and information integration. He has led a number of research projects which were awarded the Technical Accomplishment of IBM research many times and Outstanding Technical Accomplishment of IBM research in 2008 and 2010. Dr. Su was awarded the IBM Master Inventor in 2007 and currently chairs the Invention and Disclosure Board in CRL. He has published more than 50 papers in top international conferences/journals, with more than 40 patents or patents pending. Dr. Su is guest professor of APEX Lab, Shanghai JiaoTong University. He is also Vice Chairman of Technical Expert Council IBM Greater China Group. E-mail: suzhongatcn.ibm.com

Hossein Vahabi: Hossein Vahabi received his bachelor's and master's degrees in computer engineering from the University of Modena and Reggio Emilia, respectively, in 2006 (summa cum laude) and 2008 (summa cum laude). In 2012, he received a Ph.D. with European honors in computer science and engineering at the IMT Institute for Advanced Studies Lucca, Italy. Currently, Dr. Vahabi is leading his own private company H.V. His research interests cover many topics in the field of recommender systems: query recommendation, tourism point of interests recommendation, tag recommendation, tweet recommendation, and large-scale recommendation. E-mail: hossein.vahabi@imtlucca.it

Rossano Venturini: Rossano Venturini is currently a researcher at the Computer Science Department, University of Pisa. He received a Ph.D. from the Computer Science Department of the University of Pisa in 2010, with his thesis titled "On Searching and Extracting Strings from Compressed Textual Data." Dr. Venturini's research interests are mainly focused on the design and analysis of algorithms and data structures with special attention to problems of indexing and searching large textual collections. E-mail: rossano.venturini@isti.cnr.it

Haofen Wang: Haofen Wang has rich research experience in data management, Web search, and semantic Web fields. He has published more than 40 high-quality papers in the related international top conferences and journals including ISWC, WWW, SIGIR, SIGMOD, ICDE, CIKM, and Journal of Web Semantics. He has also won the best paper award of the 3rd China Semantic Web Symposium (CSWS 2009). He has been serving as reviewer for VLDB Journal, Journal of Web Semantics, and IEEE Transaction of Knowledge and Data Engineering. Dr. Wang has also served on program committees for international conferences such as ESWC 2008, ISWC 2009, EDBT 2009, ESWC 2009, ESWC 2010, ISWC 2010, EDBT 2010, ESWC 2011, ISWC 2011, ESWC 2012, ISWC 2012, WWW 2011, and WWW 2012. As a cochair, he has organized SemSearch 2009, SemSearch 2010, and SemSearch 2011, collaborated with WWW 2009, WWW 2010, and WWW 2011, respectively. As one of the deputy local chairs, he hosted the 9th International Semantic Web Conference (ISWC 2010). As a project leader, he took charge of several innovative research projects like scalable semantic search, semantic enterprise portal, and large-scale semantic data query answering using cloud computing. His education background includes a two-year IBM Ph.D. fellowship, fellowships at Hong Kong Science and Technology University and the University of Karlsruhe, Germany, and double bachelor degrees in computer science and math at Shanghai Jiao Tong University. E-mail: whfcarter@apex.sjtu.edu.cn

Yuyi Wang: Yuyi Wang received an M.Sc. in computer science in the School of Computing of the National University of Singapore, Singapore. His master's thesis concerns the nonlinearity of Boolean functions. He is currently a Ph.D. student in the MiGraNT project researching graph mining from a linear algebra point of view. E-mail: yuyi.wang@cs.kuleuven.be

Udi Weinsberg: Udi Weinsberg is a researcher and associate fellow at Technicolor Research in Palo Alto, California. He studies privacy and security, focusing on enabling practical privacy-preserving machine learning algorithms in recommender systems. He received his Ph.D. from Tel-Aviv University, Israel, School of Electrical Engineering in 2011, from where he also received his M.Sc. in 2007. During his Ph.D., Dr. Weinsberg was a member of the NetDIMES group, studying the structure and evolution of the Internet. E-mail: udi.weinsberg@technicolor.com

Ning Yu: Ning Yu is an assistant professor of the School of Library and Information Science at University of Kentucky. She received her Ph.D. in information science and a Ph.D. minor in cognitive science with an emphasis on computational linguistics at Indiana University. Dr. Yu's research interests lie broadly in information retrieval and text mining, with a focus on opinion mining (also known as sentiment analysis). She has collaborated on several information retrieval projects that produced top runs in various retrieval tasks at the Text Information Retrieval Conference (TREC), including high-accuracy document retrieval and opinion retrieval. She also has rich experience in adopting a hybrid approach to leverage human expertise and machine learning techniques for sentiment analysis on various data domains: news articles, blogs, reviews, and suicide notes. Her recent studies on semisupervised sentiment analysis have proven to be promising in solving two fundamental problems for sentiment analysis: insufficient training data and domain adaption. E-mail: nyu.yuning@gmail.com

Yong Yu: Yong Yu received his master's degree at the Computer Science Department of East China Normal University. He began to work in Shanghai Jiao Tong University in 1986. He is now the Ph.D. candidate tutor and the chairman of the E-Generation Technology Research Center (SJTU-IBM-HKU). He was the teacher of the course computer graphics and human machine interface and the course next generation Web infrastructure. As the head coach of SJTU ACM-ICPC team, he and his team have won the 2002, 2005, and 2010 ACM ICPC Championships. His research interests include semantic Web, Web mining, information retrieval, and computer vision. Email: yyu@apex.sjtu.edu.cn

Jun Zhao: Jun Zhao is a professor at the National Laboratory of Pattern Recognition (NLPR), Institute of Automation, Chinese Academy of Sciences. He received his Ph.D. degree in computer science from Tsinghua University in 1998. Prior to joining NLPR, he was a postdoctoral in Hong Kong University of Sciences and Technology. Dr. Zhao's research interests include natural language processing, information extraction, and question-answering. He has served on over 10 program committees of the major international conferences in the field of natural language processing and knowledge engineering, and also has served as an associate editor for ACM Transactions on Asian Language Information Processing (TALIP). He has won the second prize of KDD-CUP 2011. In recent years, he has published more than 20 papers in top conferences including ACL, SIGIR, IJCAI, CIKM, EMNLP, and COLING. E-mail: junzhao1001@gmail.com

Guangyou Zhou: Guangyou Zhou is an assistant professor in the NLPR, Institute of Automation, Chinese Academy of Sciences. He received his Ph.D. degree in computer science from NLPR in 2013. Before that, Dr. Zhou received his bachelor's degree from Northeast Normal University in 2008. His research interests include natural language processing and information retrieval. E-mail: gyzho@nlpr.ia.ac.cn

List of Reviewers

We are very grateful for the assistance of the following reviewers. Their valuable remarks were very helpful to improving the quality of the chapters.

Hadi Amari: Institute for Infocomm Research, Singapore

Steven Bethard: University of Alabama, United States

Tat-Seng Chua: National University of Singapore, Singapore

Xue Geng: National University of Singapore, Singapore

Karl Gyllstrom: ANATAS, Australia

Lei Hou: Tsinghua University, China

Juanzi Li: Tsinghua University, China

Zhixing Li: Tsinghua University, China

Banyong Liang: Microsoft China

Marie-Francine Moens: KU Leuven, Belgium

Jialie Shen: Singapore Management University, Singapore

Xuemeng Song: National University of Singapore, Singapore

Ivan Vulić: KU Leuven, Belgium

Zhigang Wang: Tsinghua University, China

Jianxing Yu: Institute for Infocomm Research, Singapore

List of Figures

List of Tables

Part I

Introduction

Chapter 1

Mining User Generated Content and Its Applications

Marie-Francine Moens

KU Leuven, Belgium

Juanzi Li

Tsinghua University, China

Tat-Seng Chua

National University of Singapore, Singapore

1.1 The Web and Web Trends

1.1.1 The Emergence of the World Wide Web (WWW): From Connected Computers to Linked Documents

Joseph Carl Robnett Licklider formulated the earliest ideas of a global computer network in August 1962,[1] known as the *Galactic Network*. He explained it as a set of *computers* that would be globally inter *connected* so

---

[1] http://en.wikipedia.org/wiki/J._C._R._Licklider

people could access data or programs when they wanted, which contained almost everything that the Internet is today.

Twenty-seven years later, the World Wide Web was proposed by Tim Berners-Lee. As defined in Wikipedia now,[2] it is a system of inter*linked*, hypertext *documents* that runs over the Internet. With a Web browser, a user views Web pages that may contain text, images, and other multimedia and navigates between them using hyperlinks. The proposal was meant for a more effective *European Organization for Nuclear Research* (CERN) communication system but Berners-Lee eventually realized that the concept could be implemented throughout the world. Figure 1.1 shows the architecture of the WWW that was drawn by him in the proposal.[3]

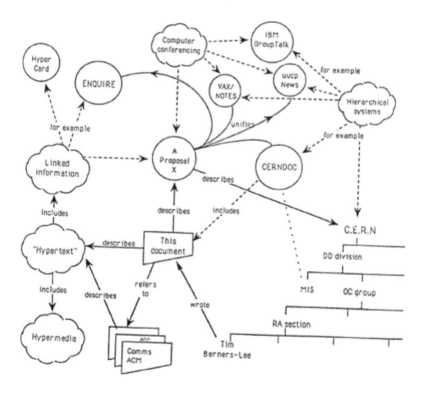

FIGURE 1.1: The architecture of the WWW in Berners-Lee's proposal.

Berners-Lee wrote the code for the WWW after that, and some essential technologies were listed as follows:

- **Hypertext and Hyperlink:** It is the key difference between documents

---

[2]http://en.wikipedia.org/wiki/World_Wide_Web
[3]http://www.w3.org/History/1989/proposal.html

on stand-alone computers. Hypertext is structured text that uses logical links (hyperlinks) between nodes containing text.

- **Resource Identifiers:** With so many various documents on the Web and elsewhere, like computer files, documents, or other resources, Berners-Lee proposed a system of globally unique identifiers for them, the universal document identifier (UDI), later known as uniform resource locator (URL) and uniform resource identifier (URI).

- **Markup Language:** As the documents on the WWW were no longer stand-alone and composed of plain text, Berners-Lee developed the publishing language HyperText Markup Language (HTML), which made the characters or codes embedded in text indicate structure, semantic meaning, or advice on presentation.

- **Transfer Protocol:** The transfer protocol is the foundation of data communication for the WWW, and thus he implemented an application protocol for distributed, collaborative, hypermedia information systems, known as HTTP.

1.1.2 The Prevailingness of Web 2.0: From "Read-Only" to Read-and-Write-Interaction

The WWW connects people to a public, shared, and "read-only" environment, but it does not facilitate direct communication between Web readers and writers, that is to say, readers can watch Web pages and subjectively comprehend the meanings, but the links between writers and readers is usually disconnected.

The term Web 2.0 was made popular by Tim O'Reilly, it was often used to refer to what some people describe as a second phase of architecture and application development for the World Wide Web. It was everything social, where "ordinary" users could meet, collaborate, and share using social software applications on the Web. Hence, it significantly increased the participating interest of Web users. In short, Web 2.0 not only connects individual users to the Web, but also connects these individual users together.

In O'Reilly's later publication *What Is Web 2.0*,[4] he provided seven features of the new Web.

1. *The Web as a platform*. Though its definition is still vague, it has a gravitational core and all the applications are based on the core. Thus, we can view the Web as a platform and a platform beats an application every time.

2. *Harnessing collective intelligence*. The central principle behind the success of Web 2.0 is embracing the power of the Web to harness collective intelligence, and some popular examples include Delicious, Digg, Flickr, Wikipedia, and so on.

---

[4]http://oreilly.com/Web2/archive/what-is-Web-20.html

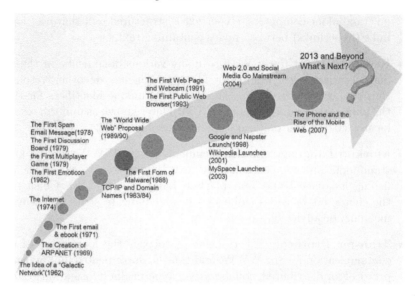

FIGURE 1.2: The evolution of the Web. **(See color insert.)**

3. *Data is the next Intel Inside.* In the Web 2.0 era, controlling data often leads to market control and financial returns.

4. *End of the software release cycle.* In the Web 2.0 era, software is often delivered as a service, not as a product, which leads to a number of fundamental changes in software release and the business model of software companies.

5. *Lightweight programming models.* It is the inevitable consequence of software as a service.

6. *Software above the level of a single device.* It is no longer limited to the PC platform. Of course, any Web application can be seen as software above the level of a single device, and more and more devices are connected to the new platform (i.e., Web 2.0).

7. *Rich user experiences.* He mainly talked about the new generation of information publishing technology, but it meant more and more as time went by.

From the above features, we can conclude that users are at the center of the Web 2.0 and interaction is the mainstream. Interactions produce different kinds of data, and how to deal with this valuable information poses a direction for the evolving Web.

1.1.3 What Will Be Next?

Figure 1.2 summarizes the evolution process of the Web. As for what the next Web will be, it is difficult to define, mainly because (a) it has not fully arrived yet, and (b) everyone has his or her own idea of what it might or might not be (as mentioned by Elise Moreau[5]).

Moreover, Moreau also predicted the future of the Web will likely be characterized by three major cumulative changes which can be interpreted as more social, more semantic, and more data. The social connects us, the semantic serves us, and the data comes from us (that is, *user generated content*). What we expect is a more meaningful Web, bringing information on the Web together and delivering it to us in a way that we can really use it because it knows us well, knows our situation, knows what we like (or do not like) and knows what we want.

Someone may ask how that happens, our answer is mining user generated content. Obviously, the straightforward way to understand a person is by talking with him but there are many more ways to achieve this goal in the Web environment. User generated content conveys all the information we need, for example, the social connections show part of the relationship, the read or view behavior tells the interests, the posts express the sentiment, and so on.

In the following sections, we will define user generated content and review the research on creating, searching, and mining it.

1.2   Defining User Generated Content

A company wants to find clients for its products and brands. Another company has a Webshop and is interested in advertising its products to potential buyers. Yet another company wants to monitor trends in lifestyles in order to more appropriately design or market its products, or it wants to link products and users in the frame of the Internet of Things in order to recommend products when a user is shopping online or offline. An academic institution has interest in studying the habitat of certain social groups. The institution also wants to build a timeline of lifestyle changes. A government is gathering data on the indicators of wealth of its citizens. All these initiatives to a large extent can rely on messages, texts, images, video, and multimedia data that people post on the World Wide Web, or to an extent on what their friends post on the Web, when the users are connected through social networks or media. Such data are currently available in abundance on social network sites, where exabytes of user generated content nowadays are commonplace rather than the exception.

The data posted by users on the Web have the following in common: they are publicly available to other users (or at least to a circle of friends), they contain a certain amount of creative effort, and they are created by the general

---

[5]http://Webtrends.about.com/od/Social-Media-Evolution/a/
The-Future-Of-The-Web.htm

public outside of their professional activities. These data are denoted as *user generated content* (UGC), also called user created content or consumer generated media (CGM). Here, we follow the definition of the Organisation for Economic Co-operation and Development (OECD) [732]. Content is considered as UGC when the content is published on a publicly accessible Web site or on a page on a social networking site that is accessible to a select group of people. There is some creative effort in putting together the work or adapting existing works in order to create a new one, which is done by one person or as a collaborative effort. Finally, there is the requirement that UGC is created outside professional routines and practices. UGC is currently distinguished from professionally generated content because a well established class of professional content providers currently have their presence on the Internet [56].

The idea of intercreativity envisioned by Berners-Lee in 1999 [153], that is, the possibility of jointly creating things or solving problems together, is very much present in today's UGC. Posting UGC gives the users the possibilities to connect with peers, to creatively express themselves, and to obtain fame and prestige within their circle of friends, or even on a global scale. UGC creation entered mainstream usage around 2005. It has boomed during the last years due to a number of external drivers [43]. Current technology can dispose of increasing bandwidth and provides tools for easy content creation and sharing. Socially, the World Wide Web is used by age groups who are "digital natives" and who have excellent information and communications technology skills. They often have the desire to create and express themselves in a digital framework and to interactively pursue certain goals. Economically, the costs of creating UGC is low due to the increasing availability of tools.

The potential gains for exploiting UGC are high, leaving room for sophisticated, targeted and user-tailored advertisement and for many new business models to monetize content. UGC even encourages unpaid contributors to provide content that a media organization can republish, promote, and profit from. Finally, as we see the rise of user licensing agreements, there are a number of institutional and legal drivers which grant copyright to users for their content.

UGC denotes any form of content such as blogs, wikis, discussion forums, posts, chats, tweets, podcasting, pins, digital images, video, audio files, and other forms of media that was created by users of an online system or service, often made available via social media Web sites. The content refers to news, encyclopedias and other reference works, movie and product reviews, problem processing, posting of consumer items and comments on them, accounts of (personal) happenings and events, fan fiction, trip planners, crowdfunding and others, and the content is often created through interaction with other users. Some authors currently prefer to use the term "personal" media instead of social media as these media are concerned with intrinsic personal motivations and sociability [422].

1.3   A Brief History of Creating, Searching, and Mining User Generated Content

Writing commentaries, messages, or notes is almost as old as the writing systems themselves, but in very ancient times writing was a privilege of elite educated persons who were professional writers. Through time many commentaries are preserved that expand literature works written in Sanskrit, Greek, or Latin and the study of these commentaries by historians had led to a better knowledge of contexts in which these works were read. They give insights into the cultural history of the times in which the commentaries were created [122]. The commentaries give very important knowledge that up until now was mostly manually mined from their sources by historians, anthropologists, and sociologists. For instance, a great deal of cultural history can be retrieved from the study of commentaries on Ovid's text of the Metamorphoses [152].

Another phenomenon interesting to mention is the graffiti that in ancient times were carved on walls with a sharp object. Although in very early times prehistoric cave paintings and pictographs using tools such as animal bones and pigments were often placed in ceremonial and sacred locations, gradually through antiquity we see that graffiti became a popular habit. Ancient graffiti displayed phrases of love declarations, political rhetoric, curses, magic spells, famous literary quotes, or simple words of thought. Examples of these were found in the ancient Greek city of Ephesus and in the ancient Roman city of Pompei. Because of historic graffiti, we are able to understand the lifestyles and culture of many societies currently and in the past [259].

In a similar way, writings, paintings, buildings and even old archives of photos and audio contribute to the study of society and culture in archaeological, historical, social, and even economic research [96]. What is left of the past in terms of material objects is somehow biased by the creations of selected groups of society, such as kings, religious groups, or wealthy citizens. Today's technologies to create digital content—whether it is in the form of text messages, photos, or videos—is within a hand's reach of a very large group of people, so the creation of UGC is done on a huge scale, making their mining with automated tools especially relevant.

The advent of the World Wide Web and "multimedia" capability in the mid-1990s heralded the area of the "new media" [34]. The new media age was boosted by the success of the hypertext markup language (HTML) as mentioned above, invented by Berners-Lee in 1989, and the hypertext transfer protocol (HTTP) and the underlying transmission control protocol and Internet protocol (TCP/IP). By choosing to put this software in the public domain, Berners-Lee gave every user the opportunity to publish their own documents via the Internet. Digital UGC started in the 1990s when Richard Stallman advocated the creation of a web-based online encyclopaedia that is collectively created and revised [158]. James Wales and Larry Singer realized this idea with the launching of Wikipedia in 2001. From then on UGC has only grown in size on the Web. With the advent of Web 2.0 users are encouraged to interact and collaborate with each other in a social media dialogue as creators of UGC in a virtual community, which was one of the original goals of Berners-Lee. To name only a few initiatives, Facebook, still the most famous social Web site, was set up by Harvard students in 2004, YouTube, a video sharing Web site, was created in 2006 and Pinterest, a pinboard-style photo-sharing Web site, started in 2009. During the last 10 years we have witnessed an explosion of social network sites, many of which offer the functionalities of self-publishing, media sharing functions, group mail, instant messaging, and novelty apps of various kinds. Facebook has possibly grown to the largest single store of personal information in human history [34]. Increasingly, UGC is characterized by intermediality, that is, the interconnectedness of media with each other and with various social institutions [316]. Stronger than in the past and in a form that is more amendable to automated processing, people more or less willingly and knowingly provide information about themselves and other persons, and about all kinds of events that previously had to be sampled and documented for distinct purposes. This has led to the phenomenon that relationships between businesses, consumers, and civil society have been reconfigured [316] and to a situation where automated tools to mine UGC are in large demand, especially from a business, academic, and governmental perspective.

To name a few highlights, in June 1993, Matthew Gray, then at MIT, produced what was probably the first Web robot, the Perl-based World Wide Web Wanderer, and used it to generate an index called Wandex. Worth mentioning is the first study on classifying text according to the sentiments that it expresses by Marti Hearst in 1992 [279]. The seminal paper of Boyd and Ellison gives a global view of social network sites and their analysis [90]. The first steps toward image mining and retrieval were taken by Chen et al. [134] and toward video mining and search by Smith and Chang [636]. The full detailed history of the development of mining and searching tools for UGC is treated exhaustively throughout the chapters of this book.

1.4   Goals of the Book

Media, game, and advertisement companies start to realize the large potential of processing UGC and the many new business models and value chains that UGC can give rise to. UGC offers enormous possibilities for business intelligence, e-commerce, marketing, and social studies. Currently, we witness that commercial firms play an increasing role in supporting, hosting, and diffusing UGC [732], and a large number of intelligent Web services emerge that empower the user to contribute to developing, rating, collaborating on, and distributing UCG. These activities foster the underlying idea that the more people who are liking, sharing, tweeting, and pinning content, the more likely it becomes that this content will come up to the top of a search engine answer list. However, we still are in need of advanced access and mining technologies in order to use UCG to its full potential so that advanced applications and new business models can be developed. Technologies that mine UGC are the subject of this book.

More specifically, the goals of this book are:

- To extensively cover and document the state-of-the-art of mining of UGC.

- To integrate insights from a variety of fields and applications when mining UGC.

- To pinpoint the bottlenecks when processing and mining UGC.

- To link the processing of UGC to the current topic of "big data" analytics.

- To yield new ideas for the development of novel technologies.

- To develop a road map for future research in mining of UGC.

The book views mining of UGC from an interdisciplinary perspective. Not only is the material that is analyzed very heterogeneous and coming from many different data sources, in addition the chapters of the book are written by prominent researchers and practitioners from the fields of social media analysis, information retrieval, natural language processing, multimedia processing, data mining, machine learning, user modeling, and e-commerce.

1.5   User Generated Content: Concepts and Bottlenecks

We introduce here a number of concepts that are central to the book and their definitions that will be used throughout its different chapters. The content that we consider in the book often refers to the blogosphere.

Blog: A blog or Web log is a Web site containing one or more posts that often interactively discuss a certain topic. The posts are usually presented in chronological order.

Microblog: A microblog is a stream of text that is written by an author over time comprising many very short updates, usually presented in reverse chronological order.

Blogosphere: Blogosphere refers to the collection of all blogs on the Web.

Another important source of UGC are the social network sites.

Social network site: A social network site is a Web-based service that allows individuals to (1) construct a public or semipublic profile within a bounded system, (2) articulate a list of other users with whom they share a connection, and (3) view and traverse their list of connections and those made by others within the system. The nature and nomenclature of these connections may vary from site to site [90].

When dealing with UGC, we often deal with large amounts of data, that is, big data.

Big data: Big data is high-volume, high-velocity, and high-variety information assets that demand cost-effective, innovative forms of information processing for enhanced insight and decision making.

To make UGC suitable for mining and search we often need to explicitly label content with descriptors. This is usually done automatically by means of machine learning techniques. When using supervised learning techniques, we need data that are manually annotated to train the systems.

Social tagging: Social tagging regards the manual and preferably automatic annotation of content found in the different media of UGC with controlled or free language tags or index terms making search and mining of the information more effective. Commonly, the social tag is a nonhierarchical keyword and is generally chosen informally and personally by the item's creator or viewer.

A typical example of automated labeling of UGC is sentiment analysis.

Sentiment analysis: Sentiment analysis regards the task of detecting, extracting and summarizing opinions, polarity, or emotions, normally based on the presence or absence of sentiment features. A typical task regards the classification of sentences or of whole discourses as opinions or facts, and in the former case the further classification of the item as positive or negative, or by more fine-grained sentiment categories (e.g., angry, happy, sad).

Knowledge extraction goes one step further and finds relationships between extracted or labeled information to make the content ready to use in knowledge bases where through reasoning additional knowledge can be inferred.

Knowledge extraction: Knowledge extraction refers to the automatic acquisition of knowledge from UGC so as to automatically construct knowledge bases.

In addition to mining UGC, searching UGC forms another important aspect of this book.

Search engine: A search engine is a software program that has the functionality of retrieving information or documents and it identifies documents or other information items in a repository that are relevant for a specific information query and often ranks these documents by their degree of relevance.

Music information retrieval: Music information retrieval aims at extracting, retrieving, analyzing, processing, and mining information about any kind of music related item or subject.

Query expansion: Query expansion regards the process of reformulating an initial search query to improve retrieval performance in information retrieval operations. In the context of UGC search engines, query expansion involves the addition or reweighing of query terms based on information found in UGC classified as relevant by the user or the search engine.

Finally, an important application of mining UGC regards recommender systems.

Recommender system: A recommender system or recommendation system is an information filtering system that seeks to predict the "rating" or "preference" that a user would give to an item (such as music, books, or movies) or social element (e.g., people or groups) they had not yet considered, using a model built from the characteristics of an item (content-based approaches) or the user's social environment (collaborative filtering approaches) [566].

The book also treats a number of bottlenecks when mining and searching UGC.

The major problem when searching or mining UGC is making sense out of this content, so that it can be appropriately indexed and described for further use. Natural language understanding, image understanding, and the understanding of video are necessary components in the construction of good mining algorithms. These technologies perform far from perfect when processing UGC. One important reason is that current tools are often developed in ideal settings where well-formed content is processed. For instance, the text of news stories is analyzed for which highly performing syntactic parsers have been trained. Once you move this technology to a more realistic setting, for example, the language that everyday people use, the performance drops substantially. Extreme cases of everyday language are UGC, often full of spelling errors and grammatical mistakes. The photos and video shots by consumers are typically of far lower quality than their professionally generated counterparts. There are problems with motion blur, defocus, and less controlled viewpoints that render recognition of people, actions, and objects more difficult.

Mining UGC becomes really interesting when content from different modalities can be combined. Although there is research on combining textual information with graph based analyses, we still know very little about how to fuse information coming from textual with information coming from visual or auditory sources. Many new business models could thrive on the aggregation of this heterogeneous content.

Finally, the algorithms for mining and searching UGC have to deal with "big data," which poses challenging scalability issues. According to the definition of Gartner,[6] the requirements for being big data regard being confronted with large amounts of data, which are created or changed at a substantial speed, and having a large diversity in the types of data. These prerequisites are currently fulfilled for UGC. There is an absolute need to search, analyze, and summarize or visualize big data. These tasks are extra difficult compared to other types of big data such as large amounts of structured data or well-formed data such as news or scientific texts.

1.6   Organization of the Book

The book is organized into four parts.

Part I is the introduction of the book, and only contains this chapter.

Part II discusses the mining of different media.

A first intuitive approach is having humans annotate UGC, so that recognizers can be trained conveniently with a goal to automatically annotate sources that are not annotated by humans. Chapter 2 on *Social Annotation* by Jia Chen, Shanghai Jiaotong University; Shenghua Bao, IBM China Research Laboratory; Haofen Wang, Shanghai Jiaotong University; Yong Yu, Shanghai Jiaotong University; and Zhong Su, IBM China Research Laboratory covers this topic. Although, social annotation of Web pages and Web media objects seems a straightforward approach, Chapter 2 delves into a number of techniques and applications. The authors propose techniques of social annotation propagation, implementing variations of random walk algorithms over the Web graph of hyperlinks and other types of links, and focuses on problems of the scalability of the propagation algorithms and integrating constraints into the random walk algorithms. The chapter also discusses several interesting applications of the proposed algorithms, such as the analysis of a folksonomy, personalized search, Web page categorization and taxonomy creation allowing for an improved search and mining.

The oldest approaches to mining UGC regard sentiment analysis. This is why this topic receives a prominent place early in the book in Chapter 3 on *Sentiment Analysis in UGC* by Ning Yu, University of Kentucky. As this topic has been studied extensively over the years, the chapter perfectly fits the need for a mature task definition, and gives an extensive overview of the state-of-the-art and literature, covering types of features, rule-based and

---

[6]http://www.gartner.com/it-glossary/big-data/

supervised learning approaches. Of specific value is the section on semisupervised learning where an overview of semisupervised methods and their results is given, which opens many paths for valuable future research.

As multimedia take a growing part in UGC, we are very pleased to introduce Chapter 4 by Markus Schedl, Johannes Kepler Universität, Linz, Austria; Mohamed Sordo, Universitat Pompeu Fabra, Spain; Noam Koenigstein, Tel-Aviv University, Israel; and Udi Weinsberg, Technicolor Research, entitled *Mining User Generated Data for Music Information Retrieval*. The chapter emphasizes the importance of mining UGC for music information retrieval. In this chapter, mining is not only restricted to music posted on social network sites, but the majority of the information regarding music, artists, their popularity, ratings instrumentation, and so on, can be extracted from Web sites, blogs, microblogs, social tag sites, and social networks. The chapter gives an overview of the most recent methodologies for mining such content with a special emphasis on recommendation applications and automatic playlist generation. The authors point to the possibilities of joint processing of several media. The conclusions provide insight into several open challenges, including coping with popularity bias, scalability, and lack of proper ground truth.

Another important modality that is prominent in social networks are graphs, a topic which is covered in Chapter 5 on *Graph and Network Pattern Mining* by Jan Ramon; Constantin Comendant; Mostafa Haghir Chehreghani; and Yuyi Wang; who are affiliated with KU Leuven, Belgium. The chapter explains the fundamentals of graph theory and graph pattern mining. Special attention is given to the complexity of the techniques and possible ways to optimize the computational complexity of the models, which is important in a large-scale social network context. Other foci are on condensed representations of the network and on algorithms for pattern matching. This compilation of network technologies is of very practical use in the many applications that mine UGC in the context of social network information.

Part III is concerned with the mining and searching of different types of UGC.

Chapter 6 discusses the mining and knowledge extraction from textual UGC. In this chapter, entitled *Knowledge Extraction from Wikis/BBS/Blogs/News Web Sites*, by Jun Zhao, Kang Liu, Guangyou Zhou, Xianpei Han, Zhenyu Qi, and Yang Liu from the Chinese Academy of Sciences, different knowledge extraction tasks are discussed in detail, including entity recognition and expansion, relation extraction, and named entity recognition. The authors point to a number of challenges such as the lack of sufficient annotated training data, the need to process the unstructured text sources in combination with other more structured information such as links and category tags, and the still difficult problem of entity disambiguation. The chapter discusses the fusion of information from heterogeneous sources such as text, Web tables, Wikipedia, query logs, and others. Again, this chapter provides an extensive literature overview and refers to interesting current competition.

Chapter 7 by Roi Blanco, Yahoo! Research Barcelona; Manuel Eduardo Ares Brea, University of A Coruna; and Christina Lioma, University of Copenhagen; covers the topic of *User Generated Content Search*. The chapter offers an extensive overview of indexing and ranking methods for UGC and focuses on the challenges that the different types of UGC, that is, blogs, microblogs, and social tags pose to the field of information retrieval. The authors also present and evaluate a novel approach for using UGC to assist searches in the form of query expansion. The authors refer to the need to evaluate such query expansion techniques in multimedia retrieval where data contain very little textual information.

Annotating Japanese Blogs with Syntactic and Affective Information constitutes Chapter 8 and is written by Michal Ptaszynski, Institute of Technology, Japan; Jacek Maciejewski and Pawel Dybala, Otaru University of Commerce, Japan; Rafal Rzepka and Kenji Araki, Hokkaido University, Japan; and Yoshio Momouchi, Hokkai-Gakuen University, Japan. The authors report on the difficult task of annotating a 5-billion word corpus of Japanese blogs with syntactic and affective information. The chapter shows the complexity of the annotation process and discusses state-of-the-art initiatives.

Part IV discusses several applications.

Chapter 9 covers the very relevant topic of question-answering search over UGC. This chapter, entitled *Question-Answering of UGC*, is written by Chin-Yew Lin of Microsoft Research Asia. In the first part, the chapter provides an extensive state-of-the-art on question-answering research where the document collections in which the answer is found consist of UGC or where similar questions are searched. The second part of the chapter proposes and evaluates many different, novel, and existing query likelihood language models that allow exploiting uncertain evidences coming from category information, structural information available in the question among which are topic-focus mixture models, entity-based translation models, syntactic information, and the integration of other evidences in the ranking function such as question quality, answer quality, and user expertise. Probabilistic retrieval models are very well suited to cope with uncertain evidences coming from a lesser quality UGC or user models. The author also points to the lack of standard test collections and to challenging future research tracks such as answer summarization, multilingual question-answering, question routing over several answer repositories, and social networks using so-called answering robots.

Chapter 10 on *Summarization of UGC*, by Dominic Rout and Kalina Bontcheva, both from the University of Sheffield, treats a difficult but very pertinent challenge given the huge amounts of UGC available on the Web that really deserves the term "big data." The authors explain why summarizing UGC is very different from classical text summarization and demands novel approaches. The authors discuss the different types of summaries that can be the product of UGC summarization and their evaluation. The last part of the chapter discusses outstanding challenges such as generating summaries that are grounded in a spatio-temporal content, exploiting implicit semantic information present in UGC, dealing with multilinguality and summarizing multilingual UGC, and building personalized summaries based on information about the user constitute very pertinent research topics. The chapter is very well documented with state-of-the-art research.

An important application that relies on UGC is discussed in Chapter 11, entitled *Recommender Systems*, with authors Claudio Lucchese, Istituto di Scienza e Tecnologie della Informazione, Italy; Cristina Ioana Muntean, Babes-Bolyai University, Romania; Raffaele Perego, Fabrizio Silvestri, Hossein Vahabi, and Rossano Venturini from the Istituto di Scienza e Tecnologie della Informazione, Italy. The chapter shows that UGC contains a tremendous amount of information for recommending products and services. The chapter gives an overview of recommendations based on different types of information including query logs, photos, blogs, Wikipedia, Twitter, and social tags. The authors also discuss several personalized services based on UGC.

Chapter 12 concludes the book with conclusions and a road map for future developments. We then focus more in depth on these issues and add some additional challenges, some of which are not treated in this book.

1.7 Mining User Generated Content: Broader Context

Mining UGC has the potential to provide companies, researchers, citizens, consumers, governments, and other interested parties with valuable information and knowledge. We already stressed the many new business models that lay ahead if successful mining of UGC is possible. In addition, UGC content tends to be collaborative and encourages sharing and joint production of information, ideas, opinions, and knowledge. Additional tools could be developed to further stimulate the creation of innovative ideas and fruitful collaborations. Making tools available that mine discussion forums and product reviews can lead to more informed users and consumer decisions. The cultural impacts of widespread mining and search tools are also far-reaching. Economic studies are interested in the diverse array of cultural content to find niche audiences. UGC can also be seen as an open platform enriching political and societal debates, diversity of opinion, free flow of information, and freedom of expression. Transparency and filtering functions may be enhanced to content creation. Citizen journalism, for instance, allows users to correct, influence, or create news, potentially on similar terms as newspapers or other large entities. Furthermore, blogs, social networking sites, and virtual worlds can be platforms for engaging electors, exchanging political views, provoking debate, and sharing information on societal and political questions. Developing technologies for improved mining and searching UGC is needed for all the above applications.

Part II

Mining Different Media

Chapter 2

Social Annotation

Jia Chen
Shanghai Jiaotong University

Shenghua Bao
IBM China Research Laboratory

Haofen Wang
Shanghai Jiaotong University

Yong Yu
Shanghai Jiaotong University

Zhong Su
IBM China Research Laboratory

The Web 2.0 is leading a new revolution on the World Wide Web, where social annotations have become more and more popular. On Web 2.0 sites, like Delicious and Flickr, various kinds of Web resources are popularly annotated by Web users with freely chosen keywords, which are also known as social annotations or tags. Such annotations not only benefit Web users, but also are helpful in many Web applications. For example, the social annotations of Web pages can be used to improve Web search [47, 735, 773], enterprise search [174], personalized search [503], Web browsing [400], and Semantic Web [729, 778]. Annotations given to other resources are also useful, for example, annotations of Flickr which are assigned to pictures can be effectively utilized for event visualization and detection [186].

2.1   Research on Social Annotations

Existing research on social annotations includes "folksonomy" [260], Semantic Web [463, 729], search and browsing [47, 174, 400, 735, 773], personalization [139, 503], event detection, visualization [186], and so on.

Early research on social annotations focuses on "folksonomy" [260]. "Folksonomy," a combination of "folk" and "taxonomy," provides user-metadata rather than the professionally created or author created metadata. Brooks and Montanez [99] analyzed the effectiveness of tags for classifying blog entries. Golder and Huberman [243] analyzed the structure of collaborative tagging systems as well as their dynamical aspects. Halpin et al. [260] produced a generative model of collaborative tagging in order to understand the basic dynamics behind tagging. Hotho et al. [296] proposed Adapted PageRank and FolkRank to find communities within the folksonomy. A general introduction of folksonomy could be found by Rattenbary et al. [563].

Some applications based on social annotations have also been explored, for example, Semantic Web [463, 729, 778], search and browsing [47, 174, 400, 735, 773], personalization [139, 503], event detection, visualization [186], and Web page classification. Dubinko et al. [186] considered the problem of visualizing the evolution of tags. They presented a new approach based on a characterization of the most interesting tags associated with a sliding time interval. P. Mika [463] proposed a tripartite model of actors, concepts, and instances for semantic emergence. Wu et al. [729] explored semantics from social annotations in a statistical way. Zhou et al. [778] further developed an unsupervised model for exploring the hierarchical semantics from the social annotations. Li et al. [400] improved the Web page browsing experiences by using social annotations. Dmitriev et al. [174] used annotations to improve the quality of intranet search. Bao et al. [47] investigated the capability of social annotations in improving the quality of Web search. Xu et al. [735] smoothed the language model for Web search using social annotations. Zhou et al. [773] proposed a unified framework to combine the modeling of social annotations with the language modeling-based methods for information retrieval. Noll and Meinel [503] adjusted the Web search for different Web users via social bookmarking and tagging. Dubinko et al. [186] considered the problem of visualizing the evolution of tags. Recently, Rattenbury et al. [563] proposed an approach for extracting place and event semantics from tags. The utilization of social annotations for Web page classification has also been addressed recently. For example, Kamishima, Hamasaki, and Akaho [329] developed a new algorithm called BaggTaming, where social annotations were considered as wild data, and labels as tame ones, to improve the accuracy of Web page classification. All the work above was conducted with the assumption of having sufficient social annotations. However, the proportion of Web resources with social annotations is still small. As a supplement, this chapter proposes a new model to propagate the social annotations to the un-annotated Web resources.

Some previous research has also been conducted on generating/extracting keywords for Web pages [230]. Different from their work, we are aiming to enrich the annotations, which consist of human knowledge. Another related work is Chirita et al.'s P-tag [139], which produced keywords relevant to both its textual content and the data residing on the surfer's desktop. In contrast with personalized tag, our approach is to propagate common understanding for Web pages.

2.2 Techniques in Social Annotations

While social annotations are useful, many applications of social annotations suffer from the annotation sparseness problem [47, 174, 735]. The Web resources with social annotations are still limited on the World Wide Web. Take Delicious as an example, more than 1 million Web users collected over 10 million Web pages with millions of social annotations. However, compared with 1.173 billion Web users and about 30 billion Web pages on the WWW, the ratio of both social annotators and annotated Web pages still remains less than 0.1%. The same annotation sparseness problem also appears in the most popular part of Web pages on the WWW. To name a few, based on our study (random sample of about 10,000 pages), more than 75% of the pages in ODP are not annotated by Web users; about 80% of pages within the top 100 most popular English sites have no annotation at all.

As a result, it is urgent to boost the social annotations and alleviate the annotation sparseness problem. Important as it is, to the best of our knowledge, no previous work has addressed this problem.

A simple way to boost social annotations is to provide more convenient tools to reduce the cost of assigning social annotations and encourage more

users to participate. However, due to the power-law distribution of the annotations [260, 400], some popular pages may have achieved a stable state and
still keep receiving new annotations (also known as "rich get richer"), while
a great amount of other pages may only have limited annotations and still
suffer from the sparseness problem. Furthermore, due to the habits of Web
users, some pages rarely get annotated since they can be easily accessed by
some other important pages, or they represent new pages that are not easy to
discover [47].

Another way to boost social annotations is to extract the key terms [230]
or to generate annotations [139] from Web pages and view them as good
summaries. Such methods can be applied to each page on the Web. However,
since it has no user knowledge at all, it cannot guarantee that the generated
key terms have the same properties and high quality as social annotations.

To alleviate the annotation sparseness problem effectively, Bao et al. [49]
propose a method, called *social propagation*, to boost social annotations automatically using propagation. The idea of propagation has been used in
other applications, like page quality evaluation [455], and relevance estimation [155, 554, 620]. While sharing the similar basic idea of propagating via
Web links, previous models are not suitable for social propagation due to
a different propagation resource and purpose. When improving the coverage of social annotations, a good social propagation model should preserve
the novel properties of social annotations, for example, the keyword property indicating that annotations are a good summary of the corresponding
Web page [47, 174, 400, 735], the popularity property indicating that the
amount of annotations represent a page's popularity [47, 186], and the complexity property, which expresses the power-law distribution of social annotations [260, 400].

2.2.1   Problem Formulation

In particular, we propose a general social propagation model based on
the random surfer. More specifically, the propagation model consists of four
surfing steps:

1. **Basic Surfing:** Basic surfing is used to model the propagation of a
   single annotation via the same type of links. Unlike previous models
   of PageRank and Relevance Propagation [620], the basic surfing here
   is aware of preserving the web pages' annotation popularity, that is, it
   prevents the case that the initially annotated pages have no annotation
   at all after propagation.

2. **Multiple-Annotation Surfing:** Most previous propagation tasks focus on only one value for each page. For example, HITS and PageR-
   ank propagate the quality value for each page. Models by Shakery and
   Zhai [620] and Qin et al. [554] propagate the relevance value of a query
   for each page. While propagation of social annotations needs to deal with

TABLE 2.1: Random Walk of a Naive Model

1. Stay at the same page with probability $(1 - \alpha)$;

2. Move to a new page by following a link from one page to another with probability α.

a higher dimension, that is, multiple annotations may be propagated to the same page. Moreover, during the propagation, different annotations should preserve their overall popularities on the whole corpus. Multiple-annotation surfing is proposed for the purposes above.

3. **Multiple-Link-Type Surfing:** The annotation can also be propagated via different types of links. Multiple-link-type surfing models the general case of propagating annotations via different types of links with different *a priori* probabilities. In our implementation, the most widely used sitemap-tree links and hyperlinks are investigated.

4. **Constraint-Guided Surfing:** Different links have different capabilities for propagation. Constraint-guided surfing is proposed to guide the annotation propagation and avoid/alleviate the annotation's topic drifting. Specifically, we study the link connection strength. The links connecting two pages more closely should have a higher priority to be propagated with.

2.2.2 Social Annotation Propagation

In this section, we start with introducing our basic model, which is able to protect a page's original annotations to some extent. Then, we elaborate its extensions from different perspectives, including multiple annotations, multiple link types, and propagation constraints. All the proposed models are based on the random surfer.

Social Propagation-Basic Model: Let's first consider a simplified configuration of propagating single social annotation via the same type of links. Assume that there is only one annotation a assigned to a page p. The purpose of a Web surfer is to collect more pages related to annotation a. Then it may have a Markovian random surfing process starting at p as seen in Table 2.1. In the model above, a is similar to the expansion factor of PageRank [3, 24]. It indicates the portion of annotation for propagation at each step. Then the probability of a Web page p owning annotation a at step $n+1$ can be derived as:

$$a^{(n+1)}(p) = (1 - \alpha)a^{(n)}(p) + \alpha \sum_{p' \to p} a^{(n)}(p') \frac{|L(p' \to p)|}{|L(p' \to *)|} \qquad (2.1)$$

TABLE 2.2: Random Walk of a Basic Model

0. Terminate surfing with probability β or continue with probability $(1 - \beta)$

If continue:

1. Stay at the same page with probability $(1 - \alpha)$;

2. Move to a new page by following a link from one page to another with a probability α.

where $a^{(n)}(p)$ means the probability of annotation assigned to page p at step n; $L(p' \to p)$ means the collection of links pointing from page p' to page p and $L(p' \to *)$ means the collection of links pointing from p'. Assuming the random surfer runs for a long enough period, the above iteration will reach an equilibrium distribution [281].

The model above is able to propagate social annotations to un-annotated pages, that is, improving the coverage of annotations. However, another problem arises where some pages initially annotated may lose all their annotations after the propagation. Such a random surfing can not guarantee the initial popularity of Web pages.

To avoid over propagation, we introduce a new step into the naive model, that is, the random surfer has an opportunity to stop with probability β and to continue with probability $(1 - \beta)$ (see Table 2.2). Then, the naive surfing can be refined as follows:

In the basic model, β is a damping factor, which preserves the Web pages' original annotations to some extent by affecting the iteration steps. The final expected distribution becomes:

$$a(p) = \sum_{i=1}^{\infty} \beta^i a^{(i)}(p) \tag{2.2}$$

In the following sections, for simplicity, we focus on extending the naive model from different aspects to fit the requirement of effective social annotation propagation.

2.2.2.1 Social Propagation-Multiple Annotations

Now, let's consider a more complicated case of social annotation propagation. Assume that there is a set of annotations $A = \{a_1, a_2, \ldots, a_n\}$. Before propagation, we have a count of c_i for each annotation a_i. In total, there are c annotations. Correspondingly, the random surfer has to decide which annotation to propagate. Table 2.3 illustrates the new random surfing process. At first, each annotation a_i has the probability c_i/c to be randomly selected. Then, the surfer follows the naive model as described in Table 2.1.

TABLE 2.3: Random Walk with Multiple Annotations

1′ Random selection of one annotation for propagation;

1 Stay at the same page with probability $(1 - \alpha)$;

2 Move to a new page by following a link from one page to another with a probability α.

Note that the random walk above preserves each annotation's popularity, that is, the total count c_i is not changed for annotation ai during the whole propagation process. Then we have the multiple-annotation propagation model as:

$$\overrightarrow{A^{(n+1)}(p)} = (1 - \alpha)\overrightarrow{A^{(n)}(p)} + \alpha \sum_{p' \to p} \overrightarrow{A^{(n)}(p')}\frac{|L(p' \to p)|}{L(p' \to *)} \qquad (2.3)$$

where $\overrightarrow{A}(p) = \{a_1(p), a_2(p), \ldots, a_n(p)\}$ is a vector that stores the probabilities of different annotations assigned to page p.

2.2.2.2 Social Propagation-Multiple Link Types

Similar to previous work on relevance propagation [30], the annotations can also be propagated via different types of links, for example, hyperlinks and sitemap-tree links. Our model can be further extended to propagating social annotations through different kinds of links. Without loss of generality, we assume that there are l types of links $L_T = \{L_1, L_2, \ldots, L_l\}$. For each link, the surfer has different probability $P(L_i)$ to follow the link according to the link's type. Then, the naive random surfer's walk can be adjusted as seen in Table 2.4.

The probabilities of a page annotated by the surfer are transformed as follows:

$$a^{(n+1)}(p) = (1 - \alpha)a^{(n)}(p) + \alpha \sum_{L_i \in L_T} P(L_i) \sum_{p' \to p \, via \, L_i} a^{(n)}(p')\frac{|L_i(p' \to p)|}{|L_i(p' \to *)|}$$

$$\sum_{i=1}^{l} P(L_i) = 1$$

(2.4)

where "$p' \to p$ via L_i" means page p' and page p are linked with link type L_i.

2.2.2.3 Social Propagation-Constraint

Links are good indicators for propagation, but they are not the whole story. The connection strength of two linked pages varies a lot. For example,

TABLE 2.4: Random Walk with Multiple Link Types

1 Stay at the same page with a probability $(1 - \alpha)$;

2′ Select a type of links L_i with probability $P(L_i)$;

2 Move to a new page by following a link of L_i with a probability α.

TABLE 2.5: Random Walk with Constraint

1 Stay at the same page with probability $(1 - \alpha)$;

2 Move to a new page by following a link from one page to another with a probability α; the selection probability of specific link $p' \to p$ is in direct proportion to $P(p' \to p)$.

some links are given to pages describing other topics. To prevent/alleviate the topic drifting, we add a constraint factor $P(p' \to p)$ to guide the surfer's walk. Table 2.5 shows the details.

The corresponding revised model with the propagation constraint is shown in Equation 2.5.

$$a^{(n+1)}(p) = (1 - \alpha)a^{(n)}(p) + \alpha \sum_{p' \to p} a^{(n)}(p') \frac{|L(p' \to p)|}{|L(p' \to *)|} P(p' \to p)$$

$$\sum_{p|p' \to p} \frac{|L(p' \to p)|}{|L(p' \to *)|} P(p' \to p) = 1 \tag{2.5}$$

In this chapter, we propose to estimate the link connection strength for the propagation as Equation 2.6.

$$P_i(p' \to p) \propto \frac{\vec{p'} \cdot \vec{p}}{|\vec{p'}||\vec{p}|} \tag{2.6}$$

where $\vec{p'}$ and $\vec{p}$ are *tf-idf* vectors of pure textual page contents.

2.2.2.4   General Model

The random surfing based models are quite flexible. The above surfing steps can be merged and we present our general social surfing process as seen in Table 2.6.

TABLE 2.6: Random Walk of a General Model

0 Terminate surfing with probability β and continue width probability $(1 - \beta)$;

If continue

1' Random selection of one annotation for propagation;

1 Stay at the same page with a probability $(1 - \alpha)$;

2' Select a type of links L_i with probability $P(L_i)$;

2 Move to a new page by following a link from one page to another with a probability α; the selection probability of specific link $p' \to p$ is in direct proportion to $P(p' \to p)$.

Then, the final distribution of annotations can be calculated by Equation 2.2, where the corresponding iteration formula is replaced as follows:

$$A^{(n+1)}(p) = (1 - \alpha)A^{(n)}(p) + \alpha \sum_{p' \to p} A^{(n)}(p') \frac{|L(p' \to p)|}{|L(p' \to *)|} P(p' \to p)$$

$$\sum_{i=1}^{l} P(L_i) = 1 \tag{2.7}$$

$$\sum_{p|p' \to p} \frac{|L(p' \to p)|}{|L(p' \to *)|} P(p' \to p) = 1$$

2.2.3 Discussion

2.2.3.1 Scalability of the Propagation

Propagation of social annotations is different from previous propagation tasks, like static quality propagation and relevance propagation. Both relevance propagation and static quality propagation focus on a single value and not on the annotation vectors, as social propagation does. From this point of view, propagation of annotations requires more computations. Assume that there are $|L|$ links and $|A_P|$ distinct annotations per page. For each iteration, the computational complexity is approximately $O(|L||A_P|)$.

Two properties of social annotations can be further utilized to accelerate the propagation. (1) Distributed propagation: in our current model, the propagation of different annotations can be processed concurrently. In addition, it is possible for partial propagation, which is especially useful in propagating some new hot annotations emerging on the Web without changing any previous propagation results. (2) Incremental propagation: as addressed by Adomavicius and Tuzhilin [11] and Agichtein et al. [12], the annotation will

become stable for some popular pages. As a result, the incremented annotations of stable pages only change their popularity of previous propagated
distribution and can skip step-by-step propagation.

2.2.3.2   Propagation through More Links

In addition to hyperlinks and sitemap-tree links, there is also other link
information available. For example, links can also be generated from manual
Web directories, like ODP. The Web pages under the same categories usually
share the same topic and, as a result, the annotations can propagate via either
links among siblings or links between parent and child pages. The proposed
model is quite flexible and such links can be easily integrated. In this paper, we
did not introduce the ODP based links yet since the connections represented by
ODP are much looser and may bring more noises. However, the links derived
from ODP can connect two sites/pages, which may not be easily connected
via hyperlinks or sitemap-tree links. We leave it as one of our future directions
in further boosting social annotations.

Another direction is to propagate the social annotations via more fine-
grained Web links. Many methods can be used to refine the link information,
for example, noise link removal and block level link detection. Noise link removal can be directly applied in our setting as a preprocessing step. As for
block level links, the initial block-level annotation for propagation is required.
The initial block-level annotation can be obtained either from page-level annotations via machine learning, or from block-level annotation services, for
example, CiteULike[1] and Technorati,[2] which allow the assignment of annotations to objects within a page. We argue that the fine-grained Web link based
annotation propagation will produce better results.

2.2.3.3   Propagation with More Constraints

As we have seen, the content based constraint does alleviate the topic
drifting effectively. In fact, more constraints can be introduced in our propagation model. First, annotations have different capabilities for propagation.
For example, some annotations only belong to the original Web pages and are
not supposed to be propagated. Second, propagation can be adjusted based
on the mutual relationship among annotations [1, 22, 34]. Third, propagation
is also affected by the similarity between annotations and content of the target page. Furthermore, different annotations may be suited for propagation
via different links. Some annotations can be propagated well via sitemap-tree
links while some others are more suitable for hyperlink based propagation.
The constraints above can help avoid topic drifting better. However, they also
introduce more computations and destroy the concurrency properties of the
current propagation model.

---

[1]http://www.citeulike.org
[2]http://technorati.com

2.2.3.4 Propagating More Information

The social annotations are usually modeled as a quad-tuple, that is, <*user, annotation, resource, time>*, which means that a *user* gives an *annotation* to a specific *resource* at a specific *time*. In this paper, we focus on the propagation of annotations over resources since they are the most useful part of the social structures. However, the user and time information may also be useful in certain applications. For example, *user* information can be used for personalized search [23, 34], browsing [18], and tag generation [5]. The time information may be used for hot topic browsing [18], visualization [8], and detection [27].

As a general framework, it is easy to incorporate user and/or time information. The simplest way is to generalize the concept of annotation as constrained annotations, that is, let the constrained annotation be $< annotation, user >$ or $< annotation, user, time >$. Then our random walk can be performed over the constrained annotations. Another way is to add a new step for the random surfer, for example, the surfer may randomly select a user or a specific time period before selecting a specific annotation for propagation. It would be interesting to see that user specific information can be extended via the propagation and support personalized search better. It would also be interesting to see whether more hot and detailed topics can be discovered from the propagated time-related annotations. We leave these as our further work.

2.3 Application of Social Annotations

2.3.1 Social Annotation for Personalized Search

In today's search market, the most popular search paradigm is keyword search. Despite simplicity and efficiency, keyword queries can not accurately describe what the users really want. People engaged in different areas may have different understandings of the same literal keywords. Teevan et al. [664] concluded that people differ significantly in the search results they consider to be relevant for the same query.

One solution to this problem is *Personalized Search*. By considering user-specific information, search engines can to some extent distinguish the exact meaning the users want to express by short queries. Along with the evolution of the WWW, many kinds of personal data have been studied for personalized search, including user manually selected interests [430], Web browser bookmarks [579], users' personal document corpus [140], search engine click-through history [177, 555, 650], and so on. In all, search personalization is one of the most promising directions for the traditional search paradigm to go further.

In recent years, there is a growing concern in the new Web 2.0 environment. One feature of Web 2.0 that distinguishes it from the classical World Wide Web is the social data generation mode. The service providers only provide platforms for the users to collaborate and to share their data online. Such services include folksonomy, blog, Wiki, and so on. Since the data are generated and owned by the users, they form a new set of personal data. In this section, we focus on exploring folksonomy for personalized search.

The term "folksonomy" is a combination of "Folk" and "Taxonomy" to describe the social classification phenomenon. Online folksonomy services, such as Delicious, Flickr, and Dogear [465], enable users to save and organize their bookmarks, including any accessible resources, online with freely chosen short text descriptors, that is, "social annotations" or "tags," in flat structure. The users are able to collaborate during bookmarking and tagging explicitly or implicitly. The low barrier and facility of this service have successfully attracted a large number of users to participate.

The folksonomy creates a social association between the users and the Web pages through social annotations. More specifically, a user who has a given annotation may be interested in the Web pages that have the same annotation. Inspired by this, Xu et al. [736] propose to model the associations between the users and the Web pages using a topic space. The interests of each user and the topics of each Web page can be mapped to vectors in the topic space. The personalized search is conducted by ranking the Web pages in two guidelines, term matching and topic matching. When a user u issues a query q, a Web page p is ranked not only by the term similarity between q and p but also by the topic similarity between u and p. The social annotations in folksonomy naturally form a social topic space. Three folksonomy properties are studied for the topic space estimation:

The categorization property. Many of the social annotations are subject descriptor keywords at various levels of specificity. The selection of proper annotations for a Web page is somewhat a classification of the Web page to the categories represented by the annotations.

The keyword property. As discussed by Golder and Huberman [243], Bao et al. [47], and Wu et al. [729], the annotations can be seen as good keywords for describing the respective Web pages from various aspects.

The structure property. In folksonomy systems, users' bookmarking actions form a cross link structure between the users and the Web pages. Since all the folksonomy data are publicly available, the structure can be fully explored.

Some of the prior studies show similar ideas. Qi et al. [555] and Ma et al. [430], use ODP taxonomy structure to represent the topics of the Web pages and the interests of the users. As a comparison, Xu et al. [736] apply ODP in their work to show whether or not the classical Web page taxonomy still perform well enough for the Web 2.0 search personalization.

2.3.1.1 Analysis of Folksonomy

What folksonomy can assist personalized search? The best way to answer this question is to analyze it.

Social Annotations as Category Names. In the folksonomy systems, the users are free to choose any social annotations to classify and organize their bookmarks. Though there may be some noise, each social annotation represents a topic that is related to its semantic meaning. Based on this, the social annotations owned by the Web pages and the users reflect their topics and interests, respectively.

Social Annotations as Keywords. As discussed in Bao et al. [47] and Wu et al. [729], the annotations are very close to human generated keywords. Thus, the social annotations usually can well describe or even complement the content of the Web pages.

Collaborative Link Structure. One of the most important benefits that online folksonomy systems bring is the collaborative link structure created by the users unconsciously. The underlying link structure of the tagging systems has been explored in many prior efforts [47, 463, 729]. The whole underlying structures of folksonomy systems are rather complex. Different researchers may reduce the complexity of modeling the structure by various simplified models, for example, in Wu et al. [729], the structure is modeled through a latent semantic layer while in Bao et al. [47], the relations between the annotations and the Web pages are modeled using a bipartite graph. In our work, since the relations between the users and the Web pages are very important, we model the structure using a user-web page bipartite graph as shown in Figure 2.1.

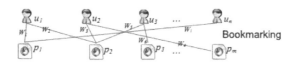

FIGURE 2.1: User-Web page bipartite structure.

where $u_i, i = 1, 2, ..., n$ denotes the n users, $p_j, j = 1, 2, ..., m$ denotes the m Web pages, $W_k, k = 1, 2, ..., l$ are the weights of the links, that is, the bookmarking actions of the users. One of the simplest implementation of the weights is the number of annotations a user is assigned to a Web page.

2.3.1.2 A Personalized Search Framework

In the classical nonpersonalized search engines, the relevance between a query and a document is assumed to be only decided by the similarity of term matching. However, relevance is actually relative for each user. Thus, only query term matching is not enough to generate satisfactory search results for various users.

Inspired by the Vector Space Model (VSM), we propose to model the associations between the users and the Web pages using a *topic space*. Each dimension of the topic space represents a topic. The topics of the Web pages and the interests of the users are represented as vectors in this space. Further, we define a topic similarity measurement using the cosine function. Let $\overrightarrow{p_{ti}} = (w_{1,i}, w_{2,i}, ..., w_{\alpha,i})$ be the topic vector of the Web page p_i, where α is the dimension of the topic space and $w_{k,i}$ is the weight of the kth dimension. Similarly, let $\overrightarrow{u_{tj}} = (w_{1,j}, w_{2,j}, ..., w_{\alpha,j})$ be the interest vector of the user u_j. The topic similarity between p_i and u_j is calculated as Equation 2.8.

$$sim_{topic}(p_i, u_j) = \frac{\overrightarrow{p_{ti}} \cdot \overrightarrow{u_{tj}}}{|\overrightarrow{p_{ti}}| \times |\overrightarrow{u_{tj}}|} \tag{2.8}$$

Based on the topic space, we make a fundamental personalized search assumption, that is, Assumption 1.

ASSUMPTION 1. *The rank of a Web page p in the result list when a user u issues a query q is decided by two aspects, a term matching between q and p and a topic matching between u and p.*

When a user u issues a query q, we assume two search processes, a term matching process, and a topic matching process. The term matching process calculates the similarity between q and each Web page to generate a user unrelated ranked document list. The topic matching process calculates the topic similarity between u and each Web page to generate a user related ranked document list. Then a merge operation is conducted to generate a final ranked document list based on the two sub ranked document lists. We adopt ranking aggregation to implement the merge operation.

Ranking Aggregation is to compute a "consensus" ranking of several subrankings [11]. There are a lot of rank aggregation algorithms that can be applied in our work. Here we choose one of the simplest, Weighted Borda-Fuse (WBF). Equation 2.9 shows our idea.

$$r(u, q, p) = \gamma \cdot r_{term}(q, p) + (1 - \gamma) \cdot r_{topic}(u, p) \tag{2.9}$$

where $r_{term}(q, p)$ is the rank of the Web page p in the ranked document list generated by query term matching, $r_{topic}(u, p)$ is the rank of p in the ranked document list generated by topic matching, and γ is the weight that satisfies $0 \leq \gamma \leq 1$.

Obviously, how to select a proper topic space and how to accurately estimate the user interest vectors and the Web page topic vectors are two key points in this framework. The next two sections discuss these problems.

2.3.1.3 Topic Space Selection

In Web page classification, the Web pages are classified to several predefined categories. Intuitively, the categories of Web page classification are very similar to the topics of the topic space. In today's World Wide Web, there are two classification systems, the traditional taxonomy such as ODP and the new folksonomy. The two classification systems can be both applied in our framework. Since our work focuses on exploring the folksonomy for personalized search, we set the ODP topic space as a baseline.

Folksonomy: Social Annotations as Topics: Based on the categorization feature, we set the social annotations to be the dimensions of the topic space. Thus, the topic vector of a Web page can be simply estimated by its social annotations directly. In the same way, the interest vector of a user can also be simply estimated by her social annotations. Obviously, if we treat the users and the Web pages as documents, the social annotations as terms, the above setting fits a SVM. Since the VSM has developed for a long time, there have been a large number of mature technologies to improve the VSM search effectiveness. All these can be easily applied here. One of the most important properties of the SVM is the weighting for document terms. Similarly, the topic weighting here is also very important. The simplest while widely used one is tf-idf. In addition to this, the $BM25$ weighting scheme is a more sophisticated alternative, which represents state-of-the-art retrieval functions used in document retrieval.

Taxonomy—ODP Categories as Topics: In Web page taxonomy, the "DMOZ" Open Directory Project (ODP) is the largest, most comprehensive human-edited directory of the Web. We choose ODP's 16 top categories as the dimensions of the topic space. However, 16 categories may be too few for our personalized search task compared to the folksonomy categories. Thus, we make another choice of a total of 1171 categories, including all the second level categories of ODP and the third level categories of TOP/Computers. The choice is based on the consideration that the data corpus we will use in experiments are mostly about computer science.

Now the question is how to estimate the topic vectors and interest vectors. All the descriptions of the Web pages under a category can be merged to create a term vector of the corresponding category. Then the topic vector of a Web page can be calculated by cosine similarity of the category's term vector and the social annotations of the Web page. Similarly, the interest vector of a user can be calculated by cosine similarity of the category's term vector and the social annotations owned by the user.

2.3.1.4 Interest and Topic Adjusting via a Bipartite Collaborative Link Structure

In Section 2.3.1.1, we have modeled the underlying collaborative structure of a folksonomy system as a bipartite graph. The bipartite structure is the result of user collaboration, which is one of the main advantages of online folksonomy service over offine desktop bookmarks. Intuitively, the topics of the Web pages that a user saved in social tagging systems exhibit the user's interests. In return, the interests of the users who saved a given Web page also imply the topics of the Web page to some extent. Furthermore, it is not difficult to infer that this process is actually iterative. We propose to fully explore this bipartite structure for adjusting the initial estimation of users' interest vectors and the Web pages' topic vectors using an iterative algorithm.

Formally, let $G = (V, E)$ be the graph, where the nodes in V represent users and Web pages, and the edges E represent the bookmarking actions. The nodes in V are divided into two subsets $U = \{u_1, u_2, ..., u_n\}$ representing the users and $P = \{p_1, p_2, ..., p_m\}$ representing the Web pages. In Table 2.7, we list all the symbols we will use in the algorithm.

TABLE 2.7: Symbols Used in the Topic Adjusting Algorithm

Symbol	Meaning
W	The adjacency matrix, in which the rows represent the users and the columns represent the Web pages. $W_{i,j}$ is set to the number of annotations that u_i gives to p_j.
W_{rn}	The row normalized version of W.
W_{cn}	The column normalized version of W.
$r_{i,j}$	The jth normalized interest of the ith user.
$t_{i,j}$	The jth normalized topic of the ith Web page.
R	The row normalized interest matrix of all the users, in which the rows represent the users and the columns represent the interests. $R_{i,j}$ is the jth interest value of u_i.
T	The row normalized topic matrix of all the Web pages, in which the rows represent the Web pages and the columns represent the topics. $T_{i,j}$ is the jth topic value of p_i.
α	The weight of the initial estimated user interest.
β	The weight of the initial estimated Web page topic.

Each iteration of this algorithm is performed in two steps.
1) User interest adjusting by related Web pages.

$$r_{i,j} = \alpha \cdot r_{i,j}^0 + (1 - \alpha) \cdot \frac{\sum_{k=1}^{m} t_{k,j} \cdot W_{i,k}}{\sum_{k=1}^{m} W_{i,k}} \qquad (2.10)$$

where $r_{i,j}^0$ is the initial value of $r_{i,j}$.
2) Web page topic adjusting by related users.

$$t_{i,j} = \beta \cdot t_{i,j}^0 + (1 - \beta) \cdot \frac{\sum_{k=1}^{n} r_{k,j} \cdot W_{k,i}}{\sum_{k=1}^{n} W_{k,i}} \qquad (2.11)$$

where $t_{i,j}^0$ is the initial value of $t_{i,j}$.

As we can see from the two equations above, we reserve in each iteration an α and a β weight of the initial interest value, and the initial topic value respectively. The reason is that since $r_{i,j}^0$ and $t_{i,j}^0$ are estimated directly from the social annotations' literal contents while $(\sum_{k=1}^{m} t_{k,j} \cdot W_{i,k})/\sum_{k=1}^{m} W_{i,k}$ and $(\sum_{k=1}^{n} r_{k,j} \cdot W_{k,i})/\sum_{k=1}^{n} W_{k,i}$ are from the link structure, they are two heterogeneous parts. The two weights, α and β, are to reserve the influence of the social annotations' literal contents in the final adjusted vectors. In addition, though the forms of the two equations above seem to be complicated, the operations are actually a linear combination. Thus, the topic vectors of the Web pages and the interest vectors of the users must be in the same scale. Thus, before the running of the algorithm we normalize all the vectors. Finally, the two equations above can be rewritten in the form of matrices as the following:

$$R^{t+1} = \alpha R^0 + (1 - \alpha)W_{rn}T^t \tag{2.12}$$

$$T^{t+1} = \beta T^0 + (1 - \beta)W_{cn}^T R^{t+1} \tag{2.13}$$

We claim that this iterative algorithm converges to a fixed point finally. In the following we give a short proof. We do not list the detailed analysis of this algorithm because of page limitation. The interested readers can refer to some prior studies by Athique [30] and Asur et al. [29], inspired from which we have the idea of this algorithm.

PROOF. Without loss of generality, we only prove R^i can converge to a fixed point. Let W_α be $(a - \alpha)W_{rn}$ and W_β be $(1 - \beta)W_{cn}^T$, we can expand Equation 2.12 as the following:

$$R^{i+1} = \alpha\{E + W_\alpha W_\beta + (W_\alpha W_\beta)^2 + ... + (W_\alpha W_\beta)^{i+1}\}R^0$$
$$+ \beta W_\alpha\{E + W_\beta W_\alpha + (W_\beta W_\alpha)^2 + ... + (W_\beta W_\alpha)^i\}T^0$$

Thus,

$$\lim_{i \to +\infty} ||R^{i+1} - R^i||$$
$$= lim_{i \to +\infty}||\alpha[W_\alpha W_\beta]^{i+1}R^0 + \beta W_\alpha(W_\beta W_\alpha)^i T^0||$$
$$= lim_{i \to +\infty}||\alpha(1 - \alpha)^{(i} + 1)(1 - \beta)^{i+1}(W_{rn}W_{cn}^T)^{i+1}R^0$$
$$+ \beta(1 - \alpha)^{i+1}(1 - \beta)^i(W_{cn}^T W_{rn})^i T^0||$$

On the one hand, consider that W_{rn} and W_{cn}^T are both row normalized, they are actually two Markov matrices, thus, $W_{rn}W_{cn}^T$, $W_{cn}^T W_{rn}$, $(W_{rn}W_{cn}^T)^{i+1}$, and $(W_{cn}^T W_{rn})^i$, are also Markov matrices. On the other hand, because $0 < \alpha < 1$ and $0 < \beta < 1$, we can derive:

$$\lim_{i \to +\infty} \{\alpha(1 - \alpha)^{i+1}(1 - \beta)^{i+1}\} = 0$$

$$\lim_{i \to +\infty} \{\beta(1 - \alpha)^{i+1}(1 - \beta)^i\} = 0$$

Thus, we can finally derive that $\lim_{i \to +\infty} ||R^{i+1} - R^i|| = 0$, that is, R^i is convergent. $\square$

2.3.2 Hierarchical Semantics from Social Annotations

Compared with the traditional metadata organization, a folksonomy represents a high improvement in lowering barriers to cooperation. A traditional taxonomy, which is predefined only by small groups of experts, is limited and might easily become outdated. Social annotation just solves these problems by transferring the burden from several individuals to all Web users. Users could arbitrarily annotate Web resources according to their own vocabularies, and largely enrich the metadata resources for the Semantic Web. Although social annotation services have a large potential to boom the Semantic Web, development of these services are impeded by their own shortcomings. Such shortcomings are mainly due to two features of folksonomy:

> Uncontrolled vocabulary. Breaking away from the authoritatively deter-mined vocabulary, a folksonomy suffers from several limitations. One is ambiguity. People might use the same word to express different mean-ings. Another phenomenon is synonym. Different tags might denote the same meaning. Given the ambiguity and synonymy of natural language terms, users might easily miss valuable information while obtaining some redundant information.

> Nonhierarchical structure. The folksonomy represents a flat but non hier-archical annotation space. This property gives difficulties when browsing Web pages, and moreover, makes it hard to bridge a folksonomy with traditional hierarchical ontologies.

Aimed at overcoming those shortcomings, much research has been con-ducted. Aurnhammer et al. [36] introduced the concept of the "navigation map," which describes the relationship between data elements. The author showed how to find semantic related images. Wu et al. [729] gave a probabilis-tic method to allocate tags into a set of parallel clusters, and applied these clusters to search and discover the Delicious bookmarks. Both of Aurnham-mer et al. [36] and Wu et al. [729] focused on exploring relations between tags in the uncontrolled vocabulary, but still did not solve the nonhierarchy prob-lem. In Li et al. [400], the authors proposed an algorithm to derive synonymic and hierarchical relations between tags, and demonstrated promising results. But the model is supervised, thus could not be effectively extended to other contexts, and also lacks a sound theoretical foundation.

In a paper by Zhou et al. [778], the authors propose an unsupervised model, which could automatically derive hierarchical semantics from the flat tag space. Although search engines which aim to derive hierarchy out of search results already exist (e.g., Vivisimo[3]), to the best of our knowledge, no work has been done before on exploring hierarchical semantics from tags. We demonstrate that the derived hierarchical semantics well compensates for the folksonomy's shortcomings.

In order to derive the hierarchical semantics, our model proceeds in a top-down way. Beginning with the root node containing all annotations, we apply the splitting process to gain a series of clusters, each of which represents a specific topic. Further apply the splitting process on each cluster, and smaller

---

[3]http://vivisimo.com/

clusters with narrower semantics are gained. It is easy to observe this recursive process to help us obtain a hierarchal structure. A probabilistic unsupervised method named the deterministic annealing (DA) algorithm is utilized in each splitting process. Unlike other clustering algorithms, the DA algorithm could well control the cluster number and each cluster's size with the help of a parameter T. We make use of this feature to ensure that each node's semantics can be identified by a few tags.

Different from previous work, our model has several important features:

- *Unsupervised model.* Without any need of training data, it could be easily extended to other social annotation services.

- *Hierarchical model.* In the derived structure, each node represents an emergent concept and each edge denotes the hierarchical relationship between concepts.

- *Self-controlled model.* In our model, the number and the size of clusters are automatically determined during the annealing process.

The hierarchical semantics derived from our model has a large number of applications. Take two for example: (1) *Semantic Web.* The derived hierarchical semantics well serves as a bridge between the traditional strict ontology and the distributed social annotations. It would make ontology more sensitive to users' interests and demands, and reflect the current trends in the Internet. (2) *Resource Browsing and Organization.* The derived hierarchical semantics could also be utilized as effective tools for resource browsing and organization. Users could easily trace the path from the root to the node which contains information they want.

2.3.2.1 Algorithm Overview

This model builds the hierarchical structure in a top-down way. Beginning with the root node, the model recursively applies the splitting process to each node until termination conditions are satisfied. In each splitting process, the DA algorithm is utilized. Figure 2.2 gives an intuitive description of this splitting process. In Figure 2.2, we observe that controlled by a parameter T, the DA algorithm splits the node in a gradual way. As T is lowered from the first to the fourth subgraph, the cluster number increases from one to four finally. This process terminates when all clusters become "Effective Cluster," or the number of "Effective Cluster" reaches an upper bound. The term "Effective Cluster" refers to those clusters whose semantics could be generalized by some specific tags. We name those tags the "Leading Tag" for this cluster. It should be noted that the effective clusters do not emerge immediately. In the second subgraph, neither of the clusters are effective clusters, because their semantics are too wide to be generalized by any tag. In the fourth subgraph, all of the clusters are effective clusters, leading tags for which are "music," "home," "Web," and "game," respectively. In our model, we design a criterion, which is given in Section 3.4, to identify an effective cluster.

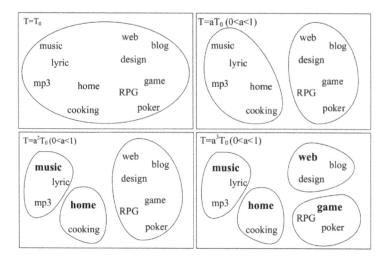

FIGURE 2.2: The emergent semantics during the annealing process.

An overview of our model is given in Algorithm 1. In Algorithm 1, we maintain a queue Q to store the information of nodes which are waiting for splitting. Vector P in the queue indicates the probability that each tag emerges

---

Algorithm 1 Deriving Hierarchical Semantics

1: Initialize Q. Q is a queue containing one N dimensions vector $P_0 = (1, 1, \ldots, 1)$

2: **while** Q is not empty **do**

3:    Pop P from Q. Let $P = (p_0, p_1, \ldots, p_N)$

4:    $\{p(c_i|t_j)|i \in [1, C], j \in [1, N]\} \leftarrow f_D(P)$

5:    **for** each cluster $c_i, i = 1, 2, \ldots, C$ **do**

6:        Extract leading tags t_{c_i} to stand for the semantics of cluster c_i

7:        **if** c_i could be further split **then**

8:            Let $P' = (p'_0, p'_1, \ldots, p'_N)$

9:

$$p'_j = \begin{cases} p_j * p(c_i|t_j) & t_j \neq t_{c_i} \\ 0 & t_j = t_{c_i} \end{cases}$$

10:           Push P' into Q.

11:        **else**

12:            The remaining tags except leading tags t_{c_i} form leaves for the current node.

13:        **end if**

14:    **end for**

15: **end while**

---

in this node. At line 1, elements of P_0 are all initialized with 1, because all tags are contained in the root node. From line 2 to 10, the algorithm recursively splits each node until the termination condition is satisfied. We finally gain a hierarchical structure and each node's semantics is identified by its corresponding leading tags.

Line 4 of Algorithm 1 is a key part of our model. The function f_D serves as a clustering machine. Input the node's information, and f_D outputs a series of effective clusters derived from this node. Each cluster is described by the value $p(c_i|t_j)$ represents the relation between the jth tag and the ith cluster. As discussed before, the DA algorithm is utilized in f_D.

2.4 Conclusion

In this chapter we have given an overview of the methods for annotating UGC and have especially focused on effective methods for annotation propagation.

Chapter 3

Sentiment Analysis in UGC

Ning Yu

School of Library and Information Science, University of Kentucky

3.1 Introduction

Freely accessible and easily customizable Web applications have made it easy and fun for people to publish and share their experiences, knowledge, opinions, and emotions. The opinions of lay users (nonexperts) may serve to balance and complement the authoritative points of view published by mainstream media such as the New York Times newspaper and CNN; and the customer moods may help make market predictions. Therefore, user generated opinions have attracted an increasing amount of interest from individuals as well as organizations. For example, people are curious about what other people think of certain products or topics; companies want to find out what their target audience likes or dislikes about their products and services;

and government officials would like to learn whether people are for or against new policies. Foreseeing the growing demand for detecting online opinion, researchers from different communities started to explore a new research area called opinion mining in the late 1990s. Dave, Lawrence, and Pennock [162], who first coined the term "opinion mining," described an opinion mining tool for online product reviews that aimed to automate the sequence of "processing a set of search results for a given item, generating a list of product attributes (quality, features, etc.) and aggregating opinions about each of them (poor, mixed, good)" (p. 519). To date, a series of opinion mining tasks have been explored, including differentiating opinions from facts, also known as subjectivity analysis [719, 722, 744, 767], detecting positive or negative opinion polarity [3, 156, 345, 371, 521], determining opinion strength [672, 724], and identifying opinion holders and opinion properties [71, 346, 371, 402, 616].

In the past few years, especially after the emergence of Twitter, the term "sentiment analysis" has seen a wider use than "opinion mining": sometimes it refers to valence analysis or the polarity detection subtask of opinion mining [242], other times it refers to emotion status identification [82, 427, 533]. Although sentiment analysis emphasizes on general feelings while opinion mining is targeted on opinion expressions, these two terms are often used interchangeably. This chapter adopts a broad definition for sentiment analysis: the task of detecting opinions, polarity and/or emotional status, and focuses on the first two subtasks, which are fundamental and well-studied in the literature.

The rest of this chapter is organized as follows. Section 3.2 lays the groundwork for later sections by defining the problem of sentiment analysis and exploring general challenges. Being a "subdiscipline at the crossroads of information retrieval and computational linguistics" [209, p. 417], sentiment analysis requires a broad range of knowledge and techniques. In the hope that readers will gain a thorough overview of this interdisciplinary research problem, Section 3.3 discusses major issues of sentiment analysis and explores a large body of sentiment analysis studies that tackled these issues. Section 3.4 concludes this chapter by pointing out future directions.

3.2 Background

3.2.1 Problem Definition

Sentiment analysis is the task of detecting, extracting, and/or summarizing opinions, polarity and/or emotions, normally based on the presence or absence of *sentiment features*. In most cases, sentiment analysis is treated as a classification problem, with the categories being *opinion* and *fact*, *positive* and *negative*, or a finer level of emotion categories (e.g., *angry*, *happy*, *sad*), and is evaluated by classification accuracy. There are also cases, such as in the context of information retrieval and information extraction, when sentiment analysis involves retrieving or extracting sentiment expressions or documents, and is evaluated by precision, recall, and/or F score. In both cases, finding important sentiment indicators and designing the proper strategy to utilize them are crucial.

Sentiment analysis can also be understood as a subtask of other nonfactual information detection tasks. *Question-answering*, an information retrieval task that returns actual answers rather than whole documents, may also overlap with the task of opinion detection when the question is sentiment-oriented [408], such as "What do people feel about the U.S.-Iraq war?" *Appraisal extraction* [78] and *affective computing* [538], both of which contain the task of identifying attitudes and emotions [78, 268, 411, 765], are also closely related to sentiment analysis.

3.2.2 Levels of Granularity

Sentiment analysis can be conducted at several levels depending on the granularity of the target text unit: the term level, the expression level, the passage level, and the document level. The level of granularity is mainly decided by the purpose of the application. For example, document level sentiment analysis is usually enough for a retrieval task, but not for an extraction or summarization task, which requires identification of sentiment at the level of sentences or passages. Granularity is also restricted by the available annotated corpus: the finer the level at which the corpus is annotated, the more levels of granularity on which one system can be trained to detect sentiment. In terms of user generated content on microblogs, distinguishing document from subdocument level of sentiment analysis is not necessary because microblogging messages are typically short.

Sentiment analysis at the term level is used to determine whether a single word or phrase falls into some sentiment categories, often within a certain context. However, in real-world applications, term-level sentiment analysis is rarely the ultimate goal. Instead, it provides a set of terms (i.e., lexicon) that can serve as features for higher level sentiment analysis.

Sentiment analysis at the expression level identifies the exact portion of text that is directly responsible for the sentiment attribute. In the manually annotated opinion expression "(Perhaps you'll forgive me) for reposting his response," the opinion expression is indicated by parenthesis [718, p. 3]. Sentiment analysis at such a fine level is an extremely difficult task for both humans and machines because the boundary of the expression is not fixed (i.e., a sentiment expression could be a single word or an entire phrase). As suggested by Wiebe et al. [718], expression-level sentiment analysis is used only during the process of manually annotating corpora for "knowledge acquisition (analysis, training, feature generation)" (p. 3).

Sentiment analysis at the passage level is the most popular approach. The passage level can include a single sentence, a passage containing multiple sentences, or any text unit of arbitrary length. Although automated passage-level sentiment analysis is feasible for user generated content, it is still quite challenging because of the difficulty of precisely truncating the passage boundary (e.g., misplaced/missing punctuation marks) and because of the sparsity of sentiment-bearing features in short text units.

Document-level sentiment analysis is directly related to many real-world applications such as retrieving opinion posts from the blogosphere. It can be easily integrated into existing Web-mining systems, which usually work with document-level information. A group of studies on document-level opinion retrieval in the blogosphere has been conducted as part of the Blog track at the Text REtrieval Conference (TREC). The Blog track is an international information retrieval contest that requires participants to carry out systematic investigation of integrating opinion retrieval tasks with traditional topical retrieval. In the Blog track, methods of finding opinion blog posts on specific topics are studied in a standardized environment: same training and testing datasets created from a blog corpus containing blog posts that have been manually classified into different opinion classes (i.e., "positive," "negative," or "neutral"), same 50 search topics (i.e., search tasks), and same evaluation matrix [509].

Other levels of granularity in opinion detection include multidocument collections and speech, which is defined as a "continuous single-speaker segment of text" [668, p. 328].

3.3   Major Issues in Sentiment Analysis

All sentiment analysis studies can be decomposed into three roughly sequential steps: (1) data preparation; (2) feature selection/extraction; and (3) algorithm deployment. This section will examine important issues associated with each step.

3.3.1   Data Annotation

Sentiment-annotated data are obviously required for creating and evaluating a supervised classifier, which is built by learning the characteristics of prelabeled data. For other approaches that do not need an annotated corpus to build sentiment analysis systems, the gold standard or ground truth is a prerequisite for empirical evaluation. When creating a sentiment-annotated dataset, manual annotation is relatively accurate but labor intensive and can be performed only on small amounts of data. In contrast, automatically generated annotated data can be noisy, but the effects of noise can be mitigated to some extent by using a large amount of data [767].

User generated data annotated at the document level are relatively easy to harvest given the emergence of review aggregation sites that provide clearly labeled opinion categories and sites that provide user tagging options. Some sentiment-annotated documents available to the research community include manually cleaned and enriched review corpora [519, 409] and nonreview corpora distributed by data retrieval or data mining competitions such as the Blog track at the TREC conference [509]. In order to automatically harvest opinion documents, Zhang and Yu [767] constructed a search query by binding together an opinion target (e.g., "Skype") with patterns such as "I like" or "I don't think" and submitted it to a general search engine such as Google, whose top results were saved as positive training examples for opinion detection; they then searched the opinion target against Wikipedia to generate negative examples (i.e., nonopinion documents). Sentence-level or token-level annotated user generated content, on the other hand, is hard to get. The widely used opinion corpus MPQA has annotated opinion expressions and emotions, but it is based on news resources, not user generated content [720]. The JDPA corpus [338] is an opinion corpus released in 2010 and it consists of fine-grain annotations of blog posts. However, the corpus is restricted to blog posts expressing opinions about automobiles and digital cameras only. User generated metadata, such as hashtags for tweets, can approximately serve as annotation [427]. The problems are that metadata are not always available and user generated metadata do not always align with targeted sentiment classes.

3.3.2 Important Sentiment Features

The sentiment analysis literature indicates that both lexicon-based and machine learning-based approaches benefit from the large number and great variety of sentiment features used as evidence in sentiment analysis. There exist three major sources of sentiment evidence: (1) *Knowledge-based* evidence, often based on researchers' understandings and observations of the use of sentiment language and generates the most intuitive features including words or phrases that are semantically opinionated or affective. Commonsense or everyday knowledge can also provide sentiment evidence, especially for the implicit sentiment. (2) *Statistical/empirical* evidence, often used in information retrieval and topical text classification, can also serve for sentiment analysis. Features extracted according to statistical sources of evidence may not always be intuitive (e.g., "try the," "off," "just"). (3) Writing *style* and document *structure*, which emerged from research in linguistics and information retrieval, are other sources of evidence for sentiment. Some instances include short forms or symbols used on the Web (e.g., ":)", or "imho") or differences in the length of positively and negatively opinionated sentences.

Based on one or more pieces of evidence, sentiment features can be extracted with *statistical methods* based on term presence or frequency in the training set or can be selected with *linguistic methods* based on word attributes, syntactic relationships, or other linguistic characteristics. Sentiment features may be used alone or with relevant scores, showing the strength of association between each feature and its corresponding sentiment class.

The evaluation of individual features is not easy, if not impossible, due to the limited number of studies that perform measurements at the level of single features and the difficulty in comparing the performance of the same features across systems that have implemented sentiment analysis differently. Several effective sentiment features that have been examined in the literature will be discussed in order of ascending complexity.

3.3.2.1   Single Word Features

The *bag-of-words* or *unigram* feature originated in the field of information retrieval. This feature is extracted from a training set according to word presence, frequency normalized by document-length, a *tf-idf* value, or a more complicated term weight computed without consideration of grammatical rules or word order. To demonstrate how the feature value is calculated, let's take a look at a simple scenario where there are only two sentences in the training set: "Mary loves the soundtrack of that movie while John loves its story!" labeled as "positive opinion" and "He regrets to watch that horrible movie" labeled as "negative opinion." And if the feature value is calculated by simply counting word occurrence, the word "loves" has a feature value of 2 under the positive category, the word "regrets" has a feature value of 1 under the negative category, and the word "movie" has a feature value of 1 under both categories, which means it can not distinguish one category from another. The bag-of-words feature is an obvious and efficient feature of topical classification, based on the assumption that when people talk about different topics, they tend to use different vocabularies (e.g., "medicine" and "patient" will occur frequently in the category of "Health," but not the category of "Arts"). This is occasionally the case in sentiment analysis. Using a basic text classifier with only length-normalized unigrams, Ng et al. [495] achieved an accuracy rate as high as 99.8% on both movie and book reviews in document-level opinion identification. A close look at their unigrams shows that the high accuracy was due to the different vocabularies used in both the review and nonreview data in their experiments. However, in most cases, the differences in vocabulary are not sufficient to distinguish sentiment from nonsentiment. The concept of opinion or sentimentalism is believed to be a complicated one for this superficial feature [521]. The use of bag-of-words alone was outperformed by a rich set of linguistic features [569] or, more often, by a combination of bag-of-words and other features tailored to the sentiment analysis task [225, 502, 519]. Therefore, bag-of-words alone is normally used in sentiment analysis detection as a baseline to estimate the difficulty of the target domain as well as to provide a basis for the fusion of features.

Nevertheless, some efforts have been made to improve the quality of the bag-of-words feature. One problem with the bag-of-words feature is that some features (e.g., date and time) may be too specific and thus carry little value in the form of individual instances, but may become a stronger feature when grouped together. In order to transform overly specific features to valuable features, Dave et al. [162] applied a series of substitutions and found that two were helpful: replacing any numerical unit with "NUMBER" and substituting instances of a product name (e.g.," Canon," "Nikon," etc.) with "_productname." However, similar substitutions did not always show improvements [753]. Similarly, *stemming*, which reduces inflected words to their root form, can be applied to overcome variation in language use. However, there is no clear gain from stemming in opinion detection [744]. One reason for this is that stemming may actually erase some subtle sentiment cues. Dave et al. [162] found that "negative reviews tend to occur more frequently in the past tense, since the reviewer might have returned the product" (p. 522), and this opinion indicator will be erased after stemming.

Based on the bag-of-words features, Yang et al. [744] created a *high-frequency* (HF) lexicon by identifying high-frequency terms from positive blog training data (i.e., opinionated blog posts) and removing those that also had a high frequency in negative blog training data (i.e., nonopinionated blog posts). The resulting set of extracted terms was then manually reviewed to filter out spurious terms and to assign polarity and strength of opinion. Examples of extracted high-frequency cues are "Skype *sucks*," "Skype *rocks*," and "Skype is *cool*." The HF lexicon contributed to the overall performance of an opinion retrieval task. Although the improvement was limited (5–7%) and there are not many reports on the benefits of using the HF feature alone, this feature serves as a good candidate for opinion lexicons considering the simplicity of generating the HF lexicon and the relatively high quality of the HF lexicon due to manual controls.

Also generated by simply looking up the word frequency as is the case for the HF feature, *unique words*, words that appear once in the corpus, are not immediately obvious indicators of sentiment. The occurrence of unique words is specific to sentiment language based on the observation that people become creative when expressing opinions and tend to use uncommon or rare term patterns [717]. Wiebe et al. [719] observed that the difference between the proportion of unique words in opinionated documents and nonopinionated documents is significant, with $p<0.001$ ($z>=22$).

Building on the same assumption, Yang et al. [744] extended the notion of unique words to *low-frequency* (LF) words in order to capture creative opinion expression, also called *opinion morphology* (OM). A semiautomatic method was used to construct an LF lexicon from a blog collection of 2.8 million posts. The LF lexicon contained patterns that could capture intentionally misspelled words (e.g., "luv," "hizzarious"), compound words (e.g., "metacool," "crazy-good"), repeated-character words (e.g., "soooo," "fantaaastic," "grrrreat"), or combinations of the three (e.g., "metacoool"). In a topical opinion finding task, a 4–5% increase was achieved over the baseline using the LF lexicon.

Unique and LF words constitute one of the few features that have been shown to work for sentiment analysis. Although this feature has low coverage due to the nature of the uniqueness, the precision is promising. When generating unique words, Wiebe et al. [719] point out that the quality of the unique words is related to the size of the corpus and only in a corpus of sufficient size are these cues informative. When the training set is small, using unique terms as features degrades performance [162], probably due to over-generalization. Therefore, Wiebe et al. [719] recommended using additional un-annotated data (e.g., the entire corpus) for identifying uniqueness features. When building the LF lexicon, the size of the corpus is less an issue since manual examination and evaluation of LF patterns are involved. But the procedure is more complicated and expert knowledge is required for pattern extraction.

3.3.2.2 Part-of-Speech Based Features

Compared to single word features, which usually ignore the meaning and function of words, part-of-speech (POS) based features offer sentiment evidence derived from the word class. *Part-of-speech* (POS) is the foundation of linguistic analysis and is often used together with grammatical rules to extract linguistically rich sentiment features. The most basic and direct usages of the POS information include: (1) employing POS directly in a bag-of-words fashion [220] based on the assumption that the distribution pattern of POS is an indicator of sentiment (e.g., a large proportion of adjectives and adverbs may be uncommon in a fact-based document); (2) attaching POS to other sentiment features such as single term features [225, 521] to reduce ambiguity caused by the fact that one word may belong to different sentiment classes when used as a different POS (e.g., "pretty" when used as an adjective is a strong positive feature, but it is neutral when used as an adverb); and, more frequently, (3) using POS as a simple criterion to select sentiment features based on the assumption that different word classes or special types of words hold different sentiment strength. Word classes and their subsets used as sentiment features in accordance with the latter approach are discussed below.

Adjectives

Adjectives have been reported to have a positive and statistically significant correlation with subjectivity in early sentiment analysis studies [102]. To reveal the relationship between adjectives and sentiment, Kamps et al. [330] generated a graph by simply using synonym relations to connect all of the adjectives in WordNet [466]. They observed that, in this graph, the group of highly connected nodes holding about 25% of all adjectives contained all the modifiers that are used to express affective or emotive meaning.

The mere presence of adjectives is normally not strong sentiment evidence in itself since adjectives include many terms that describe properties such as color or age and are not necessarily sentiment. Therefore, adjectives are typically applied along with other features or with certain selection criteria. Three types of adjectives: dynamic adjectives, gradable adjectives, and semantic-oriented adjectives, have been found to be stronger sentiment cues than adjectives as a whole [274].

Dynamic adjectives are adjectives with the "qualities that are thought to be subject to control by the possessor and hence can be restricted temporally" [558, p. 434]. For example, dynamic adjectives such as "foolish" can be used in "he is being foolish" while nondynamic (i.e., stative) adjectives such as "tall" cannot be used in "he is being tall." Bruce and Wiebe [102] assumed this stative/dynamic distinction between adjectives to be related to subjectivity and manually identified a list of 123 dynamic adjectives from about 500 sentences in the Wall Street Journal Treebank Corpus. Their examination indicates that these dynamic adjectives were indeed more subjective than the rest of the adjectives in the corpus.

Hatzivassiloglou and Wiebe [274] suggested that another type of adjectives, gradable adjectives, were also useful opinion indicators that had 13–21% higher precision than adjectives as a whole. *Gradable adjectives* are those that can participate in comparative constructs (e.g., "This movie is more exciting than the other") and accept modifying expressions that act as intensifiers or diminishers (e.g., "This game is very exciting," where "very" is an intensive modifier). Gradable adjectives can be identified manually or automatically using a statistical model, but the latter is computationally expensive because of the requirement for syntactic parsing and morphology analysis. Using the dynamic and gradable adjectives distributed by Hatzivassiloglou and Wiebe [274], Yu [753], and Yu and Kübler [755] found them to have a positive effect in classifying blog posts as well.

Unlike dynamic and gradable adjectives, which are judged by the context of usage, *semantic-oriented adjectives* can be identified more easily. Semantic-oriented adjectives are polar words that are either positive or negative. Adjectives with polarity, such as "good," "bad," or "beautiful," are inherently connected with sentiment as opposed to adjectives, such as "white," "Chinese," or "succeeding," which have no polarity. Hatzivassiloglou and Wiebe [274] and Whitelaw et al. [714] showed that a reasonably high accuracy of sentiment analysis could be achieved by using polar adjectives alone. Chesley et al. [136] also found that positive adjectives played a major role in classifying opinionated blog posts. Semantic-oriented terms, not necessarily restricted to adjectives, usually account for a large proportion of opinion lexicons; and existing opinion resources such as Wilson's subjectivity terms [722] provide semantic-oriented terms that are domain independent. There has also been a large amount of work done on automatically identifying semantic-oriented lexicons [136, 209, 226, 330, 345, 659, 678].

Pronouns

It is to be expected that *first person pronouns* may be used more frequently when an individual point of view is being expressed than when an objective statement is being made. Similar assumptions can be made about the *second-person pronouns*. Zhou et al. [775] successfully used the presence of pronouns such as "I," "you," "me," "us," and "we" occurring near target topical terms as opinion indicators in the Blog track. In contrast, Chesley et al. [136] observed a slight negative effect when applying these features in their experiments with blog data. The inconsistency in these findings may have been due to the frequent use of pronouns even in objective statements (e.g., "I heard that there is a big sale at Macy's" and "Here is the recipe you asked for"). One possible solution for the over-generalization associated with first and second person pronouns as sentiment cues is to bind this implicit/weak feature with other opinion-bearing features.

There may be more potential in pronouns when it comes to fine-level sentiment analysis. Social psychologist Pennebaker found strong correlations between the use of pronouns, along with other function words, and different emotions [532]. For example, when angry, people use more second person and third person pronouns than first person because they are likely to focus on others than on themselves.

Other POS Features

Although not as significant as adjectives, verbs are also found to be good indicators for sentiment information. *Verb classes*, the categories for classifying verbs syntactically and/or semantically, are often used for culling sentiment verbs. *Levin's verb classes*, developed on the basis of both intuitive semantic groupings and participation in valence alternations (i.e., polarity alternations) [395], are probably the most popular verb classes used as sentiment evidence [569, 570, 722, 724]. More specifically, Chesley et al. [136] found that the "asserting" and "approving" verb classes played a key role in improving the accuracy of classifying blog posts as positive opinion.

Nouns are not logically linked with sentiment, but certain subsets have proven useful for opinion detection in news articles. Riloff et al. [570] reported a high precision (77%) at sentence-level opinion detection achieved by a supervised classifier using only subjective nouns. However, recall is only moderate (64%), due either to the difficulty of creating a comprehensive lexicon for this feature or to the low probability of finding subjective nouns in a sentence.

3.3.2.3   N-Grams, Phrases, and Patterns

The greatest limitation of single words and POS-based features is that they carry no contextual information, which is crucial for sentiment analysis. Therefore, multiword features that retain word dependence have frequently been investigated based on the assumption that they are more deterministic than individual words. These features can be grouped into co-occurrence based N-grams and collocations, syntactic based phrases, and various linguistic patterns.

N-Grams and Collocations

Utilizing high order n-grams (n>1) is the simplest way to retain a word's context. So far, the contribution of n-grams has been examined mainly in polarity detection and the findings have not been consistent [162, 521]. Cui et al. [156] conjectured that the small training corpora might have hindered these previous experiments from extracting effective high order n-grams. Cui et al. [156] found that adding higher order n-grams improved the accuracy of classifying positive and negative opinions. For example, using a union of n-grams from unigram to 6-grams achieved the highest overall F-score of 0.9007, while using unigrams alone yielded a lower overall F-score of 0.8832. However, the benefits of incorporating higher order n-grams over bigrams were trivial (<=0.1% improvement over the overall F score) and might not be valuable in analyzing some types of user generated content, attributing to the problem of data sparseness, where it contains very short text and may contain no trigram features at all (e.g., tweets).

A collocation can be defined as a special kind of n-gram and has been widely adopted in sentiment analysis. Simply put, words in a collocation occur together more often than they would by chance and the meaning of the collocation as a whole is not a straightforward combination of the meanings of its parts. Common collocations include proper names (e.g., "United Nations"), verb/adjective phrases (e.g., "angry with"), and terminological expressions (e.g., "heart attack").

Collocations identified by Wiebe et al. [719] are n-grams (n=1-4) consisting of pairs of word-stem and POS (e.g., "could-modal have-verb") extracted from an annotated opinion expression. The best subjectivity feature investigated by Wiebe et al. [719] was the collocation extracted based on the unique and creative nature of the opinion expression: All unique words in collocations were replaced by a placeholder, UNIQ, with the POS kept.

Weak sentiment features can become stronger when bound with other sentiment cues. The *IU collocations* proposed by Yang et al. [744] are n-grams with IU anchor terms, which are essentially first-person pronouns (e.g., "I," "we") and second-person pronouns (e.g., "you"). IU collocations (e.g., "I believe" and "You will love") were used to mark adjacent statements as opinions (e.g., "I believe God exists," "God is dead to me") and they worked best as single features during their experiments in the Blog track. Since IU collocations are collection-independent, both blog data and movie reviews were used for IU n-gram harvest. In order to accommodate the various forms of an IU collocation (e.g., "I believe," "I cannot but believe," "I have always believed," etc.), IU collocations in the lexicon were "padded" in such a way that document texts with up to two words in between IU collocation words would be matched. Kanayama and Nasukawa [331] applied similar IU collocations to a Japanese language corpus, which suggests that IU collocations may be a language-independent feature.

Acronyms, Idioms, and Metaphors

Acronyms are very popular in Web content and have proven to be effective in information retrieval and text classification tasks as they normally convey an important concept or name. Yang et al. [744] developed an acronym lexicon, which consists of a manually filtered subset of chat acronyms and shorthand text messages from NetLingo (http://www.netlingo.com/acronyms.php) in both acronym and expanded forms (e.g., "imho"="in my humble opinion"). A sentiment acronym normally represents a long phrase that serves as a clear indicator of sentiment. Idioms, too, often express strong sentiment (e.g., "cost [somebody] an arm and a leg" [173]). In addition to idioms, which are often metaphorical, some "general metaphors" are also good sentiment cues [569]. Hearst [279] noticed that negative things are described in terms of "downness" (e.g., "quality is declining"), whereas desirable things are expressed in terms of "upness" (e.g., "being in heaven"). Zhang et al. [765] have proposed several ways of detecting those metaphors in their study. For example, calling someone an animal usually conveys an opinion, as in the statement "he is such a pig." Due to the need for deep linguistic analysis to extract metaphors, the effectiveness of this feature in sentiment analysis has not yet been fully investigated.

Adjective Phrase and Appraisal Groups

Conceptually, noun phrases are more closely associated with topics while adjective phrases may be valuable to sentiment. Surprisingly, there are few studies that have made explicit use of adjective phrases as a sentiment feature. In the related but more difficult task of identifying opinion holders, Bethard et al. [71] found that adjective phrases were tightly associated with opinion expression and that this feature was able to improve both recall and precision of identifying opinion holders by 8%. This implies that adjective phrases, when available, could be a promising feature for opinion detection. This appears to have been confirmed by the success in applying a type of sophisticated adjective phrase, appraisal groups, in opinion detection.

An appraisal group [714] is comprised of a head term with a defined attitude type and an optional list of preceding appraisal modifiers. For example, "not very happy" is an adjective appraisal group with "happy" as the head term and "not" and "very" as the two modifiers. Each appraisal group is labeled with its attitude type, orientation, force, focus, and polarity. The attitude types are assigned based on appraisal theory [446]. Whitelaw et al. [714] were able to get excellent classification accuracy (90.2%) on a corpus of movie reviews using feature sets consisting of various disjunctions of lexical items or adjective appraisal group values. Although this linguistically rich approach is limited to adjective phrases, it outperformed several previous studies of the polarity detection task using the movie review dataset [483, 521, 678]. The success of the appraisal group approach demonstrates the value of sophisticated linguistic features in sentiment analysis and should be further explored. Luckily, with reduced cost and increasing accuracy of full syntactic parsers, extracting these features from a large-scale dataset is not as difficult as a few years back.

Dependency-Based Patterns and Extraction Patterns

Whether or not a feature is a sentiment feature is often determined by how it is used. Syntactic parsing, which discovers dependencies between words in a sentence, is an intuitive resolution to clarify the specific usage of words. Hence, dependency-based patterns can be defined to restrict sentiment features in particular structures (e.g., a word modifies strong sentiment features).

Examples of complex dependency-based features used for sentiment analysis can be found by Wilson [724], Tetsuji et al. [666], and Alexander and Patrick [20]. Ng et al. [495] explored three dependency relations: adjective-noun, subject-verb, and verb-object. These dependency relations were found useful in polarity detection for reviews, but only when bigrams and trigrams were not used. Ng et al. [495] suggested that this was because "high order n-grams and dependency-based features capture essentially the same information" (p. 617). It is encouraging that simple techniques and features can achieve the same results as more complex features.

Extraction patterns, which originated in the study of information extraction, are also reliant on syntactic parsing but are not limited to predefined dependency relations. Extraction patterns are "linguistically richer and more flexible than single words or n-grams" [527, p. 105] in that they look for specific syntactic constructions produced by a shallow parser rather than exact word sequences. This is especially valuable when a single expression can exist in different forms. An example excerpted from Riloff and Weibe [569] is "<subj>was asked," which can be extracted from sentences such as "I was asked if I like this product" or "Mike was constantly asked about his new camera." The ability to catch subtle differences between the active and passive voice in subjective expressions is another advantage of extraction patterns. The pattern "<subj>was asked" was observed to have appeared only in subjective sentences. In contrast, a similar pattern in the active voice ("<subj>asked") occurred in 63% of subjective sentences. This makes "<subj>was asked" a reliable indicator of opinion even though humans may not always recognize such a pattern. In addition to serving directly as sentiment features, extraction patterns can also provide context for extracting other sentiment features, such as subjective nouns [570]. For example, extraction patterns such as "expressed <dobj>" can be used to extract subjective nouns such as "hope" or "grief," which function as the direct object of "expressed."

3.3.2.4 Other Sentiment Features

In addition to sentiment features that are specifically motivated by and directly applicable to sentiment analysis tasks, there are other features, including stylistic features, fact-based, and nonverbal features, that could potentially be useful for sentiment analysis.

Stylistic features refer to features that capture those aspects of a text which are independent of the topic. Unlike other linguistic features that either depend heavily on word meaning (e.g., most of the POS-based features) or that require linguistic parsing (e.g., appraisal patterns), stylistic features are based solely on statistical evidence and are less language specific. Encouraged by successful attempts to utilize stylistic features for user generated content in authorship identification and gender analysis, for example [772], researchers have hoped that stylistic features would uncover latent patterns for sentiment analysis.

One difficulty with sentiment analysis lies in "inferring sentiments from fact" [345], which is especially beneficial for identifying implicit sentiment (e.g., the fact that someone "returned a product" indicates that he may not like it). Commonsense, also known as real-world knowledge, refers to knowledge about everyday life. Because it is context independent, this generic knowledge has been utilized as a fact-based feature in the task of emotion identification, but it has not been applied in opinion detection. A successful application of everyday knowledge was developed by Liu et al. [411] for emotion identification in an e-mail corpus. A real-world corpus of 400,000 facts was used to capture the underlying semantic context of expressions of emotion. For example, "It feels like riding a rollercoaster" may be associated with the emotion "excitement" although no explicit cues (e.g., "exciting") appear because the commonsense corpus contains the statement that "a consequence of riding a rollercoaster may be excitement." Liu et al. [411] built four linguistic models to extract concepts (e.g., "riding a rollercoaster") and their associated emotions (e.g., "excitement") via fine-level syntactic parsing and analysis. According to their user study, when trained on commonsense concepts with valence information, the emotion identification system was able to accurately predict the emotions of sentences in e-mails.

People are often able to capture the emotions of others with ease by sensing the tone of their voice rather than by reading written text. In order to take advantage of this phenomenon, Holzman and Pottenger [290] proposed the novel feature of *speech phonemes* (i.e., the units of sound) for discriminating emotional from nonemotional content in online chat data. They used 49 phonemes (e.g., /zh/, /t/) that "represent the major units of sound used in American English speech including accents and pauses" (p. 3). Each chat message was first "read" by some text-to-speech software, and phonemes were than extracted from the resulting speech reproduction. An accuracy rate of over 90% was achieved with a supervised text classifier using the top nine phonemic features, in addition to stylistic features such as word length and punctuation marks. Holzman and Pottenger [290] found that the biggest advantage of phonemic features was that they were robust in the presence of very noisy data containing misspellings, lack of adherence to grammar rules, and so on, which made the phonemic features especially attractive for classifying conversational data on the Web. However, whether this benefit comes from the high correction capabilities of the text-to-speech system employed in their experiments or from the special characteristics of chat language (e.g., use of intentionally misspelled words that have sounds similar to the correct words, such as "sooo," "wat," and "thrut") needs to be validated via closer examination.

When present, certain Web structures, Web links, citations within documents, and "respond-to" relationships may also be good sentiment features. In the political domain, such evidence has been shown to be less noisy than text-based sources of evidence [16, 440].

3.3.2.5 Recommendation for Selecting Sentiment Features

For a particular task, which feature(s) to select is often determined by factors besides the effectiveness of the features reported in the literature. General recommendations arising from review of the literature would include: (1) Bag-of-words, or unigrams, are the most straightforward features that can be easily constructed to serve as a baseline; (2) Manually or semimanually created opinion lexicons (e.g., dynamic adjectives, gradable adjectives) are high quality but offer low coverage and may be used to capture general opinion expressions; (3) Sentiment specific features (e.g., unique words or n-grams that contain unique words, IU collocations) are strong cues and should be used whenever possible; (4) High order n-grams may be helpful to supplement unigrams if they are generated from large training corpus and are used with caution regarding their specificity; (5) Complicated linguistic collocations and patterns (e.g., appraisal groups) are effective but their success depends on the performance of syntactic parsers over user generated content; and (6) Combining weak features (e.g., IU collocation combines pronouns and general opinionated verbs) or combining diverse features (e.g., unigrams which are high-coverage and low-precision, used with manually established features which are low-coverage and high-precision) has proven to yield better performance than any feature on its own, thus supporting continued exploration of insignificant features (e.g., stylistic features) provided they are easy to construct.

Following the assumption that large-scale features are needed for sentiment analysis, many studies have adopted a "kitchen sink" approach to combine a variety of sentiment features without applying any feature selection methods. However, when features are noisy and redundant, researchers have found it beneficial to select only the most important features [3, 225, 495].

3.3.3 Sentiment Scoring and Classification

Selected sentiment features contribute either to predicting the sentiment class of a target example (classification) or to producing a score to show how likely it is that this example is sentiment (scoring). N-fold cross validation has been widely adapted for evaluation and the measurement commonly reported is the average classification accuracy; the exception is the TREC Blog track where average precision and recall are the key evaluation measures. Unfortunately, as with other information systems that are developed without standard environment, the results of sentiment analysis are not generally comparable because of the diversity of target datasets, preprocessing procedures, and evaluation methods.

3.3.3.1 Ad Hoc Rule-Based Approach

The basis of the *ad hoc rule-based approach* is the sentiment lexicon, which is a list of the terms or patterns that provide evidence for the presence of sentiment or fact. High-quality knowledge-based sentiment features normally

provide the basis for such lexicon, and statistical and structure-based sentiment features are usually added after manual inspection.

The most naive yet effective way of using a sentiment lexicon is to apply
a simple matching rule that assumes the presence of one or more sentiment
features that can serve as a proxy for the sentiment class label. For example, in
sentence-level subjective classification [274, 717], a sentence would be classified
as subjective if at least one member of a set of adjectives occurred in the
sentence; if not, it would be classified as objective. Instead of providing a
binary judgment based on simple match, an opinion score can be calculated
for the target unit by counting the total number of occurrences or summing the
scores of opinion-bearing features [226], which are sometimes normalized by
unit length. In order to handle negations and other exceptions, it is common
to introduce other rules in addition to simple matching or scoring rules [173,
345, 498]. For example, one rule can define that, if *not* occurs in a piece of
text, the semantic orientation of this text unit is to be reversed.

The strength of the ad hoc rule-based approach lies in the fact that it
is conceptually intuitive and easy to implement. As a matter of fact, recent
sentiment analysis studies in Twitter space have mostly replied on this ad
hoc rule-based approach [667, 506]. However, this strength comes with four
limitations: (1) a heavy dependence not only on the quality of sentiment features but also on the quantity and diversity of features necessary to capture
the variety of features used in sentiment expressions; (2) the need for sophisticated strategies such as linguistic-parsing to extract sentiment features and
for expert knowledge and man power to implement, maintain, and update
complex rule-based systems; (3) an inability to capture all exceptions; and (4)
the absence of obvious sentiment features in some sentiment expressions.

3.3.3.2 Supervised Learning Approach

Supervised learning is a mature and successful solution in traditional topical classification and has been adopted and investigated widely for sentiment
analysis with satisfactory results [751, 767]. With no classification techniques
developed specifically for sentiment analysis, state-of-the-art topical classification algorithms are often tailored for the task of sentiment analysis. Normally, this is done in the following way: (1) Instead of the ordinal frequency
of features, binary values (presence/absence) are considered in representing
the classifying unit. This is motivated by the extreme brevity of the text unit
when classifying short Web documents such as tweets and reviews or when
conducting subdocument level sentiment analysis. The preference for binary
values may also be due to the characteristics of sentiment analysis, where
occurrence frequency is less influential (i.e., single occurrence of sentiment evidence is enough); (2) A wider variety of evidence/features discussed in the
earlier section are investigated in addition to auto generated features (e.g.,
bag-of-words, n-grams, etc.) [225, 483, 502, 519, 714, 751]; and (3) Exhaustive
parameter optimization is not usually performed for classification models. Instead, default parameter values from some off-the-shelf toolkit are used with

or without preliminary analysis of the effect of varying the parameter values [156, 495, 521, 714, 483]. The under-utilization of parameter optimization may be the result of insufficient investigation of supervised classification in sentiment analysis to date.

Naïve Bayes and Support Vector Machine (SVM) are the most common and effective supervised learning algorithms for text classification and have been widely adapted for sentiment analysis. In order to classify large-scale Web data more effectively, an SVM model with an optimized learning algorithm such as Sequential Minimal Optimization (SMO) has sometimes been employed [3, 225, 502, 714]. In most cases, SVMs have shown marginal improvement over Naïve Bayes classifiers. One explanation for discriminative models being more appropriate for sentiment classification than generative models was given by Cui et al. [156], who argued that a discriminative classifier can differentiate mixed sentiments better than a generative classifier. However, the advantage of discriminative classifiers may be degraded when working with a small corpus that does not provide enough sample data for the discriminative model to learn from. As an added bonus, Naïve Bayes classifiers are also much faster to train than SVMs.

Pang et al. [521] made early efforts to adapt several popular supervised classification algorithms to opinion detection in the domain of movie reviews. A classification accuracy of 82.9% was obtained using an SVM classifier with bag-of-words features only. A later examination of supervised classification for polarity detection [156] tested an online version of SVM called a Passive-Aggressive (PA) algorithm with a *large-scale* dataset (near 800,000 reviews) and *high-order n-grams* and produced an overall F-score as high as 0.9007 (precision: 0.9022, recall: 0.8991). Yang et al. [742] applied an SVM to classify approximately 40 emotions (e.g., "happy," "sad," "love") based on the emoticons used in the Chinese Yahoo! blog. A classification accuracy of 75.93% was achieved when emotion categories were combined into two groups: positive and negative. Even though the performance was modest, SVM was still considered to be effective given that emotion classification is more difficult than opinion/polarity detection.

Text classification algorithms based on bag-of-words normally do not take into account the sequence or structure of text, which may hold valuable context information for sentiment analysis. Language models, on the other hand, are good at making use of such textual characteristics. Yu [753] and Yu and Kübler [754, 755] have found that a character-based language model consistently performs well for the subjectivity classification task. The literature on sentiment analysis also bears witness to some interesting experiences with supervised graphic models that make use of language structures [519]. For example, Breck et al. [94] applied a linear-chain Conditional Random Field (CRF) to construct a sequential model for tagging opinions at the expression level. Much like SVMs, CRFs are discriminative methods and are able to use a large and diverse set of features. CRFs out-performed SVMs at expression-level opinion detection in the pilot experiments owing to their context sensibility. Pang and Lee [519] built a structural model that considers not only the individual scores of every sentence generated from an Naïve Bayes classifier but also some association scores between sentences, which led to a statistically significant improvement in the accuracy of polarity detection.

The biggest limitation associated with supervised learning is that it is sensitive to the quantity and quality of the training data and may fail when training data are biased or insufficient. Sentiment analysis at the subdocument level raises additional challenges for supervised learning-based approaches because there is little information for the classifier.

3.3.3.3   Semisupervised Learning (Bootstrapping)

Most lexicon-based and supervised learning-based methods can benefit from a large-scale annotated dataset, which, unfortunately, is not always available, especially at the subdocument level. While obtaining sentiment-annotated user generated data can be expensive and difficult, fetching unlabeled user generated content in the target domain is normally cheap and easy. This is the perfect scenario for conducting semisupervised learning, which does not focus on preparing more annotated data but on automatically and simultaneously learning and labeling the unlabeled data. The main idea behind semisupervised learning is that, although unlabeled data hold no information about classes (e.g., "opinion" and "nonopinion"), they do contain information about the joint distribution over classification features. Therefore, when there is limited labeled data in the target data domain, using semisupervised learning with unlabeled data can achieve improvement over supervised learning. Although having been intensively studied in the field of computational linguistics, semisupervised learning is a relatively new approach to the sentiment analysis problem.

Self-Training

A successful application of *self-training*, the simplest semisupervised learning on sentence-level opinion detection, has been described by Riloff et al. [569, 570]: (1) build either a simple rule-based classifier using a few manually-created sentiment seeds or a baseline supervised classifier trained on a few manually labeled data and tune the classifier for high-precision performance; (2) apply this high-precision classifier on the un-annotated corpus and assume the top n returned sentences actually contain sentiment; (3) add those n sentences to the training set, based on which more sentiment features can be fetched to expand the seed set and/or the classifier can be updated; and (4) go back to step (2) to classify more sentences with the updated classifier until sufficient numbers of training data have been collected or the classification performance falls below a certain threshold. Thus, having bootstrapped a simple high-precision classifier through several iterations, the process gathers a large annotated dataset and/or rich sentiment lexicon(s), either of which can then be used in supervised or lexicon-based sentiment analysis.

Self-training is a wrapper approach that can be applied to any existing system as long as a confidence score can be produced and it avoids dealing with any inner complexities of the existing system. Self-training has been originally adopted for sentiment lexicon expansion [568] and only recently has been explicitly applied for sentence-level sentiment analysis [277, 756].

Expectation-Maximization

The Expectation-Maximization (EM) algorithm was introduced and named by Dempster et al. [168]. EM refers to a class of iterative algorithms for maximum-likelihood estimation when dealing with incomplete data. Nigam et al. [499] later combined the EM algorithm with an Naïve Bayes classifier to resolve the problem of topical classification, where unlabeled data were treated as incomplete data. One strong assumption was made when integrating EM learning into text classification: All data are generated by a mixture model and there is a one-to-one correspondence between mixture components and classes. In the case of opinion detection, this mixture model assumes that the dataset should contain two tight clusters: one corresponding to the opinion examples and the other corresponding to nonopinion examples. Apparently, the real world is more complicated and this assumption is usually violated. Nigam et al. [499] proposed two extensions to EM to deal with violated assumptions: (1) introduce a new weighting parameter for controlling the influence of unlabeled data and emphasize the clusters that are favorable to the labeled data; and (2) introduce a many-to-one correspondence between mixture components and classes to relax the one-to-one assumption. The extended EM algorithm was shown to achieve significant improvement in three real-world topical classification tasks. Detailed algorithms and a theoretical analysis can be found in Nigam et al. [499].

EM-based SSL can be understood as a special form of self-training under the mixture model assumption. Each iteration in EM-based SSL involves the following steps: (1) train the NB classifier with labeled data; (2) apply the NB classifier to each unlabeled document to assign a "probabilistically weighted" [499, p. 104] class label (i.e., the E-step); (3) retrain the NB classifier with both the originally labeled and the unlabeled data to maximize the posteriori estimate for the classification parameters (i.e., the M-step); and (4) repeat steps 2 through 4 until the NB classifier does not change. In the end, EM finds the local maximization of the likelihood of the classification parameters given all of the data.

Motivated by the success of combining EM and Naïve Bayes in text classification tasks, a few studies have used the same semisupervised learning algorithm to deal with the absence of large amounts of labeled data for sentiment analysis. EM-NB semisupervised learning has yielded better performance than either supervised approaches or unsupervised lexicon-based approaches in sentiment classification at various levels and with different data domains, including blog data [35, 226, 753, 755, 658]. Takamura et al. [658] found that the EM-NB semisupervised learning algorithm always improved the classification accuracy regardless of the quantity of labeled data (varying from 100 to 1000); it produced better results with more unlabeled data; and it extracted more contextual features when compared with the top 100 features used in the initial and final Naïve Bayes model.

Co-Training

One shortcoming of self-training and EM-NB is that the resulting training data might be biased toward the initial sentiment analysis system. In other words, the training data will be made up by those examples, which are easiest for this particular system to identify. *Co-training* solves this problem by training one classifier with examples labeled by another classifier, or more often, with examples labeled unanimously by both classifiers. Because the two classifiers have to be very different from each other, the union of classified examples is better balanced than examples resulting from using either.

According to the original co-training paper [79], for each target example to classify, there exist two views that are independent of each other and can make the right prediction alone. For example, a Web page can be represented by words appearing either on the Web page itself or on its incoming links (i.e., anchor text). During co-training iterations, features generated by each view are used to train one classifier (i.e., natural feature split). When labeling new documents, a combined classifier will be constructed by multiplying the predictions of the two final classifiers. In the case of sentiment analysis, however, it is hard to find this kind of natural split without domain knowledge. Fortunately, relaxing the original co-training assumptions or barely exploiting the redundancy in the feature set seems to suffice for co-training [768]. In a comprehensive evaluation for co-training, Nigam and Ghani [497] stated that when there is no natural split, randomly splitting the feature set will still outperform regular algorithms using a single feature set (e.g., EM), as long as there is enough redundancy in the feature set. Since the sentiment-bearing feature set is usually large and diverse, it is reasonable to assume the existence of a certain level of redundancy. When there is no natural split in the feature set, two classifiers can also be built without splitting the feature set: Goldman and Zhou [244] used two different supervised learning algorithms; Zhou and Li [779] applied two different parameter configurations on the same learning algorithm; Maeireizo et al. [435] trained two classifiers for each of the target classes (i.e., emotional and nonemotional); and Jin et al. [322] created disjoint training sets in each iteration and successfully applied the co-training algorithm to identify opinion sentences in camera reviews. Yu [753] and Yu and Kübler [754] have applied four different co-training strategies on opinion classification in movie reviews and blog posts and found that the more different the two classifiers are, the better the co-training performance.

Compared to self-training, co-training requires less labeled data than self-training since each labeled example is used twice; co-training converges faster than self-training [753, 754]; and, when there are different views for the target examples, co-training is conceptually clearer than self-training, which simply mixes features.

Semisupervised Learning Support Vector Machine

Originally known as transductive support vector machine, semisupervised learning support vector machine, *S3VM*, is a natural extension of support vector machine (SVM) in the semisupervised spectrum and are designed to find the maximal margin decision boundary in a vector space containing both labeled and unlabeled examples [66]. As depicted in Figure 3.1, the black dots correspond to unlabeled examples while the black circles with positive or negative signs correspond to labeled examples. While traditional SVMs will draw a boundary, indicated by the dotted lines, to separate the labeled examples, S3VMs will draw boundaries, indicated by the solid lines, to separate examples so as to keep the positive and negative examples apart. Mathematical descriptions for S3VMs can be found in Bennett and Demiriz [66]. S3VMs inherit the advantages of SVM while overcoming the negative impact of limited labeled data. Therefore, when an existing opinion detection system already uses SVM, it is reasonable to select S3VMs as the semisupervised learning algorithm.

Although SVMs are one of the favored supervised learning methods for sentiment analysis, S3VMs have rarely been applied for sentiment analysis directly. Dasgupta and Ng [161] used S3VMs as part of their evaluation on their unsupervised and interactive polarity classification for reviews. Their system gained some benefit from collecting user feedback and from applying S3VMs with limited labeled data. Yu [753] and Yu and Kübler [754, 755] found no benefits of applying S3VMs to the sentence-level opinion detection task in various data domains. One possible reason is the lack of S3VM optimization.

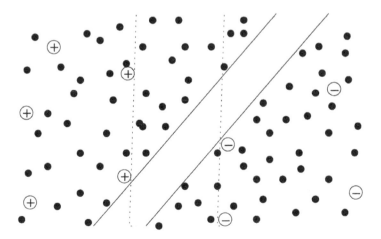

FIGURE 3.1: A visual representation of S3VMs modified from Zhu [781].

Graphic-Based Semisupervised Learning

There are also graph-based semisupervised learnings that have been adopted in sentiment analysis [16, 330, 440]. Although using a graph to describe a problem space is straightforward and intuitive, graph-based semisupervised learning is not ideal for dealing with large-scale data because it requires pair-wise calculations between all data, and the whole graph needs to be recalculated every time a new example must be classified. Furthermore, an increase in the distinct regions on a graph requires more labeled data to predict class labels for each region.

3.4 Conclusion

Sentiment analysis is a research area that has developed at the intersection of text mining and natural language processing. Immediate applications of sentiment analysis in user generated content include detecting a valence shift toward certain topics, monitoring emotion change within an online community, balancing opinions of mass media, and so on. The outcome can be used for personalized search, market predictions, or understanding certain events. In the hope that readers will gain a thorough overview of this interdisciplinary research problem, this chapter explored a brief history of sentiment analysis, listed the challenges, evaluated a variety of sentiment features, and discussed major methodologies of sentiment analysis.

In summary, most studies have suggested that a fusion of various sentiment features surpasses the use of any subset of these features. When rich sentiment features are available, both simple matching and text classification approaches have been reported to yield promising results for sentiment scoring/classification albeit inconsistently across domains. A large annotated corpus is critical both for extracting high-quality features and for training text classifiers; it can be obtained using semisupervised learning algorithms.

Although many sentiment analysis studies have explored new features and methods, researchers have not always performed adequate evaluations of results. The lack of evaluations of individual features or methods prevents researchers from drawing comparisons among features or methods, making it difficult to select and reuse features and methods. Even when they have been evaluated in the original research, it is challenging to adapt individual features or methods from other studies due to numerous factors (e.g., data cleaning strategies, evaluation measures) and system variables (e.g., data domain, level of granularity) that can impact effectiveness. This problem could be resolved, in part, at least, if researchers were to properly record all parameters and to conduct their research in controlled environments, which could be facilitated by increasing the number of free accessible sentiment-annotated user generated corpora and standardizing a sentiment analysis framework.

Another problem in studies of sentiment analysis is the lack of efforts to develop efficient fusion strategies. Although the fusion of various features has proven to be promising, features are often combined with equal treatment and without organization. In order to leverage different sources of evidence for sentiment, a close examination of which features to combine and how to combine them would improve on the current thrown together approach to fusion. For example, similar features could be grouped into one; and different weights could be assigned to emphasize the most reliable features as identified by preliminary analysis or experimentation. In the case of SVM, an SVM kernel could be used to implicitly encode feature combinations.

Chapter 4

Mining User Generated Data for Music Information Retrieval

Markus Schedl

Johannes Kepler Universität, Linz, Austria

Mohamed Sordo

Universitat Pompeu Fabra, Barcelona, Spain

Noam Koenigstein

Tel-Aviv University, Israel

Udi Weinsberg

Technicolor Research, Palo Alto, California

4.1   Introduction to Music Information Retrieval (MIR)

Music is an omnipresent topic in our society as almost everyone enjoys listening to it and many even create it. This is also underlined by the millions of users accessing online social media platforms and services to consume music, among other types of multimedia items. The recent boom of such social media services and the resulting tremendous increase of user generated content (UGC) yielded an enormous amount of this kind of data, which is frequently available through APIs. Even though this data represents a rich source for manifold data mining and information extraction and retrieval tasks, dealing with its noisiness is by no means trivial.

The research field of Music Information Retrieval (MIR) is a highly multidisciplinary one that has become quite popular during the last few years, although its origins date back only about a decade [248]. MIR research foremost aims at extracting, analyzing, processing, and mining information about any kind of music-related item or subject (for example, a song, an album, or a music artist) on any representation level (for instance, audio signal, symbolic MIDI representation, name of a music artist, or band photograph) [597]. Such information can then be used to research music retrieval algorithms and systems, an equally important aim of MIR [181].

4.1.1   User Generated Content in MIR Research

Although UGC plays a minor role in MIR research, there is a trend to exploit data sources that are not directly related to the audio signal, for instance, user generated tags, playlists, or Web pages about music, can be made out recently [248]. Another trend is considering music processing and modeling as a multimodal endeavor [605, 406]. In this vein, UGC is particularly used in the following MIR tasks: (i) feature extraction and similarity measurement; (ii) music auto-tagging; (iii) intelligent user interfaces for browsing music collections; and (iv) music popularity estimation.

Feature Extraction and Similarity Measurement. Many MIR tasks rely on two important building blocks: (i) the extraction of computational features from different music-related data sources (e.g., the audio signal, a Web page about an artist, or a microblog indicating a user's listening activity), and (ii) the measurement of similarity between the feature representations of two music items. Such music similarity measures enable applications such as intelligent browsing interfaces, automated playlist generation, music identification, and neighborhood-based music recommendation systems (see Section 4.4). However, elaborating feature extractors and similarity measures operating on the resulting features in a way that captures resemblance as perceived by humans is a nontrivial task, not the least since perception of music is highly subjective.

According to Schedl et al. [605], computational features describing aspects of human music perception can be categorized into three groups: *music content*, *music context*, and *user context*. While the music content refers to features that can be extracted from the audio signal itself (e.g., rhythm, timbre, melody, and harmony), aspects of the music context cannot be inferred directly from the signal with current technology (e.g., meaning of song lyrics or political background of an artist). The third category of aspects comprises the factors that relate to the listener himself. Applying a broad interpretation of the term user context, this also includes preference and taste as well as musical knowledge and experience. Exemplary factors for each of the three categories are shown in Figure 4.1. Given the prominence of textual data sources in research involving UGC, this chapter will focus on text-based MIR tasks, such as auto-tagging and classification, popularity estimation, and music recommendation.

Auto-Tagging. Learning models that describe the relationship between low-level feature representations of a piece of music and high-level semantic annotations such as musical genres, moods, or instruments is an important, albeit very challenging task. After having been learned, such models can be used to classify music items, that is, automatically label songs previously unseen by the system. This process is referred to as music auto-tagging. In most auto-tagging approaches, low-level features are computed from the audio signal and give coarse descriptions of rhythm or timbre. Social tags are frequently used as ground truth annotations to train the models for classifying music items. Two examples of how tag models are built using a machine learning algorithm are proposed in Eck et al. [189] and Bertin-Mahieux et al. [70].

Intelligent User Interfaces. Building intelligent user interfaces has become more and more important to manage the wealth of music available to consumers today. Such systems should offer an intuitive way, beyond pure text-based search, to sift through music collections and encounter serendipitous music experiences. An example of such a user interface is nepTune,[1] presented by Knees et al. [353], where the authors extract audio features from music files, train a neural network on these features to cluster the music collection under consideration, and visualize the resulting clusters by creating a virtual landscape of the collection. This landscape can then be navigated in the fashion of a computer game. Figure 4.2 shows a screenshot of the nepTune interface, which is available in a PC version and a version for mobile devices. It makes use of tags to describe regions of interest on the landscape, using for instance genre or instrument labels.

Another application that combines automated playlist generation with a browsing interface for mobile music consumption can be found by Schnitzer

---

[1] http://www.cp.jku.at/projects/neptune

et al. [612]. Figure 4.3 depicts a screenshot of this user interface, dubbed `Intelligent iPod`.[2] Schnitzer et al. [612] propose a content-based approach to create a circular playlist by approximating a Traveling Salesman Problem on the song similarity matrix. Such a matrix contains pairwise similarities between all songs in the collection under consideration. The resulting playlist is then visualized as a colored stripe where different colors correspond to different styles, (see 2) in Figure 4.3. User interaction is provided by using the player's scroll wheel to easily access the various music regions, (see 4) in Figure 4.3. To facilitate interpretation of the different regions, user generated tags are mined from `last.fm`[3] and attached to the corresponding regions.

Popularity Estimation. Techniques to approximate the popularity of a song or an artist are well-desired, not only by the music industry. Music listeners also make frequent use of popularity information, though often implicitly —for instance, when creating playlists for a party, striving for serendipitous music encounters, or just assessing the "mainstreaminess" of their music taste. Furthermore, geospatial estimates of music popularity are an important ingredient to understanding culture-specific music listening behavior, a task that is seeing increasing attention [618].

Solving these tasks particularly relies on UGC as demonstrated by Szabo and Huberman [655] for videos and by Schedl et al. [602] for music artists. Schedl et al. investigated several data sources to predict artist popularity in different countries. In addition to microblogs, they look into page count estimates returned by search engines, music files in shared folders of peer-to-peer networks, and playcounts on `last.fm`.

4.1.2   Organization of the Chapter

In the following, approaches to different MIR tasks that rely on UGC in a broader sense are presented. The subsequent sections are organized according to the data source harvested. In detail, we will elaborate on feature extraction, similarity measurement, music recommendation, music popularity estimation, and auto-tagging, using as data source Web pages, microblogs, explicit user ratings, peer-to-peer networks, social tags, and social networks.

4.2   Web Pages

Web pages about music items such as artists, albums, or songs represent a valuable source for contextual information. As they frequently contain UGC, Web pages might be considered to encode cultural knowledge. On the other

---

[2]http://www.cp.jku.at/projects/intelligent-ipod
[3]http://www.last.fm

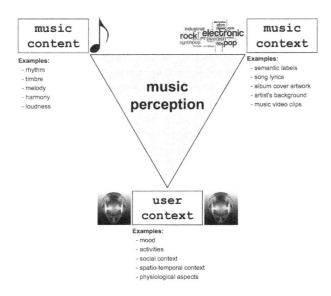

FIGURE 4.1: Different categories of factors that influence music perception. **(See color insert.)**

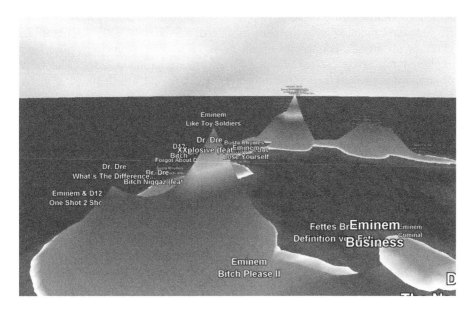

FIGURE 4.2: The nepTune music browsing interface. **(See color insert.)**

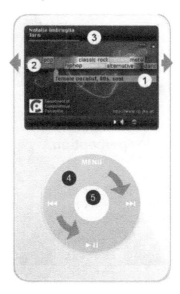

FIGURE 4.3: The `Intelligent iPod` mobile browsing interface. (**See color insert.**)

hand, Web pages are one of the most noisy data sources. In the context of MIR, music-related Web pages have mainly been used to *estimate similarity* between music artists [351, 601], although other tasks have been addressed as well, for example, automatically *extracting information* about music entities (for instance, members and instrumentation of a band [606, 352], discographies [352], or an artist's country of origin [604, 247]). Web pages have also been exploited for *artist categorization* into genres and moods [234]. The tasks of similarity measurement and information extraction are dealt with in the following.

4.2.1 Similarity Measurement

There exist two principal strategies to derive a similarity score between two music artists a and b from Web pages. The first one applies the *vector space model* [587], which means that the Web pages of each artist are modeled as a term weight vector, and a similarity function is subsequently applied to the resulting representation of a's and b's pages. Typically, such approaches comprise the following steps:

Acquiring Web pages relevant for the artists under consideration can be performed using a *focused crawler* [126], which gathers music-related pages given a number of seed URLs. Alternatively, and more often employed in MIR, related Web pages are determined by relying on the results of a *search engine* [716]. The former method tends to yield more accurate Web pages, though at higher computational costs. The latter one is easy to implement, nonetheless relying on the ranking algorithms of the search engine queried, which is usually a black box. Another problem when using a search engine is the ambiguity of artist or band names. For instance, when searching Web pages of bands such as "Nirvana," "Bush," or "Kiss," using only the band name as the query returns a lot of unrelated search results. It is thus common to add additional keywords such as "music" and "review" to the query, in order to focus the search on music-related Web pages [716, 351]. For more specific information extraction tasks, other keywords are better suited, though. To give an example, when aiming at extracting information about band members and instrumentation, Schedl and Widmer [606] show that querying for `"artist"` `music` or `"artist"` `music members` outperforms other schemes.

Modeling artists via term profiles first tries to discard Web page elements uninformative for the task, such as HTML tags. The resulting plain text representation is typically tokenized into single words, which are subsequently converted to lowercase—a process often called *casefolding*. Also stop words which occur too frequently to be meaningful for distinguishing between different Web pages, and in turn artists, are removed; this step is often called *stopping* or *stop word removal*. Typical stop words are "I," "the," "is," "to," and "and." To deal with different inflections, *stemming* algorithms [544] may be employed in order to obtain a canonical representation of each word. For instance, the words "influence," "influencing," and "influencer" are all mapped to "influenc" when applying stemming.

After these preprocessing steps, all Web pages retrieved for a particular artist a are concatenated to create a *virtual document* of a since the music entity of interest is the artist. Subsequently, a term vector representation $\mathbf{w_a}$ is created for each artist a. To this end, each term t occurring in the virtual document of a is assigned a term weight $w_{a,t}$, which represents the importance of t for a. Different ways to compute this term weight have been proposed in the literature. Most of them rely on weighting by *term frequency-inverse document frequency (tf-idf)* [39]. While the term frequency $tf_{a,t}$ estimates the sole importance of term t for artist a, for example, by counting the number of occurrences of t in a's virtual document, the inverse document frequency idf_t approximates the importance of t in the entire corpus of Web pages retrieved. The basic idea of the *tf-idf* weighting is that terms rarely occurring in the whole corpus are given a higher weight (high idf_t value). So are terms that occur often in the document of a particular artist (high $tf_{a,t}$ value). Since the $tf_{a,t}$ and the idf_t factors are multiplied to obtain the final score $w_{a,t}$, those terms that occur frequently in pages of artist a, but seldom in the entire corpus, are assigned the highest weight. This means that those terms are most representative for artist a and discriminate a best from other artists.

Computing similarity estimates is eventually performed by applying some kind of similarity measure between the term vectors $\mathbf{w_a}$ and $\mathbf{w_b}$, respectively, for artists a and b under consideration. Frequently, the cosine measure is applied for this purpose, see Equation 4.1, where T denotes the set of all terms, and θ gives the angle between a's and b's term vectors.

$$sim_{cos}(a,b) = \cos\theta = \frac{\sum\limits_{t\in T} w_{a,t} \cdot w_{b,t}}{\sqrt{\sum\limits_{t\in T} w_{a,t}^2} \cdot \sqrt{\sum\limits_{t\in T} w_{b,t}^2}} \qquad (4.1)$$

There exist a large number of different formulations for term frequency, inverse document frequency, and similarity measurement. A comprehensive investigation can be found by Schedl et al. [601] in which the authors analyze the impact of various algorithmic choices for the task of artist similarity estimation from Web pages. The overall best performing formulation when using Web pages as data source was found to be the combination of cosine similarity and the term weighting function given in Equation 4.2, where $f_{a,t}$ denotes the absolute number of occurrences of t in a's virtual document, D_t is the set of documents containing term t, F_t is the total number of t's occurrences in the corpus, and N is the total number of documents in the corpus. These findings are based on two artist collections (one comprising 224 highly popular artists from 14 genres; the second one 3000 artists from real-world collections, including lesser known ones).

$$w_{a,t} = tf_{a,t} \cdot idf_t = (1 + \log_2 f_{a,t}) \cdot \left(1 - \frac{\sum\limits_{d\in D_t}\left(-\frac{f_{a,t}}{F_t}\cdot\log_2\frac{f_{a,t}}{F_t}\right)}{\log_2 N}\right)$$
$$(4.2)$$

$$w_{d,t} = \log_e(1 + f_{d,t}) \cdot \log\frac{N - f_t + 0.5}{f_t + 0.5}$$

$$w_{d,t} = (1 + \log_e f_{d,t}) \cdot \log_e\frac{N - f_t}{f_t}$$

$$sim(a,b) = \frac{\sum_{t\in\mathcal{T}_{a,b}}(w_{a,t}\cdot w_{b,t})}{W_a \cdot W_b}$$

The second approach to artist similarity measurement from Web pages relies on *co-occurrence analysis*, that is, the similarity between a and b is inferred from the number of Web pages on which both artist names occur together. In Schedl et al. [600], it is proposed to use as the similarity estimate the conditional probability that artist a occurs on a Web page known to mention artist b. This conditional probability is approximated by estimating relative frequencies inferred from page count estimates given by a search engine. Equation 4.3 gives the corresponding similarity function, which is made symmetric.

$$sim(a,b) = \frac{1}{2}\cdot\left(\frac{c_{a,b}}{c_a} + \frac{c_{a,b}}{c_b}\right) \qquad (4.3)$$

$c_{a,b}$ denotes the number of pages on which both artist names a and b occur, whereas c_a represents the number of pages which are known to mention artist *a*. A similar approach is proposed by Zadel and Fujinaga [758], although the authors suggest to employ the similarity function given in Equation 4.4. Here the minimum is used in the denominator to account for different popularities of artists.

$$sim(a, b) = \frac{c_{a,b}}{\min{(c_a, c_b)}} \tag{4.4}$$

4.2.2 Information Extraction

Extracting music-related information from Web pages is another task in MIR, which serves, for instance, to build music information systems [607]. Reviewing the literature on music information extraction approaches mainly address the extraction of *band members and instrumentation* [606], *genre and mood* [234], *country of origin* of an artist or a band [247, 604, 603], and *discographical information* [352]. Work on the former three is briefly summarized in the following.

Band Members and Instrumentation: Identifying relations between bands, musicians, and instruments is a problem addressed by Schedl and Widmer [606], where Schedl et al. first use a list of bands to gather corresponding sets of Web pages by querying a search engine, an approach similar to the one presented in Section 4.2.1. From these pages, 2-grams, 3-grams, and 4-grams, that is, consecutive term sequences of length 2, 3, and 4, respectively, are extracted. Only *n*-grams whose terms are capitalized are retained, assuming that person names are spelled in this manner. Furthermore, *n*-grams containing common speech words are filtered. To the remaining *n*-grams and the surrounding text, rules such as `"M plays the I,"` `"R M,"` or `"M is the R"` are applied. In these rules, `M` is the potential band member (the *n*-gram), `I` is the instrument, and `R` is M's role in the band (such as "singer" or "guitarist"). To cover different notations for instruments and roles, the authors use synonym lists, for example, <"keyboardist," "keyboarder," "keyboard player">. The number of times each rule can be applied to the Web page set of the band of interest is computed, and these counts are aggregated for each pair <M,I>, mapping roles to instruments. Pairs <M,I> that occur too infrequently in a band's Web page set are discarded using a dynamic threshold. Eventually, the remaining relations between a band, its members, and their instruments are predicted.

Genre and Mood: There exists extensive literature on the MIR task of genre and mood classification. However, most of the works derive this kind of information from audio-based features. In contrast, extracting such information from Web pages is suggested by Geleijnse and Korst [234]. The authors parse Web pages to find patterns such as `"A is one of the biggest G artists,"` `"G artists such as A,"` `"M mood by A,"` or `"M style of A,"` where `A` represents an artist or band, `G` denotes a genre, and `M` is a mood term. The number of occurrences of such patterns is then used to predict the most probable genre and mood for the musician or band under consideration.

Country of Origin: Govaerts and Duval [247] analyze artist pages and biographies available from last.fm,[4] freebase,[5] and Wikipedia[6] in a more or less structured manner. They apply different heuristics, such as counting in biographies the number or positions of terms denomination locations.

Schedl et al. [604, 603] apply standard term weighting, such as *tf-idf*, to determine the most important country terms in Web pages, retrieved with an approach similar to the one presented in Section 4.2.1, that is, mining Web pages returned by search engines. As another heuristic, they also perform keyword spotting on the retrieved artist-related Web pages and subsequently use the distance between keywords such as "born" or "founded" and country names to predict the most probable origin.

4.3 Microblogs

Microblogging services, the most popular of which is certainly twitter[7] at the time of writing, have tremendously increased their user base during the past few years.[8] Hundreds of millions of users continuously inform the world of what they are currently doing or what is important for them. In comparison to Web pages and blogs, microblogging messages are restricted to 140 characters when using twitter. This generally results in more accurate messages and lower computational complexity of algorithms harvesting this data source, which makes microblogs especially interesting for the purpose of *music similarity measurement*. In addition, the timeliness of microblogs makes them suitable for the task of trend prediction. In the domain of MIR, *popularity estimation* of artists is of particular interest along this research line. Given that many tweets, that is, messages posted via twitter, are geo-localized, popularity estimates can even be computed at the granularity of regions of the world. On the downside, the people who tweet a lot are probably not the most representative group. Hence, approaches that exploit microblogs may give biased results. In the following, we will address the tasks of similarity measurement and popularity estimation.

4.3.1 Similarity Measurement

A study similar to the one reported by Schedl et al. [601] and summarized in Section 4.2.1, but using twitter posts instead of Web pages, is conducted by Schedl [598]. The study aims to determine well-performing variants

---

[4]http://www.last.fm
[5]http://www.freebase.com
[6]http://www.wikipedia.org
[7]https://www.twitter.com
[8]http://www.huffingtonpost.com/2011/04/28/twitter-number-of-users_n_855177.html

of model parameters when creating term vector representations and in turn applying a similarity function. More precisely, different formulations for *tf*, *idf*, normalization, and similarity measures are investigated. Also, two schemes for querying `twitter` are assessed—"`artist`" and "`artist`" `music`. In addition, the use of different dictionaries to index the gathered microblogs are analyzed. These dictionaries—which comprise, for instance, music-related terms retrieved from `freebase` or most frequently applied tags of `last.fm` users— effectively reduce the number of dimensions of the *tf-idf* vectors since term weights are only calculated for the dictionary entries.

The best performing term weighting variants according to Schedl's experiments are given in Equations 4.5, 4.6, and 4.7. These findings are based on two collections of artists: one containing 224 well-known artists (from 14 genres, 16 artists each), the other one comprising 3000 artists from real-world collections gathered from `last.fm`. The overall best results for similarity measurement in a typical retrieval task[9] are achieved when combining these term weighting variants with the *Jaccard coefficient* similarity function given in Equation 4.8. In these equations, N represents the total number of virtual artist documents in the corpus, $f_{a,t}$ is the number of occurrences of term t in the virtual document of artist a, f_t denominates the total number of documents containing term t, W_a is the length of a's virtual document, and $T_{a,b}$ denotes the set of distinct terms in artist documents a and b.

$$w_{a,t} = tf_{a,t} \cdot idf_t = \log_e(1 + f_{a,t}) \cdot \log_e \frac{N - f_t}{f_t} \tag{4.5}$$

$$w_{a,t} = tf_{a,t} \cdot idf_t = \log_e(1 + f_{a,t}) \cdot \log \frac{N - f_t + 0.5}{f_t + 0.5} \tag{4.6}$$

$$w_{a,t} = tf_{a,t} \cdot idf_t = (1 + \log_e f_{a,t}) \cdot \log_e \frac{N - f_t}{f_t} \tag{4.7}$$

$$sim(a, b) = \frac{\sum_{t \in T_{a,b}} (w_{a,t} \cdot w_{b,t})}{W_a^2 + W_b^2 - \sum_{t \in T_{a,b}} (w_{a,t} \cdot w_{b,t})} \tag{4.8}$$

Looking at the query scheme, the experiments showed that using only the artist name outperforms adding the keyword "music." This observation seems reasonable since space is precious in tweets, and microbloggers therefore try to omit redundancies; for instance, it is rather unlikely that someone will add "music" to a tweet about "Madonna." As for the different term dictionaries under investigation, using an amalgamation of genres, instruments, and moods gathered from `freebase` yields results that are best on average (over all combinations of other parameters) and also most stable (when varying other parameters). It can hence be concluded that dictionaries comprising domain-specific terms both reduce computational complexity, as they decrease the dimensionality of the feature vector representations, and give better retrieval results than using all the terms appearing in the corpus.

---

[9]The retrieval task used for assessment in [598] can be formulated as returning artists which belong to the same genre as the artist used as query.

Another approach to microblog-based music similarity measurement is suggested by Zangerle et al. [761] and by Schedl and Hauger [599], two works which are conceptually quite similar but carried out independently. Both first identify tweets reporting music listening activity by filtering the `twitter` stream for identifiers such as `#nowplaying`. Having determined a set of candidate tweets this way, the authors match the content of the tweets to databases of artists and tracks, such as `musicbrainz`.[10] Subsequently, Zangerle et al. [766] as well as Schedl and Hauger [604] employ *co-occurrence analysis* to identify which artists or tracks are listened to by the same user. While Zangerle et al. [766] use the absolute number of co-occurrences to build a music recommender system, Schedl and Hauger [604] evaluate different normalization strategies to account for varying popularity of artists that might distort the results of their similarity estimators. Evaluation is performed using `last.fm` similarities as ground truth and comparing the overlap between the `twitter`-based most similar artists and those returned by `last.fm`, taking as seed each artist in the collection. The best performing similarity estimator is given in Equation 4.9, where $co(a, b)$ denotes the total number of co-occurrences of artists a and b in the tweets of same users, and $occ(a)$ represents the count of artist a in the entire corpus of tweets.

$$sim(a, b) = \frac{co(a, b)}{\sqrt{occ(a) \cdot occ(b)}} \tag{4.9}$$

4.3.2   Popularity Estimation

Microblogs have also been used to predict the popularity of artists in different countries. Schedl et al. [602] investigate various data sources for this task; in addition to tweets, they look into page count estimates returned by search engines, music files in shared folders of Peer-to-Peer networks, and artist playcounts on `last.fm`. The providers of all of these data sources allow to confine to a country the retrieval of listening data. This might either be supported by their APIs (as in the case of `last.fm`) or by using additional tools such as a mapper of IP addresses to countries, in the case of Peer-to-Peer networks.

Schedl et al.'s [602] microblog-based approach first retrieves tweets that include the hashtag `#nowplaying`, which is frequently used to indicate music listening. Only tweets that include information about the user's location as <latitude, longitude> coordinates are considered further. Using a list of major cities in the world and their corresponding countries, tweets originating from a location within a certain radius around these cities are mapped to countries. Subsequently, the microblogs are scanned for occurrences of artist names, and a count corresponding to term frequency $tf_{c,a}$ is computed for each country c and artist a. Similar to the concept of virtual artist documents introduced before, this can be thought of as creating *virtual country documents* by

---

[10]http://musicbrainz.org

treating all tweets assigned to country c as one big document and calculating the $tf_{c,a}$ weights for this document. Equation 4.10 gives the popularity score for artist a in country c, where $|C|$ indicates the total number of countries and df_a represents the "document frequency" of artist a. In this interpretation, the document frequency corresponds to the number of countries in which artist a is mentioned in at least one tweet. The rightward term in Equation 4.10 thus represents an idf-factor that downranks artists that are popular regardless of the country.

$$pop(c, a) = tf_{c,a} \cdot \log_2\left(1 + \frac{|C|}{df_a}\right) \tag{4.10}$$

Finally, we would like to mention that there also exist some companies that are specialized in measuring artist, band, and song popularity, which is no surprise given the economic interests of the music industry. Such companies include **Band Metrics**[11] and **BigChampagne Media Measurement**.[12] Also traditional music charts such as the "Billboard Hot 100"[13] released weekly by the **Billboard Magazine**[14] still play an important role, even though they just provide charts for the United States.

4.4 Explicit User Ratings

Explicit ratings in music are numerical values that users give to songs, albums, artists, or even genres according to what their opinion on that item may be. When compared to implicit datasets, explicit ratings datasets are more difficult to collect because they require motivating users for active participation. For example, in personalized online radio Web sites, users care to rate songs in order to personalize their playlists (e.g., **Pandora**[15]). Still, most users do not explicitly rate every song they have listened to. Therefore, in general, explicit ratings datasets are more sparse than implicit datasets—namely the users × item matrix has more unknown values.

While implicit datasets are more easily obtained, when harnessed correctly explicit ratings can be much more informative. Ratings serve as a direct platform for users to express their preferences, therefore there is no need to make strong assumptions to interpret the data. Yet, understanding ratings is not as straightforward as it initially seems. Considering the popular 5-star rating, for example, we can assume that 1 star indicates that the user did not like the song, and 5 stars that the user did like it. However, for users that usually

---

[11] http://www.bandmetrics.com
[12] http://www.bigchampagne.com
[13] http://en.wikipedia.org/wiki/Billboard_Hot_100
[14] http://www.billboard.com
[15] http://www.pandora.com

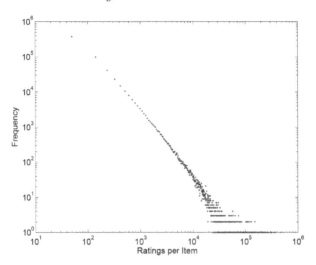

FIGURE 4.4: Frequency of ratings per item in the Yahoo! Music dataset. A linear line on a log-log graph indicates a power-law distribution.

rate low, a 3-star rating might be a positive indication, while for high raters it is probably a negative indication.

4.4.1 Characteristics of Explicit Rating Datasets

In this section we will use the publicly available Yahoo! Music dataset [183]. It consists of 262,810,175 explicit ratings of 624,961 music items by 1,000,990 users collected during 1999–2010, making it the largest publicly available explicit dataset. Ratings distributions usually follow a power-law with a "short head" of popular items that occupy the majority of the dataset. One of the main challenges is the need to handle the sparsity of information in the "long tail" [124]. In the music domain, this challenge is emphasized because the size of the catalog (number of items) is generally larger than, for instance, in the movie domain. When plotting the number of ratings per item in the Yahoo! Music dataset versus the frequency of such items, we see a clear power-law behavior (Figure 4.4).

The long tail of rare songs makes it difficult to learn and recommend items in the tail. However, users often expect a recommender system to help them explore such items (rather than presenting them with what they are already familiar with). It is therefore useful to incorporate a taxonomy that ties the rare items with other related items [661, 357]. Another approach is to combine content-based information with collaborative filtering information [175].

Let us also consider the distribution between the raters. Figure 4.5 depicts the mean rating per user versus the number of ratings that users provide. We see that as the number of ratings increase, the mean rating decreases.

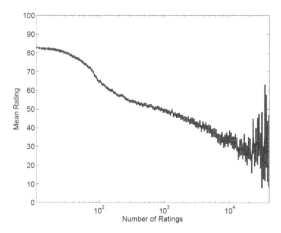

FIGURE 4.5: Users' mean rating versus popularity in the Yahoo! Music dataset.

This may be the result of heavy raters being more "critical," or the fact that because they rate more songs, they are also more likely to rate "bad" songs. Another assumption may be that there are two types of raters: those who rate every song they listened to, and those who only "remember" to rate after they hear a song they really like. The latter group is expected to have less ratings in their histories and a higher mean rate.

Explicit ratings datasets have different scales, and ratings are unevenly distributed across the possible values. A binary dataset, for example, consists of "like" or "dislike" signals. The Yahoo! Music dataset is based on a 0–100 scale, but multiples of ten are far more frequent than other values. Specifically, the values 0, 30, 50, 70, and 100 dominate the dataset, which is equivalent to a 5-star rating scale frequently used in recommendation systems.

4.4.2   Matrix Factorization Models

Explicit ratings datasets are mostly used for music recommendations and personalization [733, 357, 657]. In this context, the algorithms are similar to other domains such as movies or books. In this setting, Matrix Factorization (MF) algorithms have been shown to be more accurate than other methods such as neighborhood models, Latent Dirichlet Allocation [770], or Restricted Boltzmann Machines [586]. In the music domain, this has been recently demonstrated in the KDD-Cup '11 competition for music recommendations in which participants were required to predict music ratings based on explicit ratings to songs, albums, artists, and genres [183].

In MF models, each user u is associated with a user-traits vector $p_u \in \mathbb{R}^K$, and each item i with an item-traits vector $q_i \in \mathbb{R}^K$, where K is the dimensionality of the factorization. Each user and each item is therefore represented by a K dimensions latent vector. The user's trait vector p_u represents the user's preferences or "taste." Similarly, the item's traits vector represent the item's latent characteristics. The dot-product $p_u^\top q_i$ is the personalization component, which captures user's u affinity to item i. Predicted ratings are obtained using the rule:

$$\hat{r}_{ui} = \mu + b_i + b_u + p_u^\top q_i \tag{4.11}$$

where μ is the overall bias and b_i and b_u are scalers that represent the item and user biases, respectively.

The item bias b_i captures the item's tendency to be rated higher or lower than the average item. For example, popular songs will usually have a higher item bias due to the fact that they are highly rated by most users regardless of the rater's personal taste. Similarly, the user bias b_u captures raters' tendencies to rate on a higher or lower scale than the average user. For example, the user bias can alleviate the pattern shown in Figure 4.5.

The simple model of Equation 4.11 is not specific to music, however, a significant strength of MF models is their natural ability to easily incorporate additional domain-specific features. Both the personalization components p_u and q_i and the bias components b_i and b_u can be extended. For example, an item's bias may change over time. This can be easily incorporated into the model by adding a time dependent component to the item bias $b_i(t)$. Similarly, the user's bias may have a temporal component $b_u(t)$. Incorporating this into our model will result in the following form:

$$\hat{r}_{ui} = \mu + b_i + b_i(t) + b_u + b_u(t) + p_u^\top q_i \tag{4.12}$$

where $b_i(t)$ captures temporal drift from the static item bias b_i. The temporal item bias $b_i(t)$ can represent specific time slots in the ratings dataset (e.g., days or week numbers), or it can incorporate smooth temporal drift in the time frame that is near the given rating [367]. Alternatively, it can be based on a linear combination of temporal basis functions such as in Dror et al. [182]. Time granularity of weeks fit well with songs' temporal popularity changes [362, 182]. Similar extensions are also applicable to users and items traits [367].

Another example is items' taxonomy. Items belonging to the same taxonomy may often share similar characteristics. It is therefore useful to tie their trait vectors with a common component based on the taxonomy [182]. We can hence expand our model to the following format:

$$\hat{r}_{ui} = \mu + b_i + b_i(t) + b_u + b_u(t) + p_u^\top \left(q_i + q_{type(i)} \right) \tag{4.13}$$

where $q_{type(i)}$ is a shared trait, common to all the items of type $type(i)$. The taxonomy components allow for information to propagate more efficiently between different items of the same taxonomy and help mitigate the cold start problem (items with little ratings history). A shared taxonomy component may also be added to the item's bias. In Dror et al. [182] a hierarchical music item's taxonomy was modeled by adding multiple shared components for each level of the taxonomy (tack $\rightarrow$ album $\rightarrow$ artist $\rightarrow$ genre). The authors use *explicit* musical genres with *latent* trait vectors. This is in contrast to Yoshii et al. [748], where *latent* musical genres are learnt through an aspect model based on both collaborative filtering and content-based information.

There are various techniques for training MF models. Generally, a cost function is defined on the prediction error (e.g., RMSE) and optimization is followed by Stochastic Gradient Descent or an Alternating Least Squares algorithm. Alternatively, a probabilistic model can be defined and inference can be done by learning the posterior distributions of the parameters using Gibbs Sampling, Variational Bayes, or Expectation Propagation [646, 523].

Items' trait vectors (q_i) spans a similarity space defined by an inner product operation. We conclude by presenting an example of this space, which shed some light on how the MF model embeds the items. Figure 4.6 depicts the most popular musical tracks and genres in the Yahoo! Music dataset embedded in a 2-dimensional latent space. This figure is based on an MF model similar to Equation 4.13 with musical genres added as taxonomy feature vectors ($q_{type(i)}$). Note how the learned embedding separates Rock and similar music from Hip-Hop and similar music. In MF models, similarity is based on the inner product between items. Songs and artists in similar (close) angles have positive correlation in terms of their ratings (similar items). Orthogonal items are uncorrelated in terms of their ratings and opposite items have negative correlation. The embedding of Figure 4.6 implies positive correlation between ratings of Hip-Hop artists and between ratings of Rock artists. It also implies that ratings of these two genres are uncorrelated with the other genre. Note that the low dimensionality (which is required for a visualization) causes a small number of items to be wrongly folded near less related items (e.g., Bob Marley). Usually a much higher dimensionality is used (50 dimensions for example), which prevents such folding.

4.5 Peer-to-Peer Networks

Peer-to-Peer (P2P) networks provide a fruitful ground for MIR, including media files shared by users, search queries, and spatial and temporal changes that take place in the network. This data is often adopted as an invaluable resource for various MIR tasks, including user and content similarity, recommendation, ranking, and trend prediction.

P2P networks have a great potential as a practically unbounded source of data. The abundance and wealth of information regarding user preferences is particularly useful in recommendation techniques based on collaborative filtering, which were shown to outperform content-based approaches, given that the dataset used is sufficiently comprehensive.

Despite all their advantages, P2P networks are quite complex, making the collection of a comprehensive dataset far from being trivial, and in some

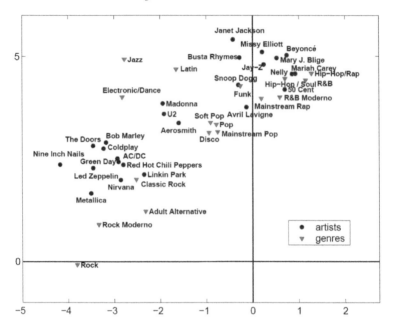

FIGURE 4.6: The most popular musical tracks and genres in the Yahoo! Music dataset are embedded into a two-dimensional space. (**See color insert.**)

cases practically unfeasible. First, P2P networks have high user churn, as users constantly connect and disconnect from the network, being unavailable for changing periods. Second, users in P2P networks often do not expose their shared data in order to maintain high privacy and security measures, therefore disabling the ability to collect information about their shared folders. Finally, users often delete content after using it, leaving no trace of its usage.

In this section, we look at the challenges and opportunities of using data obtained from P2P networks, and present some of the work that used P2P data in MIR research. The results we present in this section use data from a recent work [627], which performed a measurement study using 24 hours active crawling of 531,870 shared song files (.mp3 files) of over 1.2 million users in the Gnutella network [571].

4.5.1 P2P Data Usage

The content in file sharing networks is mostly ripped by individual users for consumption by other users. User-based interactions are a desirable property in information retrieval datasets, however, when it comes to metadata, it is the main source of ambiguities and noise. For example, in the Gnutella [571] network, which facilitates string-based search queries that are matched against metadata, only 7-10% of the queries are successful in returning useful content [759].

Koenigstein et al. [361] used the previously described dataset for studying the validity of using P2P data in MIR research, and showed that for many file types shared in P2P networks, typically there are several similar duplications available on the network. The files may be digitally identical, thus having the same hash signature, yet bearing different file names and metadata tags. Duplication in metadata tags are typically the result of spelling mistakes, missing data, and different variations on the correct values. A common hash signature can facilitate similar file groupings, nonetheless it does not solve the problem of copies that are not digitally identical.

As a result of the network size, churn, and dynamics, the authors raised a concern about the ability to collect information from a P2P network in a way that accurately captures the reality. The authors first considered the number of peers that need to be crawled in order to collect the majority of shared files. First, there is a need to correctly identify whether two files that are shared by different users are the same or not. For this end, either the file hash or, for some content, metadata can be utilized. Using the file hash is straightforward and suitable for all types of files, as every file in the P2P network has a file hash taking over its content. However, there can be slightly different copies of the same file, each with a different hash, mostly due to small changes in the creation of the file by users. In music content, for example, different disc ripping software or bit-rate result in different copies of the same song.

Metadata exists for some file types, such as music and movies, and provides additional information about the file. However, this metadata is often missing and contains spelling ambiguities and mistakes, hence it can also result in incorrect identification of similar songs. These ambiguities are common in music files, for example, Lil Wayne is also spelled as "l!l w4yne." Therefore, the authors used several techniques for identifying distinct songs. First, they used the file hash as the song id, and when hashes are exactly the same, they considered them as the same song. Second, accounting for the large number of songs with a single appearance, only hashes that appear at least twice are included, referred to as "appearance>1." Third, the metadata of the song was used, considering only songs that have both "title" (name of the song) and "artist" tags, with their concatenation as a unique song id. Finally, accounting for spelling mistakes and ambiguities, the authors use the SoundEx algorithm, which, roughly speaking, tells whether two strings sound similar.

Figure 4.7(b) depicts the number of unique songs per number of crawled users. The order of users was randomly selected to reduce any possible spatial bias. Without using any filter, almost each crawled user adds new files, which is expected since the authors show that over 90% of the songs are shared by a single user. However, for all noise reducing techniques, the figure shows varying convergence trends, indicating that the utility of crawling many users decreases.

The convergence witnessed when using metadata seems faster than when using file hashes, indicating that file hashes are more noisy than the metadata. Alternatively, this can be attributed to the observation that roughly

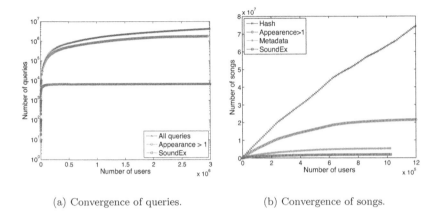

(a) Convergence of queries.   (b) Convergence of songs.

FIGURE 4.7: Convergence of queries (a) and of songs (b) per number of crawled users, using different methods for filtering noise. **(See color insert.)**

75% of the songs did not have both title and artist tags present and were therefore disregarded in that analysis. This contributes to the reduction of "noise" resulting in a more stable and quickly converging set of songs. Using SoundEx further reduces the number of shared songs and contributes to faster convergence.

Collection of queries performed by users in P2P networks is also very useful for various MIR tasks; however, it is often a much more complicated task than crawling the shared folders [350]. Hence, the authors further quantified the utility of collecting queries from an increasing number of users. Noise in queries is mostly related to either scarce keywords, or more likely, spelling mistakes. Therefore, the authors use techniques similar to the above: (a) keep only queries that appear more than once, and (b) aggregate queries using the SoundEx algorithm.

Figure 4.7(a) depicts the number of unique queries per number of crawled users. The figure shows that when all the queries are considered, the convergence is very slow (note the semilog scale), meaning that each additional user contributes some new queries. When considering only queries that appeared more than once, there is a more noticed convergence, and the overall number of unique queries goes down to less than 2 million. Applying SoundEx on the data significantly removes the number of distinct queries and results in an amazingly fast convergence. This shows that spelling mistakes are prominent in queries, in particular, much more than in metadata. This is expected, since there are significantly more users who issue queries than those that publish new content and manually enter the metadata in P2P networks.

This analysis shows that the diversity in search terms is mostly attributed to very "rare" strings that originate from single users, and to spelling mistakes, whereas the majority of common queries are repeated frequently among the different users, hence can be more easily collected. Filtering one-time queries is justified because such queries account for many of the spelling mistakes in search terms and is useless for collaborative filtering. Applying the more intense SoundEx filter almost completely mitigates duplications due to spelling mistakes, but probably groups together some different queries as well.

4.5.2   Peer Similarity Measurement

The similarity between peers is an important research topic since it is a building block for search and recommendation in P2P networks [491]. Voulgaris et al. [691] were one of the first to shift from the "network" definition of similar peers (e.g., geographical distance, packet delay, etc.), and proposed the concept of "semantic similarity" in P2P networks, that is, capture the distance of peers by looking at the files they share.

Shavitt et al. [626] studied the applicability of semantic similarity, and showed that this task is not straightforward, mainly since P2P networks are extremely sparse, and the overlap between peers is small. In fact, in their dataset, only 0.03% of possible links between users and songs (identified using metadata) actually exist, whereas in `NetFlix`, which is considered very sparse, over 1% of the possible links exist. This extreme sparseness makes it difficult to assess the similarity between any two users, which is needed in order to estimate how "like-minded" they are. The authors showed that unlike in well-structured services, the sparseness in P2P data is also the result of the difficulty to identify which files are identical. In particular, comparing the actual content of files is usually done using the MD5 hash of the files, which fails when different copies exist. Using metadata is susceptible to different tagging and spelling mistakes.

The method presented by the authors for capturing the distance between peers leverages the observation that it is possible to estimate the similarity between two files in the network by counting the number of users that share them together. This enables the transformation of the sparse collaborative matrix into a graph that connects files, and the weight of each link corresponds to the similarity between the files. The distance between peers is then computed using the maximum weighted bipartite matching.

This method captures the concept of the "wisdom of the crowds" in P2P networks—the distance between files is estimated based on the global preferences of many peers, and this, in turn, is used to estimate the distance between peers, even if they have no overlapping files.

4.5.3   Recommendation Systems

An interesting usage of P2P networks in MIR research is to leverage their massive adoption in music for improving recommendations. Recommender systems were suggested to help users find new content based on their preferences or similarity to other like-minded users. These systems have been studied extensively in recent years [565], mostly relying on the willingness of users to rank their preferences in order to provide a better recommendation. However, as mentioned above, P2P networks do not enjoy the luxury of explicit ranking of content, therefore require new methods to assess peer similarity.

Shavitt et al. [625] presented a set of methods for leveraging the song similarity graph, S, so that it can be used for content recommendation. The authors showed that by applying clustering algorithms on the song similarity graph, it is possible to identify groups of similar songs without using any metadata. Then, users are mapped to these clusters based on their known songs, and obtain recommendations from similar songs within "their" cluster.

4.5.4   Popularity Estimation

Bhattacharjee et al. [72] used P2P networks for estimating the "shelf-life" of albums, that is, the duration of a music album on the "Billboard Hot 100" chart, and showed that P2P sharing activity can be used to help predict the subsequent market performance of a music album.

Koenigstein et al. [359] demonstrated the use of geo-aware P2P query strings in the detection of emerging artists, based on the observation that some emerging artists have a stronghold of fans in their hometown area. By modeling the concept of local popularity, the authors devised an algorithm for spotting out locally popular artists on the rise, and showed it can reach a 15-30% average success percentage (a high rate in the industry's standards).

This direction was later extended by Koenigstein et al. [362], where popularity trends in P2P queries belonging to well known artists were used in order to predict singles' success on the American Billboard chart. It was shown that popularity trends in P2P networks are highly correlated with those on the Billboard. However, while in P2P networks these trends are shown immediately, on the Billboard there is a delay of about two weeks caused by the manual data collection and the time that passes from the data collection until the actual publication time. Therefore, the authors suggested replacing "old fashioned" music popularity charts by new charts based on online activity such as P2P networks [358].

4.6   Social Tags

A tag is a keyword, a free text word, or short phrase that describes a piece of information, generally a piece of Web or multimedia content. In music, tags can refer to different aspects, such as moods (*happy*, *sad*, etc.), musical genres (*rock*, *jazz*, etc.), instruments (*piano*, *guitar*, etc.), time periods (*80s*, *2000s*, etc.), usage (*music to fall asleep to*, *party*, etc.) or more subjective aspects

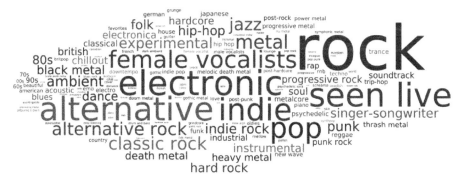

FIGURE 4.8: Tag cloud of `last.fm` top tags. **(See color insert.)**

(*seen live, sxsw, favorite*, etc.). Even though tags describe multiple facets, they are, by definition, a nonhierarchichal representation of content. Hence their job is not to organize all the information in the Web into tidy categories, but rather to add value to the huge amount of data available nowadays [60].

When these tags are entered by users (usually nonexperts) of any system (or a game [391, 441, 676, 347]), they are commonly referred to as "social tags" [384]. Examples of systems for tagging music content are `last.fm`, (Figure 4.8), `SoundCloud`,[16] and `Freesound`[17] (although the latter is more for sounds and unfinished works rather than music items). `last.fm` is a social music Web site that—among other functionalities—allows users to share information related to what they are currently listening to on their music devices. Additionally, it also allows users to tag music items (artists, albums, and tracks) either for organizational purposes or to communicate their musical taste. For instance, users of `last.fm` tagged the artist "Elton John" as *70s, 80s, pop, classic-rock, singer-songwriter, piano,* and *british,* among others.

Unlike other UGC, such as Web pages, mining or harvesting social tags is a straightforward task. When introduced by users (or media uploaders, as it is the case for `SoundCloud` and `Freesound`), tags are stored internally in the social Web site's systems in a structured fashion. As a result, these Web sites are able to publish tags through their APIs, generally in XML or JSON format.

The combination of the tags provided by thousands of music users leads to the emergence of a large body of domain-specific knowledge, usually referred to as folksonomy. Due to its informal syntax (i.e., direct assignment of tags), the tagging process allows the collective creation of very rich tag descriptions of individual music items [641]. When compared to taxonomies defined by experts, music folksonomies have several advantages. First, completeness, meaning that they ideally encompass all possible "ways to talk about music," including both lay and expert points of view. Second, due to the continuous

---

[16]http://www.soundcloud.com
[17]http://www.freesound.org

nature of the tagging process, folksonomies tend to be well updated. Third, they usually incorporate both commonly accepted and generic concepts, as well as very specific and local ones. According to Laurier et al. [388], Levy and Sandler [397], and Sordo et al. [642], when a folksonomy emerges, it tends to follow an inherent structure and is comparable to expert annotations in some cases.

Collecting tags via social networks is also a scalable approach. By the end of the year 2011, `last.fm` has collected over 11 million artist annotations, and 33 million track annotations, covering more than 2.9 million distinct tags, artists, and albums.[18] Nonetheless, social tagging has several limitations [641]. First, social tags suffer from linguistic issues such as synonymy and polysemy. As an illustrative example, the word *piano* can refer to a keyboard musical instrument or to a dynamic direction in music. Second, the intentional misuse of tags, such as spam, hacking, and malicious tagging, which try to deliberately confuse the system. Last, but especially not least, sparseness and popularity bias. While popular artists and songs get hundreds of tags, new or unpopular music resources do not get any tags or only a few tags. The term popularity in this case has a different "effect." According to Lamere [384], the typical tagger in social Web sites has a sense of popularity that may differ considerably from the music sales, a classic measure of popularity in music. The popularity bias in social tagging systems is thus strongly linked to the community bias such systems are frequently prone to, that is, distortions arising from the fact that certain systems tend to attract people with certain characteristics. To give an example, `last.fm` users tend to have on average a higher inclination toward metal music than the total population.

4.6.1 Similarity Measurement

The most common approach to infer music similarity from social tags is by using co-occurrence analysis. The rationale is that music items that share some or most of their tags are more likely to be similar. A music item (e.g., a track, an artist, or an album) is represented as a vector of tags V_t, where $V_t > 0$ ($V_t = 0$) implies the presence (absence) or importance of tag t for that music item. Similarity between pairs of music items is then modeled as a correlation of the corresponding vectors of tags. A well-known method for computing correlation between pairs of vectors is *Pearson's correlation coefficient*, which is defined as:

$$r_{12} = \frac{\sum_i (X_{i1} - \bar{X}_1)(X_{i2} - \bar{X}_2)}{\sqrt{\sum_i (X_{i1} - \bar{X}_1)^2}\sqrt{(\sum_i X_{i2} - \bar{X}_2)^2}} \tag{4.14}$$

This method, though, suffers from several limitations. First, the high dimensionality and sparseness of UGC makes the process computationally

---

[18]This information was obtained through personal communication with Mark Levy, MIR team leader at `last.fm` (2011).

expensive.[19] Second, there is the lack of sensibility to noise in the data, including the problems of spam, hacking, and malicious tagging. Third, there is the lack of flexibility and generality. For example, two documents that do not share any tags will never be considered as similar, even though some tags in both music items are similar or are correlated in some way.

To overcome these issues, several methods have been proposed in the literature. One well known method is *Latent Semantic Analysis* (LSA) [167]. This method is used to analyze the inherent structure of documents, represented here as an $M \times N$ matrix of music items and tags, where M is the number of items and N the number of tags. LSA assumes a latent semantic structure that lies underneath the randomness of word choice and spelling in noisy datasets [64]. Basically, LSA consists of two steps: a Singular Value Decomposition (SVD) of the original matrix (followed by a dimensionality reduction) and a distance measure to compute the item or term similarity.

Singular Value Decomposition: A projection of the original $M \times N$ space to a continuous space of concepts. Given the original sparse matrix, $\mathbf{M}$, the Singular Value Decomposition of $\mathbf{M}$ is computed as follows:

$$\mathbf{M} = U\Sigma V^* \tag{4.15}$$

where U is an $M \times M$ unitary matrix of $\mathbf{M}$, Σ an $M \times N$ rectangular diagonal matrix whose diagonal entries are the singular values of M, and V^* represents the conjugate transpose of V, an $N \times N$ unitary matrix of $\mathbf{M}$ [245]. Given that the first singular values of a matrix tend to encompass most of the information in this matrix, the latter technique, additionally, allows to reduce the dimensionality of the original matrix by choosing a relatively small number of singular values (L) while still preserving the similarity structure among rows or columns.

Distance measure: the distance measure used for calculating the similarity between pairs of music items. The most prominent similarity distance in the literature is the cosine distance, defined as:

$$sim(t_1, t_2) = cos(\vec{t_1}, \vec{t_2}) = \frac{\vec{t_1}.\vec{t_2}}{||\vec{t_1}|| \cdot ||\vec{t_2}||} \tag{4.16}$$

where $\vec{t_1}$ and $\vec{t_2}$ are binary vectors with all the tag concepts. The values of $sim(t_1, t_2)$ range from -1 to 1. A value closer to 1 or -1 means that $\vec{t_1}$ and $\vec{t_2}$ are very similar or dissimilar, respectively. On the other hand, if the value of $sim(t_1, t_2)$ is close to 0 it means that there is no correlation between the two music items.

One of the limitations of LSA is that it assumes that the tag distribution among music items is normally distributed. If this assumption is not justified, other techniques such as probabilistic LSA (pLSA) [289] or Latent Dirichlet

---

[19]There exist methods that deal with highly dimensional sparse vectors more efficiently (e.g., [303]).

Allocation (LDA) [77]—which model co-occurrences as mixtures of conditional distributions—are reported to give better results.

4.6.2 Use of Social Tags in MIR

Music tags have recently been the object of increasing attention by the research community [384]. A number of approaches have been proposed to associate tags to music items based on an analysis of audio data [70, 674], on the knowledge about tag co-occurrence [397], or on the extraction of tag information from community-edited resources [592, 643]. In particular, social tags enable a wide range of MIR-related tasks, including auto-tagging, recommendation, or faceted browsing.

Auto-Tagging. Music auto-tagging refers to the task of classifying music items in terms of high-level concepts, such as musical genres, moods, or instruments. In this context, social tags are used as ground truth annotations for training models to classify music items. Eck et al. [189] and Bertin-Mahieux et al. [70] are two examples of how models of tags are built using machine learning algorithms to predict tags for unseen music items. More recently, there has been a growing interest in developing multimodal or hybrid approaches—that is, methods that use more than one source of information—for music classification. As an example, Wang et al. [694] used social tags along with audio content for artist style clustering. Turnbull et al. [675] combined contextual information (social tags and Web pages) and audio content for music query-by-text retrieval. They demonstrated that using combinations of different sources of music information leads to better performance than using a single source.

Recommendation. Social tags have also been used in music recommendation. For instance, Symeonidis et al. [654] and Nanopoulos et al. [489] proposed a framework that uses a 3-order multidimensional matrix and high-order Singular Value Decomposition (HoSVD) to model the triple consisting of users, tags, and items. The resulting model is then used to recommend new music items to users.

Browsing and Navigation. Although tags are a nonhierarchichal representation of content, several studies have been conducted to find categorizations of tags—inherent to the social tagging process—which can be useful for browsing and navigating through large music collections. For instance, Levy and Sandler [397] applied dimensionality reduction techniques and latent semantic analysis to a dataset of tagged music tracks (using `last.fm` social tags) in order to obtain their corresponding compact representations in a low-dimensional space. This information is then used for genre and artist classification. Recently, Sordo et al. [643, 641] proposed a method to infer semantic facets of music social tags. Examples of facets include *musical genres, instruments, music software,* and *musical eras.* Once semantic facets are inferred, tags are then classified with respect to these facets.

4.7   Social Networks

Even though online social networks such as Facebook[20] or MySpace[21] have
become very popular during the past few years, surprisingly they have not
been used to a large extent for MIR purposes. Unlike approaches that mine
information from text, such as the ones presented in Sections 4.2 and 4.3,
scientific MIR work that exploits social networks as data source typically focus
on the friend relationships between users of the network under consideration.
Modeling these relationships as a large graph, the community structure of the
network can be assessed and used for tasks such as *music recommendation* and
playlist generation. Accordingly, these are the two tasks that will be covered
in the following.

4.7.1   Music Recommendation

Mesnage et al. [456] present a study aimed at assessing if music recommendations are better when music taste of social contacts from Facebook are
taken into account. To this end, the authors created an application dubbed
Starnet that recommends music to a user using different strategies; the recommendations are either based on positive ratings of the user's friends, on
positive ratings of others in the networks, or they are created randomly not
taking into account any ratings. Harvesting track information from last.fm
and searching for corresponding YouTube[22] video clips, the authors were able
to determine clips for about a quarter of a million tracks, which were linked to
the Starnet application. Subsequently, 68 participants used Starnet for a period of 4 months. They were asked to rate tracks on a 5-point-scale and could
also skip the current track. Furthermore, the users should indicate whether
they knew the selected track. Subsequent tracks were determined by applying
one of the three recommendation strategies mentioned above. From almost
5000 ratings received, Mesnage et al. found that people tend to prefer known
songs over unknown ones. Also collaborative recommendations, in particular
recommendations highly ranked by friends, were preferred over random ones.
While 47% of the friend-based recommendations were rated above average,
only 33% of the recommendations by other users (nonfriends) were rated so.
This rate drops to 17% when tracks were selected randomly.

4.7.2   Playlist Generation

Work by Fields et al. make use of the MySpace artist network as this is
one of the most important social networks for musicians [218, 217]. To this

---

[20]https://www.facebook.com
[21]http://www.myspace.com
[22]http://www.youtube.com

end, they sample part of the network, only considering artist pages. On each of these artist pages, up to 40 links to "top friends" within the network can be found. The authors explore the graph structure of the network via snowball sampling and also compute acoustic features for the most popular songs of each artist. Fields et al. [217] then combine acoustic information and social connections by using as edge weights for the MySpace graph the distance between the content-based feature vectors, which describe the timbre of the analyzed songs. To generate a playlist, Fields et al. [217] proposed using the *minimum cut/maximum flow* algorithm, which determines the highest weight in the narrowest path between two nodes of the network. This equals finding the smallest weight of edges, which have to be removed in order to disconnect the two nodes. These nodes represent the start and end song of the playlist to generate. The list of artists/songs in the playlist is thus identified by the nodes in the path(s) whose interconnecting edges have maximum flow value.

4.8   Conclusion

This chapter presented an introduction to Music Information Retrieval (MIR), paying particular attention to approaches exploiting user generated content. We illustrated the use of various data sources for several MIR tasks, such as similarity measurement, music retrieval, music recommendation, music information extraction, and artist popularity estimation. Advantages and shortcomings of the data sources have been discussed as well and are summarized in Table 4.1 with respect to important aspects of the data sources.

TABLE 4.1: Aspects of UGC Sources

	Web Pages	Microblogs	User Ratings
Community	no	yes	yes
Level	artist	artist,track,user	artist,track,user
Feature Dim.	very high	high	user×item
Specific Bias	low	community	community
Potential Noise	high	high	subjective scales

	P2P Networks	Social Tags	Social Networks
Community	yes	yes	yes
Level	artist,track	artist,track	artist,track
Feature Dim.	item×item	moderate	user×item
Specific Bias	community	community	community
Potential Noise	high	vandalism,hacking	yes

The first row in the table indicates whether a specific community is required to create the data. Whether the data source can be used to infer information on the level of artists or tracks is shown in the second row. The subsequent row indicates the dimensionality of the feature space in which similarities are computed, and hence reflects the complexity of the respective approaches. The penultimate row indicates whether a data source is prone to a specific bias and the last row shows its susceptibility to a specific type of noise. Furthermore, all context-based approaches suffer from general problems. First, we witness *data sparsity*, especially for artists in the "long tail." Second, there is *popularity bias*, that is, disproportionately more data is available for popular artists than for lesser known ones, which often distorts inferred similarity measures. In addition, methods that exploit UGC are prone to include only participants of existing communities in a broad sense (ranging from very specific groups like users of a certain P2P network to the huge community of the "microblogosphere"). This frequently poses a problem since members of the same community often tend to have similar music tastes. This phenomenon is known as *community bias* or *population bias*.

Open Challenges. One important challenge in MIR research is certainly to elaborate highly scalable feature extraction and similarity computation approaches. First steps into this direction have been performed, where Schnitzer [611] presents a content-based music recommendation system that is capable of dealing with millions of songs. Another challenge, which is also related to feature extraction and similarity measurement, is the automatic prediction of musical descriptors that are directly understandable to listeners. Deriving such descriptors that reflect human music perception from the audio signal is by no means a trivial task. Hence, bridging this "semantic gap" that frequently occurs between computational, low-level audio features that are easy to compute and high-level semantic descriptors that can be understood by humans is a challenging endeavor. Examples for high-level descriptors are genres, instruments, epochs, moods as well as artist, album, and track name. Striving to solve this problem, various approaches for the task of *auto-tagging* have been proposed. Auto-tagging methods typically learn relations between audio-based features and semantic concepts. The trained classifier is then used to predict the concepts for previously unseen music files [641]. One of the biggest problems in MIR (and hence one of its biggest challenges) is the lack of proper ground truths from which to develop and evaluate intelligent systems for music annotation, information extraction, and other relevant MIR tasks [681]. Typical datasets used in the Music Information Retrieval Evaluation eXchange (MIREX)[23] campaign are in the order of hundreds or a few thousands of music items. According to Urbano [681], ground truth datasets, apart from data quality, should be larger and more heterogeneous, that is, they should include sufficient examples of all possible aspects of music. Mining and leveraging user generated content can play an important role in ground truth generation and thus advancing research in MIR. The challenge lies in a proper validation and analysis of the huge amount of UGC available nowadays. A final challenge

---

[23]http://www.music-ir.org/mirex/wiki/MIREX_HOME

and recent trend is that of personalization and user-awareness. Building music retrieval systems that adapt to the user and his context, for example, by creating playlists that fit the user's current mood or activity, is a hard task but will enable new music experiences. To develop personalized systems, it is further crucial to model and understand the user and to address his particularities. For instance, the notion of music similarity is very much dependent on individual factors, such as the user's musical perception or taste. To give an example for the former, one person might judge two songs as similar due to their lyrics being both about unfulfilled love, while another might feel that the very same songs are different because of their differing rhythm. As for the influence of music taste on similarity, a fan of heavy metal music might regard two classical orchestra pieces as similar, while at the same time judging a black metal song highly dissimilar to a death metal track.

We are sure that the large and increasing amount of user generated data will help improve music retrieval and recommendation systems, thereby helping to solve some of the challenges mentioned above because this kind of data contains complementary information to common music content-based features. In addition, UGC is also suited to extract information about the user's context and in turn to enable context-aware and personalized systems.

Chapter 5

Graph and Network Pattern Mining

Jan Ramon

KU Leuven

Constantin Comendant

KU Leuven

Mostafa Haghir Chehreghani

KU Leuven

Yuyi Wang

KU Leuven

5.1 Introduction

During the last decade, ever growing databases have been constructed by both users and automated processes. In both cases, the structure of the databases is often complex, describing relations between many different objects. Therefore, data is usually represented using relational databases, graphs, or similar formalisms. Over the last decade, graph mining has emerged as a branch of data mining focusing on such graph-structured data.

One can distinguish two major types. First, in transactional graph mining one considers a collection of instances each represented by a separate isolated graph. One example is a database of molecules. Every molecule is represented with a graph, every node representing an atom, and every edge representing a bond. Other examples include drawings, scene descriptions, and local neighborhoods in a larger world.

The second setting can be called the single network setting. In this setting, all data is contained in one large graph. Instances of interest are vertices in this large graph. A typical example is the Internet. We can represent Web pages with vertices and hyperlinks with edges. Other examples are social networks, forums, and citation networks.

Graph mining research considers both algorithmic and statistical challenges. First, algorithmic challenges arise from the fact that many graph problems are intractable, for example, the subgraph isomorphism is NP-complete. Second, in a network, examples connected by edges are not (statistically) independent. For example, Web pages connected with hyperlinks are more likely to have similar topics. Therefore, the assumption of many machine learning algorithms that observations are independently and identically distributed (i.i.d.) does not hold. This poses challenges, for example, with respect to the estimation of the statistical power of a training sample.

Next to data mining methods, other approaches can also provide useful insight into network structured data. One line of research which is increasingly being adopted by the graph mining community originated from statistical physics. It studies, among other things, the asymptotic properties of networks where all participants behave in a similar way.

In this chapter, we survey graph mining methods. We focus on graph pattern mining, but also discuss a number of related topics such as generative models and the patterns emerging from them. The chapter is organized as follows. First, we review basic definitions and notations. Then, we discuss graph pattern mining in the transactional graph mining setting. In Section 5.4, we then consider mining in a single large network. Finally, we conclude and provide some pointers for further reading.

5.2 Basic Concepts

We will first briefly review some basic terminology. A more in-depth introduction to graph theory and terminology can be found [170].

Definition 1 (directed graph). *A directed graph is a tuple (V, E, λ) where V is a finite set of vertices (also called nodes), $E \subseteq V \times V$ is a set of arcs, and $\lambda : V \cup E \to \Sigma$ is a labeling function mapping every vertex and arc on a member of some label alphabet Σ. For a graph G, we will denote its vertex set with $V(G)$, its arc set with $E(G)$, and its labeling function with λ_G.*

Many different types of graphs are considered in the literature depending on what is useful in a specific situation. For instance, unlabeled graphs are graphs where Σ is a singleton. They are often represented with pairs (V, E). In some settings, edges between nodes carry a continuous-valued weight, expressing the strength of a relationship.

Undirected graphs are graphs whose arcs, called edges, do not have a direction. Often edges of such graphs are defined as sets of two vertices, that is, $E \subseteq \{e \subseteq V | \#e = 2\}$. For a directed graph, the underlying undirected graph is the graph obtained by removing the orientation of all arcs. A simple graph is a graph having at most one arc (edge) between any two vertices, and no loops (arcs connecting a node to itself). A multigraph may have several arcs between the same pair of vertices, these are then called parallel arcs. Hypergraphs are graphs where edges have one, two, or more elements. Here too, there are variants with ordered and unordered edges. For simplicity and uniformity of explanation, we will use directed labeled graphs unless explicitly stated otherwise. The theory and algorithms presented here are very similar for undirected graphs, unlabeled graphs, and hypergraphs.

As an example of how graphs are used to represent real-world data, consider a social network such as Facebook. We can represent users with nodes and friendship relations with edges. If we want to model more of Facebook, we could label the user nodes with label "person," and add also "group" nodes and "event" nodes. Accordingly, we could add edges between persons and groups representing memberships and edges between persons and events indicating participation. Some relations are not binary. For example, an invitation has a sender, a receiver, and an event to which the receiver is invited by the sender. We could distinguish between different roles in several ways. First, the node representing the event to which the receiver is invited has the label "event," which hence determines its role. To distinguish between sender and receiver, we could either use directed arcs from the sender to the invitation to the receiver, or we could label the edges with "receiver" and "sender," or we could insert additional nodes labeled "receiver" and "sender" and connect the sender, receiver, and invitation with them. Many alternatives are equivalent and the specific choice often depends on what is easiest (e.g., for implementing algorithms) and clearest (to understand the semantics of the data).

Definition 2 (incident, adjacent, degree). *An edge $\{v, w\}$ is said to be incident with the vertices v and w. v and w themselves are said to be adjacent because they are connected by an edge. The degree of a vertex is the number of edges incident with it.*

An essential concept in pattern mining is pattern matching, that is, the matching of a small graph, called the pattern, in a larger database graph. We will first introduce subgraph isomorphism and homomorphism, the most popular matching operators.

Definition 3 (subgraph). *A graph H is a subgraph of a graph G if $V(H) \subseteq V(G)$, $E(H) \subseteq E(G)$ and for all $x \in V(H) \cup E(H)$, $\lambda_H(x) = \lambda_G(x)$.*

Definition 4 (isomorphism). *Two graphs H and G are isomorphic, denoted $H \cong_i G$, iff there is a bijection $\pi : V(G) \to V(H)$ such that for all $x, y \in V(G)$, $(x, y) \in E(G) \Leftrightarrow (\pi(x), \pi(y)) \in E(H)$ and such that for all $x \in V(G) \cup E(G)$, $\lambda_G(x) = \lambda_H(\pi(x))$. Such a bijection π is called an isomorphism between the two graphs H and G. A graph H is subgraph isomorphic to a graph G, denoted $H \preceq_i G$, iff H is isomorphic to a subgraph of G.*

Definition 5 (homomorphism). *A graph H is homomorphic to a graph G, denoted $H \preceq_h G$ iff there is a (not necessarily injective) mapping, called homomorphism, $\pi : V(H) \to V(G)$ such that for all $x, y \in V(H)$, $(x, y) \in E(H)$ implies $(\pi(x), \pi(y)) \in E(G)$ and such that for all $x \in V(H) \cup E(H)$, $\lambda_H(x) = \lambda_G(\pi(x))$. Two graphs G and H are homomorphically equivalent, denoted $H \cong_h G$, iff G is homomorphic to H and H is homomorphic to G.*

As can already be expected from the notation, both relations induce a partial order and corresponding equivalence relation. Subgraph isomorphism and homomorphism is sometimes also called OI-subsumption (subsumption under object identity) and θ-subsumption (e.g., in the field of inductive logic programming [496]). Table 5.1 summarizes the terminology. Every subgraph isomorphism mapping is a homomorphism, but not every homomorphism is a subgraph isomorphism mapping. Figure 5.1 gives an example of (a) a subgraph isomorphism mapping and (b) a homomorphism.

TABLE 5.1: Isomorphism and Homomorphism Terminology

Mapping	isomorphism	homomorphism
Equivalence	isomorphic ($\cong_i$)	equiv. under homomorphism ($\cong_h$)
Partial order	subgraph isomorphic ($\preceq_i$)	homomorphic ($\preceq_h$)
logic-based	OI-subsumption	θ-subsumption

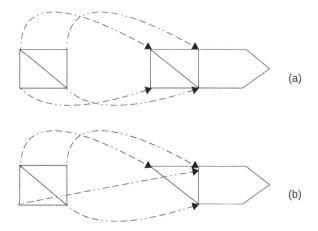

FIGURE 5.1: Isomorphism and homomorphism: (a) A subgraph of isomorphism mapping (which is also a homomorphism), (b) a subgraph of homomorphism mapping (but not isomorphism).

It is possible that a graph is subgraph isomorphic or homomorphic to another graph in several ways. The embedding and image concepts allow one to disambiguate between several such ways.

Definition 6 (embedding). *An embedding under isomorphism (resp. homomorphism) of a graph H in a graph G is a subgraph isomorphism mapping (resp. a homomorphism) from H to G. We denote the set of all embeddings of H in G with $Emb_i(H, G)$ (resp. $Emb_h(H, G)$).*

Definition 7 (image). *An image of a pattern H under some mapping π is the graph formed by the set of images of all vertices and all edges under π, that is, $\pi(H) = (\pi(V(H)), \pi(E(H)))$. An image of H under isomorphism (resp. homomorphism) in some graph G is an image $\pi(H)$ of H under some subgraph isomorphism (resp. homomorphism) π from H to G.*

It is possible that several embeddings of H in G correspond to the same image of H in G (see for example, Figure 5.2). The reverse does not hold: every embedding corresponds to only one image.

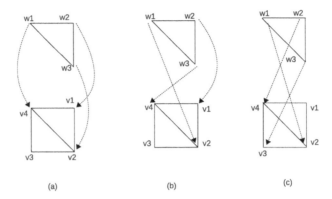

FIGURE 5.2: Embedding: (a) and (b) are two embeddings under isomorphism corresponding to the same image, (c) shows a different image.

5.3 Transactional Graph Pattern Mining

In the transactional graph mining setting, one considers a set of transactions, each represented with a graph. We do not assume dependencies between the transactions (in the terminology of machine learning theory, the transactions are independently and identically drawn from some distribution), so compared to the propositional machine learning setting and the itemset mining setting, the main additional challenge is the more complex structure of the graphs. This setting has many applications, and a good understanding of the transactional setting is a valuable prerequisite to study the more complex setting where all data is represented with a single network.

In this section, we will focus on graph pattern mining. Pattern mining is a basic task to discover patterns of interest. Once useful patterns have been generated, they can be used for a wide range of purposes. One application of pattern mining is association rule generation, where one wants to see whether certain patterns are correlated with certain target variables. Another popular application is feature generation, where every pattern can give rise to a feature which is 1 for the transactions where the pattern occurs and 0 for the other transactions. Also, if the set of generated patterns is of managable size, manual inspection can produce useful insight into the dataset.

5.3.1 The Graph Pattern Mining Problem

Depending on the situation, different settings of graph pattern mining may be considered. We therefore first identify the most important ingredients of a graph pattern mining problem.

Definition 8 (graph pattern mining setting). *A graph pattern mining setting is a triple $(L_d, L_p, \leq)$ where*

- *L_d is a class of graphs, called the database language,*

- *L_p is a subclass of L_d, called the pattern language*

- *$\leq$ is a partial order on L_d, called the matching operator*

A database for the graph pattern mining setting $(L_d, L_p, \leq)$, or shortly a database for L_d, is a multiset of graphs of L_d. For two patterns P_1 and P_2, if $P_1 \leq P_2$ then we call P_1 more general than P_2 (since P_1 will occur in all graphs where P_2 occurs) and P_2 more specific than P_1.

Figure 5.3 shows an example database of three undirected graphs over the alphabet $\{a, b, c\}$.

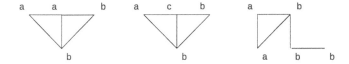

FIGURE 5.3: An example database of three undirected graphs over the alphabet $\{a, b, c\}$.

Definition 9 (graph pattern mining problem). *Let $(L_d, L_p, \leq)$ be a graph pattern mining setting. An interestingness predicate ι for $(L_d, L_p, \leq)$ is a predicate mapping every pair (D, P), where D is a database for L_d and P is a pattern from L_p, to either* **true** *or* **false**.

The problem of ι-interesting graph pattern mining for $(L_d, L_p, \leq)$ is the problem where the input is an input database D for $(L_d, L_p, \leq)$ and the task is to list all elements $P \in L_p$ for which $\iota(D, P)$ holds.

The most popular interestingness predicate is a minimal frequency constraint:

Definition 10 (pattern frequency). *Let $(L_d, L_p, \leq)$ be a graph pattern mining setting and D be a database for it. Let $P \in L_p$ be a pattern. The frequency of P in D, denoted $freq(D, P)$ is defined as*

$$freq(D, P) = |\{T \in D \mid P \leq T\}| \tag{5.1}$$

P is frequent in D w.r.t. some frequency threshold t if $freq(D, P) \geq t$

Consider, for example, the graph pattern depicted in Figure 5.4. The frequency of this graph pattern in the database of Figure 5.3 is 2.

FIGURE 5.4: An example graph pattern.

Definition 11 (frequent graph pattern mining problem). *Let* $(L_d, L_p, \leq)$ *be a graph pattern mining setting. The problem of frequent graph pattern mining for* $(L_d, L_p, \leq)$ *is the problem where the input is a database D for* $(L_d, L_p, \leq)$ *and a minimal frequency threshold t, and the task is to list all elements* $P \in L_p$ *for which* $freq(D, P) \geq t$ *holds.*

Other interestingness predicates can be considered, for example, Bringmann et al. [98] studies the constraint that patterns should have a minimal correlation with a given target attribute. The pattern mining problem is also related to combinatorial enumeration problems such as the enumeration of all molecules satisfying some specific properties [252].

A useful property for interestingness predicates is anti-monotonicity. Most of standard pattern mining algorithms rely on this property to prune their search.

Definition 12 (anti-monotone predicates). *Let* $(L_d, L_p, \leq)$ *be a graph pattern mining setting and let* ι *be an interestingness predicate for* $(L_d, L_p, \leq)$. ι *is said to be anti-monotone iff for all databases D for* L_d *and for all graphs G and H in* L_p , $G \leq H$ *and* $\iota(D, H)$ *implies* $\iota(D, G)$.

Note that while the term anti-monotone is more common in the field of pattern mining, different conventions exist. For example, in the field of graph theory the terms "monotone graph class" and "monotone predicate" are more commonly used.

5.3.2 Basic Pattern Mining Techniques

The task of pattern mining is an enumeration task in the sense that there are several solutions to a pattern mining problem and the task is to list each of them.

Most approaches perform a *search*, starting at some most general element, and then incrementally specializing it. In such a general-to-specific search, one can exploit the anti-monotonicity property. For example, the frequency of a more specific pattern will never be larger than the frequency of a more general pattern. Accordingly, if a pattern is not frequent, it is not needed to investigate any pattern which is more specific.

In order to perform a search, it is necessary to get from one candidate solution to another one. For this, an extension operator (also called refinement operator) is commonly used.

Definition 13 (minimal element). *Let $L, \leq$ be an ordered set. An element x of L is minimal iff for all $y \in L$, $y \leq x$ implies $x \leq y$.*

Definition 14 (extension operator). *Let $L_p, \leq$ be a partially ordered set. An extension operator ρ is a mapping $\rho : L_p \to L_p$ such that $\forall G \in L_p : \rho(G) > G$. We denote $\rho^1 = \rho$, $\rho^{i+1} = \rho \circ \rho^i$ and $\rho^*(x) = \cup_{i \in \mathbb{N}} \rho^i(x)$. We call ρ a complete extension operator iff $L_p, \leq$ has a finite set of minimal elements $P_\perp$ and $L_p = \rho^*(P_\perp)$, that is, by applying ρ recursively to $P_\perp$ all patterns can be generated in a finite number of steps.*

Pseudocode for a generic frequent graph pattern mining algorithm is shown in Algorithm 2. As can be seen, to perform a search in practice, the generic algorithm needs a starting point (the minimal elements $P_\perp$ of $(L_p, \leq)$) and a complete extension operator ρ. These, together with the frequency counting operator $freq(\cdot, \cdot)$ are important topics in graph pattern mining research.

Algorithm 2 is a breadth-first algorithm. We will discuss alternatives (mainly depth-first) and advantages of each search strategy later in this chapter.

Algorithm 2 Algorithm MineFrequentPatterns$((L_d, L_p, \leq), P_\perp, \rho, D, t)$

1: **Require.** a graph pattern mining setting $(L_d, L_p, \leq)$, the set $P_\perp$ of all minimal elements of L_p under $\leq$, a complete extension operator ρ, a database D and a frequency threshold t.
2: **Ensure.** all frequent patterns
3: $S_0 \leftarrow \{H \in P_\perp | freq(D, H)\}$
4: $k \leftarrow 0$
5: **while** $S_k \neq \{\}$ **do**
6:     $k \leftarrow k + 1$
7:     $S_k \leftarrow \{\}$
8:     $C_k \leftarrow \{\}$
9:     **for all** $G \in S_{k-1}$ **do**
10:         $print(G)$
11:         **for all** $H \in \rho(G)$ **do**
12:             **if** $H \notin C_k$ **then**
13:                 $C_k \leftarrow C_k \cup \{H\}$
14:                 **if** $freq(D, H)$ **then**
15:                     $S_k \leftarrow S_k \cup \{H\}$
16:                 **end if**
17:             **end if**
18:         **end for**
19:     **end for**
20: **end while**
21: **return** $\cup_k S_k$

Consider again the database in Figure 5.3. Suppose we mine all patterns under subgraph isomorphism with a frequency of at least 2. Figure 5.5 shows the resulting patterns.

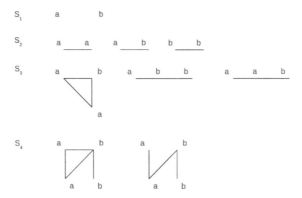

FIGURE 5.5: 2-frequent patterns (i.e., patterns occurring with a frequency of at least 2) in the database of Figure 5.3.

In general, many approaches can be seen as *generate-and-test* approaches, where first the task is to *orderly enumerate* all candidate patterns (in Algorithm 2 the patterns which are stored in C_k), and the second step is to check for each enumerated pattern whether it is *frequent* (in Algorithm 2, these patterns are added to S_k and later printed). Of course, both steps can be interleaved as in Algorithm 2. For more complex data structures, orderly enumeration may become a nontrivial problem. It is needed to enumerate all patterns, but enumerating the same pattern several times may be inefficient or produce redundant output. Usually, one tries to either define a canonical form of the patterns, or a canonical form of generating a pattern. We will present an example later when discussing concrete graph mining systems.

One can distinguish between two major types of pattern mining algorithms: breadth-first search algorithms and depth-first search algorithms. The *breadth-first* algorithms define a size function on the pattern language and generate the patterns in order of size. For example, the size of a graph could be defined as the number of edges or as the number of vertices. When a graph is generated, then one knows that all its subgraphs (which have a smaller size) have already been considered. The breadth-first algorithms therefore have the advantage that they can exploit the anti-monotonicity property better, since when a pattern is generated the frequency of all patterns, which are more general, is already counted. Therefore, there is a maximal opportunity to find out when a pattern which is more general than the one under consideration is infrequent.

On the other hand, this also means that the breadth-first algorithms store a lot of data in quickly accessible storage space. The *depth-first* approaches have the advantage that when a branch of the search is finished, one can discard all data structures concerning that branch. As a result, only a minimum of memory is required to store patterns, and available memory can be used for other optimizations. For example, when one stores for some node in the search tree all transactions matched by the associated pattern, then when counting the frequency of the more specific children one has only to check these transactions. Indeed, transactions not matched by a parent node will not be matched by its children. One example of a depth-first algorithm is FP-growth [263].

5.3.3 Graph Mining Settings

There are several significant factors influencing the characteristics of a pattern mining problem. A first factor is the *graph class*. One can either consider the fully general graph mining problem, allowing any graph as a transaction or pattern, or one can restrict graphs to some subclass such as star graphs, paths, or trees. Several settings considering restricted graph classes have been considered in the literature or are equivalent to well-studied pattern mining settings:

- Star graphs are graphs consisting of a central vertex and a number of leaf vertices connected to this central one. When considering star graphs where leaf vertices are labeled with items from some set I, mining frequent star graph patterns of at least two vertices is equivalent to itemset mining [15] where the set of items is I and the transactions are the set of leaf labels of individual star graphs. Even though problems only involving itemset mining can be handled more efficiently with a special-purpose itemset mining system, star graphs may be used to represent itemsets in problems involving more complex graphs. In that case, star graphs make all data uniform so that a graph mining system can be used.

- A (directed) path is a graph P with $V(P) = \{v_1, v_2, \ldots, v\, n\}$ and $E = \{(v_1, v_2), \ldots, (v_{n-1}, v_n)\}$. Labeled paths can be seen as sequences. Finding frequent subgraph isomorphic patterns is equivalent to finding frequent subsequences. Many subsequence mining algorithms have been proposed in the literature, among others by Agrawal and Srikant [17], Pei et al. [530], and Antunes and Oliveira [28].

- An undirected cycle is a graph C with $V(C) = \{v_1, v_2, \ldots, v_n\}$ and $E = \{\{v_1, v_2\}, \ldots, \{v_{n-1}, v_n\}, \{v_n, v_1\}\}$. A tree is a graph that does not contain a cycle as a subgraph. In the data mining literature, several types of trees are considered. Free trees are undirected trees. Rooted trees (also called rooted unordered trees) are trees where one vertex acts as the root and all edges are directed away from this root. For a vertex v of a rooted tree T, the vertices w for which $(v, w) \in E(T)$ are called children of v, and v is called their parent. Rooted ordered trees are rooted trees where for each vertex a total order is specified on its children. An attribute tree is a rooted tree for which for each vertex all its children have a distinct label. A huge amount of tree mining algorithms have been proposed in the literature [137]. Common applications include mining parse trees (in programming languages or natural language processing), XML, and many other tree-structured file formats.

- Some approaches specifically consider molecular graphs or classes of a subset of the molecular graphs. Molecular graphs do not have a very formal definition, the main idea is that all molecules occurring in practice are considered. Atoms are represented with vertices and bonds with edges. Naturally, there are some restrictions to these graphs, for example, due to the limited valency of atoms, a constraint that translates to a limited degree of vertices.

Usually, one chooses a graph class which is sufficiently expressive to represent all data in the application, but which is otherwise as restricted as possible in order to be able to exploit the structural properties of the graphs. For example, texts are normally represented with strings and HTML Web pages with rooted trees.

A second parameter is the *graph type*. One can use directed and/or undirected edges, ordinary graphs or hypergraphs, possibly allow loops (edges with the same vertex at both endpoints), and possibly allow parallel graphs (where the edge set is a multiset, making it possible to have several edges between the same pair of vertices). Often, the choice here will depend on what is most natural for the application at hand, and what types of graphs the available algorithms can process. There exist transformation methods to transform certain types of graphs into other types of graphs without loss of information and often without significant loss in efficiency. Consider, for example, a graph representing relationships between humans. It is possible that two persons (vertices) p and q are both friends and colleagues. One can represent this in a parallel graph with drawing an edge labeled "friend" between p and q, and by also drawing an edge labeled "colleague" between p and q. Alternatively, one can avoid the complexity of parallel graphs by introducing a new vertex for every relationship. One would then add vertices x (labeled "friend") and y (labeled "colleague") and connect them to both p and q.

A final important parameter of a graph mining problem is the *matching operator*. Depending on the application at hand, some matching operators may be preferred to another. The most common graph matching operator is the subgraph isomorphism operator. The homomorphism operator has been studied extensively in the field of Inductive Logic Programming [482], where it is known as the θ-subsumption operator. Other graph matching operators exist, such as the subgraph homeomorphism operator [385], but these are less frequently used in the graph mining literature. So when to use isomorphism and when to use homomorphism? It often happens that vertices represent objects in the application and edges represent relations between them. When using subgraph isomorphism, one wants different objects (vertices) of the pattern to correspond to different objects (vertices) in the matching transactions. For example, when considering molecules, saying that a molecule contains a chain of 3 carbon atoms naturally means that there are three different carbon atoms in the object. On the other hand, when using homomorphism, objects can play several roles. Consider, for instance, graphs representing relationships between people. A pattern could express that some persons p_1 and p_2 are brothers, that p_1 has a boss b_1 and that p_2 has a boss b_2 (by drawing suitable colored edges between p_1, b_1, p_2, and b_2). However, if the brothers would work in the same company they may have the same boss. In that case, one would like the pattern to match the transaction (a triangle between the boss and the two brothers). In such a situation one may prefer homomorphism.

5.3.4 Complexity

Graph mining may be very demanding for storage and computation resources. In typical data mining experiments, one attempts to mine thousands to millions of patterns, while the size of databases is constantly increasing. It is therefore important to have a better understanding of the factors determining the complexity of pattern mining, both from a theoretic and from a practical point of view. In this section, we will discuss techniques to analyze the complexity of a pattern mining algorithm and techniques to optimize it w.r.t. a naive algorithm.

5.3.4.1 Enumeration Complexity

We start with a discussion on complexity analysis. While such analysis is not necessarily predictive for the behavior of an algorithm in practice, it can provide insight and hints at improvements. For example, one may want to exploit the structure of data when it is known that this allows for a lower time or space complexity, or one may decide to restrict the representation in such a way that an efficient technique can be applied. In some cases, such decisions can make the difference between a polynomial time asymptotic complexity or solving a #P-hard problem, while in practice the running time can be improved by several orders of magnitude.

The number of solutions (frequent patterns) to a frequent pattern mining problem may be huge. Even for the itemset mining problem, in the worst case there are $2^{|I|}$ frequent itemsets, where $|I|$ is the number of items in the database. In the general case for graphs, we get roughly 2^{n*n} possible patterns with n the number of vertices, not even taking into account multiple label values. As a consequence, one can not hope to obtain a polynomial time algorithm. To perform a more refined analysis, the following complexity classes are usually considered in the literature [324]. They are based on the idea that a listing algorithm (here a pattern mining algorithm) lists its solutions (frequent patterns) one by one, and that one can study the delay between outputting two consecutive solutions. At the start, the algorithm gets a certain amount of time on the clock, for every new solution it also gets "payed" a certain amount of new time on the clock, and its goal is to never run out of time.

Definition 15 (listing complexity). *Let S be a set of cardinality N. Then its elements, say $s_1, \ldots s_N$, are listed with polynomial delay if the time until printing s_1, the time between printing s_i and s_{i+1} for every $i = 1 \ldots N$, and the termination time after printing s_N is bounded by a polynomial of the size of the input, in incremental polynomial time if the time between printing s_i and s_{i+1} for every $i = 1 \ldots N$ (resp. the termination time after printing s_N) is bounded by a polynomial of the combined sizes of the input and $s_1, \ldots, s_i$ (resp. $s_1, \ldots, s_N$), in output polynomial time (or polynomial total time) if S is printed in a time bounded by the combined sizes of the input and the entire set S.*

Clearly, polynomial delay implies incremental polynomial time, which, in turn, implies output polynomial time. We also note that, in contrast to incremental polynomial time, an output polynomial time algorithm may have in the worst case a delay time exponential in the size of the input before printing the i-th element for any $i \geq 1$.

5.3.4.2   Complexity Results

For several settings, one has investigated whether efficiency with respect to one of the above classes could be obtained. As a simple example, in the case of mining general graph patterns under subgraph isomorphism, one can use the following simple argument to show that (unless P=NP) no algorithm exists to list all frequent subgraph patterns in output polynomial time [293]. Consider a database with two transactions. The first one is a cycle with length n, and the second transaction is an arbitrary graph on n vertices. Let the minimal frequency threshold be 2. There are at most $n + 1$ frequent patterns (the paths of length 0 to $n - 1$ and the cycle of length n). Suppose that there is an algorithm which lists all frequent subgraph patterns in output-polynomial time. Then, given that we can bound the output size by a polynomial in the input size $n + 1$, we could bound the total running time by a polynomial in the input size. This would mean that we could decide whether there is a cycle of length n in the arbitrary graph of size n in polynomial time. However, this problem, known as the Hamiltonian cycle problem, is known to be NP-complete. Therefore, unless P=NP we reach a contradiction.

On the other hand, if the pattern matching operator $\leq$ can be executed in polynomial time, Algorithm 2 will run with polynomial delay if the candidate generation can be performed efficiently (i.e., ρ and the test in line 10 of Algorithm 2 takes only polynomial time). This has been shown to be the case for itemsets [17], paths, and trees. For larger classes of graphs, the situation depends on some other factors.

Consider, for example, the class of bounded treewidth graphs. Treewidth is a graph property measuring how much a graph resembles a tree.

Definition 16 (treewidth). *A tree decomposition of a graph G is a pair (T, X) where T is a rooted tree and $X = \{X_x\}_{x \in V(T)}$ is a family of subsets of $V(G)$ satisfying (i) $\cup_{x \in V(T)} X_x = V(G)$, (ii) for every $\{u, v\} \in E(G)$, there is a*

$x \in V(T)$ *such that* $u, v \in X_x$ *and (iii)* $X_x \cap X_y \subseteq X_z$ *for every* $x, y, z \in$ $V(T)$ *such that* z *is on the path between* x *and* y. *The treewidth of* (T, X) *is* $max_{x \in V(T)}|X_x| - 1$ *and the treewidth of* G *is the minimal treewidth over all tree decompositions of* G.

Let w be a constant. If G has treewidth at most w and H is connected and has bounded degree, then one can decide whether H is a subgraph of G in polynomial time (the constant w appearing in the exponent). However, in general, subgraph isomorphism between connected graphs of treewidth at most w (for w at least 2) is NP-complete [448]. Despite this negative result, it can be shown that frequent connected subgraphs of treewidth at most w can be listed in incremental polynomial time [295]. The homomorphism matching operator has a lower time complexity. For (not necessarily connected) graphs of bounded treewidth, not necessarily of bounded degree, homomorphism can be decided in polynomial time and hence mining is possible with polynomial delay.

The graph class and the matching operator are not the only parameters that have an influence on the complexity. The search strategy may imply or prohibit that some computations can be shared. For example, the incremental polynomial time result for graphs [295] uses a breadth-first approach. For a depth-first approach, incremental polynomial time can not be reached.

5.3.4.3 Optimization Techniques

There are a large number of common strategies to improve the computational complexity of graph pattern mining. Some techniques affect the asymptotic behavior, others only affect the practical running time. In our discussion, we will focus on the frequency counting since for sufficiently large databases, this forms the dominating cost.

Restricting the graph classes. A first technique consists of restricting the class of the data graphs or of the pattern graphs. Such restriction may be possible due to several reasons. First, in many applications, one may have prior knowledge on the structure of the data. This may include hard rules (e.g., molecules have bounded valency, mRNA molecules can be represented as outerplanar graphs [294]) or general knowledge to which there are exceptions (for example, 96% of the molecules are outerplanar graphs [294], traffic networks are almost planar graphs). Second, one may feel that only patterns from a particular subclass are sufficiently valuable, because other patterns are too complex to interprete afterwards. For example, domain experts will often prefer free patterns rather than closed patterns because free patterns are smaller and hence easier to understand (see below for a definition of "free pattern"). In each of these cases, one can make assumptions on the graph class of the data and the patterns. This may allow one to use specialized algorithms which exploit the known structure and are therefore more efficient.

Storing information to avoid recomputation. Typically, several computations need to be repeated. One strategy which has been explored is to store some of these results to avoid recomputation. However, since memory is limited, one usually has to make an intelligent choice regarding which information to store and which information to recompute. Information which is stored often includes the following:

- The identifiers of transactions matching smaller patterns, since only those have to be considered when checking superpatterns;

- Embeddings of smaller patterns, since to obtain an embedding of a superpattern one can start from an embedding of a smaller pattern;

- Association rules already discovered, since these allow one to derive in certain cases the frequency of patterns from the frequency of smaller patterns [164].

Heuristics. Solving hard problems may be unavoidable, and in that case intelligent search can help. Consider, for example, the problem of pattern matching. Subgraph isomorphism checking is the most expensive part of most large-scale graph mining processes. Even though it is NP-complete in general, different heuristic strategies may vary strongly in efficiency. The most common strategy is to map the pattern in the database graph, node by node, backtracking when no solution can be found. A classical search heuristic is to first map the node for which the number of available alternatives is the smallest [680].

Prioritizing the more important patterns. Even though it does not influence the total cost, delivering the most important patterns first may be more desirable than treating all patterns equally. This is even more true in the case where the number of patterns is so large that the mining process is expected to be terminated before outputting all answers. Also, when the time needed to find patterns diverges strongly, finding the easier to find patterns first may be called for. One example is described by Nijssen and Kok [500] where paths are mined first, then trees and only at the end, cyclic graphs.

Hierarchical approaches. In some cases, sets of nodes can be grouped together into larger entities, and working with such groups is more efficient than working with individual nodes. For example, in molecules, atoms are often grouped together in functional groups such as rings and chains [294],[87],[163]. Also, in traffic networks, streets may be grouped into districts or cities, an approach which is typically used in routing applications [233].

5.3.5 Condensed Representations

When performing pattern mining, one is usually only interested in the most valuable patterns. For example, patterns may be processed afterwards, either by a human or an algorithm performing a next step of data mining. In both cases, it is undesirable to have a too large set of mined patterns. Therefore, a huge amount of literature has considered the question of how to remove from the set of all patterns those which are redundant according to certain criteria. In this section, we will review two directions of research. First, we will consider free and closed patterns as a way to represent all information using fewer patterns. Next, we will discuss different criteria which can be used to select the most useful patterns, thereby discarding part of the information.

5.3.5.1 Free and Closed Patterns

Recall that the language L_p of patterns is equipped with a partial order $\leq$, and that the frequency measure is anti-monotonic w.r.t. this order. Consider two patterns P and Q such that $P < Q$. In some cases, Q may (informally stated) occur everywhere where P occurs. For example, the pattern Q in Figure 5.6 matches in all graphs of the database in Figure 5.3 where pattern P from Figure 5.6 matches. In such cases, it is not necessary to output both patterns with their frequency, as they are identical. We will call the pattern P from Figure 5.6 a frequency-free (f-free for short) pattern, as the pattern description does not contain redundant information. Pattern Q in Figure 5.6 is not free, as removal of an edge gives a pattern with the same frequency. On the other hand, pattern Q in Figure 5.6 is a maximal pattern with frequency 2. We will therefore call Q a f-closed pattern. More formally:

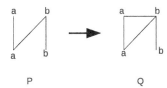

FIGURE 5.6: In the database of Figure 5.3, the association rule $P \rightarrow Q$ holds (i.e., whenever P is a subgraph, Q is also a subgraph). Therefore, Q is a closed pattern but P is not.

Definition 17 (f-free pattern). *Let D be a database and let $P \in L_p$ be a pattern. P is a f-free w.r.t. D iff there is no pattern $Q < P$ such that $freq(D, Q) = freq(D, P)$.*

Definition 18 (f-closed pattern). *Let D be a database and let $P \in L_p$ be a pattern. P is a f-closed w.r.t. D if there is no pattern $Q > P$ such that $freq(D, Q) = freq(D, P)$.*

The notion of closed pattern is most interesting when it is related to a so-called closure operator. An operator $cl : L_p \rightarrow L_p$ is a closure operator if it satisfies the following properties:

- Idempotency: $\forall P \in L_p : cl(cl(P)) = cl(P)$

- Extensivity: $\forall P \in L_p : cl(P) \geq P$

- Monotonicity: $\forall P, Q \in L_p : P \leq Q \Rightarrow cl(P) \leq cl(Q)$

A pattern P is called *cl*-closed if $cl(P) = P$.

The importance of closure operators becomes clear when one considers the complexity of mining all closed patterns. In particular, for a closure operator cl, under reasonably weak assumptions, it is possible to mine all *cl*-closed patterns in output polynomial time.

For itemsets and a number of other settings such as attribute trees [32], there is a closure operator such that the corresponding closed patterns coincide with the definition of f-closed patterns above. For more complex graph classes, however, the situation is more complicated.

Garriga et al. [232] showed that when every pair of patterns in L_p has a unique least upper bound, a closure operator exists and one can mine all f-closed patterns efficiently. This holds in particular for graph patterns under homomorphism. The least upper bound of two graph patterns under homomorphism is their product graph. In fact, this least upper bound is well-known in the field of Inductive Logic Programming as the least general generalization of two logical conjunctions [540]. Unfortunately, the size (as well as the treewidth) of the least upper bound of a set of graph patterns under homomorphism is in general not bounded by a polynomial in their total size. As a consequence, computing the least upper bounds and checking their frequency prohibits efficient mining of closed graph patterns under homomorphism.

Nevertheless, the relation between homomorphism and logical subsumption is an important one which allows for using very expressive languages. For example, De Raedt and Ramon [164] describe how to combine mining of closed logical conjunctions with a background theory, which may represent prior domain knowledge of the user.

For a closure operator cl, one can also define *cl*-free patterns (these are patterns P such that for all $Q < P$, $cl(Q) \neq cl(P)$). However, even though the set of free patterns is a subset of the set of all patterns, the number of closed patterns is smaller than the number of free patterns. This may explain why closed patterns got more attention in the literature on condensed representations.

When a notion of closed patterns is used which does not correspond to some closure operator, the so-called "early termination" technique, the usual pruning strategy for closed pattern mining algorithms, can not be used. In the general case, this may mean that one has to mine all frequent patterns, and then to filter out those which are closed. Given that the number of frequent patterns may be exponential in the number of closed patterns, one can not expect such an approach to run in output polynomial time.

If it is not needed that the solution set is a lossless compression of the set of all patterns with their frequency, then stronger compression is possible in the sense that smaller sets of patterns can be generated from which one can not reconstruct the frequency of all patterns. One possible approach is to mine δ-closed patterns. A pattern P is δ-closed if each of its superpatterns has a frequency which is smaller than $freq(P) - \delta$. The notion of δ-closed patterns can also be extended to graphs [164].

5.3.5.2 Selection of Informative Patterns

Closed patterns are a powerful concept to reduce the number of patterns without losing information. However, often the number of patterns is still huge. Moreover, in a number of settings there are no known strategies to skip the nonclosed patterns (achieving output-polynomial time), and one has to revert anyway to a generate-and-test strategy.

Therefore, another research direction is to select patterns or association rules on the basis of some useful quality criteria. These criteria include:

- Correlation of the pattern or association rules with some target attribute [782, 98]

- Association rule quality (e.g., lift, confidence, leverage)

- Additional information provided by the pattern and its frequency compared to a set of already selected patterns

Typically, one can start from the set of all frequent patterns and then filter them using the given selection criteria. In some cases, one can perform some pruning in the search space. For example, Zimmermann and De Raedt [782] describe a method to prune when searching for patterns correlating with the target attribute.

5.3.6 Transactional Graph Mining Systems

One of the first graph mining systems was AGM [305], mining induced subgraphs and its variants such as AcGM. This system used a matrix-based canonical form, and introduced operations to join the canonical form of smaller patterns into the canonical form of a larger pattern. In particular, patterns are represented with their adjacency matrices. Given a graph G with an ordered set of vertices $V(G) = \{v_1, v_2, \ldots, v_n\}$, the adjacency matrix A of G is an $n*n$ matrix with $A_{i,j} = 1$ iff $(v_i, v_j) \in E(G)$ and $A_{i,j} = 0$ otherwise. For example, consider Figure 5.7. On the right-hand side one can see the adjacency matrix for the pattern on the left-hand side (with the vertices ordered 1,2,3,4,5). AGM defines the code for an adjacency matrix A as follows:

$$code(G) = A_{1,1}A_{2,1}A_{2,2}A_{3,1}A_{3,2}A_{3,3}\ldots A_{n,n-1}A_{n,n}$$

For example, in Figure 5.7, the code is shown below the adjacency matrix of the pattern. The canonical code of a graph is the minimal code which can be obtained from an adjacency matrix of that graph over all orderings of its vertices. The interesting property of a canonical form is that whenever two graphs are isomorphic, they have the same canonical code. This property can be used to ensure that every pattern is generated exactly once. The code in Figure 5.7 is canonical.

AGM is a breadth-first pattern miner. A new pattern of size n is generated from two patterns of size $n - 1$ sharing a common $(n - 2) * (n - 2)$ block in the top left of their canonical adjacency matrix. In particular, if

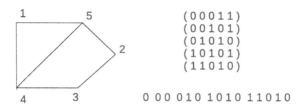

FIGURE 5.7: A pattern and its canonical adjacency matrix and code.

$$A = \begin{bmatrix} X & y \\ y^T & z \end{bmatrix}$$

and

$$B = \begin{bmatrix} X & u \\ u^T & v \end{bmatrix}$$

then the newly generated pattern is of the form

$$C = \begin{bmatrix} X & y & u \\ y^T & z & w \\ u^T & w & v \end{bmatrix}$$

where w is either 0 or 1. Several subsequent algorithms also exploited this idea of only generating new patterns from the combination of two smaller patterns which differ only at one vertex. This limits the number of new candidate patterns to consider. AcGM [304] extends AGM by allowing for both induced subgraph isomorphism and normal subgraph isomorphism, and by considering hierarchies of labels.

gSpan [741] is one of the most popular graph mining systems. It uses a depth-first algorithm. This system is also based on an orderly generation of patterns using a canonical form, called depth-first search (DFS) code. New patterns are generated by extending a single smaller pattern in such a way that every pattern is generated from exactly one parent pattern. The depth-first approach has been shown to have advantages on not too large datasets as it allows for storing information on embeddings of the parent pattern in the database graphs, which can then be exploited when counting the frequency of larger patterns.

The Gaston system [500] has been shown to be one of the most efficient graph pattern mining systems. One of its most important features is that it first mines all paths and trees before mining cyclic structures. The main advantage of this approach is that in a range of practical datasets, such as molecule datasets, most frequent patterns are acyclic. Gaston also employs a depth-first search algorithm.

Some approaches add more than one vertex at a time, making larger steps in the search space. Examples are the MoSS system [286] and the FOG system [294], both of which treat cyclic fragments separately from linear fragments, an approach which turns out to be useful in chemo-informatics applications [609].

Some researchers consider special purpose graph mining systems. For example, Kuramochi and Karypis [378] describe gFSG, aimed at mining geometric patterns, that is, patterns where vertices have spatial coordinates.

5.4 Single Network Mining

Up to now, we considered the transactional setting of graph mining, where a database consists of separate, independent transaction graphs. In practice, not all graph data can be structured in this way. Consider, for instance, the Internet, news forums, traffic networks, protein interaction networks and citation networks. In all these cases, the data is made up by one large graph or network, where instances are the nodes. For instance, in a social network, the users may be represented by nodes and their interactions with edges. One may be interested both in global properties of the networks or in properties of individual nodes. We will discuss both of them in the following sections.

Global properties include parameters such as the average distance between nodes, the connectivity, the occurrence of clusters of highly connected nodes, the degree distribution, and so on. The field of complex systems, originating from statistical physics, has produced a large body of literature on this topic.

When considering the properties of individual nodes, pattern mining questions similar to those in the transactional setting can be considered. However, there are several additional challenges compared to that simpler setting. First, since the neighborhoods of the nodes overlap heavily, they are not independent. In order to perform correct statistics, it is important that examples are independent and hence generalizing over nodes of a network is a nontrivial task. A second problem is that in the large network case, the graph at hand is usually much larger than the graphs considered in the transactional setting, and hence more care is needed w.r.t. computational complexity.

5.4.1 Network Models

While in the transactional setting a lot of data consists of descriptions of static objects, many large networks are evolving. Even more, often one assumes that the evolution in all parts of the network is somehow similar. For instance, consider a social network. Motivations to become friends, such as recommendation of other friends and common interests, are relevant for each of the users in the network, and hence to some extent two users with similar properties in a similar context may act similarly.

Network models, of which we will discuss some simple examples in Section 5.4.1.2, have been studied with methods originating from statistical physics (where particles too are assumed to behave all similarly). Interestingly, when a fixed local process is repeated a large number of times, certain patterns and structures arise in the network. In Section 5.4.1.1, we will discuss a number of properties commonly used to measure the characteristics of networks.

When no model of the network is available, it is possible to learn a model from data. Here, one can consider both predictions of future evolutions in the dynamic network and the learning of statistical patterns in a static snapshot of the network. In both cases, pattern mining, that is, the discovery of interesting local patterns, is a first step. We will discuss pattern matching and pattern mining in later sections.

5.4.1.1   Network Property Measures

One of the most popular statistics for networks is the diameter. It is most commonly defined as the longest shortest path in the graph. This definition is problematic for real-world networks, as they often contain several components, that is, for each vertex of the graph, there exist vertices that are not reachable via the edges. In such situations one usually considers the giant connected component of the graph, that is, the connected component having the biggest number of nodes. In many applications, the diameter of the network has been shown to be surprisingly small. From a pattern mining point of view, the diameter is an indication for the diameters of "local patterns" which make sense or could be efficiently matched against the network.

There has been significant interest in the degree distribution of networks, which is the distribution of the number of direct neighbors (vertex degree) of the network's nodes. While straightforward to collect, this statistic gives important insight into the underlying network generation process.

Finally, Watts and Strogatz [705] introduce the clustering coefficient as a measure of "cliquishness of a friendship circle," which they define as the average over the rate of existing to possible edges among the direct neighbors of every node [705]. The clustering coefficient has a direct relation to the number of triangles in the graph, a topic which has been researched in the data mining community as we discuss below.

While many more statistics over a network are possible, the ones discussed above are the most common in the literature concerning statistical models of graphs and are well studied.

5.4.1.2   Network Models

Erdős-Rényi model. The simplest model from a conceptual point of view is the random-graphs model, attributed to Erdős and Rényi, in which all missing edges have the same (uniform) probability of appearing (in contrast with the Bernoulli model first introduced by Gilbert [237] for which the ER-model is often confused [84]; interestingly though, many properties are common for graphs from either graph probability space [83]). In a series of papers [204, 205], they study this model thoroughly and provide asymptotic bounds on many of its properties (degree distribution, probability of all the nodes to belong to the giant component, number of edge-choosing steps until the graph becomes fully connected). A number of graph properties have received significantly more attention, as to the researchers' surprise empirical observations strongly disagreed with the predictions and it is both what spurred a new wave of interest in the area of statistical models of networks and serve as a basis for classifying the networks as not being random. These properties are the degree distribution, the clustering coefficient, and the diameter of the graph.

Erdos proved that the degree distribution of a graph generated by the ER-model follows a Poisson distribution [205]. The bounds on the diameter are significantly more involved, and we will only mention that several small ($\sim log\ n$) values for the graph diameter are possible, depending on the value of model parameters [83].

Watts-Strogatz model. A distinguishing feature of many real-world networks is that, while having short diameters akin to random graphs, their clustering coefficient (and hence the frequency of triangles, and in fact also of other dense patterns) is significantly higher than what the ER-model predicts. This observation has led Wang and Ramon [705] and Watts and Strogatz [705] to formally introduce the small-world model.

An interesting property of this model is that it allows one to vary the degree of "randomness" of the network it generates. The generation process is extremely simple and proceeds as follows: a regular graph (e.g., a ring lattice with fixed node degree d) on n nodes is generated, after which each edge is rewired with probability p [705]. This procedure has the effect of significantly reducing the diameter of the graph without having significant effect on the clustering coefficient (in a particular range of p).

While the WS-model represents a step forward in the understanding of real-world graphs, it captures a small number of statistical properties of interest.

Barabási-Albert model. The observation that a number of networks do not match the predictions of the ER-model for the degree distribution has been reported by Barabási and Reka [51]. The authors suggest that two important processes occurring in real-world large-scale networks—network growth and preferential attachment to existing nodes—is not being accounted for and propose a model that incorporate said processes.

Since its introduction, the scale-free property has been confirmed in a large number of networks from a wide range of domains: biology, technological networks, citation networks, networks of chemical interactions, and so on. A detailed analysis of the network of scientific collaborations [50] has prompted the authors to introduce further refinements to this model, namely that "internal links" creation is also governed by the "rich get richer" scheme.

5.4.2 Pattern Matching in a Single Network

We now continue our discussion of pattern mining, building on the insights gained in the transactional graph mining setting; and keeping in mind the statistical properties described in the previous section.

Given a database graph (a large network) D, the frequent subgraph pattern mining in D aims to find the set S of all the patterns P whose support is not less than a predefined threshold σ, that is,

$$S = \{P | f(D, P) \geq \sigma\},$$

where f is the support of the pattern P in the database graph D.

This problem of pattern mining poses two main chanllenges, pattern matching and frequecy counting. The first is related to deciding where a pattern occurs in the data, while the latter concerns the summarization of the occurrences in one single number, which makes sense statistically. First, in this section, we will consider the pattern matching problem. In the next section, we survey work on support measures for single network pattern mining.

In particular, we need to find embeddings of a pattern P in the database graph G. The studied approaches can be divided into three main categories: *small pattern matching*, *exact matching*, and *approximative matching*.

5.4.2.1 Matching Small Patterns

Due to the huge size of the networks, many studies only consider small patterns and either apply brute force or devise more efficient methods.

Triangles. Counting triangles has received quite some interest recently in the field of data mining, as it is the smallest nontrivial pattern matching problem, and is related to the calculation of the clustering coefficient. Furthermore, many interesting graph mining tasks are based on counting the number of triangles in the graph. For example, in Becchetti et al. [58], a method based on triangles was proposed for detecting spamming.

Both exact and approximate triangle counting algorithms have been proposed. In this section, we assume that G is an undirected loop-free graph with $n = |V(G)|$ and $m = |E(G)|$.

Exact triangle counting. The brute-force method, checking for every triple of vertices, whether it forms a triangle, runs in $O(n^3)$ time.

The most efficient algorithms for counting triangles are based on matrix multiplication. The asymptotic time complexity of the fastest existing (theoretical) method for matrix multiplication takes $O(n^{2.37})$ time and $\Theta(n^2)$ space [149]. For sparse graphs, in Alon et al. [22], an $O(m^{1.41})$ time and $\Theta(n^2)$ space algorithm, NODEITERATOR, is proposed. It computes for each node its neighborhood and then checks how many edges exist among its neighbors. In [308], Itai and Rodeh exploited the NODEITERATOR idea to present an algorithm that counts the number of triangles in $O(m^{\frac{3}{2}})$ time. This algorithm computes spanning trees of the graph and removes edges while checking that every triangle is listed exactly once.

Approximate triangle counting. Tsourakakis et al. [673] propose a sampling approach. In particular, the proposed algorithm samples edges independently with probability p, counts the triangles in the resulting sparser graph, and divides the result by p^3. If p is not too small and triangles are sufficiently uniformly distributed, one can show that the result is a close approximation.

In Buriol et al. [107], the authors present estimators for the number of triangles in the graph when the input is provided as a stream which is too large to store.

Network motifs. *Network motifs* are subgraphs which occur much more often than they occur in random networks [628]. Several researchers have studied in moderately large application domains motifs which are sufficiently small to match without significant computational challenges.

Shen-Orr et al. [628] found that much of a gene regulation network is composed of repeated appearances of three highly significant motifs. They showed that each network motif has a specific function in determining gene expression. Similarly, Maayan et al. [431] presented a model of signaling pathways in hippocampal CA1 neurons, and found a high fraction of positive and negative feedback loop motifs.

In Milo et al. [469], the authors found network motifs in networks from biochemistry, neurobiology, ecology, and engineering. They saw that the motifs shared by ecological food Webs were distinct from the motifs shared by the genetic networks of Escherichia coli or from those found in the World Wide Web.

5.4.2.2 Exact Pattern Matching

The subgraph isomorphism problem has been shown to be #P-complete in general, and almost all practical testing procedures are based on search with backtracking. An old but still widely used backtracking algorithm is described by Ullmann [680]. In Larrosa and Valiente [386], the search method exploits a heuristic derived from *constraint satisfaction* to reduce the cost. VF and its successor VF2 [150] are two search algorithms implementing a number of efficiently computable heuristics, and have been used in several transactional graph mining systems. There are algorithms using other strategies, for example, decision tree based techniques [518]. The reader is referred to Messmer and Bunke [457] for a short review of subgraph isomorphism algorithms. When the database graph is large and has a high average degree, these matching algorithms become intractable even for reasonably small patterns.

5.4.2.3 Approximative Algorithms for Pattern Matching

When exact pattern matching for pattern mining is too expensive, one can resort to approximative algorithms. One option is to exploit statistical regularity in the graph. For instance, for certain pattern classes, there exist efficient algorithms which provide good approximations on almost all random graphs [223].

On the other hand, recent work on fixed parameter tractability has shown that there are algorithms, often randomized ones, whose asymptotic complexity is exponential in the pattern size but only polynomial (e.g., linear) in the network size. This is especially appealing in mining patterns, which are usually small, in large networks.

For instance, if the patterns are trees, the subgraph isomorphism problem still remains #P-complete. However, based on recent advances in parameterized complexity theory, Kibriya and Ramon [340] proposed a randomized algorithm for mining rooted trees in large networks. This method finds all the homomorphisms first, and then with high probability removes those which are not isomorphisms exploiting properties of a specific algebraic structure [368]. This algorithm can mine all frequent rooted trees with delay linear in the size of the network and only mildly exponential in the size of the patterns.

5.4.2.4   Algorithms for Approximate Pattern Matching

Inexact matching is also called error-tolerant graph matching. The major motivations of inexact matching algorithms are that (1) the collected data may have noise, and (2) patterns may have several variations. The tree search based strategy is also widely used in inexact matching and most of the algorithms are based on the *edit distance* (e.g., [105] and [588]). In order to compute the edit distance of two graphs, we first have to define a set of allowed operations with different costs on graphs. Usually, insertions, deletions, and substitutions of vertices and edges are standard choices, and according to the applications, we also use other operations, like merging and splitting of vertices. Using these operations, a graph can be transformed to another graph, and different paths may exist. The graph edit distance of two graphs is the minimum cost path, and in most applications, to compute the optimal solution is extremely expensive. Practical approaches just find the suboptimal solution by relaxation [327]. Other strategies include continuous optimization, spectral methods, artificial neural networks, relaxation labeling, and so on. We do not list all the algorithms here. See Conte et al. [148] for a comprehensive survey of pattern matching.

5.4.3   Pattern Mining Support Measures

Pattern matching, discussed in the previous section, allows one to list all embeddings (or images) of a pattern P in a network G. A support measure (or frequency measure) is a function summarizing the embeddings of P into a single number reflecting how often P occurs in G.

The support of a pattern in the transactional setting is the number of graphs in the database which are supergraphs of that pattern. However, defining an appropriate support measure in a single graph is more challenging because two or more images of the pattern may overlap. If we count all the embeddings (or images) the support may not be anti-monotonic, which is problematic as usually the anti-monotonicity allows for the most pruning in the pattern search space. In fact, only anti-monotonicity is not enough for a practical support measure. For example, a support measure just returning a constant number is anti-monotonic, but not informative. Therefore, we often require a support measure to be *normalized*, that is, it should return the number of images if there are only nonoverlapping images.

An important class of normalized anti-monotonic support measures relies on the *overlap graph*. The nodes of an overlap graph G_P^D are the images of the pattern P in the database graph D, and two nodes are adjacent if the corresponding images overlap, that is, they share at least a common edge (*edge-overlap*) or a common vertex (*vertex-overlap*).

Vanetik et al. [686] introduced the maximum independent set (MIS) support measure, measuring the size of the maximum independent set of the overlap graph. Fiedler and Borgelt [216] proved that the MIS measure is anti-monotonic and claim that some cases of overlap can be ignored without affecting the anti-monotonicity of resulting support measures. Given a pattern $P = (V(P), E(P))$, there exists a *harmful overlap* of embeddings ϕ and ϕ' if there is a vertex $v \in V(P)$ such that $\phi(v), \phi'(v) \in \phi(V(P)) \cap \phi'(V(P))$. Vanetik et al. [686] gave a necessary and sufficient condition for anti-monotonicity of overlap graph based support measures. We cannot take the MIS support measure into practice directly because it is NP-hard to compute, and remains so even when the degree of the overlap graph is bounded. Kuramochi and Karypis [377] designed two practical mining algorithms using the MIS support measure. In their algorithms, the MIS support is computed approximately.

Bringmann and Nijssen [97] examined the expense of computing the MIS of overlap graphs, and then described another support measure *minimum image based support*, which does not use overlap graphs. Given a pattern $P = (V(P), E(P))$, the minimum image based support is defined as,

$$minImage(D, P) = \min_{v \in V(P)} |\{\phi_i(v) | \phi_i \text{ is an embedding of } P \text{ in } D\}|.$$

This support measure is anti-monotonic, and it can be computed very efficiently. However, compared to overlap graph based support measures, the minImage overestimates the statistical evidence. For example, consider the following embeddings of some pattern: $(1, 11)$, $(2, 11)$, $(3, 11)$, $(4, 11)$, $(5, 11)$, $(6, 12)$, $(6, 13)$, $(6, 14)$, $(6, 15)$, and $(6, 16)$. The minImage returns 6 as the support of the pattern while MIS returns 2. From a statistical point of view, all embeddings either depend on vertex 6 or on vertex 11, so there are only two independent observations (if we consider embeddings which do not overlap as independent observations of some phenomenon). Therefore, the notion of independence has some advantages.

Calders et al. [112] generalized the conditions for anti-monotonicity of overlap graph based support measures. They showed that the conditions can be used whenever the matching operator is isomorphism, homomorphism, or heomomorphism. In addition, the authors proposed two normalized anti-monotonic support measures. One is the MCP, that is the minimum clique partition of the overlap graphs, which is also NP-hard to compute. Another is the Lovász theta value ϑ, which can be computed with semidefinite programming, and hence in polynomial time. However, existing methods are still very expensive to compute ϑ [348, 309, 300]. We point out that the Schrijver theta value ϑ' [613] can be also used as a normalized anti-monotonic support measure. It is very similar to the ϑ, and we always have $MIS \leq \vartheta' \leq \vartheta \leq MCP$.

Wang and Ramon [702] observed that those images which share a common vertex (vertex-overlap) or a common edge (edge-overlap) build a clique in the overlap graph, and proposed the overlap hypergraph whose nodes are the images and hyperedges are these cliques. They introduced an overlap hypergraph based normalized anti-monotonic support measure s that is the solution of a (usually sparse) linear program, which can be solved very efficiently using recently interier-point methods. More recently, they showed that this measure also has a natural statistical interpretation [703].

5.4.4 Applications

The literature has a huge amount of articles describing the analysis of large networks in a wide range of application domains. Here we only give a few examples:

- In *co-author networks*, two people are connected if they published a paper together [450].

- In *citation networks*, articles are represented with vertices and citations with edges. One example of such a network is DBLP.[1]

- In *molecule interaction networks*, two molecules are connected if they interact during at least one experiment. For instance, Chen et al. [131] describe a protein interaction network.

- In *communication networks*, two people are connected if they had at least one contact during a certain observation period. This can concern phone calls, SMS messages [184], e-mails, etc.

Several other types of networks can be found in the SNAP repository.[2] Often such networks are represented with undirected graphs, even though in many cases (e.g., when sending e-mail from one person to another one) the relationship is directed.

In addition to the tasks described in detail in this chapter, typical other tasks include the discovery of communities (clusters of vertices being strongly connected while the connection with other parts of the network is relatively weak), and classification of vertex properties (e.g., prediction of the area of research based on the areas of co-authors).

---

[1]http://www.informatik.uni-trier.de/ley/db/
[2]http://snap.stanford.edu/data/

5.5 Conclusion

In this chapter, we have provided an introduction to and an overview of graph pattern mining techniques. An important issue in graph mining is the computational cost. We outlined strategies for analyzing and improving the complexity. Our discussion was illustrated with a few of the many applications of graph mining.

Clearly, many challenges are remaining in the field of graph mining. First, despite the significant progress during the last decades, graph mining is still computationally demanding. More algorithmic insights are needed to handle the challenge of generating in reasonable time good (approximative) results. A second challenge lies in the transformation of the gained information in terms of patterns and statistics into insight into the applications at hand. It is not because we can predict the actions of users that we understand his motivations and will still be able to predict well in a changing context. We anticipate that the exploration of expert advice and causal inference may be interesting paths in future work.

5.6 Additional Reading

This chapter focused on graph pattern mining. Rossi et al. [576] survey prediction problems in graphs. Graphs from a probabilistic model point of view are studied in the fields of statistical relational learning [236].

The field of graph mining is related to many other fields in the literature which deserve reading. First, there are the fields of graph theory [171, 711] and algorithmic graph theory [355]. Many, often old, results provide excellent inspiration for improving graph mining algorithms. A work providing references classified by problem type is by Gross and Yellen [250]. Second, there is a large literature on techniques investigating large graphs and networks. Recent work in this direction can easily be found in the proceedings of recent editions of major data mining conferences such as KDD, ICDM, SDM, and PKDD.

Part of the work on large networks is based on properties of the adjacency matrix. One example of this is by Prakash et al. [545]. The field investigating the properties of the adjacency matrix of graphs is called spectral graph theory [142].

5.7 Glossary

Association rule: A rule representing a correlation between two patterns, the antecedent and the consequent.

Asymptotic complexity: An expression indicating how the cost of a method depends on the input parameters (usually size) for very large inputs.

Canonical form: The assignment of a unique string representation to patterns, such that all equivalent patterns obtain the same string.

Complexity: The cost of a method in terms of time or space.

Frequent: A property is called frequent when it occurs often in a database graph.

Graph: A mathematical object consisting of a set of vertices and a set of edges between some of these vertices.

Mining: Discovering interesting patterns in data.

Motif: *See* Pattern.

Network: The term network usually refers to a very large graph.

Pattern: A motif or substructure which can occur in a database.

Powerlaw: Dependency of the form $f(x) = bx^a$ for some constants a and b.

5.8 Acknowledgments

This work has been supported by the ERC StG 240186 project "MiGraNT: Mining Graphs and Networks, a Theory-Based Approach."

Part III

Mining and Searching Different Types of UGC

Chapter 6

Knowledge Extraction from Wikis/BBS/Blogs/News Web Sites

Jun Zhao, Kang Liu, Guangyou Zhou, Zhenyu Qi, Yang Liu

NLPR, Institute of Automation, Chinese Academy of Sciences

Xianpei Han

Institute of Software, Chinese Academy of Sciences

6.1 Introduction

Understanding the meaning of texts, capturing the intention of users, and precisely providing information services are the crucial techniques for manifold Web applications, however, they are not trivial problems. On the Web, texts often have the characteristics such as diversified structures, multifarious noises, variant language expressions, data sparseness, and so on, which make difficulties for textual understanding. To this day, although many researchers have employed multiple resources (synonym lexicons, etc.) and methods (exquisite designed patterns and natural language processing techniques) to understand the texts, the problem is far from being solved.

Employing knowledge is possible to be a new breakthrough for deeply capturing the meaning of texts. As widely known, the meaning of texts can be represented by keywords (nouns and noun phrases). However, these nouns or noun phrases are often ambiguous. If we could map these linguistic units into the appropriate entities in a knowledge base, we could obtain the fine-grained information, such as entity attributes, types, related entities, and so on, so that the exact meaning of the texts are refined. Based on these advantages of a knowledge base, much research has been devoted to the techniques or methods used for digging knowledge from texts and constructing knowledge bases automatically, shortly named as *Knowledge Extraction* (KE). For example, the research group led by Professor Mitchell focuses on the "Read the Web" project,[1] which is a self-learning system to extract entities and relations from the Web. Meanwhile, Etzioni has also researched a similar project, "Machine Reading" [507], which called extract relation knowledge from the Web.

---

[1] http://rtw.ml.cmu.edu/rtw/

FIGURE 6.1: An example Web page with UGC. **(See color insert.)**

In addition, Google has constructed a huge knowledge base named Knowledge Graph, which contains more than 500 million entities and relations. Based on Knowledge Graph, Google expects to promote the intelligence of its search engine. Informatik Institute constructed a Knowledge Base named Yago[2] in Saarbrcken, Germany, through extracting knowledge from Wikipedia and constructing the mapping between it and WordNet [649].

KE is related to traditional techniques such as information extraction (IE), natural language processing (NLP), Semantic Web, machine learning, and so on. The most important problem in KE is how to obtain knowledge which has wide coverage and can support various applications. The Web contains substantial resources. Furthermore, with the rapid development of Web 2.0, much UGC data originate from the Web, which provide new opportunities and challenges for knowledge harvesting. Texts in UGC data, like Wikipedia, BBS, blogs, and so on, are often different from the traditional texts. First, they often have informal expressions, variant structures, links, and so on. Second, from the pages in UGC Web sites, we can also find specific information which does not occur in the traditional Web pages, like hashtags, infoboxes, open categories, and so on. Figure 6.1 shows a Web page in Wikipedia, where we can observe some specific information in UGC Web sites. Therefore, how to exploit these specific textual characteristics in UGC Web sites and extract knowledge from them is a big challenge.

It is worth noting that, from different UGC Web sites, we can extract different kinds of knowledge. For example, Wikipedia and news Web sites often contain lots of facts. In blog Web sites, in addition to facts, opinions are embedded. And BBS Web sites often contain conversation knowledge. Mining opinions are discussed in Chapter 4 in Part II of this book. Therefore, this chapter mainly focuses on extracting factual knowledge from UGC data.

---

[2]http://www.mpi-inf.mpg.de/yago-naga/yago/

Without special a description, "Knowledge" means "Factual Knowledge" in this chapter.

What is the aim of knowledge extraction? What subtasks are included in this research field? What are the challenges we must meet? And how can we extract knowledge effectively from UGC contents? The rest of the chapter will answer these questions.

6.1.1   Task Descriptions

Knowledge Extraction (KE) is a task related to many research fields, such as information extraction, natural language processing, Semantic Web, and so on. Therefore, according to the emphasis of different related research fields, there are various definitions. In comprehensive consideration, we use the definition in Wikipedia as follows.

> *Knowledge extraction is the creation of knowledge from structured (relational databases, XML) and unstructured (texts, documents, images) sources. The resulting knowledge needs to be in a machine-readable and machine-interpretable format and must represent knowledge in a manner that facilitates inferencing. Although it is methodically similar to Information Extraction (NLP)[3] and ETL[4] (Data Warehouse), the main criteria is that the extraction result goes beyond the creation of structured information or the transformation into a relational schema. It requires either the reuse of existing formal knowledge (reusing identifiers or ontologies) or the generation of a schema based on the source data.*

This definition means that Knowledge Extraction is not only to convert unstructured texts into structured format, but also manage them in a specific format, which has the mechanism to generate new knowledge through inference. A piece of knowledge is often comprised of two entities and a relationship between them, so that knowledge can be represented as triples and often described using knowledge representation languages such as RDF and OWL [739]. For example, from the sentence "Yao Ming was born in Shanghai," we can extract a knowledge triple (Yao Ming, be born in, Shanghai), where "Yao Ming" and "Shanghai" are two entities, and "be born in" denotes the relationship. By this observation, KE is not only to simply extract textual elements from texts, but also to find the semantic meanings behind the texts. To this end, KE contains several special subtasks, which we will briefly demonstrate as follows.

Entity recognition: An entity is the basic element of knowledge. Thus, identifying entities is an important task in KE, which aims to locate and identify the entity elements (often nouns or noun phrases) in texts.

---

[3]Natural Language Processing

[4]Extraction-Transformation-Loading

Previous work mainly focused on named entity recognition (NER), which usually constrained entities to seven classes, including location, organization, person, number, time, quantities, monetary values, and percentage. But for Web applications, these seven classes are far from sufficient. Thus, recent applications aim to extract open types of entities.

Entity set expansion: Entity expansion refers to expand a given seed set entity to a more complete set that belongs to the same semantic class. For example, by given some entities like "Saint Louis," "Los Angeles," "Atlanta," the system needs to find other American cities, such as "New York," "Seattle," "Orlando," and so forth. This task is important for the knowledge base population, which can expand more similar knowledge according to the given knowledge. One of the difficulties of this task is how to compute the semantic similarity between potential items and the given seeds. Another difficulty is how to avoid semantic drift in the expansion process. For the example mentioned above, the cities, like "New York," "London," "Tokyo," which are not American cities, are apt to be extracted as the results because they all have held the Olympic Games.

Relation extraction: Relationships are defined over two or more entities. For the example mentioned above, the person "YaoMing" is involved in a "be born in" relationship with the location "ShangHai." In a knowledge base, the types of the relation often include "Attribute," "Part-of-Whole," "SubClass," "InstanseOf," and so on. The "be born in" relation in the above example belongs to the relation of "Attribute," which means that the birthplace is an attribute of a person. Relation Extraction aims to identify a relationship by providing two or more entities from texts, or extract entities by providing an entity and the specific relationship type. A typical task of relation extraction is event extraction, which identifies event arguments by providing the predefined event framework.

Entity disambiguation: Entities are often ambiguous, which raises serious problem for the usage of the knowledge base. In many situations, the similar textual surfaces may refer to different entities. For example, the name "Michael Jordan" can represent more than 10 people in Google search results, such as "Michael (Jeffrey) Jordan (Basketball Player)," "Michael (I.) Jordan, (Professor of Berkeley)," "Michael (B.) Jordan (American Actor)," and so on. If we do not know the real referent entity, we cannot obtain the precise knowledge. Thus, entity disambiguation has become a more and more popular research topic.

In addition to the four subtasks mentioned above, KE also includes some other subtasks (e.g., knowledge inference, ontology mapping, etc.). Due to the space limitation, we will not describe these subtasks in this chapter.

6.1.2 Important Challenges

For the subtasks mentioned above in knowledge extraction, there are three important challenges which we must face, especially for UGC data. **The first**

challenge is how to exploit the structure of the pages in UGC Web sites when extracting knowledge. Most traditional knowledge extraction methods often focus on extracting information from unstructured texts. However, UGC Web sites often contain structured or semistructured texts in addition to unstructured texts. The texts in UGC Web sites are often labeled by users or linked to each other, such as the open category tags and links in Wikipedia. Therefore, how to employ these special information in UGC Web sites to extract knowledge is an important challenge.

The second important challenge is how to find extracted targets for extraction and obtain sufficient data for training statistical models. In traditional information extraction, the extracted targets are predefined. However, in UGC Web sites, because of the openness of domain, the extracted targets are no longer predefined, which means that they need to be predefined. Furthermore, we still face another difficulty, the lack of labeled data for building extractors. Traditional knowledge extraction approaches relied on sufficient labeled data for training the statistical models. However, for knowledge extraction on the Web, especially on UGC, we cannot label sufficient training data in each domain and cannot predefine complete knowledge types for extraction. Thus, the traditional knowledge extraction approaches have limitations for the texts in UGC Web sites. How to automatically generate labeled training data is one of the biggest difficulties for knowledge extraction from UGC Web sites.

The third challenge is entity ambiguity. As mentioned above, entity disambiguation is an important subtask in KE. Entity ambiguity suffers from the name variation problem and the name ambiguity problem. Name variation means that an entity can be mentioned in different ways such as full name, aliases, acronyms, and misspellings. For example, the entity *Michael Jeffrey Jordan* can be mentioned using more than 10 names, such as *Michael Jordan*, *MJ*, *Jordan*, and so on. The name ambiguity problem is related to the fact that a name may refer to different entities in different contexts. For example, the name *Bulls* can refer to more than 20 entities in Wikipedia, such as the NBA team *Chicago Bulls*, the football team *Belfast Bulls*, and the cricket team *Queensland Bulls*. Thus, entity disambiguation is not a trivial task.

6.1.3 Organization of the Chapter

The subsequent sections are organized according to the subtasks mentioned above. In the second section, we will elaborate on the methods on entity recognition and entity expansion. The third section will present the approaches on relation extraction on structured, semistructured, and unstructured texts. In the last section, we will introduce the details on entity disambiguation.

6.2   Entity Recognition and Expansion

Named entities are important meaningful units in texts. The recognition and analysis of named entities is of great significance in the field of Web information extraction, Web content management, knowledge engineering, and so on. In this section, we will introduce some key technologies of entity recognition and extraction systems.

6.2.1   Entity Recognition

In this section, we focus on the entity recognition, especially for named entity recognition. Generally speaking, the task of named entity recognition (NER) is to identify three main categories (entity class, time class, and digital class) and seven small categories (person, location, organization, time, date, monetary, and percentage) of named entities in the text. Among these types, time, date, monetary, and percentage are relatively easy to recognize. So, NER usually refers to the recognition of a person, location, and organization.

There have been many studies on NER [731, 730, 76]. Totally speaking, they can be divided into two kinds. The first kind is based on manually generated rules [370]. This kind of method usually takes a lot of human labor and time to design rules, and the performance mainly relies on experienced linguists. The main shortage is that when transplanted to a new field or language, these systems need a lot of artificial modification on rules. The second kind is based on machine learning methods, which often design effective features and use statistical models (Hidden Markov Model, Maximum Entropy, Conditional Random Field, Decision Tree, etc.) to indicate named entities.

To evaluate the performance of these different methods, researchers organized several well known tests including MUC (Message Understanding Conference),[5] SIGHAN (the Special Interest Group for Chinese Information Processing of the Association for Computational Linguistics),[6] CoNLL (Conference on Computational Natural Language Learning),[7] and ACE (Automatic Content Extraction),[8] and so on. The results of MUC show that entity recognition systems for English have already obtained the ability to deal with large scale texts. The system developed by Language Technology Group Summary won No. 1 in MUC-7 (1998), the precision and recall of their system reached 95% and 92% individually [138]. The performance for Chinese is around 88% of precision and 84% of recall, according to BACKOFF-3 [396].

With the increase of Web applications, people expect that the NER systems are able to find more types of entities. In ACE 2007 [501], the organizer

---

[5]http://www.itl.nist.gov/
[6]http://www.sighan.org/
[7]http://ifarm.nl/signll/conll/
[8]http://www.itl.nist.gov/iad/894.01/tests/ace/

extended target entity types to 7 classes and 45 subclasses including new classes such as weapons, vehicles, and airports. Under this circumstance, traditional methods showed limitations: for every new class, these methods have to train a new model or construct a new set of rules, which are time-consuming and labor-intensive. In addition, scalability of these methods remains a big problem. The training set and test set are usually small and domain dependent. So in a real application environment, the performance of these methods will be greatly reduced.

To solve the above problem, some recent studies focus on "Entity Set Expansion" [507, 45, 698]. This task aims to extract target entities from large scale texts (Web-scale, for instance). The type of target entities is not predefined but open. We will introduce the main technologies and methods in the next section.

6.2.2 Entity Set Expansion

In this section, we will discuss the problem of "Entity Set Expansion." This problem can be defined as follows.

Given a partial set of entities (called "seed entity"), the system should expand it into a more complete set which belongs to the same category. For example, given a few elements like "Gold," "Mercury," and "Xenon" as seeds, the entity set expansion system should discover other elements such as "Silver," "Oxygen," and so on, based on the given seeds.

According to the input, the problem has some transformations. In some cases, the input is the name of category instead of seeds. Back to our example, now the input is "Elements" not "Gold," "Mercury," and "Xenon." At this time, the problem is also called "Set Instance Extraction" or "Hyponymy Relation Extraction" [700].

These collections of entities are used in many commercial and research applications. For instance, question-answering systems can use the expansion tools to handle list questions [701]; search engines can collect large sets of entities to better interpret queries [515].

Considerable progress has been made in developing high-quality entity set expansion systems. These methods often include three important steps: (1) generating high-quality seeds; (2) extracting candidates which have the same semantics with the given seeds or category name; (3) refining the candidate set. The result is a list of candidate strings ranked by their similarity scores. Figure 6.2 is a map sketch of a typical entity set expansion system. We will introduce the system part by part.

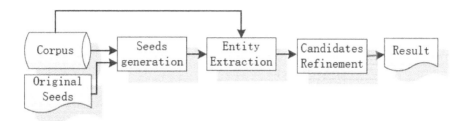

FIGURE 6.2: A typical entity set expansion system.

6.2.2.1 Seed Generation

As we discussed above, almost all open entity extraction methods need some original entities as seeds. Previous studies show the quality of seeds has a great influence on the extraction performance. So it is very important to generate high-quality seeds. A prominent work about better seed selection is proposed by Vishnu et al. [683]. They measured each seed according to the following three factors: (1) *Prototypicality*, which weighs the degree of a seed's representation of the concept; (2) *Ambiguity*, which measures the polysemy of a seed; (3) *Coverage*, which measures the degree of the amount of semantic space which the seeds share in common with the concept. Then, they designed three methods, each of which deals with one factor.

This method has two limitations: (1) They only choose relatively better seeds from original ones but cannot generate new, high-quality seeds. Unfortunately, if original seeds are not of high-quality, they can only obtain a poor performance. (2) In many situations, it is hard to get enough original seeds for selection since seeds are provided by humans. To solve the above problems, Qi et al. [553] proposed a method to automatically generate high-quality seeds.

First, Qi et al. [553] measured the quality of seeds by the following three factors: (1) *Semantic relatedness*—High-quality seeds should have high semantic relatedness among each other; (2) *Ambiguity*—Good seeds should have less ambiguity; (3) *Population*—High-quality seeds should not be sparse. And they presented three algorithms to respectively measure these factors.

(1) To measure the semantic relatedness of two entities, they adopted the method described by Milne and Witten [426], which exploited the links in Wikipedia. Based on the idea that the higher semantic relatedness two entities share, the more common links they have, this method measures the semantic relatedness of two seeds a and b as follows:

$$sr(a,b) = 1 - \frac{\log(\max(|A|,|B|)) - \log(|A \cap B|)}{\log(|W|) - \log(\min(|A|,|B|))}$$

where a and b are the two entities of interest, A and B are sets of all entities that are linked to a and b, respectively, and W is the entire Wikipedia.

Given a seed set S and one seed $s \in S$, the semantic relatedness of $s \in S$ is approximated as the average semantic relatedness of s and all other given original seeds in S.

$$Rel(s) = \frac{\sum_{s \in S, s' \neq s} sr(s, s')}{(M - 1)}$$

where S is the given seed set, s is a seed, and M is the size of S.

(2) To calculate the ambiguity of a seed s, they use

$$Amb(s) = \frac{count(< s, d >)}{\sum_{d' \in D} count(< s, d' >)}$$

where d is the article which describes s in Wikipedia. And $count(< a, d >)$ is the number of times that the seed s is linked to the article d, and D is the article set.

(3) They used the following formula to calculate the popularity of a seed:

$$Pop(s) = \frac{count(s)}{\max_{s' \in S}[count(s')]}$$

where $count(s)$ of each seed s is the number of Web pages returned when s is used as a query to a searching engine. S refers to the given seeds set.

Based on the above factors, they designed a three stage strategy to generate new, high-quality seeds. First, they linked original seeds to Wikipedia articles. Second, they measured seed quality to decide which seed should be replaced. Finally, they leveraged Wikipedia semantic knowledge and Web corpus frequency to generate new high-quality seeds and replace old ones (Figure 6.3).

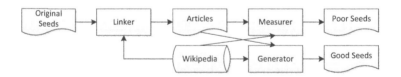

FIGURE 6.3: Flowchart of the seeds rewriting system.

The *Linker* links every seed in the original seed set to the article d, which describes it in Wikipedia. This can be seen as a procedure of disambiguation. The *Measurer* measures the quality of each seed and decides which seed should be replaced based on the above three scores ($Rel(a)$, $Amb(s)$, and $Pop(s)$). The *Generator* generates new seeds using Wikipedia's category structure and semantic knowledge, and returns the most high-quality one as a result. In the following, we introduce each component step by step.

Linker

In order to use the semantic knowledge of Wikipedia articles, the Linker needs to find out the exact articles which describe the seeds. These articles should have high semantic relatedness among themselves because they all describe instances of the same concept. Moreover, the probability of the articles being linked to should also be considered. So the following method is designed to solve this problem: For each seed in S, we use it as an anchor, then we can get an article set including all articles that link to it. So for three input seeds we get three article sets A_1, A_2, A_3. For every possible article group $G = \{A_1(i), A_2(j), A_3(k)\}$, we use the following formula to compute its confidence and choose the group which gets the highest score as the final result.

$$Conf(G) = Relatedness(G) + Probability(G) + Category(G)$$

where $Relatedness(G)$ is the average relatedness of each two articles in G. $Probability(G)$ is the product of the probabilities of the articles in G, $Category(G)$ represents the common category label of all these articles; if there exists a common category label for all the articles, the value is set to 1, otherwise the value is set to 0. Finally, we choose the group that has the highest confidence and link seeds s_1, s_2, s_3 to their related articles $A_1(i), A_2(j), A_3(k)$.

Measurer

For every seed, after linking it to article s in Wikipedia, the Measurer measures its quality according to the above three factors: semantic relatedness, population, and ambiguity. Then the original seed with the lowest quality is filtered out and replaced. The quality of newly generated seeds is also judged by this method.

Generator

The Generator generates new, high-quality seeds. It extracts candidate new seeds using the category structure of Wikipedia and then measures their quality and returns the one with the highest quality. A schematic diagram is shown in Figure 6.4.

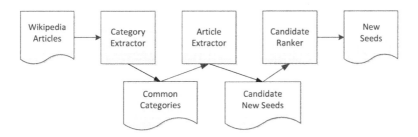

FIGURE 6.4: Flowchart of the new seed generation procedure.

Given the three original articles, the Category Extractor gathers their common category labels for further processing. If there is no common category for all three articles, it gathers common category labels for every two articles. The Article Extractor collects all the articles belonging to the common category labels and using their titles as candidate new seeds. The Candidate Ranker uses the following combined formula to measure the quality of every candidate new seed generated according to the previous three factors. Last, the Generator returns the one with the highest score as the new seed and replaces the old poor-quality seed.

$$Qua(s) = Rel(s) + Pop(s) + Amb(s)$$

By using the new seed sets, they can improve entity expansion performance by up to average 9.1% over original randomly picked seed sets on the test set of six concept lists extracted from Wikipedia [553].

6.2.2.2   Entity Extraction

Entity Extraction finds entity candidates in Web texts and ranks them according to the given entity seeds. Then the candidates with higher ranks will be extracted as the results, which are regarded as having the same semantic category with the original seeds. In detail, entity extraction can be divided into four kinds according to the resources they used: (1) extraction from query logs; (2) extraction from Web documents; (3) extraction from Web tables; and (4) extraction from multiple sources. We will introduce them one by one.

(1) Extraction from Queries

Some researchers made productive studies on mining entities from queries [514, 513]. The reason is quite convincing: (1) Named entities constitute a significant fraction of queries; (2) It is easy to collect large amount of queries since millions of people submit their queries every day; (3) Queries have more timeliness than traditional domain-dependent corpus. You can extract the newly created entities or terminologies from them.

The main idea is to construct context-vectors for seeds and candidates as the description features, and then use these vectors to compute the similarity between seeds and candidates for validating candidates. A typical algorithm to discover entities from Web search queries is proposed by Pasca [514]. First, he identified queries that contain a seed entity and found query templates from these queries. And then he used these query templates to extract entity candidates. For each candidate, he constructed a search-signature vector, which is made of the query contexts of the candidate. After pooling these vectors together, he got a search signature vector for the target semantic category. Finally, he got a ranked list of entities using the vector for the category. Experimental results on 10 classes show a 0.96 value for *Prec*@50, 0.90 for *Prec*@150, and 0.80 for *Prec*@250.

(2) Extraction from Web Documents

A main kind of method is the pattern-based one. The key idea of this kind of method is using seeds to find useful patterns and then using patterns to find candidates.

Pattern-based methods originated from Hearst [278] who defined six kinds of semantic templates. Nowadays, researchers have developed more effective methods based on this idea. Sarmento and Jijkoun proposed a method of entity set expansion from free text [593]. They used predefined semantic patterns to find candidates. And then they constructed a presentation vector for every candidate. Finally, they gave each candidate a score by computing the similarity in the vector space. Experiments on 3219 classes generated by the "Wikipedia List pages" get an average precision of 0.424.

Different from those methods dealing with unstructured text, Wang et al. proposed a language-independent system called SEAL which can automatically find structure-patterns from structured Web pages and use them to extract entities [700, 701, 699, 698]. SEAL contained three parts: the fetcher, the extractor, and the ranker. The fetcher found Web pages which contain all seed entities by crawling the top 100 Web URLs, which are returned by Google API. Then the extractor learned page-dependent patterns (which are called "wrapper") and extracted candidate entities. Finally, the ranker built a graph and ranked the extracted mentions globally based on the weights computed in the graph walk. SEAL obtained a mean average precision of more than 94% for English queries, more than 93% for Japanese queries, and 95% for Chinese queries.

In addition to these pattern-based methods, some researchers develop methods based on distributional features. The key idea of this kind of methods is to construct a distribution matrix for a given corpus. And then the system uses this matrix to compute the average similarity between each term and given seed entities. Durme and Pasca constructed the term-context matrix from 100 million Web free texts [684]. Then they proposed a cluster-like method which could generate $< instance, classlabel >$ pairs. They reported 91% accuracy for 440 classes and 86% accuracy for 8572 classes. Pantel et al. proposed a method which could compute Web-scale distributional similarity and solved the entity set expansion problem based on this similarity [515]. They used NP chunks as terms. For each term w, they constructed a pointwise mutual information vector $PMI(w) = \{pmi_{w1}, pmi_{w2}, \ldots, pmi_{wm}\}$ where pmi_{wf} is the pointwise mutual information as follows:

$$pmi_{wf} = \log \frac{c_{wf} * N}{\sum_{i=1}^{n} c_{if} * \sum_{j=1}^{m} c_{wj}}$$

where c_{wf} is the frequency of feature f occurring for term w, n is the number of unique terms, and N is the total number of features for all terms.

Given 10 seeds, they can generate a ranked list of candidates belonging to the same category. They got 0.404 in R-PREC for 50 randomly picked classes.

(3) Extraction from Web Tables

With the development of the Web, hundreds of millions of Web tables are generated. These structural or semistructural resources contain rich semantic information. Items in the same column of a table have a high probability to belong to the same category. Some researchers explore the power of these Web tables and design methods for entity set expansion from them [256, 700].

He et al. proposed a method which computes similarity between candidates and seeds based on information from Web tables [256]. The key idea is: (1) the produced set should be similar to the given seeds. (2) The set should also be coherent because its elements represent a consistent concept. First, they built a bipartite graph using Web tables and Web search queries. One kind of node is candidate and the other kind of node represents Web tables or queries. Based on the following two facts they constructed the produced entities set R: (1) Terms in the same column of a Web table have a high probability belonging to the same class. (2) Terms with similar contexts also have a high probability belonging to the same class. Second, given a seed set S, they computed the similarity from two aspects: relative score and coherent score.

$$Q(R, S) = \alpha * S_{rel}(R, S) + (1 - \alpha) * S_{coh}(R)$$

$$S_{rel}(R, S) = \frac{1}{|R| * |S|} \sum_{r \in R} \sum_{s \in S} Sim(s, r)$$

$$S_{coh}(R) = \frac{1}{|R| * |R|} \sum_{i=1}^{|R|} \sum_{j>i}^{|R|} Sim(r_i, r_j)$$

where $r_i \in R$ and $r_j \in R$ represent the two different seeds, $Q(R, S)$ is the quality of the expanded set R with respect to the seed set S, $S_{rel}(R, S)$ is the relevance of the expanded set and the seed set, $S_{coh}(R)$ is the coherence of R.

Finally, the system returned a ranked list as a result. Experiments in four classes obtained 0.9 of *Prec@20*.

(4) Extraction from Multiple Sources

Different from the above methods, this kind of methods employed multiple resources. The basic idea of this kind of methods was that combining information sources and information extraction algorithms usually leads to improvements in open-domain information extraction (IE). In detail, they usually designed separate features for different resources according to their different characteristics. Then they combined the scores to get a final result.

Talukdar used free texts and Web table data as knowledge resources [660]. For free texts, they used the template-based method to extract candidates, and used the distribution-based method to give each candidate a similarity score. For Web tables, they supposed that every column was a candidate and used the relation between columns and tables to give candidates the similarity scores. Then they built a graph and leveraged a random walk algorithm to compute the final scores. They reported 0.55 of MRR (mean reciprocal rank) on 38 classes.

Pennacchiotti and Pantel proposed a framework for information extraction which can deal with multisources containing Web texts, Wikipedia articles, query logs, and Web table data [513]. For different knowledge sources, they used different features and designed relevant algorithms to compute a confidence score. Then they used a mixed model to aggregate the results. They reported a 0.85 MAP (mean average precision) for three classes.

6.2.2.3   Result Refinement

Even for the highest quality expansions, errors still occur and manual refinements are necessary for most practical uses [692]. So it is also valuable to design methods which can effectively refine expansion set with less human labor.

Vyas and Pantel found that the main reason of the errors was the ambiguity of seeds [692], especially for the bootstrapping strategy. They designed a system using the bootstrapping strategy but only resorting to the human editors to point out a mistake for all candidates in each iteration. They reported an improvement on R-precision from 26% to 51%.

6.2.3   Summary

In this section, we briefly introduce an important subtask in Knowledge Extraction: Entity Recognition and Expansion. Specifically, to satisfy the need of knowledge extraction in opened UGC data, the entity recognition should not constrain to the traditional predefined entity types. Thus, we discuss the key techniques in entity set expansion, which includes seed generation, entity extraction, and result refinement. Then we get the following conclusions:

- Expansion systems always include two important components: (1) Find the candidates which may have the same semantic category with the given seeds; (2) Estimate the average similarity between each candidate and the given seeds.

- Seeds have a great impact upon the expansion performance. And ambiguity is the most important factor for measuring the quality of seeds. It affects expansion performance a lot, especially when you are using a bootstrapping method.

6.3   Relation Extraction

6.3.1   Introduction

Knowledge is not isolated but is related with each other. Therefore, relation extraction has explicit needs for knowledge extraction. For example, it is not satisfied to only find occurrence of people names and location names, but to identify whether there are "born in" relations between them. Relation extraction is an important task, since the entity attributes (e.g., "Is-A" relation) are important components for constructing KB, and the relationships are also useful for understanding the meaning of texts.

The types of relation include binary and multiway according to the number of arguments. Binary relation means that the relation involves two entities or concepts. Multiway relation means that the relation occurs among several entities. Typical examples of multiway relations are event extraction, record extraction, and semantic role labeling [590]. In this section, we mainly focus on binary relation extraction. The task of binary relation extraction can be divided into two different cases according to the different inputs. The first case is when given an entity e and a specific relation r, the task aims to extract the entity with which the entity e has the relation r; or to identify relations by two given specific entities e_1 and e_2.

Most previous methods on relation extraction demand that the relation name or type is predefined, which needs sufficient labeled data to train the extraction models. This constraint limits the application of relation extraction from the Web, especially from UGC Web sites. As mentioned in the first section, texts in UGC Web sites cover much more domains and classes, which means that we cannot list all relation types for all the domains and cannot manually label sufficient training instances. Therefore, many researchers have paid more attention to open information extraction (Open IE). Open IE faces two challenges. The first challenge is how to extract the relation types and automatically generate the labeled instances from the UGC data. The second challenge is how to exploit the Web structures in UGC Web sites for open-domain relation extraction. This section first describes the mainstream methods on traditional relation extraction (predefined relation extraction). Then we present several typical techniques for open-domain relation extraction from UGC data in details.

6.3.2 Predefined Relation Extraction

As mentioned above, there are two levels for predefined relation extraction, which will be presented as follows, respectively.

6.3.2.1 Identify Relations between the Given Entities

In this level, relation extraction refers to the task of detecting and classifying prespecified relations between two entities in texts. The formal task definition is described by Sarawagi [590]: given a text snippet x and two marked entities e_1 and e_2 in x, identifying whether there is the relationship r between e_1 and e_2. For example, the text fragment "please call Alice from CompanyA Inc. at her cell phone (123) 456-7890" contain three entities "Alice," "CompanyA Inc.," and "(123) 456-7890," the task is to decide whether there is an "EmployeeOf" relation between "Alice" and "CompanyA Inc.," and "Person-Phone" relation between "Alice" and "(123) 456-7890." "EmployeeOf" and

"PersonPhone" are two predefined relation types. For the Knowledge Base (KB) population, the relations are often entity attributes, so the task is also named as Attribute Extraction or Slot-Filling.

Generally, the approaches of relation extraction can be divided into two categories.

Feature-based methods: Feature-based approaches regard relation extraction as a problem of classification or sequence labeling. These methods assume that the relations between any entities can be represented with several different level features, such as contextual words (word surfaces, unigram, bigram, etc.), the word type features (part-of-speech, word sense, etc.), the syntactic relation between words, and so on. Therefore, for a specific relation type, the task can be regarded as a sequence labeling process. The relation identification process is to label whether the words in a sentence is the relation argument by using the classical machine learning methods [253, 648, 590]. Since the relation types are predefined, these previous methods need sufficient training data to train the classifier. However, manually labeling data for each relation is time-consuming and labor-intensive.

Kernel-based methods: From feature-based methods for relation extraction, many researchers realize that the syntax-based features are much more effective for indicating relations. Its key problems are how to represent the syntactic structure in feature representation and how to compute the similarity between instances based on syntactic structure features. Based on these observations, several approaches exploited kernels to model the syntactic relations between words and compute the similarity between two different syntactic trees, such as dependency tree kernel [157], or a convolution tree kernel [766]. Furthermore, kernels have also been proposed to combine the similarity among not only between syntactic trees, but also different kinds of structures including sequences, parse trees, dependency graphs, and so on.

6.3.2.2   Identify Entity Pairs for Given Relation Types

In this level, relation extraction is to extract two entities which have the given relation types. For example, by given "Is_A" relation, the system is to extract such entity pairs as ("cat," "animal"), ("car," "vehicle"), ("man," "human"), where "cat" is an "animal," "car" is a kind of "vehicle," and "man" is a "human." To implement this process, previous methods often adopt a pattern-based strategy, which uses patterns to extract potential entities for a given relation type, where patterns can be represented using the regular expression combining with lexical, syntactical, or ontological information [487]. However, the key problem is how to expand more patterns for a specific relation. Most approaches adopt a bootstrapping strategy to find patterns and example seeds, such as SNOWBALL [14]. However, because of the semantic drift of patterns, the extracted entities may not be related to the given relation. To solve the above problem, Zhu et al. [780] exploited the Markov Logic Network to perform result verification and filter the incorrect entity pairs.

TABLE 6.1: ACE08 Relation Types and Subtypes

Type	Subtype
ART (artifact)	User-Owner-Invertor-Manufacturer
GEN-AFF (General affiliation)	Citizen-Resident-Religion-Ethnicity, Org-Location
METONYMY	*None*
ORG-AFF (Org-affiliation)	Employment, Founder, Ownership, Student-Alum, Sports-Affiliation, Student-Alum, Sports-Affiliation, Investor-Shareholder, Membership
PART-WHOLE (part-to-whole)	Artifact, Geographical, Subsidiary
PER-SOC (person-social)	Business, Family, Lasting-Personal
PHYS (physical)	Located, Near

6.3.2.3 Evaluations on Predefined Relation Extraction

In this section, we demonstrate several typical competition tracks involving relation extraction tasks, such as MUC, ACE TAC-KBP, WePS, SemEval, and so forth.

MUC (1987–1997): The task involving relation extraction in MUC (Message Understanding Conference) is the Template Relation (TR) Task, which aims to extract relational information on employee_of, manufacture_of, and location_of. The corpus they used is New York Times News Service. The best system achieved is *Precision* = 87%, *Recall* = 65% in TR task.

ACE (1999–2008): The research objective for ACE (Automatic Content Extraction, ACE) program was the detection and characterization of Entities, Relations, and Events. The tasks in ACE are Entity Detection & Recognition (EDR), Entity Mention Detection (EMD), Relation Detection & Recognition (RDR), Relation Mention Detection (RMD), Event Detection & Recognition (VDR), and Event Mention Detection (VMD). People, organizations, geopolitical entities, facilities, and locations are the five main ACE entity types. There are seven main types of relations in ACE, including artifact, general affiliation, metonymy, org-affiliation, part-to-whole, person-social, and physical, shown in Table 6.1. The source data used for evaluation contains the following domains: newswire, broadcast news, broadcast conversations, weblogs, usernet newsgroud/discussion groups, and conversational telephone speech transcripts. The best system that participated in ACE 2008 achieved the overall ACE value score of 50.8% in LEDR (local Entity Detection & Recognition), and 3.8% in LRDR (local Relation Detection & Recognition). The best system that participated in ACE 2008 achieved the overall ACE value score of 13.4% in VDR (Event Detection & Recognition), 82.9% in EMD (Entity Mention Detection), 33.4% in RMD (Relation Mention Detection), and 24.1% in VMD (Event Mention Detection).

Knowledge base population (KBP): In TAC-KBP, slot-filling task aims to extract the value for the predefined slot (attribute) of query entities

TABLE 6.2: The Types of Entities Defined in KBP

Person		Organization
per:alternate_names	per:title	org:alternate_names
per:date_of_birth	per:member_of	org:political/religious_affiliation
per:age	per:employ_of	org:top_members/employees
per:country_of_birth	per:religion	org:number_of_employees/members
per:stateorprovince_of_birth	per:spouse	org:members
per:city_of_birth	per:children	org:members_of
per:origin	per:parents	org:subsidiaries
per:date_of_death	per:siblings	org:parents
per:country_of_death	per:other_family	org:found_by
per:stateorprovince_of_death	per:charges	org:found
per:city_of_death		org:dissolved
per:cause_of_death		org:country_of_headquaters
per:countries_of_residence		org:stateorprovince_of_headquaters
per:stateorprovince_of_residence		org:city_of_headquaters
per:cities_of_residence		org:shareholders
per:schools_attended		org:Website

from the given document collections. The type of entities is confined to PER-SON and ORGANIZATION. Slots of interests are shown in Table 6.2, such as birth place, age, schools, and so on, for PERSON, top_members, founders, affiliations, and so on, for ORGANIZATION.[9]

Attribute extraction track in WePS: The goal of Attribute Extract (AE) task of Web People Search (WePS2) is to extract 18 kinds of "attribute values" of target individuals (person type) from the given Web pages. The goal of WePS3 is much more complicated, as systems are requested to link each attribute to a person (cluster of documents) instead of just listing the attributes obtained from each document. Slots of interest include Date of birth, Birth place, School, and so on.[10] The best system in WePS3 achieved a performance of $Precision = 0.22$, $Recall = 0.24$, $F - measure = 0.18$.

Semantic evaluation exercises (SemEval): SemEval5 is evolved from the SensEval (word sense disambiguation evaluation) series. The SemEval-2 (2010) task 8 focuses on the classification of semantic relations between noun-phrase pairs, which aims to predict the relation for a given sentence and a pair of nominals. Evaluating phrasal semantics task in SemEval-4 (2013) task 5 is to characterize and predict the meaning for a given pattern, which is also called relation paraphrase or mapping.[11]

6.3.3 Open Domain Relation Extraction

As mentioned above, traditional relation extraction approaches assume that the relation is predefined. However, for Web texts, especially for UGC, there has been great interest in scaling IE to a broader set of relations and

---

[9]http://www.nist.gov/tac/2012/KBP/task_guidelines/index.HTML
[10]http://nlp.uned.es/weps/
[11]http://www.cs.york.ac.uk/semeval

to far larger corpora [45, 288, 472, 116, 210]. Recently, Open Information Extraction (Open IE) has become more and more popular [45]. Furthermore, mining relations on the Web is different from those on the unstructured texts, due to the diversely structured Web pages, especially on UGC Web sites. In this section, we will describe the typical techniques of open domain relation extraction on structured (semistructured) and unstructured UGC Web pages, respectively.

6.3.3.1 Relation Extraction in Structured/Semistructured Web Pages

Text in Web sites, especially in UGC Web sites, are often not completely unstructured, much structured or semistructured information is contained as well. In UGC Web sites, texts are usually decorated by HTML tags like HTML tables and HTML lists, and so on. If we can construct some special patterns according to the Web site's structure (HTML tags), mining relations will be easier. Therefore, how to exploit the structure of the Web pages is the key issue for relation extraction. Now we will describe the relation extraction from different structured/semistructured Web pages.

(1) Relation Extraction from Data Records

Data records are displayed with some fixed templates in UGC Web sites [257]. Mining the knowledge from such data records is an important task of relation extraction because objects in the data records often denote the object's attributes, such as products' properties. Relation extraction from data records is to learn specific patterns or templates from Web pages. The basic idea is that the structures of the data records in a specific Web site are often stationary and most pages in this Web site contains the similar structure. Therefore, through page matching, we can mine the common parts among the same Web site.

ROADRUNNER aims to generate a wrapper for a set of HTML pages, which corresponds to infer a grammar for the HTML code (a regular grammar) [154]. It works with two or more HTML pages belonging to the same Web site at a time. Pattern generation is based on the similarity and dissimilarity between the pages.

The matching algorithm works on two objects (a list of tokens and a wrapper, that is, one union-free regular expression) in Web pages at a time. Given two HTML pages belonging to the same Web site, one randomly picks page P_1 as an initial version of wrapper W. Then, the wrapper is progressively refined to find a common regular expression by applying W on the other page P_2. A mismatch happens when some tokens in P_2 does not comply to the grammar specified by wrapper W. Mismatches can help to discover the essential information about the wrapper. Whenever one mismatch is found, the original wrapper W is generalized to solve the mismatch. Totally, there are two kinds of mismatches (string mismatches and tag mismatches) that can be generated in ROADRUNNER [154].

ROADRUNNER is specially designed for extracting relation knowledge from multiple pages in the same site. However, there are some pages which contain the record lists. To extract relation knowledge from this kind of pages, previous researchers often detect the partial data region about a record list by using the tree alignment algorithm [257].

(2) Relation Extraction from General Web Pages

Relation extraction from data records assumes that the data records in the Web sites are explicitly given. However, in many cases, the users do not know where to obtain such pages or Web sites. Yoshinaga and Torisawa [750] proposed to extract knowledge from the semistructured HTML documents. In this method, the extracted items are constrained to entity attributes, shortly named as AVPs (Attribute Value Pairs). First, it searches the lists or tables in Web pages containing the AVPs through the given attribute seeds. Then the patterns can be learned in the retrieval pages. Finally, the AVPs are extracted based on the learned patterns.

In fact, there are three steps to acquire the class attributes [749]: (1) Sampling pages that are likely to include class attributes; (2) Extracting the class attribute candidates by using the learned patterns; and (3) Filtering out the erroneous attribute candidates.

- **Sampling Web pages from the Web:** Web pages that show catalogs or specifications of the objects are collected because these pages often contain attributes of the objects.

- **Extracting of attribute candidates:** According to the sampled Web pages, the attributes are likely to be emphasized through HTML tags, which are employed as the clues. Noun sequences surrounded by the particular HTML tags or braces are extracted as candidate attributes.

- **Filtering the acquired class attributes:** Finally, it uses the statistics and hit counts of a commercial search engine to filter out the erroneous attribute candidates, and then obtains a final set of attributes used by many Web authors to describe the objects.

Extracting of attribute candidates is the most important part of Yoshinaga and Torisawa's research [749]. First, it collects pages that include AVPs through a commercial search engine with a query consisting of the entity, the class, and the class attributes. Then it identifies the tables or lists containing the object's AVPs from the sampled Web pages. It follows the hypothesis that AVPs for a given entity are likely to appear jointly in a small number of regions (AVP blocks) enclosed by HTML block tags. After locating the AVP blocks, it induces AVP's extraction patterns from each block. The algorithm in Yoshinaga and Torisawa [749] assumes that the attribute name immediately precedes the attribute value, and the AVP immediately follows the value in an AVP block. Furthermore, when an attribute in an AVP block is emphasized by some HTML tags and braces, the same symbols are used to emphasize other attributes in the same block. Based on this hypothesis, the procedure induces a regular expression as a generic pattern to extract the attributes and their values [749, 750].

6.3.3.2   Relation Extraction from Unstructured Texts

Now, we will describe the typical methods focusing on extracting open relation knowledge from unstructured texts. Compared with traditional predefined relations, the difficulties of open relation extraction are: (1) How to generate the relation types; and (2) For each relation type, how to generate the training data, which is used to train the extractor. Furthermore, compared with the structured or semistructured texts, unstructured texts do not have such structured indicators, such as HTML tags, links, and so on. In this case, how to exploit the intrinsic features in texts, such as tokens, part-of-speech, and syntactic information for open relation extraction is a big challenge. This section will present some representative open domain relation extraction systems, such as TextRunner [45], NELL [116], YAGO [649], and PATTY [487].

(1) TextRunner

Here, we introduce a famous OpenIE system named as TextRunner [45]. The basic idea of TextRunner is that most sentences contain highly reliable syntactic clues to their meaning. For example, relationships in sentences are often expressed through verbs (such as "invented," "married," or "elected") or verbs followed by prepositions (such as "invented by," "married to," or "elected in"). It is often quite straightforward for a computer to locate the verbs in a sentence, identify entities related by the verb, and use them to create statements of fact. To validate the feasibility, the authors of TextRunner select a sample of 500 sentences at random from an IE training corpus developed by Bunescu and Mooney [104], and express the binary relationships using a compact set of relation-independent lexicon-syntactic patterns, and then quantify their frequency. They found that 95% of the patterns could be grouped into the categories listed in Table 6.3.

In total, TextRunner consists of three key modules [45].

1. Self-Supervised Learner: TextRunner creates a learner to find and label a set of tuple of the form of $t = (e_i, r_{ij}, e_j)$, where e_i and e_j are strings denoting entities, and r_{ij} denoting a relationship between them. In this process, some heuristics are used to label each pair of noun phrases (e_i, e_j) from the parsed tree of the sentence. It is difficult to anticipate the form of relation and its arguments in a general manner. Therefore, they tried some heuristics, which only cast constraints on parse structure and the part-of-speech tags. Then these positive or negative extracted tuples are used as training examples to train a classifier. The features for each tuple are as follows [45], including

TABLE 6.3:   Taxonomy of Binary Relationships (Nearly 95% of 500 randomly selected sentences belongs to one of the eight categories [45].)

RelativeFrequency	Category	SimplifiedLexico-SyntacticPattern
37.8	Verb	E1 Verb E2 (X established Y)
22.8	Noun+Prep	E1 NP Prep E2 (X settlement with Y)
16.0	Verb+Prep	E1 Verb Prep E2 (X moved to Y)
9.4	Infinitive	E1 to Verb E2 (X plans to acquire Y)
5.2	Modifier	E1 Verb E2 Noun (X is Y winner)
1.8	Coordinaten	E1 (and—,-—:) E2 NP (X-Y deal)
1.0	Coordinatev	E1 (and—,) E2 Verb (X , Y merge)
0.8	Appositive	E1 NP (:—,)? E2 (X hometown : Y)

part-of-speech tags, token number, stopwords number, pronoun number, and part-of-speech tags of contextual words.

2. Single-Pass Extractor: The Single-Pass Extractor extracts tuples for all possible relations in a single pass over the entire corpus. It first tags the part-of-speech of each word and identifies the noun phrases in sentences [45]. Then relations are found by examining the text between a pair of noun phrases by using Conditional Random Field (CRF) [381]. Each candidate will be sent to Self-Supervised Learner, and the ones labeled as trustworthy are retained.

3. Redundancy-Based Assessor: The Assessor assigns a probability to each retained tuple based on a probabilistic model of redundancy in text introduced by Downey et al. [180].

The final outputs are trustworthy tuples like (*Berkeley, locatedin, Bay Area*), with a value between [0, 1] indicating the confidence of this extraction. These tuples are further classified as concrete or abstract. Concrete means that the truth of the tuple is grounded in particular entities, for example, (*Tesla, invented, coiltransformer*). Abstract tuples are under specified, such as (*Einstein, derived, theory*), or imply properties of general classes, such as (*executive, hiredby, company*) [45].

In addition, there are some other open domain relation extraction systems, such as Kylin [725], WOE [726], ReVerb [507], and so on. Kylin extracted relations from Wikipedia, which exploited the Wikipedia infobox to automatically create training examples to learn the relation-specific extractors. WOE builds on Kylin, which automatically learns the extracted patterns from Wikipedia texts. ReVerb is an extension of TextRunner and WOE. It implements some constraints in the extraction system to resolve the problem of uninformative and incoherent extractions. Because of space limitations, we will not introduce them in detail in this chapter.

(2) NELL

NELL means never-ending language learning, which comes from the "Reading the Web" [116] project at Carnegie Mellon University (CMU). The motivation of this project is that the vast redundancy of information on the

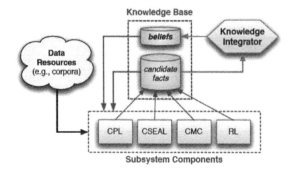

FIGURE 6.5: CMU NELL system architecture [116].

Web (e.g., many facts are stated multiple times in different ways) will enable a system with the right learning mechanisms to succeed. The never-ending language learning system runs 24 hours per day, 7 days per week, performing reading and learning tasks each day [116].

NELL acquires two types of knowledge: (1) Knowledge about which noun phrases refer to which specified semantic categories, such as countries, cities, and companies, and (2) knowledge about which pairs of noun phrases satisfy which specified semantic relations, such as $locateIn(city, location)$. To these aims, NELL learns free text patterns for extracting knowledge from sentences on the Web. It also learns to extract the knowledge from semistructured Web data such as tables and lists [116]. It tries to learn morphological regularities of instances of categories, and the probabilistic horn clause rules to make inference for new relations which do not explicitly occur in texts.

Figure 6.5 shows the main architecture of the CMU NELL system. Based on the description by Carlson et al. [116], there are four main components as follows.

- **Coupled pattern learner (CPL):** This component is to learn the useful contextual patterns for extracting relation instances, such as "chairman of X" and "X born in Y," which utilizes co-occurrence statistics between the noun phrase and the contextual words (both defined using part-of-speech tags) to learn extraction patterns, and then uses those patterns to find additional instances of each predicate. The details of this component is described in by Carlson et al. [116, 117].

- **Coupled SEAL (CSEAL):** It is a semisupervised extractor, which fully utilizes the Web page structure information. It mainly aims to extract instances of the corresponding predicate from lists and tables in Web pages. At the same time, this component uses mutual exclusion relationships to provide negative examples, which are used to filter out general lists and tables [116, 117, 697].

- **Coupled morphological classifier (CMC):** The aim of this component is to make validation on the extracted candidates to ensure high precision [116]. CMC contains a set of binary regularized logistic regression models, which are used to classify candidates based on various morphological features (words, capitalization, affixes, part-of-speech, etc.).

- **Rule learner (RL):** This component is a relational learning algorithm, which learns probabilistic horn clauses to generate inference rules. The learned rules are used to infer new relation instances from other relation instances [116].

(3) YAGO

In 2007, the Max Planck Institute in Saarbrücken, Germany, developed a huge knowledge base with high coverage and precision, named "YAGO" [649]. YAGO was automatically derived from Wikipedia and WordNet, which currently contains more than 1 million entities and 5 million facts. By employing the synsets in Wordnet, YAGO can organize the extracted concepts from Wikipedia category pages into a taxonomy with a hierarchical structure, where the concepts from Wikipedia are labeled by the WordNet taxonomic synset. Recently, YAGO was extended to the new version YAGO2, which contains more than 10 million entities and 120 million facts about these entities [287].

Futhermore, Nakashole et al. [487] presented PATTY, a large resource for textual patterns that denote binary relations between entities. PATTY aims to generate the semantical type for each relational pattern, and organizes them into a subsumption taxonomy. Moreover, it aims to generalize syntactic variations such as "sings her <song>" and "sings his <song>" into a more general pattern "sings [prep] <song>"[487]. Also, it tries to find out the hyponymy relations between patterns. For example, it automatically infers that the above patterns are semantically subsumed by the pattern "<musician> performs on <musical composition>." On Wikipedia corpus, they reported that it has obtained 350,569 pattern synsets with 84.7% precision [487].

6.3.4   Comparison

In this section, we compare the above three representative open domain information extraction systems in different perspectives. TextRunner constrains patterns to verbs or verb phrases that end with prepositions, while PATTY can learn arbitrary patterns [487]. Also, the methods in the TextRunner are blind to the ontological dimension of the entities in the patterns, while PATTY aims to organize the patterns into synonymous patterns and constructs a taxonomy. NELL learns to extract suitable noun-phrase pairs from a large Web corpus based on the predefined relations with type signatures (e.g., *locateIn* :< *organization* > × < *city* >). In contrast, PATTY discovers patterns for relations that are *a priori* unknown [487].

6.3.5 Summary

The goal of Open Domain Relation Extraction is to extract all instances of all meaningful relations from Web pages. The extractions are noncanonical facts: (1) It does not disambiguate words to entities; (2) The relations are not well-defined, as they are usually verbs or verb phrases ending with prepositions. In this section, we have briefly introduced some typical systems for relation extraction from the Web, including TextRunner [45], NELL [116], YAGO [649], and PATTY [487].

6.4 Named Entity Disambiguation

As mentioned in the first section, named entity disambiguation is one of the difficult problems to be solved. For example, the name "Michael Jordan" represents more than 10 people in the Google search results. Some of them are shown below:

Michael (Jeffrey) Jordan, Basketball Player
Michael (I.) Jordan, Professor of Berkeley
Michael Jordan, Footballer
Michael (B.) Jordan, American Actor

The name ambiguity has raised serious problems in automatic knowledge base population. Ambiguous names are not unique identifiers for specific entities and, as a result, there are many confounders in the construction of knowledge base. So, there is an urgent demand for efficient, high-quality named entity disambiguation methods.

6.4.1 Task Description

Formally, the task of entity disambiguation can be defined using a six-tuple as follows

$$M = \{N, E, D, O, K, \delta\}$$

where $N = \{n_1, n_2, \ldots, n_l\}$ is the set of the entities to be disambiguated, for example, {Michael Jordan, NBA, MVP, ... }; $E = \{e_1, e_2, \ldots, e_k\}$ is the set of the referent entities in the real world, for example,

Michael (Jeffrey) Jordan: Basketball Player;
Michael (I.) Jordan: Professor of Berkeley;
Michael Jordan: Footballer;
Michael (B.) Jordan: American Actor;
NBA: National Basketball Association;

NBA, National Bicycle Association;

MVP: Most Valuable Player;

MVP: Health Care

In practical application, the set of referent entities are often given in the form of knowledge bases such as Wikipedia[12] and Freebase.[13] But, in some cases, there is no such set of target objects.

$D = \{d_1, d_2, \ldots, d_n\}$ is a document collection containing the entities to be disambiguated, for example, the top 100 Web pages of Google for the search query of *"Michael Jordan"*;

$O = \{o_1, o_2, \ldots, o_m\}$ is the set of mentions of entities to be disambiguated in D. For example, in *"Michael Jordan is an American former professional basketball player,"* *"Michael Jordan"* is a mention of the target object *"Michael (Jeffrey) Jordan: Basketball Player."* The contexts of an entity mention (surface name) can be the texts inside the specified window around the mention, or the whole text where the mention occurs, and so on.

K is the background knowledge of the entity disambiguation task. Because the information supplied by the literal meaning of the target referent entity is not enough to support the disambiguation task, the background knowledge is needed. The background knowledge regards texts which describe the target referent entity. For example, the following two Wikipedia texts can respectively be used as the background knowledge of *"Michael (Jeffrey) Jordan: Basketball Player"* and *Michael Jordan: Footballer."*

Michael (Jeffrey) Jordan: *Basketball Player: Michael Jeffrey Jordan (born February 17, 1963), also known by his initials, MJ, is an American former professional basketball player, entrepreneur, and majority owner and chairman of the Charlotte Bobcats. His biography on the National Basketball Association (NBA) Web site states, "By acclamation, Michael Jordan is the greatest basketball player of all time." Jordan was one of the most effectively marketed athletes of his generation and was considered instrumental in popularizing the NBA around the world in the 1980s and 1990s.*

Michael Jordan: *Footballer: Michael William Jordan (born 7 April 1986) is an English football goalkeeper born in Cheshunt, Hertfordshire. He made seven appearances in the Football League for Chesterfield, having started his career as a trainee at Arsenal.*

According to whether the set of the target referent entity is given or not, the entity disambiguation task is divided into two categories: clustering-based disambiguation and entity-linking based disambiguation.

---

[12]http://www.wikipedia.org/

[13]http://www.freebase.com/

Clustering-based disambiguation: This kind of methods group all mentions for a certain target referent entity into a cluster, and each cluster corresponds to a specific entity.

Entity-linking based disambiguation: This kind of methods link each name mention in a document with a referent entity in a knowledge base. Because the referent entities are unambiguous, the mentions are disambiguated through linking.

6.4.2 Evaluation of Entity Disambiguation

Currently, there are two main evaluation platforms: WePS (Web Person Search Clustering Task) evaluation [314][315] and TAC KBP [453]. WePS evaluates the clustering-based entity disambiguation systems. TAC KBP aims at the evaluation of entity-linking based entity disambiguation systems.

6.4.2.1 WePS Evaluation

WePS mainly evaluates the person name disambiguation methods. For the input of person name searching results (usually top 100 or 150 Web pages of a search engine for given person name), the disambiguation systems group these Web pages into clusters so that each cluster corresponds to a specific person.

WePS used *Purity* and *Inverse Purity* as the evaluation metrics [314].

Purity focuses on the frequency of the most common category in each cluster, and rewards the clustering solutions that introduce less noise in each cluster.

$$Purity = \sum_i \frac{|C_i|}{n} \max Precision(C_i, L_j)$$

$$Precision(C_i, L_j) = \frac{|C_i \cap L_j|}{|C_i|}$$

where $C = \{C_1, C_2, \ldots, C_n\}$ denotes the clusters automatically obtained, $L = \{L_1, L_2, \ldots, L_m\}$ denotes the clusters manually annotated.

Inverse Purity focuses on the cluster with maximum recall for each category, rewarding the clustering solutions that gather more elements of each category in a corresponding single cluster.

$$InversePurity = \sum_i \frac{|L_i|}{n} \max Precision(L_j, C_i)$$

6.4.2.2 TAC KBP Evaluation

TAC KBP evaluated the Entity Linking task, which links each name mention in a document with the referent entity in a knowledge base (Wikipedia). The dataset of TAC KBP Entity Linking task includes two parts: Reference Knowledge Base and Evaluation Data [453].

The main evaluation metric of the Entity linking task is micro-averaged accuracy, the average precision of all the linkings computed as

$$Mirco = \frac{\sum_{q \in Q} \Sigma(L(q), C(q))}{|Q|}$$

where Q is the set of all the queries, $L(q)$ is the ID of the referent entity automatically given for query q, $C(q)$ is the ID of the referent entity manually annotated, $\Sigma(L(q), C(q))$ is used to determine whether $L(q)$ and $C(q)$ are equal.

6.4.3 Clustering-Based Entity Disambiguation

Given the set of the mentions of the entities to be disambiguated $O = o_1, o_2, \ldots, o_k$, a clustering-based on an entity disambiguation system often works using the following steps.

- For each entity mention in a text, extract the features in the context, such as words, entities and concepts, and so on, and represent them as a feature vector;

- Compute the similarities between each pair of entity mentions;

- Cluster the entity mentions using some clustering algorithm, so that each cluster corresponds to a referent entity.

In this process, the key is to compute the semantic similarity between entity mentions. According to the similarity computation methods, there are three kinds of methods as follows. (1) Entity mention similarity computation based on textual features in the context; (2) Entity mention similarity computation based on social networks; and (3) Entity mention similarity computation based on background knowledge.

6.4.3.1 Entity Mention Similarity Computation Based on Textual Features

This kind of method disambiguated names based on the bag-of-words (BOW) model. Bagga and Baldwin [41] represented a name as a vector of its contextual words, then the similarity between two names was computed through cosine equation, and finally two names were predicted to be the same entity if their similarity is above a threshold. Mann and Yarowsky [443] extended the name's vector representation by extracting biographic facts. Pedersen et al. [528] employed significant bigrams to represent the context of a name. Fleischman [221] trained a Maximum Entropy model to give the probability that two names represent the same entity, then used a modified agglomerative clustering algorithm to cluster names using the probability as the similarity.

6.4.3.2   Entity Mention Similarity Computation Based on Social Networks

All the BOW model based methods mentioned above only employed the contextual terms, while other semantic relations like social relatedness between entities and associative relatedness between concepts are ignored. Recent research has investigated social networks as background knowledge for disambiguation. Bekkerman and McCallum [61] disambiguated names based on the link structure between a set of socially related persons in the Web pages, their model leveraged hyperlinks, and the content similarity between Web pages. Malin and Airoldi [438, 439] measured the similarity based on the probability of walking from one ambiguous name to another in the social network constructed from corpora. Einat et al. [195] disambiguated names in e-mail documents by building a social network from e-mail data, then employed a random walk algorithm to compute the similarity. Joseph et al. [325] used the relationships from DBLP to pinpoint names in the research domain to the persons in DBLP. Kalashnikov et al. [328] enhanced the similarity measure by collecting entity co-occurrence information via Web search. Social networks can only capture a special type of semantic relations: the social relatedness between persons, which has the limitation of coverage. To overcome this deficiency, several researchers used other resources as the background knowledge, such as Wikipedia.

6.4.3.3   Entity Mention Similarity Computation Based on Background Knowledge

To overcome the deficiency mentioned above, many works exploited Wikipedia as the background knowledge for entity disambiguation, which surpasses other knowledge bases by the coverage of concepts, rich semantic information, and up-to-date content. By leveraging Wikipedia's semantic knowledge like social relatedness between entities and associative relatedness between concepts, the similarity between name observations can be measured more accurately. Therefore, there are mainly two problems: (1) How to represent the name observations as the feature vectors for clustering; and (2) How to compute the similarity between name observations.

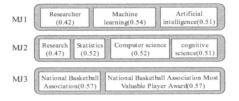

FIGURE 6.6: The concept representations of MJ1, MJ2, and MJ3.

(1) Representing name observations as Wikipedia concept vectors

Intuitively, if two name observations represent the same entity, it is highly possible that the Wikipedia concepts in their contexts are highly related. In contrast, if two name observations represent different entities, the Wikipedia concepts in their contexts will not be closely related. Thus, a name observation o can be represented by the Wikipedia concepts in its context, that is, a Wikipedia concept vector $o = \{(c_1, w(c_1, o)), (c_2, w(c_2, o)), \ldots, (c_m, w(c_m, o))\}$, where each concept c_i is assigned a weight $w(c_i, o)$ indicating the relatedness between c_i and o.

The key component in this process is to recognize the Wikipedia concepts in the context of the name observations. In the method of Milne and Witten [468], the recognition takes three steps: (1) Identifying surface forms; (2) Mapping them to Wikipedia concepts; and (3) Concept weighting and pruning for a better similarity measure. For example, given the following three observations MJ1, MJ2, and MJ3 of "Michael Jordan," their concept vector representations are shown in Figure 6.6.

- MJ1: **Michael Jordan** is a leading researcher in machine learning and artificial intelligence.

- MJ2: **Michael Jordan** has published over 300 research articles on topics in computer science, statistics, and cognitive science.

- MJ3: **Michael Jordan** wins NBA MVP.

FIGURE 6.7: The semantic related concepts of Berkeley professor Michael I. Jordan in the constructed semantic network.

(2) Measuring the similarity between name observations by leveraging Wikipedia semantic knowledge

After obtaining the concept vector representations of name observations, previous methods' similarity measures can be applied to compute the similarity of two name observations. Different from the traditional BOW model based methods and the social network based methods, Han and Zhao [265], Strube and Ponzetto [647], Gabrilovich and Markovitch [224], and Milne and Witten [467] took into account the full semantic relations indicated by hyperlinks within Wikipedia, rather than just term overlap or social relatedness between entities. Milne and Witten [467] mentioned that links between articles are only tenuously related. Therefore, two Wikipedia concepts are considered to be semantic related if there are hyperlinks between them. In this way, a semantic network can be constructed based on the hyperlinks between Wikipedia articles, where the linked concepts in this graph are semantically related. For example, Figure 6.7 shows a part of the constructed semantic network, which contains all the semantic related concepts of Berkeley's professor Michael Jordan.

Milne and Witten [467] compute the semantic relatedness based on links in Wikipedia articles, which is based on the idea that the higher semantic related Wikipedia concepts will share more semantic related concepts. This method measures the semantic relatedness as:

$$sr(a,b) = \frac{\log(\max(|A|,|B|)) - \log(|A \bigcap B|)}{log(|W|) - \log(\min(|A|,|B|))}$$

Han and Zhao [265] extended this method and proposed a robust semantic relatedness measure, which captured the semantic overlap between different concepts in Wikipedia. Given two concepts o_k and o_l, the semantic relatedness between them can be computed as follows.

$$SR(o_k \rightarrow o_l) = \frac{\sum_{c \in o_k} w(c,o_k) \times w(Align(c,o_l),o_l) \times sr(c,Align(c,o_l))}{\sum_{c \in o_k} w(c,o_k) \times w(Align(c,o_l),o_l)}$$

$$Align(c,o_l) = argmax_{c_i \in o_l} sr(c,c_i)$$

where o_l and o_k means the concept representation of the different entities, c denotes the concept in Wikipedia and $sr(c,c_i)$ can be computed by using Milne and Witten's method [467].

(3) Grouping name observations using hierarchical agglomerative clustering

Given the computed similarities, name observations are disambiguated by grouping them according to their represented entities by using clustering algorithms. In this process, the hierarchical agglomerative clustering (HAC) algorithm was widely used in prior disambiguation research and evaluation tasks (WePS1 and WePS2), because it does not need setting of a fixed number of clusters.

In addition to the studies mentioned above on clustering-based entity disambiguation in recent years, the increasing availability of large-scale, rich semantic knowledge sources (such as Wikipedia and WordNet) creates new opportunities to enhance the entity disambiguation by developing algorithms which can exploit these knowledge sources at best. The problem is that these knowledge sources are heterogeneous and most of the semantic knowledge within them is embedded in complex structures, such as graphs and networks. Therefore, researchers focused on computation of structural semantic relatedness (SSR), which can enhance the entity disambiguation by capturing and leveraging the structural semantic knowledge in multiple knowledge sources [266].

6.4.4   Entity-Linking Based Entity Disambiguation

Entity linking (EL) is to link a text mention of an entity to the referent entity in the knowledge base. Specifically, if the knowledge base does not contain the referent entity for the mention, the mention will be linked to NIL. Let $M = \{m_1, m_2, \ldots, m_k\}$ denote a collection of name mentions. Each name mention m in M is characterized by its name $m.S$, its local surrounding context $m.C$, and the document containing it $m.D$. Given a knowledge base KB containing a set of entities $\{e_1, e_2, \ldots, e_n\}$, the objective of EL is to determine the referent entities in KB of the name mentions in M. Specifically, we use $m.E$ to denote the referent entity of a mention m. For example,

Name Mentions: m_1 = *Bulls*, m_2 = *Jordan*, m_3 = *Space Jam*

Document: During his standout career at the Bulls, Jordan also acts in the movie Space Jam.

Knowledge Base: Wikipedia

Here, an EL system should identify the referent entities of the name mentions as $m1.E$=*"Chicago Bulls,"* $m2.E$=*"Michael Jordan,"* and $m3.E$=*"Space Jam."*

The entity linking task, however, is not trivial due to the name variation problem and the name ambiguity problem. Name variation means that an entity can be mentioned in different ways such as full name, aliases, acronyms, and misspellings. For example, the entity *Michael Jeffrey Jordan* can be mentioned using more than 10 names, such as *Michael Jordan*, *MJ*, *Jordan*, and so on. The name ambiguity problem is related to the fact that a name may refer to different entities in different contexts. For example, the name *Bulls* can refer to more than 20 entities in Wikipedia, such as the NBA team the *Chicago Bulls*, the football team the *Belfast Bulls*, and the cricket team the *Queensland Bulls*.

In recent years, much research has focused on the EL problem. Depending on how they model and exploit the interdependence between EL decisions, the existing EL work can be classified into the following two broad categories.

6.4.4.1   Independent Entity Linking

This kind of methods regarded the name mentions in the texts are isolated. Their algorithms often processed only one mentions once a time. Initial approaches mainly focused on the use of local compatibility based on some contextual features. The idea is to extract the discriminative features of an entity from its textual description, then link a name mention to the entity which has the highest contextual similarity with it. Mihalcea and Csomai [559] proposed a Bag-of-Words (BOWs) model based method, the compatibility between a name mention and an entity was the cosine similarity between them. Cucerzan [582], Bunescu and Pasca [103], and Fader et al. [1] extended the BOW model by incorporating more entity knowledge such as its categories. Zhang et al. [693] and Mihalcea and Csomai [559] computed the compatibility using classification algorithms. Zheng et al. [757], Dredze et al. [428], and Zhou et al. [738] employed learning-to-rank techniques, which can take into account the relative rank between the candidate entities. The main drawback of the local compatibility based approaches is that they do not take into account the interdependence between EL decisions.

Medelyan et al. [505] and Milne and Witten [468] have proposed to compute the mention-to-entity compatibility by leveraging the interdependence between EL decisions. The idea was that the referent entity of a name mention should be coherent with its unambiguous contextual entities. Medelyan et al. [505] determined the compatibility using the semantic relatedness between the candidate entity and the contextual entities, where the computation of semantic relatedness is based on the link structure in Wikipedia. Milne and Witten [468] extended the method of Medelyan et al. [505] by adopting learning-based techniques to balance the semantic relatedness, the commonness, and the context quality. In addition, Han and Zhao [265] proposed a framework including three factors which could be considered in EL decisions as follows.

The probability of a name mention m (its context is c and its name is s) referring to a specific entity e in a knowledge base can be expressed using the following formula (here s and c are assumed to be independent given e):

$$e = \arg\max_{e} P(m, e) = \arg\max_{e} P(s, c, e) = \arg\max_{e} P(e)P(s|e)P(c|e)$$

This model incorporates three types of entity knowledge: $P(e)$ corresponds to the popularity knowledge, $P(s|e)$ corresponds to the name knowledge, and $P(c|e)$ corresponds to the context knowledge.

$P(e)$ denotes the popularity of the entity. The idea behind this is that if an entity e_1 is more popular than another entity e_2, e_1 has higher probability to be linked to mention than e_2. We can use the occurrence frequency of the entity in Wikipedia to estimate this information as follows.

$$P(e) = \frac{Count(e) + 1}{|M| + N}$$

where $Count(e)$ is the count of the name mentions whose referent entity is e in Wikipedia, $|M|$ is the total name mention size, and N is the total entity number.

$P(s|e)$ encodes the name knowledge of entities, that is, for a specific entity e, its more frequently used name should be assigned a higher $P(s|e)$ value than the less frequently used name, and a zero $P(s|e)$ value should be assigned to those never used names. Intuitively, the name model can be estimated by first collecting all (entity, name) pairs from the name mention dataset, then using the maximum likelihood estimation:

$$P(s|e) = \frac{Count(s, e)}{\sum_s Count(s, e)}$$

where $Count(s, e)$ means that the count of the name mentions whose referent entity is e and name is s.

$P(c|e)$ encodes the context knowledge of entities, that is, it will assign a high $P(c|e)$ value if the entity e frequently appears in the context c, and will assign a low $P(c|e)$ value if the entity e rarely appears in the context c. The maximum likelihood estimation can be used to estimate this information, where semantic relatedness between entity and the contextual entities can be computed by using the link relationships between concepts in Wikipedia.

Nevertheless, the drawbacks of the approaches mentioned above are that they have a strong assumption that the contextual mentions are unambiguous and the EL decision is made independent. However, this assumption is usually limited in real documents and the contextual mentions are often ambiguous. Specifically, the entities in a topical coherent document are usually semantically related to each other [583]. For the example in the above section, the three entities contained in the document, the *NBA player Michael Jordan*, the *NBA team Chicago Bulls*, and the *Movie Space Jam* are all related to each other. In such a case, figuring out the referent entity of one name mention may in turn give us useful information to link other name mentions in the same document. For example, knowing the mention *"Bulls"* refers to the *NBA team Chicago Bulls* could help us link the mention *"Jordan"* to the *NBA player Michael Jordan* since only this candidate referent entity is semantically related to the *Chicago Bulls*. Similarly, knowing *"Jordan"* refers to the *NBA player Michael Jordan* could in turn help us figuring out the mention *"Bulls"* referring to the *NBA team Chicago Bulls*. Therefore, the entity linking performance could be improved by resolving the entity linking problems in the same document jointly, rather than independently. In this way, the collective entity linking is needed.

6.4.4.2 Collective Entity Linking

Collective entity linking is to exploit the interdependence between the different EL decisions within a document. There are two kinds of methods: (1) Pair-wise collective approaches and (2) Graph-based collective approaches.

- **Pair-Wise Collective Approaches**

Kulkarni et al. [583] proposed to resolve the collective EL as an optimization problem, where the interdependence between EL decisions is modeled as the sum of their pair-wise dependencies. Two approximation solutions were also proposed to resolve the NP-hard problem of their inference process. We can see that the interdependence between EL decisions can provide critical evidence for accurate EL decisions. But Kulkarni's method only modeled and exploited the pair-wise interdependence between EL decisions, and does not exploit the global interdependence, which is the main drawback of the pair-wise collective entity linking approaches. In detail, the limitations are as follows. First, the pair-wise interdependence model cannot exploit the global interdependence between EL decisions, that is, the structural properties of this interdependence. For instance, in the example mentioned above, the pair-wise dependence model cannot take into account the implicit dependency between the mention "Bulls" and the mention "Space Jam," since there is no direct relation between their referent entities Chicago Bulls and Space Jam. Second, by modeling the interdependence in the pair-wise fashion, the number of computation grows exponentially and the inference process is NP-hard, which makes the pair-wise model too time-consuming to the realworld applications. Recent pair-wise model based methods [583, 468, 505] usually resolved the inference problem using approximate algorithms, which mostly cannot make the purely collective inference. Recently, column generation techniques offer the possibility to model exact inference [62].

- **Graph-Based Collective Entity-Linking Model**

To overcome deficiencies of the traditional methods, a graph-based collective entity linking method was proposed by Han et al. [264], which can effectively and efficiently model and exploit the global (rather than the pair-wise) interdependence between different EL decisions. Specifically, Han et al. [264] first proposed a graph-based representation, called a Referent Graph, which can model the global interdependence between different EL decisions as its graph structure. Then a purely collective inference algorithm was proposed, which can jointly infer the referent entities of all name mentions in the same document by exploiting both the global interdependence between different EL decisions and the local mention-to-entity compatibility.

Constructing a Referent Graph

To capture both the local mention-to-entity compatibility and the global interdependence structure between different EL decisions, a Referent Graph is proposed. A referent graph is a weighted graph $G = (V, E)$, where the node set V contains all name mentions in a document and all the possible referent entities of these name mentions, with each node representing a name mention or an entity; each edge between a name mention and an entity represents a compatible relation between them; each edge between two entities represents a semantic related relation between them.

In this referent graph, the local dependency between a name mention and an entity is encoded as the edge between the nodes corresponding to them, with an edge weight indicates the strength of this dependency. For example, the dependency between (*Bulls*, *Chicago Bulls*) is represented with an edge between them. Notice here the dependency between name mention and entity is asymmetric: only the entity depends on the name mention, but the name mention does not depend on the entity.

By connecting candidate referent entities using the semantic related relation, the interdependence between EL decisions is encoded as the graph structure of the referent graph. In this way, the referent graph allows us to deduce and use indirect and implicit dependencies, and can take the structural properties of the interdependence into consideration. For example, the name mention *Bulls* is related to the entity *Chicago Bulls*, which in turn is related successively to the entity *Michael Jordan*. An indirect relation between *Bulls* and *Michael Jordan* could be established and used in the EL when necessary. Such indirect relations cannot be identified using an approach based on pair-wise dependence modeling.

Collective Entity-Linking Algorithm

With respect to the Referent Graph representation, the referent entity of a name mention m should be an entity node which has: (1) A strong compatible relation with the node corresponding to the name mention m; and (2) Many strong semantic related relations with the nodes corresponding to the other referent entities.

Observe that if we know that the referent entities of *Bulls* and *Space Jam* is *Chicago Bulls* and *Space Jam*, then the semantic related relation between (*Chicago Bulls, Michael Jordan*) and between (*Space Jam, Michael Jordan*) can provide more evidence for the entity *Michael Jordan* to be the referent entity of *Jordan*. In contrast, the entity *Michael B. Jordan* lacks the semantic related relations with *Chicago Bulls* and *Space Jam*, which suggests that it is not likely to be the referent entity of *Jordan*, even if it has a stronger compatible relation with the mention *Jordan*. But it seems that our method faces a "chicken-and-egg" problem: The referent entity of a name mention depends on the other referent entities in the same document, and in turn the other referent entities depend on the referent entity of this name mention itself. Han et al. [264] resolves such a problem by making a purely collective inference as the following steps.

(1) The initial evidence for an entity is collected to be the referent entity of a name mention.

(2) The evidence is simultaneously reinforced by propagating them between related EL decisions using the interdependence structure in Referent Graph. In detail, the author used random walk with restart algorithm to compute the probability of linking a mention to an entity.

(3) The final EL decisions is decided according to the highest probability based on the reinforced EL evidence.

6.4.5   Summary and Future Work

Entity ambiguity is an important problem not only for knowledge extraction, but also for understanding text semantics. In this section, we briefly introduce the task description of entity disambiguation and some typical methods. The previous methods can be divided into two classes: clustering-based methods and entity-linking based methods. However, we do not discuss the NIL entity problem of the entity disambiguation task, that is, the referent entity of a name mention may not be contained in the given knowledge base. The problem is also important and needs to be answered in future work.

6.5 Conclusion

This chapter presented an introduction about knowledge extraction from online contents, especially from UGC Web sites such as Wikipedia, blogs, and so on. We roughly illustrated three major tasks in knowledge extraction, including "Entity identification and expansion," "Relation extraction," and "Entity disambiguation." And we described several typical methods for extracting knowledge from UGC contents as well. We believe that the extracted knowledge from the Web can provide an opportunity for text understanding on the web, and increase the intelligence of the search engine. The key challenge is how to obtain the multiple knowledge with high accuracy. For UGC contents, exploiting heterogeneous Web information, including the structure of UGC Web sites, the links in texts, and tags provided by users, and so on. will be helpful to understand the meaning of texts. In the future, how to improve the extraction precision, avoid semantic drift, and obtain the semantics of relationships are still big challenges for knowledge extraction.

Chapter 7

User Generated Content Search

Roi Blanco

Yahoo! Research Barcelona

Manuel Eduardo Ares Brea

University of A Coruna

Christina Lioma

University of Copenhagen

7.1   Introduction

Due to developing technologies that are now readily available, user generated content (UGC) is growing rapidly and becoming one of the most prevalent and dynamic sources of information on the Web. Increasingly, more data appears online representing human judgment and interpretation about almost every aspect of the world: discussions, news, comments, and other forms of "socializing" on the Web. The increasing availability of such UGC from heterogeneous sources resembles a *terra incognita* of data and drives the need for advanced information retrieval (IR) technology that enables humans to search and retrieve it, navigate through it, and make sense of it. As such, UGC crosses paths with information retrieval (IR): it creates new IR scenarios, needs, and expectations.

This chapter presents (i) an overview of the main challenges and the respective state-of-the-art (Section 7.2), and (ii) a novel and effective approach for using UGC in IR (Section 7.3).

7.2   Overview of State-of-the-Art

Three representative types of UGC are: *blogs* (short texts), microblogs (short sentences or phrases), and *social tags* (keywords). Each of these poses different challenges to IR, and requires different solutions.

7.2.1   Blogs

Definition 19. A *blog* (Web log) is a discussion or informational Web site consisting of discrete entries (*posts*) typically displayed in reverse chronological order (the most recent post appears first). The collection of all blogs on the Web is referred to as *blogosphere*.   □

The emergence of blogs in the late 1990s coincided with the advent of Web publishing tools that facilitated the posting of content by nontechnical users. Previously, knowledge of such technologies as HTML and FTP had been required to publish content on the Web. As a result of this open publishing paradigm, today, the blogosphere is produced by millions of independent bloggers.

Retrieving information from the blogosphere is referred to as *blog distillation, blog search*, or *blog feed search* [434]. To facilitate research in this area, in 2006 the Text REtrieval Conference (TREC [687]) started a new track for blog retrieval [511]. This blog track has provided the infrastructure necessary for large-scale evaluation of blog retrieval methodologies: large test collections of blogs with corresponding information needs and relevance assessments.

The blog distillation task is defined as identifying blogs that show a central, recurring interest in a given topic. The task has two main characteristics: (i) the retrieval units are blogs rather than single posts; (ii) in order to be considered as relevant, a blog should not just mention the topic of the user query sporadically, but rather it must contain a significant number of posts concerning this topic. Additional difficulties are posed by these factors: (a) The topics of each post may change over time, hindering the estimation of topical relevance to the query. (b) Posts are time-stamped, so ideally a blog with more recent relevant posts should be ranked higher. (c) Blog posts can have viewer generated comments that can change the relevance of the blog to the query if these are considered as part of the content of the blog.

Different methods have been applied to address these challenges in blog retrieval. We give a brief survey of the state-of-the-art below, focusing on blog indexing (Section 7.2.1.1), ranking blog posts (Section 7.2.1.2), blog-specific features (Section 7.2.1.3), and document representation (Section 7.2.1.4). More extensive information on blog retrieval can be found in the 2012 survey of Santos et al. [589].

7.2.1.1 Blog Indexing

The information needs of users searching the blogosphere fall into two general categories: the need to find individual blog posts regarding a topic, or the need to identify blogs that frequently publish posts on a given topic [276]. These categories mirror the short term versus long term interest distinction observed by Mishne and de Rijke [476] in their study of blog search behavior. Analogously to this distinction, different blog retrieval approaches may use as indexing unit either (a) an entire blog or (b) a blog post. The former views a blog as a single document, disregarding the fact that a blog is constructed from multiple posts. The latter takes all or certain samples of posts from blogs and combines their information to produce a single blog score.

When treating each blog as one long document created by the concatenation of all its posts, standard ad-hoc search methods can be used to find relevant blogs to a specific topic. For instance, Efron et al. take this approach and, given a query, they derive a score for each blog in the corpus using the negative KL-divergence between the query language model and the language model of a blog as a whole [194]. Elsas et al. [201] report an interesting comparison of the two approaches: they experiment with a *large document model* in which entire blogs are the indexing units, and a *small document model* in which evidence of relevance of a blog is harvested from individual blog posts. They also experiment with combining the two models, obtaining the best performance [31].

Currently, both approaches are in use; however, Weerkamp reports that the option of concatenating all blog posts is considered practically unrealistic by most researchers [707].

7.2.1.2   Ranking Blog Posts

Most approaches rank blogs by making a decision on the relevance scores of all or some of the posts associated with each blog. Different approaches have been proposed.

One idea is to consider blog search as a voting process. A blogger with an interest in a topic is likely to blog regularly about the topic; hence, these blog posts will be retrieved in response to a query topic. Each time a blog post is retrieved in response to a query topic, that can be seen as a weighted vote for that blog to have an interest in the query topic. Then these votes can be combined using data fusion to compute the final relevance score of each blog. This idea has been implemented in a family of voting models [269, 432, 433], which aggregate the relevance score of posts for each blog. These voting models are ported from the area of expert search[1] and effectively treat blogs as the equivalent of experts.

An alternative approach is inspired by the idea that a few posts that are highly relevant to a given topic may sufficiently represent the blog relevance [394]. This approach deals with blog distillation as a resource selection problem, and is mainly inspired by resource selection in distributed information retrieval. Distributed information retrieval uses server selection algorithms to avoid the expensive process of searching all servers for each query [275]. Queries are sent to servers that have more relevant documents to the query. Several studies have ported this idea to blog search by modeling each blog as a collection of posts and then selecting or sampling the best posts [31, 201]. This approach of sampling a few relevant posts is reported to outperform using all the posts in the blog [202, 334, 335, 707]. An interesting proposal in this area is the work of Seo and Croft [617], called *Pseudo Cluster Selection*, where they create topic-based clusters of posts in each blog and select blogs which have the most similar clusters to the query. Also inspired by resource selection approaches, Seo and Croft use diversity penalties: blogs with a diverse set of posts receive a penalty.

7.2.1.3   Blog-Specific Features

In addition to standard term frequency statistics, a number of other blog-specific features, like user comments and recency, have been explored for blog retrieval [475, 709], either during reranking, or in the first retrieval stage [707, 708]. For instance, Gao et al. [229] explored both heuristic features (e.g.,

---

[1]*Expert Search* is a task in the TREC Enterprise Track, where systems are asked to rank candidate experts with respect to their predicted expertise about a query, using documentary evidence of the expertise found in the collection [638].

Average Permalink, Sentence Length, Comment Number, Organization Numbers, Opinion Rule, etc.) and lexicon-extracted features such as Cyber Words and Cyber Emoticons (using the SentiWordNet and Wilson Lexicon). Elsas et al. have also used an external resource, namely the Wikipedia, to perform query expansion on blogs [200]. Other approaches include using topic maps [393], or random walks to model connections between blogs, posts, and terms [333].

An interesting feature of blogs is their time aspect. Keikha et al. [337] propose a method that uses time-dependent representations of queries and blogs to measure the recurring interest of blogs. In a separate study, they also successfully use the time interval between blog posts when investigating the effect of content-based similarity between posts [336]. Seki et al. also try to capture the recurrence patterns of a blog using the notion of time and relevance [615], while Nunes et al. use temporal span and temporal dispersion as two measures of relevance over time [504].

Topical cohesion is also another feature that has received attention in blog search. The voting model of Hannah et al. [269] incorporated *cohesiveness*, defined as how different each post is from the blog as a whole on average. He et al. [276] proposed a coherence score which captures the topical clustering structure of a set of documents as compared to a background collection. Applied to blogs, this coherence score was found to reflect topical consistency successfully.

7.2.1.4 Blog Representations

Blog posts can be represented in different ways. Different approaches use syndicated content (i.e., RSS or ATOM feeds) instead of permalinks (HTML content) [200, 201, 475]; Macdonald et al. [434] examine whether indexing only the XML feed provided by each blog (and which is often incomplete) is sufficient, or whether the full-text of each blog post should be downloaded. Results of which representation works better are mixed. Other ways of representing documents are, for example, a title-only representation, or an (incoming) anchor text representation. Weerkamp [707] shows that considering multiple content representations can improve blog search.

7.2.2 Microblogs

Definition 20. A *microblog* is a stream of text that is written by an author over time. It comprises many very brief updates that are presented to the microblog's readers in reverse-chronological order. $\square$

Microblog services let users broadcast brief textual messages online. Twitter is a popular microblogging service that enables its users to send and read text-based messages of up to 140 characters, known as *tweets*. Although microblogging is increasingly popular, methods for organizing and searching microblog data are still relatively new.

Effectively searching microblogs poses a number of issues for traditional retrieval approaches, such as ill-formed language,[2] limited document term statistics and spam [214]. The best performing microblog retrieval techniques attempt to utilize both semantic and temporal aspects of documents.

To facilitate research in this area, in 2011 the Text REtrieval Conference (TREC [687]) started a new track for microblog retrieval.[3] This track aims to provide the infrastructure necessary for the large-scale evaluation of microblog retrieval methodologies: A test collection of microblogs from Twitter with corresponding information needs and relevance assessments.

Different methods have been applied to address challenges in microblog retrieval. We give a brief survey below, focusing on query expansion (Section 7.2.2.1), readily available microblog search engines (Section 7.2.2.2), and microblogs as aids to standard search (Section 7.2.2.3). A more extensive review of microblog search can be found [192]. See Abel et al. [5] for more on faceted search for microblogs.

7.2.2.1   Microblog Expansion

Several studies have investigated pseudo relevance feedback for microblogs, either using standard textual features (for instance, [191, 447]), or enhanced with temporal information (for instance, [715]). The temporal element of microblogs has also been researched independently of pseudo relevance feedback. For instance, Jabeur et al. [312] propose a Bayesian network retrieval model that interprets tweet relevance as a conditional probability and estimates it using text similarity measures, the microblogger's influence, the time magnitude, and the presence of hashtags. In another interesting study, Metzler et al. [459] focus on microblog search of past events over microblog archives. Rather than retrieving individual microblog messages in response to an event query, they propose retrieving a ranked list of historical event summaries by distilling high quality event representations using a novel temporal query expansion technique. Specifically, their method takes a query as input and returns a ranked list of structured event representations. This is accomplished in two steps, timespan retrieval and summarization. The timespan retrieval step identifies the timespans when the event happened, while the summarization step retrieves a small set of microblog messages for each timespan that are meant to act as a summary.

Instead of query expansion, Efron et al. [193] propose a document expansion model for microblogs that models not only lexical properties, but also temporal properties of documents. Finally, Liang et al. [403] present an approach that models for the query and the document and combine it with temporal reranking.

---

[2]http://engineering.twitter.com/2012/05/related-queries-and-spelling.html
[3]https://sites.google.com/site/microblogtrack/

7.2.2.2 Microblog Search Engines

Even though microblog search is not one of the oldest UGC search tasks, there already exist several out-of-the-box engines, tailored to this type of content. For instance, QuickView [415] is a microblog search platform, which includes Natural Language Processing (NLP) functionalities, such as tweet normalization, named entity recognition, semantic role labeling, sentiment analysis, tweet classification, and so on. It also includes several interface options (such as clustering search results) to facilitate the display and interaction of the user with the information retrieved.

Another example is Twinder [662], which implements features such as topic-tweet semantic relatedness, as well as syntactic, semantic, sentiment, and contextual properties of the microblogs. The team behind Twinder has also created Twitcident [7], a framework for filtering, searching, and analyzing microblog information about real-world incidents or crises. This framework is currently used with data from emergency broadcasting services in the Netherlands, however, the technology powering it can be ported to other languages.

The actual search engine powering Twitter's own search is Early bird [111]. In this paper, Busch et al. describe its indexing structure and operations, pointing to the important challenge of dynamically ingesting content and making it searchable immediately, while also concurrently supporting low-latency, high-throughput query evaluation. Related to this issue of efficiently indexing real-time microblogs is the work of Bahmani and Goel [42], who present a partitioned multi-indexing scheme for efficient microblog indexing.

7.2.2.3 Microblogs as Aids to Standard Searches

In addition to searching among microblogs, the content of microblogs can also be used to facilitate standard document search. Shuai et al. [630] present an approach that uses information from tweets to rerank news search. They propose a Community Tweets Voting Model (CTVM) that effectively re-ranks Google and Yahoo! news search results on the basis of open, large-scale Twitter community data.

A different approach is proposed by Rowlands et al. [578]. The authors present a Web search system based on hyperlinks retrieved from microblogs. When a Twitter message contains a URL, they use the Twitter message as a description of the URL's target, that is, as an additional form of annotation. Their method is shown to be effective in improving overall retrieval performance.

7.2.3 Social Tags

Definition 21. A *social tag* is a nonhierarchical keyword or term assigned to a piece of information (such as an Internet bookmark or digital image). This kind of metadata helps describe an item and allows it to be found again by browsing or searching. Tags are generally chosen informally and personally by the item's creator or viewer.   □

Early forms of collaborative tagging can be traced back to medieval times, when manuscripts were annotated before being passed down to generations in a "cumulative scholarship" process [313]. That type of annotation was considered complementary to the scholarly value of the manuscripts and hence was thought to augment the value of the manuscripts. Similar to that, the type of collaborative tagging found on the Web today can also be seen as a kind of hypermedia augmentation [89]. Furthermore, the notion of annotating the Web is not new: in NCSA Mosaic, one of the earliest browsers, Web pages could be privately tagged with tags being stored on the user's machine [89]. Independently to NCSA Mosaic, the idea of asking users to tag text freely was initially developed by Hidderley and Rafferty [284], who aimed to index particularly subjective forms of information where full-text searching was failing, such as multimedia or fiction objects. Hidderley and Rafferty developed the idea of aggregating users' indexing terms to create a generalized overall view of the resources, which today has been adapted by working collaborative tagging systems. The plethora of current collaborative tagging systems cover different domains (e.g., CiteULike, Connotea[4]) and media (e.g., YouTube, Last.fm[5]) as well as different applications (e.g., integrated into enterprise search like ConnectBeam or recommender systems like Amazon[6]).

The field of IR has also shown interest in collaborative tagging from 2006 onward [476]. Several commercial IR systems now include recommendation functionalities based on user tags, for example, Amazon uses tags to suggest relevant products to online buyers. In addition, studies investigate analogies between users-products in recommender systems and queries-documents in IR systems [474, 695]. We provide a brief overview of the uses of social tags for IR, focusing on (i) social tags as aids to text search (Section 7.2.3.1), and (ii) social tags as aids to image search (Section 7.2.3.2).

7.2.3.1   Social Tags for Text Search

The motivation behind using social tags for textual IR is to try and induce the extra information (user perspective, opinion, assessment) represented in it as a potentially valuable source of information about the relevance between a query and a document. For instance, Bao et al. [48] proposed optimizing Web IR with tags in two ways. First, they used tags as an indicator of Web page popularity, and second, they computed the similarity between tags and queries. They incorporated both types of information into document ranking in two variants of PageRank called SocialPageRank (SPR), and SocialSimRank (SSR), respectively. They reported significant improvements in

---

[4]http://www.citeulike.com, http://www.connotea.org
[5]http://www.youtube.com, http://www.lastfm.com
[6]http://www.connectbeam.com, http://www.amazon.com

performance, using real-world datasets (50 manual queries and 3000 automatically generated queries on a dataset crawled from Delicious).

A different approach was proposed by Zhou et al. [774]. They used tags to enhance document ranking in Web IR as follows: topics are modelled in documents and also in tags, and then the information of the tag topics is incorporated into retrieval as a Bayesian Inference Network. Significant improvements in retrieval performance are shown over traditional approaches.

Jin et al. [321] proposed a query expansion technique that uses social tags to expand queries. They fetch and filter social tags from Delicious, and then compute their similarity to the query terms before using them for query expansion.

Finally, Carman et al. [118] investigated the use of tag data for evaluating personalized retrieval systems involving thousands of users. Using data from the social bookmarking site Delicious, they effectively rated the quality of personalized retrieval results. They also reported that user profiles based on the content of bookmarked URLs are generally superior to those based on tags alone.

7.2.3.2 Social Tags for Image Search

For similar motivations to above, social tags have also been used to enhance the effectiveness of image search. These approaches are, however, also driven by the general sparsity of textual annotations among the most image collections.

Van Zwol et al. [685] used social tags for improving large-scale image retrieval on the Web. They propose a query model that is estimated from the distribution of social tags, so that the dominant sense of the query is enhanced. They find that social tags are particularly useful in the case of ambiguous queries.

Pedro et al. (2012) [529] proposed another approach for exploiting the similarity between the query and the social tag metadata of images. They used social tags to infer an aesthetic rating for the images, which can enhance overall retrieval performance. A user study involving 58 participants has confirmed the effectiveness of social tags as an aesthetic predictor for images.

7.3 Social Tags for Query Expansion

The previous sections reviewed the main challenges and the respective state-of-the-art in UGC retrieval. Next, we present a novel approach for using UGC to assist standard search in the form of query expansion. This method differs from the approach of Jin et al. [321] on several points, which are detailed in Section 7.3.2. Section 7.3.1 describes our model, and Section 7.3.2 presents and discusses the experimental evaluation.

7.3.1   Problem Formulation

We now introduce a model for expanding queries with salient social tags. The aim is to approximate the informative salience of τ. We posit that the more informative a social tag τ is, the more useful it may be as a query expansion term when estimating the relevance of a document d to a query q.

We estimate tag salience using three different robust term weighting schemes: (i) an adaptation of the Inverse Document Frequency (*idf*) scheme; (ii) an adaptation of the Term Frequency-Inverse Document Frequency (*tf-idf*) scheme; and an adaptation of the probabilistic Bose 1 (Bo1) scheme from the Divergence from Randomness (DFR) framework [24]. Each of these weighting schemes computes a tag weight $w(\tau)$, which represents the estimated significance of the tag.

Using *idf*, $w(\tau)$ is computed as follows:

$$w(\tau) = \log_2 \frac{N}{n_\tau} \tag{7.1}$$

where N is the number of documents in the collection and n_τ is the number of documents that contain τ.

We extend Equation 7.1 to compute a *tf-idf* variation of tag significance as follows:

$$w(\tau) = \tau f_x \cdot \log_2 \frac{N}{n_\tau} \tag{7.2}$$

where τf_x is the tag frequency in the top x (pseudo relevant set of) documents.

We use Bo1 to estimate the divergence of the tag occurrence in the pseudo relevant set of documents from a random distribution of documents. Bo1 is based on Bose-Einstein statistics, and has been shown to be similar to Rocchio [574]. Using Bo1 we estimate the weight of a tag $w(\tau)$ as:

$$w(\tau) = \tau f_x \cdot \log_2 \frac{1 + P_n}{P_n} + \log_2(1 + P_n) \tag{7.3}$$

where $P_n = \frac{F}{N}$ where F is the frequency of the tag in the collection. Equation 7.3 is the same as Amati's original Bo1 formula with the sole difference that, in the original, he used tf_x (term frequency in the top x retrieved documents), whereas we use τf_x (tag frequency in the top x retrieved documents). The complete derivation of the Bo1 formula, going back to first principles, is presented by Amati [24].

Next, we present how we use the tag weights computed with Equations 7.2–7.3 for query expansion. First, we give the general ranking formula:

$$R(d, q) = \sum_{t \in q} w(t, d) \cdot w(t, q) \tag{7.4}$$

where $R(d, q)$ is the approximation of the relevance between the document and the query, t is a term in q, $w(t, d)$ is the weight of term t for a document

d, and w(t, q) is the query term weight. w(t, d) can be computed by different weighting models in different ways, for instance, using BM25 [573]. w(t, q) can be computed as: w$(t, q) = \frac{\text{qtf}(t,q)}{qtf_{max}}$, where qtf$(t, q)$ (qtf_{max}) is the term frequency (maximum term frequency) in the query. Very often, especially in short queries, qtf(t, q) will be equal to qtf_{max}, and hence w$(t, q) = 1$.

We integrate the tag weights into the estimation of w(t, q) as follows:

$$w(t, q) = \alpha \cdot \frac{\text{qtf}(t, q)}{qtf_{max}} + (1 - \alpha) \cdot \frac{w(\tau)}{w_{max}(\tau)} \tag{7.5}$$

where w(τ) is the tag weight computed with Equations 7.1 to 7.3, $w_{max}(\tau)$ denotes the maximum among w(τ), and α is a smoothing parameter ($0 < \alpha \leq 1$) to control the balance between the old and the new weights.

Equation 7.5 expands queries only with social tags. In order to expand queries with both social tags and also traditional expansion terms, we use:

$$w(t, q) = \alpha \cdot \frac{\text{qtf}(t, q)}{qtf_{max}} + (1 - \alpha) \cdot \frac{w(\tau)}{w_{max}(\tau)} + \frac{w(t)}{w_{max}(t)} \tag{7.6}$$

where w(t) is the new weight of a term in the expanded query, and $w_{max}(t)$ is the maximum w(t) of the expanded query terms. If the expanded term was not in the original query, then qtf$(t, q) = 0$. Note that the term-PRF terms and weights are obtained using the original query q and not the query expanded with tag-PRF.

7.3.1.1 Jin's Method

In Jin et al. [321], they propose a query expansion approach which uses collaborative tags, which we have used as a baseline in this chapter.

Given a query q to expand composed by k query terms $q_1, q_2, ...q_k$ the first step of their method is querying the collaborative online tagging system (Delicious in this case) with each of the individual terms, obtaining k results sets (lists of tagged documents r) $L_1, L_2, ...L_k$. After cleaning the obtained tags by manually removing ill-formed tags and splitting ill-formed compound-tags with the help of a dictionary, they calculate a score for each remaining tag t in any of the L_k in order to determine which tags will be used in query expansion. This score is calculated as:

$$\text{score}(t, q|C) = \sum_{q_j \in q} \text{idf}(q_j, C) \ \text{idf}(t, C) \ \log(\text{codegree}(t, q_j|L_j) + 1) \tag{7.7}$$

where idf(q_j, C) and idf(t, C) respectively measure the uncommonness of the query term q_j and the tag t in C, the union of all the L, and are calculated as:

$$\text{idf}(\alpha, C) = \log \frac{|C|}{\text{df}(\alpha, C) + 1} \tag{7.8}$$

and being codegree($t, q_j | L_j$) a measure of the relation between t and q_j, calculated as:

$$\text{codegree}(t, q_j | L_j) = \frac{\sum_{r \in L_j} (\log(\text{tf}(t, r) + 1) \ \log(\text{tf}(q_j, r) + 1))}{|L_j|} \qquad (7.9)$$

Once the scores have been calculated the t_{Jin} tags with the highest score are used to expand the original query q creating a new query q'. The weight of each of the terms of this expanded query (composed by the selected tags as well as the original terms of q) is calculated as:

$$\text{w}(q'_m, q') = \alpha \cdot \text{w}(q'_m, q) + (1 - \alpha) \cdot \frac{\text{score}(q'_m, q | C)}{score_{max}} \qquad (7.10)$$

where $score_{max}$ is the maximum score and $\alpha \in [0, 1]$ is a parameter which controls the balance between the original and the expanded weights.

Using this approach, Jin et. al. [299] have reported consistent gains in MAP and P@10 on TREC 2008 feedback data (264 queries) over the nonexpanded queries, although they do not compare against any other query expansion approaches.

Methodology

1. Given a query q and an expansion collection C_{tag}, we retrieve a ranked list of tagged documents L_{tag} in response to the whole query q. C_{tag} is an online dynamic collection of collaboratively tagged documents, for which we have no prior knowledge of relevant or nonrelevant documents to our query. We have no knowledge of the statistics of that collection either. Retrieval takes place online using a freely available IR system that supports collaborative tagging, which we cannot modify, but only use as a black-box. Furthermore, we disregard any knowledge of the ranking function of that system.

2. We collect the t_{tag} tags, which appear in more documents in L_{tag}. The tags collected in this way for a query are denoted T_L.

3. We expand the initial query q with the tags in T_L associated to q, and we weight these tags according to their significance.

4. The expanded query is used to retrieve a new ranked list of documents L' from a retrieval collection C. C is a static collection (e.g., TREC collection) for which we have prior knowledge of relevant and nonrelevant documents to a given query in order to perform evaluation. Retrieval takes place offline using a ranking function that we can modify.

7.3.2 Experimental Evaluation

7.3.2.1 Methodology and Settings

Tag selection. We collect social tags from Delicious and YouTube, two popular online systems where users collaboratively tag resources, respectively, Web-links and videos.

Note that, even though we use Delicious and YouTube as black-boxes in order to collect tags, tags are then processed and weighted according to the method used for tag-PRF.

Hence, both methods do not use the tags for expanding a query straight out of the black-box, but they compute their significance and use them accordingly. It should be noted also that the process used to gather the tags is different in each case, as each method proposes a different treatment of the original query in order to query the online systems. In our case, and because we collect tags from online black-box systems, the collection statistics are not publicly available to count statistics of tags over Web pages (certain collaborative tagging systems, such as Delicious, provide the most popular URLs and tags only). Hence, we measure the collection statistics of the retrieval collection instead of the tagged collection. This is supported by studies showing that there are similarities in the vocabulary used for tagging and for searching content on the Web [119].

Datasets. We use three standard TREC collections of different domain, size, and timeframe, namely *Los Angeles Times* (LAT) (475MB), WT2G (2GB), and BLOG06 (25GB). LAT represents a sampling of approximately 40% of the articles published by the *Los Angeles Times* during 1989–1990, hence it is assumed to be fairly homogeneous. WT2G contains text crawled from the Web in 1997. BLOG06 is a blog crawl of 753,681 feeds, and associated permalink and homepage documents, resulting in approximately 3 million documents from late 2005 and early 2006.

WT2G and BLOG06 are representative of everyday language found on the Web, which is itself a heterogeneous source. Overall, the three collections belong to different domains (journalistic, everyday Web, blog). The size of the collections also differs significantly (475 MB–25 GB).

For each collection, we use its associated set of queries, shown in Table 7.1. We experiment with short queries (title portion) only, because they are more representative of real user queries on the Web [512].

These datasets have been used in three different TREC retrieval scenarios, namely ad-hoc search (LAT), Web search (WT2G), and blog search (BLOG06). By using them, we aim to test the applicability of our technique in these scenarios.

Retrieval settings. For retrieval we use the Terrier IR system [510]. We match documents to queries with an established and widely-used model, Best Match 25 (BM25) [573]. BM25 computes the relevance of a document d to a

TABLE 7.1:   Characteristics of the Four TREC Datasets Used
(These characteristics vary across collections.)

Collection	LA Times	WT2G	BLOG06
Queries	401–450	401–450	901–950
Size	475 MB	2 GB	25 GB
Documents	131,896	247,491	3,215,171
Terms	189,545	1,002,586	4,968,020
Task	Ad-hoc news	Ad-hoc Web	Blog IR
Year	1989–1990	1997	2005–2006

query q as:

$$R(d,q) = \sum_{t \in q} \log \left(\frac{N - n + 0.5}{n + 0.5} \right) \cdot \frac{(k_3 + 1) \cdot \text{qtf}(t,q)}{k_3 + \text{qtf}(t,q)} \cdot \text{tfn}(t,d) \qquad (7.11)$$

where k_3 is a parameter, $\text{qtf}(t,q)$ is the query term frequency, N is the number of all documents in the collection, n is the number of documents containing term t, and $\text{tfn}(t,d)$ is the normalized term frequency in a document, given by:

$$\text{tfn}(t,d) = \frac{(k_1 + 1) \cdot \text{tf}(t,d)}{\text{tf}(t,d) + k_1 \cdot (1 - b + b \cdot \frac{l}{l_{avg}})} \qquad (7.12)$$

where k_1 and b are parameters, $\text{tf}(t,d)$ is the term frequency in the document, and l (l_{avg}) is the document length (average document length in the collection).

For weighting the expanded query terms in the second pass retrieval, we use the following models:

For standard term-PRF, we use the original Bo1 formula [24]:

$$w(t) = tf_x \cdot \log_2 \frac{1 + P_n}{P_n} + \log_2(1 + P_n) \qquad (7.13)$$

where $w(t)$ is the term weight to be computed, tf_x is the term frequency in the top x documents used for PRF, and $P_n = \frac{F}{N}$, where F is the term frequency in the collection, and N is the number of documents in the collection.

For tag-PRF, we use Jin et al.'s [299] method and the method proposed in this paper. In the former, the weighting method is summarized in Section 7.3.1.1, Equations 7.7–7.10, whereas in the latter the IDF, *tf-idf*, and Bo1 extensions proposed in Section 7.3.1, Equations 7.1–7.3, respectively, are used.

Evaluation measures. We evaluate retrieval performance using Mean Average Precision (MAP) and Precision at 10 (P@10).

7.3.2.2   Parameter Tuning

Our experiments will vary with the following parameters:

- BM25 (Equation 7.11) includes k_1 and k_3, which have little effect on retrieval, and b, which normalizes the relevance score of a document for a query across document lengths [573].

- Term-PRF includes t_x, which is the number of terms used for PRF, and d_x, which is the number of top-retrieved documents used for PRF.

- Jin et al.'s [299] PRF includes two parameters, t_{Jin}, the number of terms using for PRF, and α, which controls the balance between the original and the expanded weights.

- Tag-PRF includes the same two parameters, t_{tag}, the number of terms using for PRF, and α, which controls the balance between the original and the expanded weights.

Note how the three PRF methods used in the experiments have all two parameters in order to keep the comparison between them as fair as possible. For instance, we have chosen not to also tune the amount of documents used in the case of the Tag-PRF approaches, using directly the ones returned by each query to Delicious or YouTube instead. For each method the values of its two parameters are estimated heuristically by tuning in order to select the optimal values to use for PRF. This kind of heuristic tuning is standard in the area [24].

We perform experiments with tuned and cross-validated parameters separately.

Tuned. We tune parameters so as to optimize MAP on the basis of the corresponding relevance assessments available for the queries and collections employed as follows.

- For BM25, we vary b between 0-1, in 10 intervals of 0.1. We do not tune k_1 or k_3 because they have little effect on retrieval performance.

- For term-PRF with Bo1, we vary $t_x \in \{1, 2, ...50\}$, and $d_x \in \{1, 2, ...10\}$.

- For Jin et al.'s [299] PRF, we vary $t_{\mathrm{Jin}} \in \{1, 2, ...50\}$ and $\alpha \in \{0.1, 0.2, ...0.9\}$

- For our tag-PRF, we vary $t_{tag} \in \{1, 2, ...50\}$ and $\alpha \in \{0.1, 0.2, ...0.9\}$

In the cases involving PRF, the parameters were tuned using Coordinate Ascent [458], a technique which iteratively solves alternatively one-dimensional searches in each parameter until convergence. For example, let us take the example of optimizing term-PRF. Starting from certain initial values for BM25's b and term-PRF's t_x and d_x, Coordinate Ascent proceeds by first testing all possible values of b, obtaining and saving the one which yields the best performance (in our case the best MAP). Afterward, all the possible values of t_x are tested for that value of b and the initial value of d_x, saving the one providing the best MAP. Then, all the possible values of d_x are tested using the saved values of b and t_x. This value is saved and the process starts again, this time with the saved values.

When using both term-PRF and tag-PRF (the second experiment) only b is tuned; the parameters of the two PRF methods are the ones obtained by

TABLE 7.2: No PRF versus with Term-PRF versus Tag-PRF (Performance shown in MAP with tuned and cross-validated settings, using tags from Delicious (Del) and YouTube (Yt).)

LAT

	no PRF	term-PRF		Jin et al. [299] tag-PRF	tag-PRF Idf	*tf-idf*	Bo1
Tuned	0.2566	**0.3033**	Del	0.2678	0.2613	0.2572	0.2572
			Yt	0.2598	0.2809	0.2720	0.2718
Crossval	0.2462	**0.2912**	Del	0.2525	0.2539	0.2477	0.2476
			Yt	0.2554	0.2748	0.2695	0.2643

WT2G

	no PRF	term-PRF		Jin et al. [299] tag-PRF	tag-PRF Idf	*tf-idf*	Bo1
Tuned	0.3167	**0.3427**	Del	0.3233	0.3239	0.3225	0.3228
			Yt	0.3213	0.3413	0.3414	0.3400
Crossval	0.3167	0.3266	Del	0.3210	0.3222	0.3197	0.3180
			Yt	0.3185	0.3348	**0.3384**	0.3366

BLOG06

	no PRF	term-PRF		Jin et al. [299] tag-PRF	tag-PRF Idf	*tf-idf*	Bo1
Tuned	0.3487	0.3601	Del	0.3516	0.3490	0.3490	0.3487
			Yt	0.3588	0.3722	**0.3760**	0.3754
Crossval	0.3487	0.3337	Del	0.3500	0.3489	0.3450	0.3460
			Yt	0.3577	0.3625	**0.3723**	0.3662

tuning each of them on their own for experiment 1. For instance, the "Tuned" value of term-PRF + Jin et al.'s [299] PRF is obtained using t_x, and d_x is obtained when tuning term-PRF alone and t_{Jin}, and α is obtained when tuning Jin et al.'s method alone.

Cross-validation. The cross-validated performance values were obtained by using the values of the parameters tuned in the corresponding collection. The cross-validated values for collection LAT and BLOG06 are those tuned in WT2G, whereas the ones used in WT2G are the parameters cross-validated in BLOG06. Hence, the reported cross-validated MAP and P@10 values for term-PRF in BLOG06 use the b, t_x, and d_x parameters tuned for term-PRF in WT2G.

TABLE 7.3: No PRF versus with Term-PRF versus Tag-PRF (Performance shown in P@10 with tuned and cross-validated settings (for MAP), using tags from Delicious (Del) and YouTube (Yt).)

LAT

	no PRF	term-PRF		Jin et al. [299] tag-PRF	tag-PRF Idf	tf-idf	Bo1
Tuned	0.2844	**0.3067**	Del	0.2956	0.2956	0.2911	0.2889
			Yt	0.2844	0.2956	**0.3067**	0.2844
Crossval	0.2822	0.2956	Del	0.2800	0.2800	0.2800	0.2800
			Yt	0.2800	**0.3044**	0.2889	0.3067

WT2G

	no PRF	term-PRF		Jin et al. [299] tag-PRF	tag-PRF Idf	tf-idf	Bo1
Tuned	0.4660	0.5000	Del	0.4740	0.4860	0.4740	0.4760
			Yt	0.4780	**0.5040**	0.5000	0.5000
Crossval	0.4660	0.4960	Del	0.4720	0.4860	0.4680	0.4700
			Yt	0.4740	**0.5100**	0.5060	0.4980

BLOG06

	no PRF	term-PRF		Jin et al. [299] tag-PRF	tag-PRF Idf	tf-idf	Bo1
Tuned	0.6220	0.6320	Del	0.6340	0.6200	0.6200	0.6160
			Yt	0.6500	**0.6760**	0.6520	0.6720
Crossval	0.6220	0.5880	Del	0.6320	0.6240	0.6180	0.6160
			Yt	**0.6580**	0.6560	0.6500	0.6360

7.3.2.3 Findings and Discussion

We now highlight the main outcome of the experiments. First, we discuss how the proposed method measure up with existing approaches, comparing the performance of pseudo relevance feedback using terms, using social tags with that of the baseline method without expansion.

Table 7.2 (MAP) and Table 7.3 (P@10) report on the results of the two flavors of pseudo relevance feedback and the baseline methods alone. The method that uses social tags (*tag-PRF*) is able to improve consistently the No-PRF baseline method, being the differences more remarkable when tags are retrieved from the YouTube service. This might be due to the fact that this service has a higher number of tags, which in turn results in higher quality tags.

TABLE 7.4: Best single PRF versus Term-PRF + Tag-PRF (Performance shown in MAP with tuned and cross-validated settings, using tags from Delicious (Del) and YouTube (Yt).)

LAT

		best single PRF	Jin et al. [299] tag-PRF	term-PRF + tag-PRF		
				Idf	*tf-idf*	Bo1
Delicious	Tuned	0.3033	0.3068	**0.3080**	0.3073	0.3070
	Crossval	**0.2912**	0.2792	0.2824	0.2750	0.2752
YouTube	Tuned	0.3033	0.3042	**0.3163**	0.3134	0.3132
	Crossval	**0.2912**	0.2835	0.2885	0.2843	0.2859

WT2G

		best single PRF	Jin et al. [299] tag-PRF	term-PRF + tag-PRF		
				Idf	*tf-idf*	Bo1
Delicious	Tuned	0.3427	0.3439	**0.3453**	0.3452	0.3439
	Crossval	0.3266	**0.3273**	0.3245	0.3264	0.3259
YouTube	Tuned	0.3427	0.3450	0.3501	**0.3506**	0.3500
	Crossval	0.3266	0.3245	0.3342	**0.3367**	0.3362

BLOG06

		best single PRF	Jin et al. [299] tag-PRF	term-PRF + tag-PRF		
				Idf	*tf-idf*	Bo1
Delicious	Tuned	0.3601	**0.3614**	0.3581	0.3596	0.3596
	Crossval	0.3337	**0.3400**	0.3385	0.3369	0.3381
YouTube	Tuned	**0.3760**	0.3645	0.3671	0.3676	0.3670
	Crossval	**0.3723**	0.3434	0.3368	0.3431	0.3425

When comparing the two social-tag expansion methods, Jin et al.'s has a slight advantage in some of the runs on the Delicious collection, but underperforms when using the larger collection to retrieve tags (YouTube). In any case, *tag-PRF* provides the best overall results on both collections. The comparison with respect to term-PRF is somewhat mixed, being the numbers of WT2G and BLOG06 comparable. However, on the LATimes collection, term-PRF

TABLE 7.5: Best single PRF versus Term-PRF + Tag-PRF (Performance shown in P@10 with tuned and cross-validated settings (for MAP), using tags from Delicious (Del) and YouTube (Yt).)

LAT

		best single PRF	Jin et al. [299] tag-PRF	term-PRF + tag-PRF Idf	tf-idf	Bo1
Delicious	Tuned	0.3067	**0.3156**	0.3111	0.3133	0.3111
	Crossval	0.2956	**0.3067**	0.2867	0.3000	0.3000
YouTube	Tuned	0.3067	0.3133	**0.3200**	**0.3200**	**0.3200**
	Crossval	0.2956	0.2889	0.2956	0.3022	**0.3067**

WT2G

		best single PRF	Jin et al. [299] tag-PRF	term-PRF + tag-PRF Idf	tf-idf	Bo1
Delicious	Tuned	**0.5000**	0.4940	0.4860	0.4940	0.4920
	Crossval	0.4960	**0.5040**	0.4920	0.4940	0.4940
YouTube	Tuned	0.5000	0.4980	**0.5060**	0.4960	0.4960
	Crossval	0.4960	0.5000	**0.5260**	0.5140	0.5180

BLOG06

		best single PRF	Jin et al. [299] tag-PRF	term-PRF + tag-PRF Idf	tf-idf	Bo1
Delicious	Tuned	0.6320	**0.6460**	0.6440	0.6320	0.6340
	Crossval	0.5880	0.5980	0.5980	0.5940	**0.6000**
YouTube	Tuned	0.6520	0.6460	**0.6600**	0.6500	0.6440
	Crossval	**0.6500**	0.6020	0.6120	0.6060	0.6000

is consistently better. This is due to the odd nature of this collection and the vocabulary mismatch between the social tags collections, which are newer and, in general, return results (tags) that are not present as terms in LATimes. Furthermore, the differences between the three weighting schemes (idf, *tf-idf*, and Bo1) are negligible in most of the cases.

Finally, we address the question of whether we can combine terms and tags successfully for PRF or not. Tables 7.4 (MAP) and 7.5 (P@10) compare retrieval performance using a combination of tags and terms for PRF. The combination outperforms best single PRF at most times and is consistently better than the baseline, except for the LATimes collection. This indicates that tag-PRF contributes something extra to term-PRF, which benefits retrieval performance. The fact that tags are beneficial for retrieval is particularly apparent in the newer BLOGS06 collection when using the YouTube tags, where adding terms to tags actually decreases the quality of the results (it should be noted, however, that the values of the parameters are not optimized for the term+tag combination). This indicates that both PRF approaches are able to improve overall retrieval performance (note that all the scores in the Tables outperform the retrieval model baseline). Earlier observations regarding collections and retrieval models remain valid here. BLOG06 benefits more than the other collections and MAP benefits more than P@10. This consistency indicates that the combination of the two PRF methods is successful and does not disrupt retrieval in any way.

7.4   Conclusion

In this chapter we first surveyed current state-of-the-art approaches for ranking user generated content. As an example application, we proposed a method to use collaborative tags to perform Pseudo Relevance Feedback (PRF). PRF is an IR technique that expands the query with assumed relevant terms and resubmits it for retrieval to the system. We present three different extensions of established term weighting schemes to measure tag salience, different from a previous effort in the same field. We ask whether our proposed tag-PRF approach can enhance performance compared to a standard baseline retrieval model, compared to a competitive term-based PRF model, and compared also to an existing tag-based PRF model. A thorough evaluation of the methods on their own and also combined with term-PRF, on three different TREC collections, using two different tag sources and an established retrieval model with tuned and cross-validated settings, indicates that our tag-PRF model can enhance retrieval performance consistently, improving the results of an existing tag-PRF method and rivaling with the established term-PRF method. The proposed tag-PRF model is especially beneficial when retrieving blogs from the recent BLOG06 collection, which indicates that the lower performance with older collections may be due to the difference in the language of those collections and current language use on the Web.

Given the free availability and increasing popularity (hence amount) of collaborative tagging, further research into incorporating this type of evidence in IR may be fruitful.

Possible next research steps in this direction include investigating the effect of outdated collections upon tag-PRF in a more principled way or how to refine the PRF weighting proposed in this chapter by integrating statistical estimates of the similarity between the query and a tag. Another future research question of interest is to apply tag-PRF to multimedia IR, where the data contains little textual information. In that case, tags could be a way to boost the textual description of the informative content.

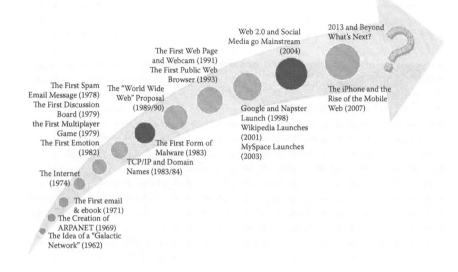

FIGURE 1.2: The evolution of the Web.

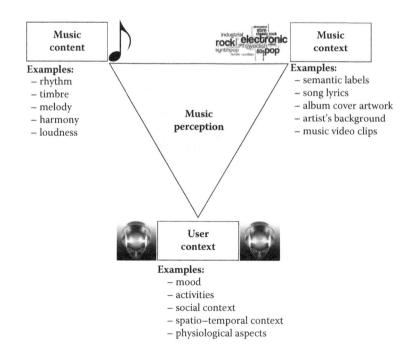

FIGURE 4.1: Different categories of factors that influence music perception.

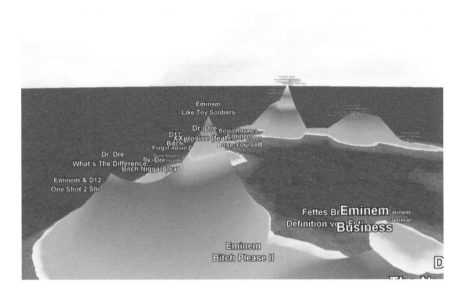

FIGURE 4.2: The nepTune music browsing interface.

FIGURE 4.3: The Intelligent iPod mobile browsing interface.

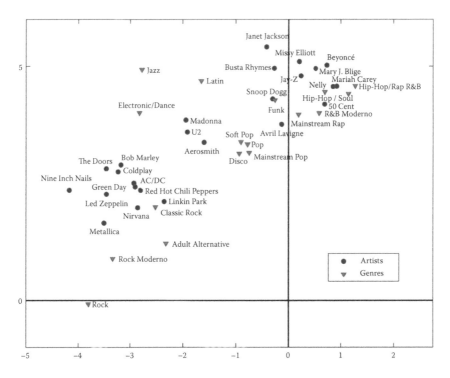

FIGURE 4.6: The most popular musical tracks and genres in the `Yahoo!` Music dataset are embedded into a two-dimensional space.

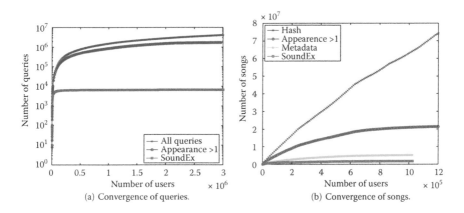

FIGURE 4.7: Convergence of queries (a) and of songs (b) per number of crawled users, using different methods for filtering noise.

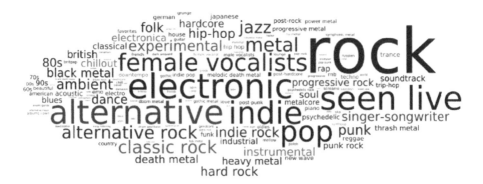

FIGURE 4.8: Tag cloud of `last.fm` top tags.

FIGURE 6.1: An example Web page with UGC.

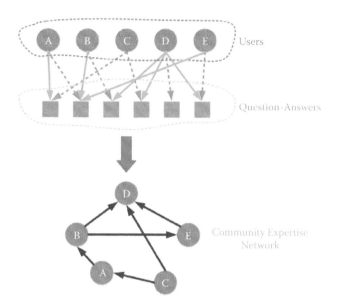

FIGURE 9.2: A sample CQA post-reply (or question-answer) network and community expertise network (CEN). A dashed line links an asker to a question and a solid line connects an answerer to a question [764].

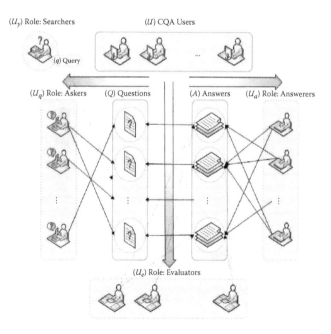

FIGURE 9.5: User roles, asker, answerer, evaluator, in CQA and interactions between questions and answers.

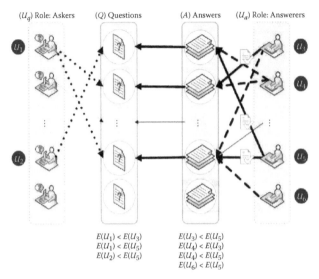

$E(U_1) < E(U_3)$ $E(U_3) < E(U_5)$
$E(U_1) < E(U_5)$ $E(U_4) < E(U_3)$
$E(U_2) < E(U_5)$ $E(U_4) < E(U_5)$
                         $E(U_6) < E(U_5)$

Best Answerer vs. Asker   Best Answerer vs. Answerer

FIGURE 9.6: Competition-based expertise score estimation, Liu et al. [412]: (1) Expertise of a best answerer (solid line) is greater than its asker (dotted line); (2) Expertise of a best answerer (solid line) is greater than other answerers (dashed line). $E(U_i)$ is the expertise score of user U_i.

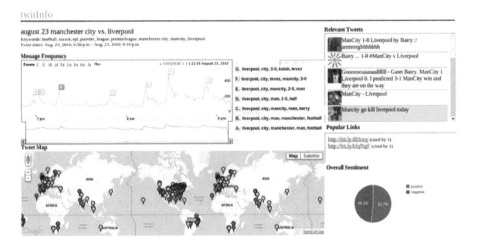

FIGURE 10.1: TwitInfo tracks a football game (http://twitinfo.csail.mit.edu/).

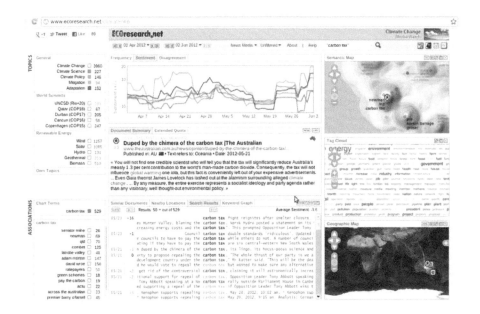

FIGURE 10.2: Media watch on climate change portal (http://www.ecoresearch.net/climate).

FIGURE 10.3: The Twitris social media event monitoring portal (http://twitris.knoesis.org).

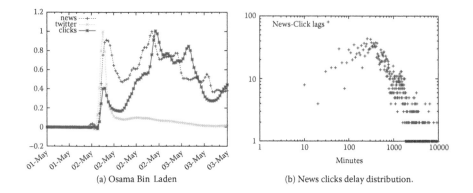

(a) Osama Bin Laden

(b) News clicks delay distribution.

FIGURE 11.4: Trends on Twitter and news streams.

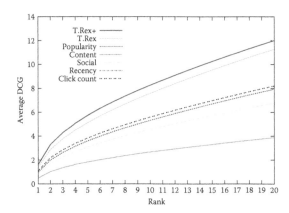

FIGURE 11.5: Average discounted cumulated gain on related entities given the top 20 ranks.

Chapter 8

Annotating Japanese Blogs with Syntactic and Affective Information

Michal Ptaszynski and Yoshio Momouchi

Hokkai-Gakuen University, Sapporo, Japan

Jacek Maciejewski

Independent Researcher

Pawel Dybala

Otaru University of Commerce, Otaru, Japan

Rafal Rzepka and Kenji Araki

Hokkaido University, Sapporo, Japan

8.1   Introduction

Text corpora are some of the most vital linguistic resources in the field of natural language processing (NLP). These include newspaper corpora, like Wall Street Journal Corpus [128] or Mainichi Shinbun Corpus [437], conversation corpora, like the BC3 corpus [311] or the CSJ corpus [151], as well as corpora of literature, such as Aozora Bunko [29]. The importance of corpora is widely recognized and numerous corpora have been compiled so far for different languages. However, comparing to major world languages, like English, there are few large corpora available for the Japanese language [206]. Moreover, the grand majority of them are based on newspapers or legal documents. Unfortunately, they are usually unsuitable for the research on emotion processing as emotions are rarely expressed in this kind of texts. Although there exist speech corpora, such as Corpus of Spontaneous Japanese [151], which could become suitable for emotion processing research, due to the difficulties with compilation of such corpora they are relatively small.

Recently, it has been noticed that user generated content (UGC), such as online forums, product reviews, or blogs, are good material for NLP research because of their richness in open access raw language material. One type of UGC is blogs, open diaries in which people encapsulate their own experiences, opinions, and feelings to be read and commented by other people. Recently, blogs have come particularly into focus of opinion mining, or sentiment and affect analysis [4, 272, 473, 449, 23, 160, 556]. Therefore, creating a large blog-based emotion corpus could become a solution to overcome two problems: the lack in quantity of corpora and applicability of corpora in the research on emotions. However, there have only been a few small Japanese emotion blog corpora developed so far [272]. Other existing Japanese emotion corpora are usually even smaller (e.g., the corpus by Minato et al. [471] contained only 1200 sentences), which makes them unsuitable for most applications. On the other hand, there exist several somewhat large Web-based corpora (containing several million words), such as JpWaC [206] or jBlogs [54]. However, since access to them is usually allowed only by means of a Web interface, it is difficult to additionally annotate them with affective information. Finally, although there exist very large resources, like Google N-gram Corpus [376], the textual datasets in such resources are usually short (up to 7 grams) and do not contain any contextual information (such as snippets with the closest content a particular n-gram appears in). This makes them unsuitable for emotion processing research, since most of contextual information, so important in expressing emotions [550] is lost. Therefore, there was a clear need for a large-scale blog corpus able to be queried locally (e.g., when looking for word or sentence patterns) with access to all contextual information and containing annotations of all kinds of information, syntactic and affective.

We decided to create YACIS, a new up-to-date 5-billion word blog corpus from scratch. The raw texts obtained from the Web were processed in several ways, including sentence and word segmentation and several kinds of annotations, like parts-of-speech, dependency structure, and affective information. We aimed at creating a corpus that could serve as a source of various statistical data as well as a base for creating more detailed subcorpora.

In the following sections, we first describe in detail the related research done in corpora distinguishable for their large scale, domain, language, and types of annotations (with separate focus on corpora annotated with affective information). Next, we present the tools and procedures used for compiling the corpus. Further, we will present detailed statistical data of our corpus. We will finalize the chapter by presenting a handful of applications in which the corpus has already proved to be useful, and propose possible further improvements to the corpus.

8.2   Related Research

This section presents some of the most relevant research related to ours. There has been no billion-word-scale corpus annotated with affective information before. Therefore, we needed to divide the description of the related research into "Large-Scale Corpora" and "Emotion Corpora."

8.2.1   Large-Scale Corpora

The notion of a "large scale corpus" has appeared in linguistic and computational linguistic literature for many years. However, study of the literature shows that what was considered as "large" 10 years ago does not exceed 5% (border of statistical error) when compared to present corpora. For example, Sasaki et al. [595] in 2001 reported a construction of a question-answering (QA) system based on a large scale corpus. The corpus they used consisted of 528,000 newspaper articles. YACIS, the corpus described here, consists of 12,938,606 documents (blog articles). The rough estimation indicates that the corpus of Sasaki et al. cover less than 5% of YACIS (in particular 4.08%). Therefore, we mostly focused on research scaling the meaning of "large" up to around a billion words and more.

Liu and Curran [414], followed by Baroni and Ueyama [54], indicate at least two types of research dealing with large-scale corpora. The first is using popular search engines, such as Google[1] or Yahoo!.[2] The second is crawling the World Wide Web and downloading its contents for further analysis.

---

[1] http://www.google.com
[2] http://www.yahoo.com

In the former type of research one gathers estimates of hit counts for certain keywords to perform statistical analysis, or wider contexts of the keywords, called "snippets" (a short, three line long text containing the keyword), to perform further analysis of the snippet contents. This refers to what has generally developed as the "Web mining" field. An example could be the research by Turney and Littman [679]. They claim to perform sentiment analysis on a hundred-billion-word corpus. By the corpus they mean roughly estimated size of the Web pages indexed by the AltaVista search engine.[3] However, this kind of research is inevitably constrained with limitations of the search engine's API. Pomikálek et al. [541] indicate a long list of such limitations. Some of them include limited query language (e.g., no search by sophisticated regular expressions), query-per-day limitations (e.g., Google allows only one thousand queries per day for one IP address, after which the IP address is blocked for 24 hours—an unacceptable limitation in linguistic research), search queries are ordered with a manner irrelevant to linguistic research, and so on. Kilgariff [341] calls uncritical relying on search engine results a "Googleology" and points out a number of problems search engines will never be able to deal with (such as duplicated documents). Moreover, only Google employees have unlimited and extended access to the search engine results. Kilgariff also proposes an alternative, building large-scale corpora locally by crawling the World Wide Web, and argues that it is the optimal way of utilizing the Internet contents for research in linguistics and computational linguistics.

As for the corpora created by crawling the World Wide Web, there have been several initiatives to build billion-word scale corpora for different languages. Two large corpora has been presented by Google. One is the "Web 1T (trillion) 5 gram" English corpus [93], published in 2006. It is estimated to contain one trillion of tokens and 95 billion sentences gathered from the Web. Unfortunately, the contents available for users are only n-gram s, from 1 (unigrams) to 5 (pentagrams). The corpus was not processed in any way except tokenization. Also, the original sentences are not available. This makes the corpus, although unmatchable when it comes to statistics of short word sequences, not interesting for language studies, where a word needs to be processed in context. The second one is the "Google Books 155 Billion Word Corpus"[4] published in 2011. It contains 1.3 million books in English published between 1810 and 2009 and processed with OCR. This corpus has a larger functionality, such as a part-of-speech annotation and lemmatization of words. However, it is available only as an online interface with a daily access limit per user (1000 queries). The tokenized-only version of the corpus is available, also for several other languages,[5] unfortunately only in the n-gram form (no context larger than 5 grams).

Among corpora created with Web crawling methods, Liu and Curran [414] created a 10-billion word corpus of English. Although the corpus was not

---

[3]In 2004, AltaVista (http://www.altavista.com/) became a part of Yahoo!
[4]http://googlebooks.byu.edu/
[5]http://books.google.com/ngrams/datasets

annotated in any way, except tokenization, differently to Google's corpora it is sentence based, not *n*-gram based. Moreover, it successfully proved its usability in standard NLP tasks such as spelling correction, or thesaurus extraction.

The **WaCky** (**W**eb as **C**orpus **k**ool **y**nitiative) [54, 53] project started gathering and linguistically processing large-scale corpora from the Web. In the years 2005–2007 the project resulted in more than five collections of around 2 billion word corpora for different languages, such as English (ukWaC), French (frWaC), German (deWaC), or Italian (itWaC). The tools developed for the project are available online and their general applicability is well established. Some of the corpora developed within the project are compared in Table 8.1.

BiWeC [541], or **Big We**b **C**orpus, has been collected from the whole Web contents in 2009 and consists of about 5.5 billion words in English. The authors of this corpus aimed to go beyond the border of 2 billion words set by the WaCky initiative[6] as a borderline for corpus processing feasibility for modern (32-bit) software.

Billion-word scale corpora have also been recently developed for other languages, such as Hungarian [258], Brazilian Portuguese [591], or Polish [239].

As for large corpora in Japanese, despite the fact that Japanese is a well recognized and described world language, there have been only few corpora of a reasonable size.

Srdanović Erjavec et al. [644] used the **WAC** (**W**eb **A**s **C**orpus) Toolkit[7] and Kilgariff et al.'s Sketch Engine [342], a tool for thesauri generation from large-scale corpora. They gathered JpWaC, a 400-million word corpus of Japanese. Although JpWaC covers only about 7% of YACIS (400 million versus 5.6 billion words), it shows that freely available tools developed for European languages are to some extent applicable also for languages of a completely different typography, like Japanese.[8] However, the researchers faced several problems, such as normalization of character encoding for all Web pages[9] (Ameba blog service, on which YACIS was based, is encoded by default in Unicode).

Baroni and Ueyama [54] developed **jBlogs**, a medium-sized corpus of Japanese blogs containing 62 million words. They selected four popular blog services (Ameba, Goo, Livedoor, Yahoo!) and extracted nearly 30 thousand blog documents. Except part-of-speech tagging, which was done by a Japanese POS tagger ChaSen, the whole procedure and tools they used were the same as the ones developed in WaCky. In the detailed manual analysis of jBlogs, Baroni and Ueyama noticed that blog posts contained many Japanese emoticons, or *kaomoji*.[10] They report that ChaSen is not capable of processing them, and separates each character adding a general annotation tag "symbol." This

---

[6]http://wacky.sslmit.unibo.it/

[7]http://www.drni.de/wac-tk/

[8]Languages like Chinese, Japanese, or Korean are encoded using 2-bite characters.

[9]Japanese can be encoded in at least four standards: JIS, Shift-JIS, EUC, and Unicode.

[10]For a more detailed description of Japanese emoticons, see [549].

TABLE 8.1: Comparison of Different Corpora, Ordered Arbitrary by Size (Number of Words/Tokens)

Corpus Name	Scale (in words)	Language	Domain	Annotation
Liu and Curran [414]	10 billion	English	whole Web	tokenization;
YACIS	5.6 billion	Japanese	Blogs (Ameba)	tokenization, POS, lemma, dependency parsing, NER, affect (emotive expressions, Russell-2D, emotion objects);
BiWeC [541]	5.5 billion	English	whole Web (.uk and .au domains)	POS, lemma;
ukWaC [53]	2 billion	English	whole Web (.uk domain)	POS, lemma;
PukWaC (Parsed-ukWaC) [53]	2 billion	English	whole Web (.uk domain)	POS, lemma, dependency parsing;
itWaC [54, 53]	2 billion	Italian	whole Web (.it domain)	POS, lemma;
Gigaword [258]	2 billion	Hungarian	whole Web (.hu domain)	tokenization, sentence segmentation;
deWaC [53]	1.7 billion	German	whole Web (.de domain)	POS, lemma;
frWaC [53]	1.6 billion	French	whole Web (.fr domain)	POS, lemma;
Corpus Brasiliero [591]	1 billion	Brazilian Portuguese	multidomain (newspapers, Web, talk transcriptions)	POS, lemma;
National Corpus of Polish [239]	1 billion	Polish	multidomain (newspapers, literature, Web, etc.)	POS, lemma, dependency parsing, named entities, word senses;
JpWaC [644]	400 million	Japanese	whole Web (.jp domain)	tokenization, POS, lemma;
jBlogs [644]	62 million	Japanese	Blogs (Ameba, Goo, Livedoor, Yahoo!)	tokenization, POS, lemma;

results in an overall bias in parts of speech distribution, putting symbols as the second most frequent (nearly 30% of the whole jBlogs corpus) tag, right after "noun" (about 35%).

They considered the frequent appearance of emoticons a major problem in processing blog corpora. In our research we dealt with this problem. To process emoticons we used CAO, a system for detailed analysis of Japanese emoticons developed previously by Ptaszynski et al. [549].

8.2.2   Emotion Corpora

The research on affect analysis, or affect sensing from text, has resulted in a number of affect analysis systems developed within several years [449, 546, 23]. Unfortunately, most of such research usually ends in proposing and evaluating a certain system. The real-world application that would be desirable, such as annotating affective information on linguistic data, is limited to processing a usually small test sample in the evaluation part of the system. The small number of annotated emotion corpora that exist are mostly of limited scale and are annotated manually. Below we describe and compare some of the most notable emotion corpora. As an interesting remark, six out of seven emotion corpora described below are extracted from blogs.

Quan and Ren [556] created a Chinese emotion blog corpus called **Ren-CECps1.0**.[11] They collected 500 blog articles from various Chinese blog services, such as sciencenet blog[12] or qq blog.[13] The articles were annotated with a large variety of information, such as emotion class, emotive expressions, polarity level, or emotion object. Although the syntactic annotations were simplified to tokenization and POS tagging, this corpus is the most comparable to YACIS in the overall variety of annotations.

Wiebe et al. [721, 723] report on creating the **MPQA** corpus of news articles. The corpus contains 10,657 sentences in 535 documents.[14] The annotation schema includes a variety of emotion-related information, such as emotive expressions, emotion valence, intensity, etc. However, Wiebe et al. focused on detecting subjective (emotive) sentences and classifying them into positive and negative. Thus, their annotation schema, although one of the richest, does not include emotion classes (joy, fear, anger, etc.).

A corpus of Japanese blogs, similar to YACIS in the amount of annotated information, has been developed by Hashimoto et al. in 2010 and published in 2011 [272]. The corpus was developed jointly by the National Institute of Information and Communications Technology, Kyoto University, and the NTT Communication Science Laboratories. The KNB[15] corpus contains about 67

---

[11] Abbreviation of **Ren**'s **C**hinese blogs **E**motion **C**orpus.

[12] http://blog.sciencenet.cn/

[13] http://blog.qq.com/

[14] The new MPQA Opinion Corpus version 2.0 contains an additional 157 documents, 692 documents in total.

[15] Abbreviation of **K**yoto University and **N**TT Lab **B**log Corpus.

TABLE 8.2:   Detailed Comparison of Different Japanese Corpora, Ordered by the Number of Words/Tokens

Corpus Name	Scale (in words)	Number of Documents (Web pages)	Number of Sentences	Size (uncompressed in GB, text only, no annotation)	Domain
YACIS	5,600,597,095	12,938,606	354,288,529	26.6	Blogs (Ameba);
JpWaC [644]	409,384,411	49,544	12,759,201	7.3	whole Web (11 different domains within .jp);
jBlogs [54]	61,885,180	28,530	[not revealed]	.25 (compressed)	Blogs (Ameba, Goo, Livedoor, Yahoo);
KNB [272]	66,952	249	4,186	450 kB	Blogs (written by students exclusively for the purpose of the research);
Minato et al. [470]	14,195	1	1,191	[not revealed]	Dictionary examples;

TABLE 8.3: Comparison of Emotion Corpora Ordered by the Amount of Annotations (Abbreviations: T = tokenization, POS = Part-of-Speech Tagging, L = Lemmatization, DP = Dependency parsing, NER = Named Entity Recognition)

Corpus Name	Scale (In sentences / Docs)	Language	Emotion Classes (standard)	Annotated Affective Information					Syntactic Annotations
				Emotive Expressions	Emotive/ Nonemot.	Valence/ Activation	Emotion Intensity	Emotion Objects	
YACIS	354 mil./13 mil.	Japanese	10 (language and culture based)	○	○	○/○	○	○	T,POS,L,DP,NER
Ren-CECps1.0 [556]	12,724/500	Chinese	8 (Yahoo! news annotation standard)	○	○	○/×	○	○	T,POS
MPQA [721]	10,657/535	English	none (no standard)	○	○	○/×	○	○	T,POS
KNB [272]	4186/249	Japanese	none (no standard)	○	×	○/×	×	○	T,POS,L,DP,NER
Minato et al. [470]	1191 separate sentences	Japanese	8 (chosen subjectively)	○	○	×/×	×	×	POS
Aman& Szpakowicz [23]	5205/173	English	6 (face recognition)	○	○	×/×	○	×	×
Das& Bandyopadhyay [160]	12,149/123	Bengali	6 (face recognition)	○	×	×/×	○	×	×
Wakamono Kotoba [449]	4773 separate sentences	Japanese	9 (6 from face recognition plus 3 added subjectively)	○	×	×/×	×	×	×
Mishne [473]	815,494 blog posts	English	132 (LiveJournal annotation standard)	×	×	×/×	×	×	×

thousand words in 249 blog articles. Although it is not a large-scale corpus (0.12% of YACIS compared by words/tokens), it developed a certain standard for preparing corpora, especially blog corpora for sentiment and affect-related studies in Japan. The corpus contains all relevant syntactic and morphological annotations, including POS tagging, dependency parsing, or named entity recognition (NER). It also contains sentiment-related information. Words and phrases expressing emotional attitude were annotated by laypeople as either positive or negative. One disadvantage of the corpus, except its small scale, is the way it was created. Eighty-one students were employed to write blogs about different topics especially for the need of this research. It could be argued that since the students knew their blogs will be read mostly by their teachers, they could select their words more carefully than they would in private.

Aman and Szpakowicz [23] also constructed a small-scale English blog emotion corpus. However, they focused not on the grammatical annotations, but on the affect-related annotations. As an interesting remark, they were some of the first to recognize the task of distinguishing between emotive and nonemotive sentences. This problem is usually one of the most difficult in text-based affect analysis and is therefore often omitted in such research. ML-Ask, a system applied in annotation of YACIS, was proved to discriminate between emotive and nonemotive sentences with sufficient accuracy.

Das and Bandyopadhyay constructed an emotion annotated corpus of blogs in Bengali [160]. The corpus contains 12,149 sentences within 123 blog posts extracted from Bengali Web blog archive.[16] It is annotated with Ekman's 6 class emotion annotation standard for face recognition.

Matsumoto et al. [449] report on construction of **Wakamono Kotoba** (Slang of the Youth) Corpus. The corpus contains separate sentences extracted manually from *Yahoo! blogs*.[17] Each sentence contains at least one word from a slang lexicon and one word from an emotion lexicon, with additional emotion class tags added per sentence. Both lexicons were created manually. The emotion class used for annotation (9 emotion classes) was set by applying the 6 emotion types from face recognition research [198] and adding an additional three of their subjective choice.

Mishne [473] collected a corpus of English blogs from the LiveJournal[18] blog service. The corpus contains 815,494 blog posts, from which many are annotated with emotions (moods) by the blog authors themselves. The LiveJournal service offers an option for its users to annotate their mood while writing the blog. The list of 132 moods include words like "amused" or "angry." The LiveJournal mood annotation standard offers a rich vocabulary to describe the writer's mood. However, this richness, without any generalization to emotion classes, has been considered too troublesome, both for users in making the annotation choice, and for researchers to generalize the data in a meaningful manner [556].

---

[16]http://www.amarblog.com/
[17]http://blog-search.yahoo.co.jp/
[18]http://www.livejournal.com/

Finally, Minato et al. [470] collected a 14,195-word/1191-sentence-corpus and annotated it manually. The corpus is a collection of dictionary examples from "A short dictionary of feelings and emotions in English and Japanese" [285]. It is a dictionary created for the need of Japanese language learners. Differently to the dictionary we applied in our research, "Emotive Expression Dictionary" created by Nakamura [486], is "A short dictionary..." Sentence examples were mostly written by the author of the dictionary himself. Finally, the dictionary does not propose any coherent emotion class list, but rather the emotion concepts are chosen subjectively. Although the corpus by Minato is the smallest corpus of all mentioned in this section, differently to others Minato et al. provide a full statistical analysis of the corpus. Therefore, in this chapter we use their research as one of the Japanese emotion corpora to compare with YACIS. We understand that a 14-thousand word scale is not representative enough to compare it to a 5.6-billion word scale, therefore, where it was possible we compared all available corpora. The detailed comparison is given in Section 8.4.2.2.

All of the above corpora were annotated manually or semiautomatically. In this research we performed the first attempt to annotate affect on a large scale corpus automatically. We performed this with systems positively evaluated for their performance, and with standardized emotion class typology.

8.3   YACIS Corpus Compilation

The corpus, named **YACIS**, or **Y**et **A**nother **C**orpus of **I**nternet **S**entences, was assembled using data obtained automatically from the pages of Ameba Blog (http://ameblo.jp/, below referred to as Ameblo). There were two main reasons for using Ameblo. First, the users are mostly Japanese so the risk that the links may lead to pages written in a language other than Japanese is small. Second, Ameblo has a clear structure of HTML source code, which makes it easy to extract only posts and comments omitting the irrelevant contents, such as advertisements or menu links.

All tools used for compiling this corpus were developed especially for the purpose of this research. Although there existed several other solutions, all of them were created for crawling the whole Web and included some parts irrelevant for crawling blog service URLs like Ameblo (such as the detection of "robots.txt" file, which specifies that no crawling robots should visit any URL from the domain, used for privacy protection), or parts that can be done more easily if the crawling domain is restricted to one blog service (such as HTML code boilerplate deletion). All these parts slow down the crawling process, and sometimes influence the corpus extraction (e.g., general rules for HTML code deletion are less precise than specific rules for deletion of the HTML code that appears in Ameblo). Therefore, the available tools, very useful as they are, were insufficient for our needs. All tools were written in C# and are operating under MS Windows systems.

We developed a simple but efficient Web crawler designed to crawl exclusively Ameblo Web pages (Figure 8.1). The only pages taken into account were those containing Japanese posts (pages with legal disclaimers, as well as posts written in English and other languages were omitted). Initially, we fed the crawler with a thousand links taken from Google (response to one simple query: 'site:ameblo.jp'). All the pages were saved to disk as raw HTML files (each page in a separate file) to be processed later. All of them were downloaded within 3 weeks between the 3rd and 24th of December 2009. Next, we extracted all the posts and comments and divided them into sentences.

Although sentence segmentation may seem to be a trivial task, it is not that easy when it comes to texts written by bloggers. Blog authors often use improper punctuation, for example, the periods at the end of sentences are often omitted. In that case we assumed that if the given parts of text are separated by two or more <br /> tags (markers of a new line) then those parts will be two separate sentences. This does not solve the problem in all cases. Therefore, we rejoined previously separated parts if the first part ended with a comma or if the quotation marks or parenthesis were opened in the first part and closed in the second.

Unfortunately, these modifications were still not perfect and in several cases parts of the text remained not split while others were segmented erroneously. One of the possible improvements was to take into consideration emoticons. We observed that if an emoticon is present in the sentence it usually appears at the end of it. Even in the cases the emoticon did not appear on the very end of the sentence, it still separated two clauses of a different meaning. Moreover, the meaning of the emoticon was always bound with the clause preceding it. This suggested separating sentences after emoticons. To do that we used a CAO emoticon analysis system developed by Ptaszynski et al. [549]. Observations showed this coped with most of the remaining sentence segmentation errors. In a random thousand sentence sample, less than 1% remained erroneously separated. Analysis of errors showed these were sentences separated by blog authors in a nonstandard way and without any particular rule.

The data is stored in modified-XML format. Although it looks like XML, it does not comply with all XML standards due to the presence of some characters forbidden by XML specification, such as apostrophes (') or quotation marks ("). Those modifications were made to improve the communication with natural language processing tools used in further processing of the corpus, such as a text parser, part-of-speech tagger (e.g., MeCab [375]), affect analysis system (ML-Ask [546]), and others. Each page was transformed into independent XML blocks between <doc></doc> tags. The opening tag of the <doc> block contains three parameters: URL, TIME, and ID, which specify the exact address from which the given page was downloaded, download time, and unique page number, respectively. The <doc> block contains two

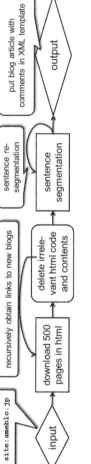

FIGURE 8.1: Flowchart representing the mechanism of the Web crawler.

```
<doc url="http://ameblo.jp/capo-del-rosso/entry-000000.html" time="2009-12-05 21:11:46" id="2000001">
        <post>
                <s>今日から十月です。</s>
                [Its October from today.]
                <s>なんか、九月はいつもよりアッという間に過ぎたような気がするなぁ。</s>
                [I have a strange feeling September passed faster than usual.]
                ...
        </post>
        <comments>
                <cmt>
                        <s>色々と忙しいですね～！</s>
                        [Oh, you've been busy, weren't you?]
                        ...
                </cmt>
                <cmt>
                        <s>お疲れサマです(^0^)</s>
                        [Well done! Cheers for good work (^o^)]
                        ...
                </cmt>
        </comments>
</doc>
```

FIGURE 8.2: An example of an XML structure of the main blog corpus.

TABLE 8.4: General Statistics of the YACIS Corpus

# of Web pages	12,938,606
# of unique bloggers	60,658
average # of pages per blogger	213.3
# of pages with comments	6,421,577
# of comments	50,560,024
average # of comments per page	7.873
# of characters (without spaces)	28,582,653,165
# of characters (with spaces)	34,202,720,910
# of words (tokens)	5,600,597,095
# of all sentences	354,288,529
# of sentences < 500 characters	353,999,525
# of sentences after correction of sentence segmentation errors	371,734,976
# of words per sentence (average)	15
# of characters per sentence (average)	77

other tag types: <post> and <comments>. The <post> block contains all the sentences from the given post where each sentence is included between <s></s> tags. The block <comments> contains all comments written under a given post placed between <cmt></cmt> tags, which are further split into single sentences placed between <s></s> tags. An example XML structure of the corpus is represented in Figure 8.2.

The corpus is stored in 129 text files containing 100,000 <doc> units each. The corpus was encoded using UTF-8 encoding. The size of each file varies and is between 200 and 320 megabytes. The size of raw corpus (pure text of sentences without any additional tags) is 27.1 gigabytes. Other primary statistics of the corpus are represented in Table 8.4.

As mentioned in Table 8.4, the average sentence length is 77 Japanese characters. Kubota et al. [373] divide sentences in Japanese according to their

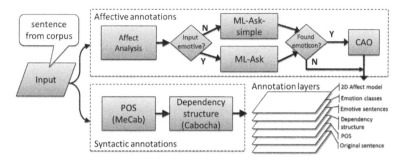

FIGURE 8.3: The flowchart representing the whole annotation process.

intelligibility into easily intelligible short sentences (up to 100 characters) and difficult long sentences (over 100 characters long). The sentences in our corpus fit in the definition of short sentences, which means they are easily understandable. Before the correction of sentence segmentation errors the average sentence length was 80 characters. After exclusion of very long sentences (consisting of over 500 characters) the number of sentences did not change significantly and was 353,999,525 (99.91%), and the final number of sentences after correction was 371,734,976 with an average length of 77 characters. This suggests the corpus is balanced in the length of sentences.

8.4   YACIS Corpus Annotation

The corpus, in the form described in Section 8.3, was further annotated with several kinds of information, such as parts-of-speech, dependency structure, or affective information. The tools we used are described in detail below, followed by a section describing corpus annotation statistics, evaluation, and comparison to other corpora. The flowchart representing the annotation process is represented in Figure 8.3.

8.4.1   Annotation Tools

8.4.1.1   Syntactic Information Annotation Tools

MeCab [375] is a standard morphological analyzer and part-of-speech (POS) tagger for Japanese. It is trained using a large corpus on a Conditional Random Fields (CRF) discriminative model and uses a bigram Markov model for analysis. In addition to MeCab, there are several POS taggers for Japanese, such as Juman[19] or ChaSen.[20] ChaSen and MeCab share the same

---

[19]http://nlp.ist.i.kyoto-u.ac.jp/EN/index.php?JUMAN
[20]http://chasen.naist.jp/hiki/ChaSen/

corpus base for training and use the same default dictionary (ipadic[21] based on a modified IPA Part-of-Speech Tagset. However, ChaSen was trained on a Hidden Markov Model (generative model), a full probabilistic model in which at first all variables are generated, and thus is slower than MeCab (based on a discriminative model), which focuses only on the target variables conditional on the observed variables. Juman, on the other hand, was developed separately from MeCab on different resources. It uses a set of handcrafted rules and a dictionary (Jumandic) created on the basis of Kyoto University Text Corpus.[22] Both MeCab and Juman are considerably fast, which is a very important feature when processing a large-scale corpus such as YACIS. However, there were several reasons to choose the former. MeCab is considered slightly faster when processing large data and uses less memory. It also allows partial analysis (a way of flexible setting of word boundaries in nonspaced languages, like Japanese). Finally, MeCab is more flexible when using other dictionaries. Therefore, to annotate YACIS we were able to use MeCab with the two different types of dictionaries mentioned above (Ipadic and Jumandic). This allowed us to develop POS tagging for YACIS with the two most favored standards in morphological analysis for Japanese today. An example of MeCab output is represented in Figure 8.5 (the results were translated into English according to "IPA POS code in Japanese and English"[23]).

Cabocha [374] is a Japanese dependency parser based on Support Vector Machines (SVM). It was developed by MeCab creators and is considered to be the most accurate statistical Japanese dependency parser. It uses a Cascaded Chunking Model, which parses a sentence deterministically focusing on whether a sentence segment modifies a segment on its right-hand side [374]. This makes the analysis efficient for the Japanese language. Other dependency parsers for Japanese, such as KNP,[24] use statistical probabilistic models, which makes them inefficient for complex sentences with many clauses. As an option, Cabocha uses IREX[25] (Information Retrieval and Extraction Exercise) standard for Named Entity Recognition (NER). We applied this option in the annotation process as well. An example of Cabocha output is represented in Figure 8.5. Table 8.5 represents all tag types included in IREX.

8.4.1.2   Affective Information Annotation Tools

Emotive Expression Dictionary [486] is a dictionary developed by Akira Nakamura over a 20-year time period. It is a collection of over 2000 expressions describing emotional states collected manually from a wide range of literature. It is not a tool per se, but was converted into an emotive expression database by Ptaszynski et al. [546, 547] in their research on affect analysis of utterances in Japanese. Nakamura's dictionary also proposes a classification

---

[21] http://sourceforge.jp/projects/ipadic/
[22] http://nlp.ist.i.kyoto-u.ac.jp/index.php
[23] http://sourceforge.jp/projects/ipadic/docs/postag.txt
[24] http://nlp.ist.i.kyoto-u.ac.jp/EN/index.php?KNP
[25] http://nlp.cs.nyu.edu/irex/index-e.html

TABLE 8.5:   Named Entity Tag Types Included in the IREX Standard

<opening tag>contents</closing tag>	Explanation
<ORGANIZATION>...</ORGANIZATION>	organization or company name including abbreviations (e.g., Toyota, or Nissan);
<LOCATION>...</LOCATION>	name of a place (city, country, etc.);
<PERSON>...</PERSON>	name, nickname, or status of a person (e.g., Lady Gaga, or "me," "grandson", etc.);
<ARTIFACT>...</ARTIFACT>	name of a well recognized product or object (e.g., Van Houtens Cocoa, etc.);
<PERCENT>...</PERCENT>	percentage or ratio (90%, 0.9);
<MONEY>...</MONEY>	currencies (1000 dollar, 100 yen);
<DATE>...</DATE>	dates and its paraphrased extensions (e.g., "4th July," but also "next season," etc.)
<TIME>...</TIME>	hours, minutes, seconds, etc.

TABLE 8.6:   Distribution of Separate Expressions across Emotion Classes in Nakamura's Dictionary (Overall 2100 Ex.)

Emotion Class	Number of Expressions	Emotion Class	Number of Expressions
dislike	532	fondness	197
excitement	269	fear	147
sadness	232	surprise	129
joy	224	relief	106
anger	199	shame	65
		sum	**2100**

of emotions that reflects the Japanese language and culture. This classification is applied to the lexicon itself. All expressions are classified as representing a specific emotion type, one or more if applicable. In particular, Nakamura proposes 10 emotion types: 喜 *ki/yorokobi* (joy, delight; later referred to as **joy**), 怒 *dō/ikari* (**anger**), 哀 *ai/aware* (sorrow, sadness, gloom; later referred to as **sadness**), 怖 *fu/kowagari* (**fear**), 恥 *chi/haji* (shame, shyness, bashfulness; later referred to as **shame**), 好 *kō/suki* (liking, fondness; later referred to as **fondness**), 厭 *en/iya* (dislike, detestation; later referred to as **dislike**), 昂 *kō/takaburi* (**excitement**), 安 *an/yasuragi* (**relief**), and 驚 *kyō/odoroki* (surprise, amazement; later referred to as **surprise**). The distribution of separate expressions across all emotion classes is represented in Table 8.6.

A frequent manner in text-based Affect Analysis research is applying a list of emotion classes based on other modalities than linguistic, such as face recognition, or simply creating a new class list for the need of a particular research (see Table 8.3 for details). In our research, we aimed at contributing to the standardization of the emotion class list in the research on emotions in Japanese. Therefore, we selected Nakamura's emotion type list as the most appropriate for our research.

ML-Ask, or *eMotive eLement and Expression Analysis system*, is a keyword-based language-dependent system for automatic affect annotation on utterances in Japanese constructed by Ptaszynski et al. [546, 547]. It uses a two-step procedure:

1. Specifying whether a sentence is emotive, and

2. Recognizing the particular emotion types in utterances described as emotive.

ML-Ask is based on the idea of a two-part classification of realizations of emotions in language into:

(1) *Emotive elements* or *emotemes*, which indicate that a sentence is emotive, but do not detail what specific emotions have been expressed. For example, interjections such as "whoa!" or "Oh!" indicate that the speaker (producer of the utterance) have conveyed some emotions. However, it is not possible, basing only on those words, to estimate precisely what kind of emotion the speaker conveyed. Ptaszynski et al. include in emotemes such groups as interjections, mimetic expressions, vulgar language, and emotive markers. The examples in Japanese are, respectively: *sugee* (great!—interjection), *wakuwaku* (heart pounding—mimetic), *-yagaru* (syntactic morpheme used in verb vulgarization), and "!", or "??" (sentence markers indicating emotiveness). Ptaszynski et al. collected and handcrafted a database of 907 emotemes. A set of features similar to what is defined by Ptaszynski et al. as emotemes has also been applied in other research on discrimination between emotive (emotional/subjective) and nonemotive (neutral/objective) sentences [721, 23, 723].

(2) *Emotive expressions* are words or phrases that directly describe emotional states, but could be used to both express one's emotions and describe the emotion without emotional engagement. This group is realized by such words as *aijō* (love—noun), *kanashimu* (to feel sad, to grieve—verb), *ureshii* (happy—adjective), or phrases such as: *mushizu ga hashiru* (to give one the creeps [from hate]) or *ashi ga chi ni tsukanai* (walk on air [from happiness]). As the collection of emotive expressions ML-Ask uses the database created on the basis of Nakamura's *Emotive Expressions Dictionary*.

With these settings ML-Ask was able to distinguish emotive sentences from nonemotive with a very high accuracy (over 90%) and to annotate affect on utterances with a sufficiently high precision (85.7% compared to human annotators), but low recall (54.7%) [547, 546]. The low recall is a disadvantage of the system, but we assumed that in a corpus as big as YACIS there should still be millions of annotations. Another reason to choose ML-Ask is that it is the only present system recognized to fully implement the idea of Contextual Valence Shifters (CVS) in Japanese.

The group recognized that CVS contain negation phrases and words like "not," "never," and "not quite," which change the valence of evaluative words (e.g., from positive to negative). ML-Ask fully incorporates the negation CVS with 108 syntactic negation structures. Examples of CVS negations in Japanese are structures such as: *amari -nai* (not quite-), *-to wa ienai* (cannot say it is-), or *-te wa ikenai* (cannot+[verb]-). Finally, the last distinguishable feature of ML-Ask is implementation of Russell's two dimensional affect space [580]. It assumes that all emotions can be represented in two dimensions: the emotion's valence (positive/negative) and activation (activated/deactivated). An example of negative-activated emotion could be "anger"; a

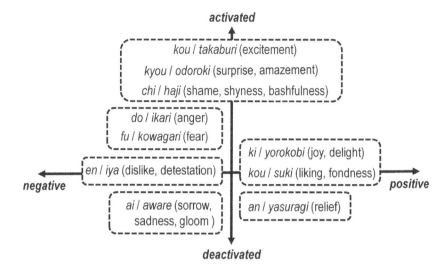

FIGURE 8.4: Mapping of Nakamura's classification of emotions on Russell's 2D space. Emotion classes placed on borderlines can be realized in more than one dimension. For example, one can be surprised positively, as well as negatively.

positive-deactivated emotion is, for example, "relief." The mapping of Nakamura's emotion types on Russell's two dimensions proposed by Ptaszynski et al. [546] was proved reliable in several research studies [549, 546, 548]. The mapping is represented in Figure 8.4. An example of ML-Ask output is represented in Figure 8.5.

We also compiled a simpler version of ML-Ask, not using emotemes, only the emotive expression dictionary with CVS and Russell's emotion space (called ML-Ask-simple) and performed additional annotations without distinguishing between emotive and nonemotive sentences. This was done for three reasons. Firs, to check how many of nonemotive sentences contain emotive expressions, which information is often provided in research on emotion corpora [470], and therefore is useful in comparison of corpora. Second, although ML-Ask distinguishes between emotive and nonemotive sentences with high accuracy, a system could be made that does this better in the future. Finally, in research on opinion mining and sentiment analysis, it has been shown that it is possible to predict sentiment without considering emotiveness of sentences [679]. Therefore, annotations performed with ML-Ask-simple could be applied in such research.

CAO is a system for the estimation of emotions conveyed through emoticons[26] developed by Ptaszynski et al. [549]. Emoticons are sets of symbols

---

[26]In particular Japanese emoticons called *kaomoji*.

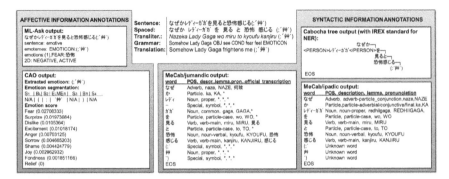

FIGURE 8.5: The examples of outputs for all annotation systems used.

widely used to convey emotions in text-based online communication, such as blogs. **CAO**, or *emotiCon Analysis and decOding of affective information system*, extracts an emoticon from an input (a sentence) and determines specific emotion types expressed by it using a three-step procedure. First, it matches the input to a predetermined emoticon database containing over 10,000 unique emoticons. The emoticons, which could not be estimated using only the database, are automatically divided into semantic areas, such as representations of the "mouth" or "eyes." The areas are automatically annotated according to their co-occurrence in a database. The performance of CAO was evaluated as very high [549] (exceeding 97%), which proved CAO as a reliable tool for the analysis of Japanese emoticons. In the annotation process, CAO was used as a supporting procedure in ML-Ask to improve the performance of affect annotation and add detailed information about emoticons appearing in the text. An example of CAO output is represented in Figure 8.5.

8.4.2 YACIS Corpus Statistics

8.4.2.1 Syntactic Information

In this section we present all relevant statistics concerning syntactic information annotated on YACIS. Where it was possible we also compared YACIS to other corpora. All basic information concerning YACIS is represented in Table 8.4. Information on the distribution of parts of speech is represented in Table 8.7. We compared the use of two dictionaries (Ipadic and Jumandic) when annotating other Japanese corpora (jBlogs and JENAAD newspaper corpus) and in addition, partially to British and Italian Web corpus (ukWaC and itWaC, respectively).

Ipadic versus Jumandic: There were major differences in the numbers of each part-of-speech types between the dictionaries. In most cases, Ipadic provided more specific annotations (nouns, verbs, particles, auxiliary verbs, exclamations) than Jumandic. For example, in Ipadic annotation there were nearly

TABLE 8.7:   Comparison of POS Distribution across Corpora

Part of Speech	YACIS-ipadic		YACIS-Jumandic		jBlogs (approx.)	JENAAD (approx.)	ukWaC	itWaC
	Percentage	(Number)	Percentage	(Number)				
Noun	34.69%	(1,942,930,102)	25.35%	(1,419,508,028)	34%	43%	1,528,839	941,990
Particle	23.31%	(1,305,329,099)	19.14%	(1,072,116,901)	18%	26%	[not provided]	[not provided]
Verb	11.57%	(647,981,102)	9.80%	(549,048,400)	9%	11%	182,610	679,758
Auxiliary verb	9.77%	(547,166,965)	2.07%	(115,763,099)	7%	5%	[not provided]	[not provided]
Adjective	2.07%	(116,069,592)	3.70%	(207,170,917)	2%	1%	538,664	706,330
Interjection	0.56%	(31,115,929)	0.40%	(22,096,949)	<1%	<1%	[not provided]	[not provided]
Other	18.03%	(1,010,004,306)	39.55%	(2,214,892,801)	29%	14%	[not provided]	[not provided]

2 billion nouns, while in Jumandic only about 1.5 billion (see Table 8.7 for details). The reason for these differences is that the dictionaries are based on different approaches to part-of-speech disambiguation. Jumandic was created using a set of handcrafted rules and therefore in a corpus as large as YACIS there are situations where no rule applies. On the other hand, Ipadic was created on a large corpus and thus provides disambiguation rules using contextual information. This is clearly visible when the category "other" is evaluated, which consists of such annotations as "symbols," or "unknown words." The number of "other" annotations with Jumandic is over two times larger than with Ipadic and covers nearly 40% of the whole corpus. The detailed analysis also revealed more generic differences in word coverage in the two dictionaries. Especially when it comes to abbreviations and casual modifications, some words do not appear in Jumandic. For example, an interjection いや *iya* ("oh") appears in both, but its casual modification いやー *iyaa* ("ooh") appears only in ipadic. Jumandic splits the word in two parts: いや and a vowel prolongation mark ー, which is annotated by Jumandic as "symbol."

YACIS versus jBlogs and JENAAD: It is difficult to manually evaluate annotations on a corpus as large as YACIS.[27] However, the larger the corpus is the more statistically reliable are the observable tendencies of annotated phenomena. Therefore, it is possible to evaluate the accurateness of annotations by comparing tendencies between different corpora. To verify part-of-speech tagging we compared tendencies in annotations between YACIS, jBlogs mentioned in Section 8.2.1, and JENAAD [682]. The latter is a medium-scale corpus of newspaper articles gathered from the Yomiuri daily newspaper (years 1989–2001). It contains about 4.7 million words (approximately 7% of jBlogs and 0.08% of YACIS). The comparison of those corpora provided interesting observations. jBlogs and JENAAD were annotated with ChaSen, while YACIS with MeCab. However, as mentioned in Section 8.4.1.1, ChaSen and MeCab in their default settings use the same Ipadic dictionary. Although there are some differences in the way each system disambiguates parts of speech, the same dictionary base makes it a good comparison of Ipadic annotations on three different corpora (small JENAAD, larger jBlogs, and large YACIS). The statistics of POS distribution is more similar between the pair YACIS (ipadic)–JENAAD ($\rho = 1.0$ in Spearman's rank setting correlation test) and YACIS (Ipadic)–jBlogs ($\rho = 0.96$), than between the pairs YACIS (Jumandic)–jBlogs ($\rho = 0.79$), YACIS (Jumandic)–JENAAD ($\rho = 0.85$) and between both versions of YACIS ($\rho = 0.88$).

Japanese versus British and Italian: As an interesting additional exercise we compared YACIS to Web corpora in other languages. In particular, we analyzed ukWaC and itWaC described by Baroni et al. [53]. Although not all the information on part-of-speech statistics is provided for those two corpora,

---

[27]Having one second to evaluate one sentence, one evaluator would need 11.2 years to verify the whole corpus (354 mil.s.).

TABLE 8.8: Evaluation Results of ML-Ask, CAO, and ML-Ask Supported with CAO on the Test Set

	Emotive/ Nonemotive	Emotion Classes	2D (valence and activation)
ML-Ask	98.8%	73.4%	88.6%
CAO	97.6%	80.2%	94.6%
ML-Ask + CAO	100.0%	89.9%	97.5%

the available information shows interesting differences between part-of-speech distribution among languages.[28] In all compared corpora the largest statistic is the number of "nouns." However, differently to all Japanese corpora, the second frequent part-of-speech in British English and Italian corpus was "adjective," while in Japanese it was "verb" (excluding "particles"). This difference is the most vivid in ukWaC. Further analysis of this phenomenon could contribute to the fields of language anthropology, and philosophy of language in general.

8.4.2.2 Affective Information

In this section we present statistics of affective information annotated on YACIS. We also evaluate these annotations in three ways. First, we used a sample of a thousand sentences randomly extracted from the corpus and annotated by laypeople. Second, we compared YACIS annotations to other emotion corpora. The third evaluation was application of the corpus to different tasks described in Section 8.5.

Evaluation of Affective Annotations: First we needed to verify the system's actual performance on YACIS, since the performance is often related to the type of test set used in evaluation. ML-Ask was previously positively evaluated on separate sentences and on an online forum. It was not yet evaluated on blogs. Moreover, the version of ML-Ask supported by CAO has not been evaluated thoroughly as well.

In the evaluation we used a test set created by Ptaszynski et al. [549] for the evaluation of CAO. It consisted of a thousand sentences randomly extracted from YACIS. They were manually annotated with emotion classes by 42 layperson annotators in an anonymous survey. There were 418 emotive and 582 nonemotive sentences. We compared the results on those sentences for ML-Ask, CAO (described in detail [549]), and ML-Ask supported with CAO. The results showed accuracy calculated as a ratio of success to the overall number of samples which are summarized in Table 8.8.

First, we verified the performance of discrimination between emotive and nonemotive sentences. The result of the ML-Ask baseline was a high 98.8%,

---

[28]We do not get into a detailed discussion on differences between POS taggers for different languages, neither the discussion on whether the same POS names (like noun, verb, or adjective) represent similar concepts among different languages (see, for example, [291] or [100]). These two discussions, although important, are beyond the scope of this chapter.

which is much higher than in the original evaluation of ML-Ask (around 90%). This could indicate that sentences with which the system was not able to deal with appear much less frequently on Ameblo. As for CAO, although it does not include such a procedure per se, it does detect the presence of emoticons in a sentence, which partially accounts for detecting emotive sentences (emoticons are one type of emoteme in ML-Ask).

The performance of CAO was also high, 97.6%. This was due to the fact that a grand majority of emotive sentences from the test set contained emoticons. Finally, ML-Ask supported with CAO achieved a remarkable 100% accuracy. This was a surprisingly good result, although it must be remembered that the test sample contained only 1000 sentences (less than 0.0003% of the whole corpus), and should be considered as partial confirmation of the system performance on the type of data contained in YACIS.

Next, we verified emotion class annotations on sentences. The baseline of ML-Ask achieved slightly better results (73.4%) than in its primary evaluation in [546] (67% of balanced F-score with P=85.7% and R=54.7%). CAO achieved 80.2%. Interestingly, this makes CAO a better affect analysis system than ML-Ask. However, the condition is that a sentence contains an emoticon. The best result, close to 90%, was achieved by ML-Ask supported with CAO. We also checked the results when only the dimensions of valence and activation were taken into account. ML-Ask achieved 88.6%, CAO nearly 95%. Support of CAO to ML-Ask again resulted in the best score, 97.5%.

Statistics of Affective Annotations: After verifying the system performance we calculated the statistics of affective annotations. First we checked the statistics of emotive and nonemotive sentences, and its determinant features (emotemes). There were nearly twice as many emotive sentences than nonemotive (ratio 1.94). Moreover, when all sentences are considered, there was approximately one emoteme class per sentence in general (ratio 0.92). This suggests that the corpus is biased in favor of emotive contents. In previous research it was often assumed that blogs make a good base for creating emotion corpora as they contain much of emotive contents. The statistics we provide here could be considered as the first attempt to confirm those claims. When it comes to statistics of each emoteme class, the most frequent class was interjections. This includes interjections separated by MeCab (see Table 8.7) and was included in the ML-Ask database. The second frequent was the punctuation marks class, which includes punctuation marks suggesting emotive engagement (such as "!" or "??"). The third frequent emoteme class consisted of emoticons, followed by endearments. As an interesting remark, the emoteme class that was present least frequently was the one consisting of vulgarities. As one possible interpretation of this result we propose the following. Blogs operate in a social space, where people describe their experiences to be read and commented by other people (friends, colleagues). The use of vulgar expressions could discourage potential readers from leaving comments and further reading, and therefore making the blog less popular.

TABLE 8.9:   Statistics of General Emotiveness of Sentences (Including: Ratio of emotive sentences to nonemotive sentences, number of emoteme classes per emotive sentence, and per sentence in general.)

# of emotive sentences	233,591,502
# of nonemotive sentence	120,408,023
ratio (emotive/nonemotive)	1.94
# of sentences containing emoteme class:	
- interjections	171,734,464
- exclamative marks	89,626,215
- emoticons	49,095,123
*) overall number of emoticons:	66,830,574
- endearments	12,935,510
- vulgarities	1,686,943
# of different emotemes in sentences	325,078,255
ratio (emoteme classes per emotive sentence)	1.39
ratio (emoteme classes per any sentence)	0.92

Second, we checked the statistics of the emotion classes annotated on both emotive sentences (annotated by ML-Ask) and on all sentences (annotated by ML-Ask-simple). The results are compared in Table 8.10. The most frequent emotions were joy (31%), dislike (20%), and fondness (19%). These emotions are the ones related the most to appraising events and experiences in a straightforward manner. They are also the most typical positive and negative emotions according to Russell's 2-dimensional scale (for details see the description of the ML-Ask system in Section 8.4.1.2). Only the three emotion classes covered over 70% of all emotion class annotations.

However, it could happen that the number of expressions included in each emotion class database influenced the number of annotations (a database containing many expressions has higher probability to gather more annotations). Therefore, we verified if there was a correlation between the number of annotations and the number of emotive expressions in each emotion class database. The verification was based on Spearman's rank correlation test between the two sets of data. The test revealed no statistically significant correlation, with ρ=0.38 in both cases, which proves that the number of expressions in each emotion class database did not influence the number of annotations.

Next, we compared two sets of results provided by ML-Ask and ML-Ask-simple. The latter annotates an emotion class on a sentence even if the sentence is nonemotive and was not written to express any emotion. Sentences like these are usually used to, for example, deliberate about a particular emotion, or express a piece of nonemotive opinion.

It was predictable that ML-Ask-simple would provide more annotations. However, it could happen that for some emotion types there were larger differences, which would suggest that emotive sentence discrimination in ML-Ask is worse for some emotion classes. For example, if the differences between

TABLE 8.10: Comparison of Emotion Class Annotations on Emotive Sentences (ML-Ask) and on All Sentences (ML-Ask-simple), Including Their Separate Percentage and Partial Sums or Percentages

	Emotion	ML-Ask			ML-Ask-Simple			% of Sentences with Emotive Expressions	
Rank	Class	Number of Sentences	%	% (partial sum)	Number of Sentences	%	% (partial sum)	Emotive	Nonemotive
1	joy	16,728,452	31%	31.40%	22,100,500	31%	30.90%	75.693%	24.307%
2	dislike	10,806,765	20%	51.68%	14,184,697	20%	50.73%	76.186%	23.814%
3	fondness	9,861,466	19%	70.19%	13,817,116	19%	70.04%	71.371%	28.629%
4	fear	3,308,288	6%	76.40%	4,496,250	6%	76.33%	73.579%	26.421%
5	relief	3,104,774	6%	82.23%	4,116,234	6%	82.08%	75.428%	24.572%
6	excitement	2,833,388	5%	87.55%	4,026,645	6%	87.71%	70.366%	29.634%
7	surprise	2,398,535	5%	92.05%	3,108,017	4%	92.06%	77.173%	22.827%
8	gloom	2,144,492	4%	96.07%	2,881,166	4%	96.09%	74.431%	25.569%
9	anger	1,140,865	2%	98.21%	1,564,059	2%	98.27%	72.943%	27.057%
10	shame	952,188	2%	100.00%	1,235,358	2%	100.00%	77.078%	22.922%
sum		53,279,213		sum	71,530,042		average	**74.425%**	**25.575%**

$p < .01$

the two annotation sets were similar for most emotion classes, but differed greatly for one or two emotion classes, it could be assumed that some of those sentences are in fact emotive, but ML-Ask was unable to discover that. This phenomenon was noticed by Ptaszynski et al. [546] in their analysis of the Japanese online forum *2channel*. In particular, they report that in the test set (containing about 2000 sentences from a single forum thread) ML-Ask annotations were statistically similar to a gold standard (human annotations) for eight out of ten emotion classes. Detailed analysis of the two problematic outliers revealed that the cause was the result of an enormous number of emoticons used to express excitement and dislike, which their version of ML-Ask could not process. In our research we supported ML-Ask with CAO (emoticon analysis system), which solves the problem for the majority of cases.

We compared the percentage of emotion class annotations on emotive sentences and on all sentences to find potential outliers. Although we assumed there would be some differences, surprisingly for all emotion classes the results were similar, with emotive sentences being approximately 75% of all annotated sentences (25% were nonemotive sentences containing emotive expressions). Even after excluding the lowest and the highest results, the average still remained the same (74.589% emotive and 25.411% nonemotive). The annotations were well balanced, which proves that ML-Ask, although not ideal, is a reliable and stable affect annotation system.

The annotations of ML-Ask-simple, with the exception of providing statistical proof for ML-Ask performance, have another potential applicability. Among nonemotive sentences containing emotive expressions some sentences are representations of opinions. If the opinion sentences could be separated from purely neutral ones, they could become useful as additional training data in fields like opinion mining and sentiment analysis.

Comparison with Other Emotion Corpora: First, we compared YACIS to KNB [272]. The KNB corpus was annotated mostly for the needs of sentiment analysis and therefore does not contain any information on specific emotion classes. However, it is annotated with emotion valence for different categories valence can be expressed in Japanese, such as *emotional attitude* (e.g., "to feel sad about X"=negative, "to like X"=positive), *opinion* (e.g., "X is wonderful"=positive, "not convinced to X"=negative), or *positive/negative event* (e.g., "X broke down"=negative, "X was awarded"=positive). We compared the ratios of sentences expressing positive valence to the ones expressing negative valence. The comparison was made for all KNB valence categories separately and as a sum. In our research we do not make additional subcategorization of valence types, but used in the comparison ratios of sentences with only positive/negative valence and including the mostly positive/negative sentences (situations when one sentence contains numerous expressions, majority of which is either positive or negative). The comparison is presented in Table 8.11. In KNB for all valence categories except one the ratio of positive to negative sentences was biased in favor of positive sentences. Moreover, for

TABLE 8.11: Comparison of Positive and
Negative Sentences between KNB and YACIS

		Positive	Negative	Ratio
KNB	emotional attitude	317	208	1.52
	opinion	489	289	1.69
	merit	449	264	1.70
	acceptation or rejection	125	41	3.05
	event	43	63	0.68
	sum	1,423	865	1.65
YACIS	only	22,381,992	12,837,728	1.74
(ML-Ask)	only+ mostly	23,753,762	13,605,514	1.75
(ML-Ask-	only	31,071,945	17,496,901	1.78
simple)	only+ mostly	32,752,589	18,442,602	1.78

most cases, including the ratio taken from the sums of sentences, the ratio was similar to the one in YACIS (around 1.7 in favor of positive contents). Although the scale of compared sentences differ greatly, the fact that the ratio remains similar across the two different corpora suggests that the Japanese express in blogs more positive than negative emotions.

Next, we compared YACIS to the corpus created by Minato et al. [470]. This corpus was prepared on the basis of an emotive expression dictionary. Therefore, we compared its statistics not only to YACIS, but also, where it was possible, to the emotive lexicon used in our research (see Section 8.4.1.2 for details). Emotion classes used in Minato et al. differ slightly to those used in our research (YACIS and Nakamura's dictionary). For example, they use the class name "hate" to describe what in YACIS is called "dislike." Moreover, they have no classes such as "excitement," "relief," or "shame." On the other hand, they use the class name "respect," which is not present in YACIS. To make the comparison possible we excluded all emotion classes not appearing in both and unified all class names. The results are summarized in Table 8.12. There was no correlation between YACIS and Nakamura (ρ=0.25), which confirms the results calculated in Section 8.4.2.2, part "Statistics of Affective Annotations." A medium correlation was observed between YACIS and Minato et al. (ρ=0.63). Finally, a strong correlation was observed between Minato et al. and Nakamura (ρ=0.88), which is the most interesting observation. Both Minato et al. and Nakamura are in fact dictionaries of emotive expressions. The fact that they strongly correlate suggests that for the compared emotion classes there could be a tendency in the language to create more expressions to describe some emotions rather than the others (dislike, joy, and fondness are often some of the most frequent emotion classes). This phenomenon needs to be verified more thoroughly in the future.

TABLE 8.12: Comparison of Number of Emotive Expressions Appearing in Different Corpora: Minato et al. [470], YACIS and Nakamura's Dictionary [486], with the Results of Spearman's Rank Correlation Test (Emotion classes marked with "*" were omitted to avoid unfair comparison.)

	Minato et al.	YACIS	Nakamura
dislike	355	14,184,697	532
joy	295	22,100,500	224
fondness	205	13,817,116	197
sorrow	205	2,881,166	232
* relief	0	3,104,774	106
* excitement	0	2,833,388	269
anger	160	1,564,059	199
fear	145	4,496,250	147
* respect	45	0	0
surprise	25	3,108,017	129
* shame	0	952,188	65
	Minato et al. and Nakamura	Minato et al. and YACIS	YACIS and Nakamura
Spearman's ρ	0.88	0.63	0.25

8.5 Applications

8.5.1 Emotion Object Ontology Generation

One of the applications of large corpora is to extract from them smaller subcorpora for specified tasks. Ptaszynski et al. [552] have applied YACIS for their task of generating a robust emotion object ontology. They used cross-reference of annotations of emotional information described in this chapter and syntactic annotations done by Ptaszynski et al. [551] to extract only sentences in which expression of emotion was preceded by its cause, as in the example below.

彼女に振られたから悲しい...
Kanojo ni furareta **kara** <u>kanashii</u>...
Girlfriend DAT dump PAS CAUS sad ...
I'm <u>sad</u> **because** my girlfriend dumped me...

The example can be analyzed in the following way. Emotive expression (<u>*kanashii*</u>, "<u>sad</u>") is bound with sentence contents (*Kanojo ni furareta*, "my girlfriend dumped me") with a causality morpheme (**kara**, "**because**"). In such a situation the sentence contents represent the object of emotion. This can be generalized to the following metastructure,

$$O_E \quad CAUS \quad X_E,$$

(8.1)

TABLE 8.13:　　A Few Examples of Success and Failure of the Emotion Object Extraction Procedure

success	failure
友達にアルバム貸してなかなか返ってこなくて怒り気味のむろびでした-_-笑 I lent a CD album to my friend, but he/she wouldn't give it back, so I've been kind of angry lately -_- laugh	怒りと悲しさでイッパイです(*_*) I'm so full of anger and sadness (*_*)
自然災害は予測しにくいので怖いですよね(-.-;) Natural disasters are scary because they are difficult to predict (-.-;)	自分で着てみた時の物悲しさ(/_-。 The melancholy I felt when I put it on (/_-。
雨続くとホンマ嫌ですよね(ノ_ヽ I don't like when the rain just keeps pouring all the time (ノ_ヽ	でも握力が無いので、こそばゆいだけかも~(^-^)/ But without a strong grip it felt just like tickling (^-^)/
歯医者って怖いですよね m(__)m I'm really scared of dentists m(__)m	怒られる要因がなくても無理に怒り出すから、もうしばらくは プライベートも静かにしてなきゃ(T-T) He bursts with anger, even when there is no reason to get angry, so I need to sit alone quietly for some time (T-T)
ipod はないと嫌だからすぐに充電だよ！！ I hate not having the ipod [with me], so got to recharge now!!	
上の娘が来月から小学生なのでちょっと心配です(;^ω^A My oldest daughter is going to primary school next month, so I'm kind of anxious (;^ω^A	

emotion object, **causality form**, emotive expression

where O_E=[Emotion object], $CAUS$=[**causal form**], and X_E=[expression of emotion].

The causal phrases were cleaned of irrelevant words like stop words to leave only the object phrases. The evaluation showed that we were able to extract nearly 20 million object phrases, from which roughly 80% were extracted correctly with a reliable significance. Thanks to rich annotations on YACIS corpus the ontology included such features as emotion class (joy, anger, etc.), dimensions (valence/activation), and POS or semantic categories (hypernyms, etc.). A few examples of successful and erroneous extraction of emotion objects are represented in Table 8.13.

8.5.2　Moral Consequence Retrieval

Another application that uses the YACIS corpus, which is annotated with affect- and sentiment-related information, regards retrieval of moral consequences of actions, first proposed by Rzepka and Araki [581] and recently developed by Komuda et al. [365].[29] The moral consequence retrieval agent was based on the idea of Wisdom of Crowd. In particular, Komuda et al. [365] used a Web-mining technique to gather consequences of actions and apply causality relations, like in the research described in Section 8.5.1, but with a reversed algorithm and lexicon containing not only emotional but also ethical notions. They cross-referenced emotional and ethical information about a certain phrase (such as "To kill a person") to obtain the statistical probability for emotional ("to feel sad," "to be in joy," etc.) and ethical consequences ("to be punished," "to be praised," etc.). Initially, the moral agent was based on the whole Internet content. However, multiple queries to the search engine API made by the system caused constant blocking of an IP address and in effect critical errors. The system was tested on over 100 ethically significant real-world problems, such as "To kill a man," "To steal money," "To bribe

---

[29]See also a mention in *Scientific American*, by Anderson and Anderson [26].

someone," "To help people," or "To save environment," resulting in a precision of 86% of correct recognitions.

8.6   Discussion

The research on large scale corpora has been gaining interest during the last several years. One of the problems that one needs to address in such research concern copyrights of the downloaded material. We follow in this matter the research of Erjavec et al. [206] and Baroni et al. [53].

According to Erjavec et al. [206] and Baroni et al. [53], downloading texts and presenting various statistics obtained from them is an activity similar to those performed by search engines. Therefore, there is no need for asking the authors of the crawled Web pages for permission to use their texts in the corpus, as the contents are already open to the public. In research on crawled corpora based on the whole Web, such as in [414, 53, 541], there is one privacy-related problem. It is the problem of detecting the "robots.txt" file which, located in a domain, means that the domain owners or Web page authors ask the robot or search engine crawler to neglect visiting the page. In our research, however, this was not the issue, since blogs in general are public and no official blog service known to the authors, including Ameblo, uses the "robots.txt" file.

YACIS corpus is meant to be used for pure scientific purposes and is not planned to be available on sale. However, we wish to contribute with it to other research. Therefore, we are open to make the corpus available to other researchers after contacting us and specifying applicable legal conditions by obtaining full usage agreement. In the near future we also plan to release an *n*-gram version of the corpus, which would be available online without any restrictions.

8.7   Conclusions and Future Work

In this chapter we presented our research on the creation and annotation of YACIS, a large scale corpus of Japanese blogs compiled for the need of research in NLP and emotion processing in text.

First, we performed a survey on Web-based corpora, with a focus on large-scale corpora containing a billion words or more. We compared some of their features and the amount of annotations. Additionally, we compared some of the Web-based corpora of Japanese language and separately emotion corpora.

Next, we presented our research in compiling and annotating YACIS, a large corpus of Japanese blogs, with syntactic and affective information. We developed a set of tools for corpus compilation and successfully compiled the large scale corpus from Ameba blogs.

The syntactic information we annotated included tokenization, parts of speech, lemmatization, dependency structure, and named entities. The syntactic information annotated on the corpus was compared to two other corpora in Japanese, and additionally to two corpora in different languages (British English and Italian). The comparison revealed interesting observations. The three corpora in Japanese, although different in size, showed similar POS distribution, whereas for other languages, although the corpora were comparable in size, the POS distribution differed greatly. We plan to investigate these differences in more detail in the future.

The affective information annotated on YACIS include emotion classes, emotive expressions, emotion valence and activation, and emotion objects. The systems used in the annotation process include ML-Ask, a system for affect analysis of utterances and CAO, a system for affect analysis of emoticons. The evaluation on a test sample of annotations showed sufficiently high results. Statistics of the affective annotations were compared to other emotion corpora. The comparison showed similarities in the ratio of expressions of positive to negative emotions on both small and large scale corpora. We also observed a high correlation between two different emotive expression dictionaries.

The YACIS corpus, containing over 5.6 billion words, is a valuable resource and could contribute greatly to numerous research, including research on emotions in language, sentiment, and affect analysis. Some of the applications of the corpus include automatically constructing a robust ontology of emotion objects [552] or emotional and moral consequence retrieval [581, 365].

In the near future we plan to improve the annotations, as there is still some amount of noise introduced by automatic annotation systems. We are considering to apply active learning techniques to optimize ambiguous annotations (such as emotive sentences with no specified emotion labels). Also, we plan to improve POS and dependency annotations by retraining syntactic analysis tools on blogs (originally the systems were designed as "all-purpose" tools and were trained on different types of data). We also plan to release an additional n-gram version of the corpus to be freely accessible from the Internet without limitations and provide an interactive online interface allowing corpus querying for all types of information.

8.8   Acknowledgments

This research was partially supported by (JSPS) KAKENHI Grant-in-Aid for JSPS Fellows (Project number: 22-00358) and (JSPS) KAKENHI Grant-in-Aid for Scientific Research (Project number: 24600001).

Part IV

Applications

Chapter 9

Question-Answering of UGC

Chin-Yew Lin

Microsoft Research Asia

9.1 Introduction

Building machines that are capable of answering natural language questions is one of the biggest challenges in natural language processing and has a history dating back to the late 1950s [634]. A renewed interest in question-answering started in 1999 with a series of NIST-sponsored TREC Question-Answering (QA) Tracks, large-scale evaluations of domain-independent question-answering[1] that produced a few high performance question-answering systems capable of answering factoid and list questions

---

[1]See TREC QA Collections at: http://trec.nist.gov/data/qa.html

[525, 478, 283]. In 2011, IBM's open-domain question-answering system, Watson [215], beat the two highest ranked Jeopardy![2] players, marking a significant milestone in the more than 60-year quest to create a viable question-answering machine.

Despite the success of Watson, state-of-the-art question-answering systems are yet to replace the services offered by community question-answering (CQA) sites such as Yahoo! Answers,[3] Naver,[4] Baidu Zhidao,[5] and Quora,[6] where users can ask and answer questions of any kind. Question-answering in UGC (user generated content) sites such as Yahoo! Answers allows users to post questions and wait for answers from others. After a sufficient number of answers are collected, either the asker selects the best answer or users in the community cast votes to choose the best answer. CQA sites have accumulated large collections of questions and answers. For example, Yahoo! Answers announced that it has reached 1 billion answers in May 2010[7] after 5 years of operation. These question and answer collections, along with their user interaction data, have drawn the interest of natural language processing [417, 68], information retrieval [317, 737, 629], and social network [8, 488] research communities.

In this chapter, we summarize the major research efforts in question-answering of UGC in the following three areas: (1) question search [317, 737, 185, 696, 113, 776]; (2) question and answer quality [319, 640, 74, 13, 75, 585]; and (3) user expertise [416, 764, 326, 412]. Research efforts into question-answering of UGC do not limit themselves to CQA data. However, we concentrate on CQA related efforts. Readers interested in question-answering beyond CQA can refer to FAQs [261, 637, 320, 343] and online forums [145, 172, 746].

We first introduce some common concepts in CQA. Figure 9.1 shows a sample of question threads from Yahoo! Answers. Asker A posted the question "What is the best way to get into Taipei from Toayoun Airport?" This part is called the *question title* or simply the *question* of a question thread. Yahoo! Answers limits the length of a question to 75 characters. He also provides more details by indicating that his flight will arrive around 6:40 AM and he had checked the airport bus information on a Web site but wanted advice from the community. This part is called the *question details*. Users are not required to enter question details. In the original question thread on Yahoo! Answers, six answers are listed. Only two are included here for illustration purposes. One is the Best Answer posted by Answerer X, which was chosen by the asker as the best answer. The other is an alternative answer entered by Answerer Y. After a close examination of these two answers, we have determined they are equally informative. However, as the asker noted in his/her feedback at the end of the Best Answer block, he chose Answerer X because Answerer X

---

[2]For more information about Jeopardy!, please see: http://www.jeopardy.com
[3]See: http://answers.yahoo.com
[4]Yahoo! Answers: http://www.naver.com
[5]Baidu Zhidao: http://zhidao.baidu.com
[6]Quora: http://www.quora.com
[7]http://yanswersblog.com/index.php/archives/2010/05/03/1-billion-answers-served

replied earlier and gave him a 4 star rating ("Asker's Rating"). Notice that one anonymous user voted that Answerer X's answer was good ("1 person rated this as good"). In addition to the information shown in Figure 9.1, each CQA question typically is assigned to a predefined question category. The question in Figure 9.1 is located in the "Travel.Asia_Pacific.Taiwan" category. The pairing of a question, the question details, its answers, and associated user interaction information such as Best Answer selection, user votes, the question category, and the asker rating of answers, forms a richer retrieval target than a plain document in traditional question-answering or information retrieval. In addition, the coupling of a question with its answers, especially a user selected or elected Best Answer, reduces question-answering in CQA to a question search problem [317, 318]. Given a question as a query, question search in CQA aims to return previously asked questions that are semantically similar to the query. The challenge is how to compute similarity between two questions asking for the same thing but expressed in different words. For example, the following two questions [318] are looking for similar answers but use different expressions:

Q1: I'd like to insert music into PowerPoint.

Q2: How can I link sound in PowerPoint?

Section 9.3 summarizes a series of models designed to tackle this question paraphrase [67] problem.

For the question posted by Asker A in Figure 9.1, the name of the airport is mistakenly written as "Toayoun." The correct name is "Taoyuan." This is a question quality problem. To ensure that questions posted on CQA sites are of high quality is an important task for managing CQA sites. We expect a high quality question should attract more user participation and more answer responses. This in turn will increase overall user engagement of CQA sites. Comparing the two answers shown in Figure 9.1, the Best Answer seems to have higher quality. Answerer X first suggests that more details can be obtained if Asker A's end destination is specified. He then suggests how to reach Taipei and explains why it is a good recommendation, that is, the least number of stops and low cost. He wishes Asker A has a good trip at the end. With hundreds of millions of question threads such as this, researchers are investigating ways to automatically determine the quality of answers [319, 13, 75]. However, the best answer is not always reliable [585] and reusable [417]. Table 9.1 shows a case where the same question "Which actress has the most seductive voice?" posted in two different categories, that is, Polls & Surveys and Movies, and resulted in two different Best Answers chosen by the same asker. This case reminds us that we cannot solely depend on Best Answer selection as the single metric for answer quality.

CQA sites such as Yahoo! Answers can be viewed as a type of post-reply (or question-answer in CQA) network as described by Zhang et al. [764].[8] This

---

[8]Zhang et al. used Java Forum as an example, http://www.java-forums.org

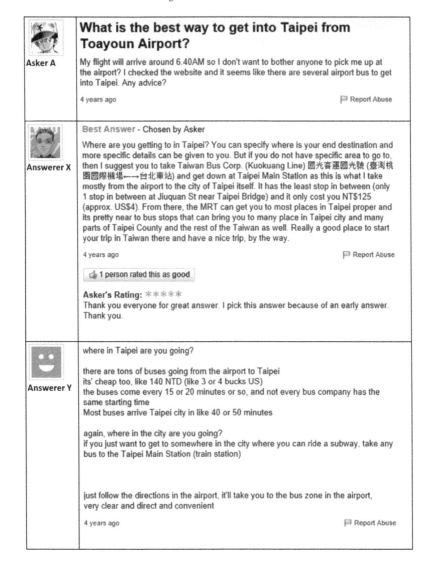

FIGURE 9.1: A sample question thread in Yahoo! Answers includes a question, the best answer chosen by the asker, and an alternative answer. The asker's and answerer's names are replaced with pseudonyms.

post-reply network reflects its members' shared interests. The answerers on this network have superior expertise on the topics that they reply to. Zhang et al. calls this community expertise network or CEN. Figure 9.1 shows a sample CEN. User expertise or reputation can be computed using link analysis methods such as PageRank [516] or HITS [349]. Intuitively, users with higher

TABLE 9.1: A Question Has Two Best Answers

Question Title	Which actress has the most seductive voice? ... could range from a giggly goldie hawn ... to anne bancroft?
Question Detail	or any other type of voice that you find alluring ...
Best Answer (Polls & Surveys)	Fenella Fielding, wow!!!!
Best Answer (Movies)	i think joanna lumlley has a really sexy voice

expertise should offer answers of better quality. However, this is not always true [13] as expertise is topic dependent, as Suryanto et al. [653] confirmed in their experiments. Section 9.4 summarizes related work in estimating question quality, answer quality, and user expertise. How to incorporate these quality metrics to improve question search is also discussed in that section.

In the rest of this chapter, we formally provide the rationale for question search and explain the need for evaluating question and answer quality in Section 9.2. Section 9.3 introduces different question search models without considering question and answer quality. In Section 9.4, we show how to compute question quality, answer quality, and user expertise and how quality features can be added to the quality-agnostic models introduced in Section 9.3. We conclude this chapter in Section 9.5.

9.2   Question-Answering by Searching Questions

The idea of answering a question by searching a collection of previously asked questions is not new. It was exploited by Hammond et al. [261] and Burke et al. [110] in the 1990s as an effective way for retrieving Frequently Asked Questions (FAQs) in USENET newsgroups. FAQ files are put together by newsgroup contributors and have a high reusable value to USENET users. Similarly, hundreds of millions of question threads in CQA sites might also benefit CQA users if effective and efficient retrieval mechanisms are developed and deployed. However, we cannot guarantee that questions and answers or even Best Answers in CQA sites always have high quality as we have briefly discussed in the introduction. Therefore, two very important questions to ask are: 1. whether previously asked questions and their answers in CQA sites are reusable and 2. what is the quality of CQA answers.

Liu et al. [417] conducted an experiment on the four most popular Yahoo! Answers categories, Computers & Internet (C&I), Entertainment & Music (E&M), Health, and Society & Culture (S&C), by manually examining 100

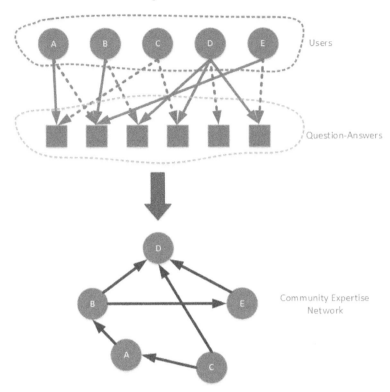

FIGURE 9.2: A sample CQA post-reply (or question-answer) network and community expertise network (CEN). A dashed line links an asker to a question and a solid line connects an answerer to a question [764]. (**See color insert.**)

questions and their answers from each category. For each question, they asked "whether the answer selected by its asker or voted by the community can be used as a good answer when a similar question is asked again. Their results show that answers are reusable in 78–90% of the cases. Among them, 84% in C&I, 38% in E&M, 83% in Health, and 33% in S&C were asking for factual information; 4% in C&I, 40% in E&M, 7% in Health, and 50% in S&C were asking for opinions. However, reusable answers might not be the best answers in a context different from their original settings. For example, the correctness of an answer might be time dependent or person dependent, that is, "the richest person in the world" or "the best movies in the summer."

Agichtein et al. [13] investigated the interaction between editor-graded question quality and answer quality on a dataset consisting of 6665 questions and 8366 question/answer pairs from Yahoo! Answers. They found that *"good answers are much more likely to be written in response to good questions, and bad questions are the ones that attract more bad answers."* Their results are shown in Table 9.2.

TABLE 9.2: Interaction between Question and Answer Quality Reported by Agichtein et al. [13] (Q: question quality, A: answer quality.)

Quality	Q High	Q Medium	Q Low
A High	41%	15%	8%
A Medium	53%	76%	74%
A Low	6%	9%	18%
Total	100%	100%	100%

A comprehensive evaluation of answer quality was reported by Sakai et al. [585] in the NTCIR-8 Community pilot QA task [307] (NTCIR-8 CQA). The NTCIR-8 CQA task was conducted over a test set consisting of 1500 questions from 15 top categories of Yahoo! Chiebukuro[9] data version 1.0 and their associated 7443 answers. Four assessors were asked to judge the quality of answers according to the following criteria [307]:

- Grade A: A satisfactory answer to the question

- Grade B: A partially relevant answer, or a partially irrelevant answer

- Grade C: An answer that is unrelated to the question

Each assessor assigned a grade A, B, or C to an answer, the results were shown in Table 9.3 with 9-level graded relevance mapping proposed by Sakai et al. [585]. We have found that CQA answers have varying degrees of quality. More informative results in Table 9.4, compiled by Sakai et al. [585], indicate that even the Best Answers selected by askers or voted by the community also have a varying degree of quality. Only about 64.8% (598+372+2=972 out of 1500) of the Best Answers were rated grade A by at least three assessors.

The results from Liu et al., Agichtein et al., and Sakai et al. validate the question search approach and also suggest the importance of question and answer quality. We summarize the major question search models in the next section.

9.3 Question Search

Question search assumes the existence of a CQA archive and it aims to automatically return relevant questions and their answers given a question query. As indicated by Hammond et al. [261] and Jeon et al. [318], the major challenge of question search is how to find semantically similar questions in a question-answering archive where input questions and their similar questions

---

[9]This is the Japanese version of Yahoo! Answers, see: http://chiebukuro.yahoo.co.jp

TABLE 9.3:   NTCIR-8 7443 Answer Grades [307]
and Their Mapping to 9-Level Graded Relevance [585]

Grade	# of Answers	Mapping	Level	# of Answers
AAAA	1301	8	L8	1301
AAAB	1505	7	L7	1505
AAAC	2	6	L6	1527
AABB	1525	6		
AABC	14	5	L5	1399
ABBB	1385	5		
AACC	1	4	L4	1318
ABBC	76	4		
BBBB	1241	4		
ABCC	7	3	L3	238
BBBC	231	3		
ACCC	1	2	L2	106
BBCC	105	2		
BCCC	32	1	L1	32
CCCC	17	0	L0	17
Total	7,443		Total	7,443

TABLE 9.4:   NTCIR-8 Best Answers
Mapping to 9-Level Graded Relevance [585]

L8	L7	L6	L5	L4	L3	L2	L1	Total
598	372	245	156	99	22	7	1	1500

might not be expressed in the same way. Hammond et al. used a machine-readable dictionary WordNet[10] to compute the semantic distance between two questions using a maker-passing algorithm [575]. This approach has not been developed further since the late 1990s [110]. The dominant approach since 2000 has been retrieval models based on the language modeling approach [542] or translation model approach [318] coupled with word-to-word [318] or phrase-to-phrase [776] translation probabilities learned through IBM Model 1 [101] to address the word mismatch problem. An important subproblem is how to construct "parallel corpora" from CQA archives. A pooled approach proposed by Xue et al. [737], which created a parallel corpus from both question-to-answer pairs and answer-to-question pairs, achieved the best results. In the rest of this section, we introduce major variants of question retrieval models.

9.3.1   Query Likelihood Language Models

Following Xue et al. [737], given a CQA archive C consisting of a collection of question-answer pairs $(D, a)_i$ and a user question or query q, the

---

[10]See: http://wordnet.princeton.edu

task of question retrieval is to rank $(D, a)_i$ according to $score(q, (D, a)_i)$. In the language modeling framework, $score(q, (D, a)_i)$ can be estimated from the probability of q given $(D, a)_i$, or $P(q|(D, a)_i)$. For a model that does not consider the answer of a question-answer pair, $P(q|(D, a)_i)$ is reduced to $P(q|D_i)$ or simply to $P(q|D)$. Table 9.5 lists 3 major ways of computing $P(q|D)$ and one way to incorporate an answer language model, $P_{ml}(w|a)$, using the answer portion of question-answer pairs. $\#(w, D)$ is the number of words w occurring both in question D and query q. $\#(w, C)$ is the number of words w occurring both in the entire collection C and query q. $|D|$ and $|C|$ are the total number of words in a question D and in the collection C, respectively. α, β, and γ are smoothing parameters and $\alpha + \beta + \gamma = 1$ in Equation 9.10.

Equations 9.1, 9.2, and 9.3 compose the baseline unigram language model (LM) for question retrieval used by the majority of research in this area. λ is a smoothing parameter to avoid the zero probability of $P(w|D)$ due to data sparsity. Equation 9.2 is a form of Jelinek-Mercer smoothing. If we replace λ with $\frac{\lambda}{|D|+\lambda}$, it becomes Dirichlet smoothing [737]. The effects of choosing different smoothing methods are investigated in detail by Zhai and Lafferty [763]. The weakness of the LM model can be explained by the maximum likelihood estimation of $P_{ml}(w|D)$ shown in Equation 9.3. $\#(w, D)$ is zero when there are no common words between a query and a question. This is the case when a query and a question have the same meaning but are expressed in different words, that is, the paraphrase problem, which leads to poor question retrieval performance.

Berger et al. [67] proposed a translation model (TR) to address this problem as shown in Equation 9.4 and 9.5. The TR model replaces the maximum likelihood estimation of $P_{lm}(w|D)$ in Equation 9.3 with $P_{tr}(w|D)$ in Equation 9.5. The index term t in Equation 9.5 acts as a *bridge* between word w in a query and words in question D. $P(w|t)$, the translation probability between w and t, typically is estimated using IBM Model 1 [101] using the following three equations [318]:

$$P(t|s) = \lambda_s^{-1} \sum_{i=1}^{N} c(t|s; J^i) \tag{9.11}$$

$$c(t|s; J^i) = \frac{P(t|s)}{P(t|s_1) + ... + P(t|s_n)} \#(t, J^i) \#(s, J^i) \tag{9.12}$$

$$\lambda_s = \sum_{t} \sum_{i=1}^{N} c(t|s; J^i) \tag{9.13}$$

$P(t|s)$ is the translation probability that we want to estimate. λ_s is a normalization factor to make sure the sum of translation probabilities given s to all ts, that is, $\sum_t P(t|s)$, is equal to 1. N is the number of training samples. J^i is the ith training pair. s_i is a word from the source in J^i. t is a word in the target. $\#(t, J^i)$ is the number of times that t occurs in J^i. $\#(s, J^i)$ is the

TABLE 9.5: Question Retrieval Models (LM: Language Model, TR: Translation Model, TransLM: Translation-Based Language Model, and TransLM+QL: TransLM Plus Answer Language Model [737])

LM

$$P(q|D) = \prod_{w \in q} P(w|D) \qquad (9.1)$$

$$P(w|D) = (1 - \lambda)P_{ml}(w|D) + \lambda P_{ml}(w|C) \qquad (9.2)$$

$$P_{ml}(w|D) = \frac{\#(w, D)}{|D|}, P_{ml} = \frac{\#(w, C)}{|C|} \qquad (9.3)$$

TR

$$P(w|D) = (1 - \lambda)P_{tr}(w|D) + \lambda P_{ml}(w|C) \qquad (9.4)$$

$$P_{tr}(w|D) = \sum_{t \in D} P(w|t)P_{ml}(t|D) \qquad (9.5)$$

TransLM

$$P(w|D) = (1 - \lambda)P_{mx}(w|D) + \lambda P_{ml}(w|C) \qquad (9.6)$$

$$P_{mx}(w|D) = (1 - \beta)P_{ml}(w|D) + \beta P_{tr}(w|D) \qquad (9.7)$$

TransLM+QL

$$P(q|D, a) = \prod_{w \in q} P(w|D, a) \qquad (9.8)$$

$$P(w|D, a) = (1 - \lambda)P_{mx}(w|D, a) + \lambda P_{ml}(w|C) \qquad (9.9)$$

$$P_{mx}(w|D, a) = \alpha P_{ml}(w|D) + \beta P_{tr}(w|D) + \gamma P_{ml}(w|a) \qquad (9.10)$$

TABLE 9.6: Question Retrieval Models Comparison Reported by Xue et al. [737]

Model	Trans Prob	MAP	P@10
LM		0.3217	0.2211
TR	$P(Q|A)$	0.3546	0.2500
TR	$P(A|Q)$	0.3658	0.2526
TransLM	$P(Q|A)$	0.3790	0.2658
TransLM	$P(A|Q)$	0.4059	0.2684
TransLM	P_{pool}	0.4238	0.2868
TransLM+QL	P_{pool}	0.4885	0.3053

number of times that s occurs in J^i. GIZA++[11] is a useful tool to estimate word-to-word translation probabilities. Please refer to Brown et al. [101] for other translation models and methods of estimating parameters.

Xue et al. [737] showed that the way training samples are created will affect overall question retrieval performance. They found that pooling question-to-answer pairs and answer-to-question pairs together to form the training samples and then using Equations 9.11, 9.12, and 9.13 to compute translation probabilities achieved the best empirical results.

The translation-based language model (TransLM) shown in Table 9.5 is proposed to effectively calculate the self-translation probability, that is, $P(w|w)$, which tends to be underestimated by IBM Model 1. Jeon et al. [318] always set $P(w|w)$ to 1 to compensate but it caused instability in the TR model. TransLM linearly combines maximum likelihood estimation of $P_{ml}(w|D)$ and translation-based estimation of $P_{tr}(w|D)$, that is, Equation 9.7, to avoid underestimation. The transLM model is further extended by Xue et al. by adding the language model from the answer part, that is, $P_{ml}(w|a)$. The complete TransLM+QL model is shown in Table 9.5.

Table 9.6 summarizes the relevant results reported by Xue et al. [737] on a collection of 1 million Wondir CQA question and answer pairs with mean average precision (MAP) and a precision of 10. Fifty questions from the TREC-9 QA track were used for testing. $P(Q|A)$ indicates that the answer portion of a question answer pair is used as the source and the question portion as the target to estimate translation probabilities; while $P(A|Q)$ is the opposite. P_{pool} uses both as training samples. The results confirm the effectiveness of TR, TransLM, TransLM+QL, and P_{pool}.

9.3.2 Exploiting Category Information

Cao et al. [114] tried to further improve question retrieval models by exploiting category information of a question. For example, the sample question shown in Figure 9.1 is in the Yahoo!_Answers.Travel.Asia_Pacific.Taiwan[12]

---

[11]See: http://www.fjoch.com/GIZA++.html
[12]We substitute space with "_" in category name for clarity.

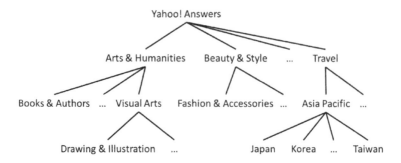

FIGURE 9.3: Part of Yahoo! Answers category tree.

leaf category. Figure 9.3 shows part of the Yahoo! Answers category tree where Yahoo!_Answers is the root category. The intuition is that the category information of a query has different significance in computing global relevance and local relevance [113]. For example, given a query "Family-friendly things to do in Paris?"—questions in the "Yahoo!_Answers.Travel. Europe.France.Paris" category are more likely to be relevant than in the "Yahoo!_Answers.Travel.United_States.Los_Angeles" category, where a very similar question "Family-friendly activities in Los Angeles area?" might exist. The word "Paris" is a discriminative word to help zoom into to the "Yahoo!_Answers.Travel.Europe.France.Paris" category but it loses its discriminative power to distinguish questions within the category.

Cao et al. [114] proposed three models to leverage category information, which are summarized in Table 9.7. Compared to LM in Table 9.5, the smoothing term $P_{ml}(w|C)$ in the LM-L model is replaced with $(1-\beta)P_{ml}(w|K(D))+ \beta P_{ml}(w|C)$ where $P_{ml}(w|K(D))$, Equation 9.18, is the maximum likelihood estimation of word w given the question collection in category $K(D)$. Parameter β is used to emphasize the significance of term w in its local relevance, $P_{ml}(w|K(D))$, or global relevance, $P_{ml}(w|C)$. The question classification language model, LM-QC, applies a category probability term $P(K(D)|q)$, the probability of q belonging to category $K(D)$, to the LM model. $Path(K(D))$ is the path from category $K(D)$ to the root of the category tree, where $P(q|k_i)$ is greater than a threshold for all categories k_i on the path. LM-LQC combines LM-L and LM-QC by multiplying question classification probability with LM-L model. Cao et al. [114] reported that LM-LQC (+19.8% MAP) and LM-L (+21.3% MAP) significantly outperform LM. LM-QC (+6% MAP) does not do much better than LM due to the fact that the relevant questions are already highly ranked by LM, as well as the classification errors and relevant questions coming from other nonrelevant categories. Cao et al. [113] explicitly modeled global relevance and local relevance using a model combination. They found that the combination of a Vector Space Model [783] for estimating global relevance and a TransLM model with leaf category smoothing for estimating local relevance perform the best.

TABLE 9.7: Question Retrieval Models Exploiting Category Information (LM-L: Language Model with Leaf Category Smoothing, LM-QC: Language Model with Query Classification, LM-LQC: Language Model with Leaf Category Smoothing and Query Classification [114])

LM-L

$$P(q|D) = \prod_{w \in q} P(w|D) \qquad (9.14)$$

$$P(w|D) = (1 - \lambda)P_{ml}(w|D) + \lambda P_{ks}(w|D) \qquad (9.15)$$

$$P_{ks}(w|D) = (1 - \beta)P_{ml}(w|K(D)) + \beta P_{ml}(w|C) \qquad (9.16)$$

$$P_{ml}(w|D) = \frac{\#(w, D)}{|D|}, P_{ml} = \frac{\#(w, C)}{|C|} \qquad (9.17)$$

$$P_{ml}(w|K(D)) = \frac{\#(w, K(D))}{|K(D)|} \qquad (9.18)$$

LM-QC

$$P(q|D) = P(K(D)|q) \prod_{w \in q} [(1 - \lambda)P_{ml}(w|D) + \lambda P_{ml}(w|C)] \qquad (9.19)$$

$$P(K(D)|q) = \prod_{k_i \in Path(K(D))} P(q|k_i) \qquad (9.20)$$

LM-LQC

$$P(q|D) = P(K(D)|q) \prod_{w \in q} [(1 - \lambda)P_{ml}(w|D) + \lambda P_{ks}(w|D)] \qquad (9.21)$$

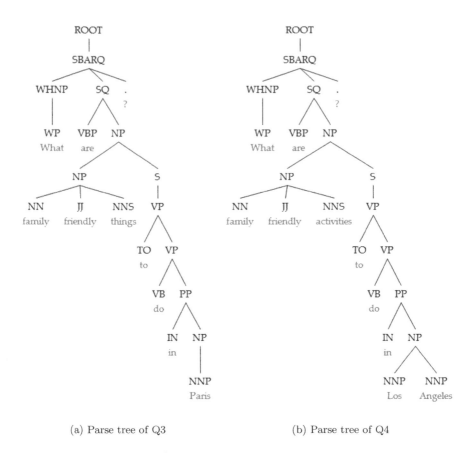

(a) Parse tree of Q3   (b) Parse tree of Q4

FIGURE 9.4: Parse trees of Q3 and Q4.

9.3.3   Structured Question Search

All models introduced in the previous sections are based on bag-of-word unigram models that ignore the structure of queries. However, structure is important for distinguishing the two sample queries below:

Q3: What are family friendly things to do in Paris?

Q4: What are family friendly activities to do in Los Angeles?

These two queries have many words in common but are very different requests. Q3 looks for family friendly things to do in Paris while Q4 focuses on Los Angeles. Figure 9.4 shows the parse trees of Q3 and Q4 generated by the Stanford Parser[13] in Penn Treebank [445] format. Q3 and Q4 have very similar

---

[13]http://nlp.stanford.edu:8080/parser/index.jsp

TABLE 9.8: Topic-Focus Mixture Models, Question Retrieval Models Exploiting Question Structure by Duan et al. [185] (LM-TF: Topic-Focus Language Model, $P_{lm}(q|D)$ Follows LM Model in Table 9.5; TR-TF: Topic-Focus Translation Model, $P_{tr}(q|D)$ Follows TR Model in Table 9.5)

LM-TF

$$P(q|D) = \lambda P_{lm}(T(q)|T(D)) + (1 - \lambda)P_{lm}(F(q)|F(D)) \quad (9.22)$$

TR-TF

$$P(q|D) = \lambda P_{tr}(T(q)|T(D)) + (1 - \lambda)P_{tr}(F(q)|F(D)) \quad (9.23)$$

syntactic structure and can be seen as consisting of two parts: (1) "What are family friendly (things | activities)" and (2) "to do in (Paris | Los Angeles)." The first part is the *focus* and the second part is the *topic* of these questions. In this example, the focuses are very similar but the topics are quite different. Intuitively, we would like to make sure both parts, especially the topic, are as similar as possible in question retrieval.

9.3.3.1 Topic-Focus Mixture Model

Duan et al. [185] proposed topic-focus mixture models to exploit this question structure. Their models are summarized in Table 9.8. $T(q)$ is the topic part of a query; $T(D)$ is the topic part of a question; $F(q)$ is the focus part of a query; $F(D)$ is the topic part of a question. The calculation of $P_{ml}(\cdot)$ and $P_{tr}(\cdot)$ follows equations in Table 9.5. Duan et al. [185] found that setting λ to 0.9 achieved the best performance. This result confirms the intuition that the topic part of a question or a query is more important than its focus. Table 9.9 summarizes the results reported from over 200 test questions each from two Yahoo! Answers categories, that is, Travel (TR) and Computer & Internet (CI), where the LM-TF model outperforms LM. Extending the topic-focus mixture model with TransLM, TransLM-QL, LM-L, LM-QC, and LM-LQC should be very straightforward. We just need to replace $P_{lm}(\cdot)$ with the intended modeling method. One challenge of applying topic-focus mixture models is how to detect the topic and focus portions of a question. Duan et al. [185] described a MDL-based tree cut method to address this problem. Please refer to their original paper for more details about the automatic detection of question topic and focus.

9.3.3.2 Entity-Based Translation Model

Singh [635] proposed an entity-based translation model, $ETLM^{wiki}$, leveraging entity co-citation information in Wikipedia to measure relatedness

TABLE 9.9:   Topic-Focus Language Model Evaluation
Results [185] (VSM: Vector Space Model [587]; LM: Language
Model; LM-TF: Topic-Focus Language Model; TR-TF:
Topic-Focus Translation Model)

Methods	Travel			Computer & Internet		
	MAP	R-Precision	MRR	MAP	R-Precision	MRR
VSM	0.198	0.138	0.228	0.236	0.175	0.289
LM	0.203	0.154	0.248	0.248	0.191	0.304
LM-TF	0.236	0.192	0.279	0.279	0.230	0.341
TR-TF	0.266	0.225	0.308	0.282	0.236	0.337

between entities. Given a query:

$$\underbrace{What}_{ne_q} \; \underbrace{is}_{ne_q} \; \underbrace{user \; generated \; content?}_{e_q}$$

The query terms "user generated content" are tagged as a Wikipedia entity,
for example, "e_q," while the other terms are not, for example, "ne_q." Based
on the TR model shown in Table 9.5, the entity-based translation model is
shown in Table 9.10 where $co(e_i, e_j)$ is the co-citation count of e_i and e_j in
Wikipedia; $df(e_i, e_j)$, the number of Wikipedia pages containing both e_i and
e_j; $tf_{e_i,wiki(e_j)}$: term frequency of e_i in the Wikipedia document where e_j
occurs; $wiki(e_i)$, the Wikipedia page where entity e_i occurs; $\gamma > 0.5$ when
$e_i = e_j$ otherwise $\gamma = 0$. γ is introduced to ensure $P_{et}(e_i|e_i) > P_{et}(e_i|e_j)$
when $i \neq j$ is always true. Singh reported that ETLM^{wiki} (MAP: 0.441)
outperformed TransLM (MAP: 0.394) relatively 11.9% in terms of MAP.

9.3.3.3   Syntactic Tree Matching

In addition to topic-focus mixture and entity-based translation models,
other methods for computing tree-to-tree similarity can also take advantage
of the question structure. Intuitively, the more tree fragments or subtrees
two trees have in common, the more similar they are to each other. However,
simply counting the number of matches might not be good enough [144]. Comparing the parse trees of Q3 and Q4 shown in Figure 9.4, most of the subtrees
are exactly the same, except for subtrees with terminal node "things," "activities," "Paris," "Los," and "Angeles." An ideal tree-to-tree similarity calculation method should reward the high overlapping of tree fragments, allow
synonyms ("things" ~ "activities"), and penalize the mismatch of key concepts
("Paris" $\neq$ "Los Angeles"). Wang et al. [696] proposed a tree kernel-based syntactic tree matching (STM) method with semantic smoothing (STM+SEM)
to compute tree-to-tree similarity as shown in Table 9.11.

Equation 9.31 computes the tree-to-tree similarity score from the node
matching score, $M(r_1, r_2)$, from subtrees rooted at r_1 in T_1 and r_2 in T_2.
Equation 9.32 normalizes $sim(T_1, T_2)$ so it is less sensitive to subtree size. δ_i

TABLE 9.10: Entity-Based Translation Model for Question Retrieval [635]

ETLM^{wiki}

$$P(q|D) = \prod_{\substack{t_q \in q \\ t_q = e_q \cup ne_q}} P(t_q|D) \qquad (9.24)$$

$$P(t_q|D) = (1 - \lambda)P_{et}(t_q|D) + \lambda P_{ml}(t_q|C) \qquad (9.25)$$

$$P_{et}(t_q|D) = \sum_{\substack{t_D \in D \\ t_D = e_D \cup ne_D}} P_{et}(t_q|t_D)P_{ml}(t_D|D) \qquad (9.26)$$

$$P_{et}(e_q|e_D) = \gamma + (1 - \gamma)\frac{co(e_q, e_D)}{\sum_{e_i} co(e_i, e_D)} \qquad (9.27)$$

$$P_{et}(ne_q|ne_D) = \gamma + (1 - \gamma)\frac{df(ne_q, ne_D)}{\sum_{ne_i} df(ne_i, ne_D)} \qquad (9.28)$$

$$P_{et}(ne_q|e_D) = \frac{tf_{ne_q, wiki(e_D)}}{|\, wiki(e_D)\,|} \qquad (9.29)$$

$$P_{et}(e_q|ne_D) = \frac{tf_{ne_D, wiki(e_q)}}{\sum_{e_i \in E} tf_{ne_D, wiki(e_i)}} \qquad (9.30)$$

is a weighting factor to emphasize different types of nodes. All terminal verb or noun nodes are given higher weight. θ_k is a weighting coefficient and is the production of all weighting factors of node i in tree fragment k. S_i is the size of subtree i with an adjusted weighting factor λ. D_i is the depth of the tree fragment with $D_{root} = 1$ and an adjusted weighting factor μ. TF_i is a tree fragment and its weight, $wt(TF_i)$ is the production of $\theta_i, \lambda^{S_i}, \mu^{D_i}$, Equation 9.35. The weight of a pair of tree fragments, $wt(TF)$, is the production of the weight of its matching fragments, $wt(TF_1)$ and $wt(TF_2)$, Equation 9.36. The tree-to-tree matching score, $M(r_1, r_2)$, for nonidentical nodes is zero, Equation 9.37. η is the total number of tree fragments, $nc(n)$ is the total number of children of node n, and $ch(n, j)$ is the j-th child of node n. The $M(r_1, r_2)$ for identical nodes can be computed using Equation 9.38 with dynamic programming.

TABLE 9.11:   Syntactic Tree Matching Similarity and Node Matching Score Proposed by Wang et al. [696]

$$sim(T_1, T_2) = \sum_{r_1 \in T_1} \sum_{r_2 \in T_2} M(r_1, r_2) \tag{9.31}$$

$$sim2(T_1, T_2) = sim(T_1, T_2)/\sqrt{sim(T_1, T_1)sim(T_2, T_2)} \tag{9.32}$$

$$\delta_i = \begin{cases} 1.2 & \text{if node } i \text{ has POS tag VB? or NN?} \\ 1.1 & \text{if node } i \text{ has tag VP or NP} \\ 1.0 & \text{all other types of nodes} \end{cases} \tag{9.33}$$

$$\theta_k = \prod_{i \in fragment\ k} \delta_i; \quad or \quad \theta_k = \delta_k \prod_{j \in fragment\ k} \theta_j \tag{9.34}$$

$$wt(TF_i) = \theta_i \lambda^{S_i} \mu^{D_i} \tag{9.35}$$

$$wt(TF) = wt(TF_1)wt(TF_2) \qquad \text{if } TF_1 \text{ and } TF_2 \text{ are identical} \tag{9.36}$$

$$M(r_1, r_2) = \begin{cases} 0 & \text{if } r_1 \neq r_2 \\ \prod_{i=1}^{\eta} wt(TF_i(r_1, r_2)) & \text{otherwise} \end{cases} \tag{9.37}$$

$$M(r_1, r_2) = \begin{cases} \delta_{r_1} \delta_{r_2} \lambda^{S_1+S_2} \mu^{D_1+D_2} & \text{if } r_1, r_2 \text{ are terminals} \\ \delta_{r_1}^{\eta} \delta_{r_2}^{\eta} \lambda^{2\eta} \mu^{\eta[2-(1+nc(r_1))(D_1+D_2)]} \\ \quad \times \prod_{j=1}^{cn(r_1)} M(ch(n_1, j), ch(n_2, j)) & \text{otherwise} \end{cases} \tag{9.38}$$

$$Sem(w_1, w_2) = 1 - distance(w_1, w_2)/2D \tag{9.39}$$

$$M_z(r_1, r_2) = \begin{cases} Sem(w_1, w_2)\delta_{r_1} \delta_{r_2} \lambda^{S_1+S_2} \mu^{D_1+D_2} & \text{if } r_1, r_2 \text{ are terminals} \\ \delta_{r_1}^{\eta} \delta_{r_2}^{\eta} \lambda^{2\eta} \mu^{\eta[2-(1+nc(r_1))(D_1+D_2)]} \\ \quad \times \prod_{j=1}^{cn(r_1)} M(ch(n_1, j), ch(n_2, j)) & \text{otherwise} \end{cases} \tag{9.40}$$

STM as defined by Equation 9.31 or Equation 9.32 uses exact matching. To allow fuzzy matching of semantically similar nodes such as "things" and "activities," a WordNet [213]-based semantic distance factor $Sem(w_1, w_2)$ is introduced. $Sem(w_1, w_2)$ is based on Leacock's measure [392]. D is the maximum depth of the WordNet taxonomy and the $distance(w_1, w_2)$ is the shortest

TABLE 9.12: Syntactic Tree Matching (STM) Evaluation Results [696] (BoW: Bag-of-Word; BoW+STM: Bag-of-Word and Syntactic Tree Matching Model; BoW+STM+SEM: Bag-of-Word, STM, and Semantic Smoothing Model)

Metric	BoW	BoW+STM	BoW+STM+SEM
MAP@10	79.08%	85.67%	86.41%
Precision@1	81.67%	81.67%	88.33%

length between two synsets, w_1 and w_2. Wang et al. [695] also allowed partial matching of production rules, such as "NP → DT·JJ·NN" matching "NP → DT·NN" in Equation 9.40 (STM+SEM). Comparing STM and STM+SEM to a simple bag-of-word model,[14] BoW [696], in Table 9.12, adding STM and STM+SEM to BoW achieved a better MAP@10 score. However, BoW+STM has the same performance as BoW according to Precision@1. This might be due to a property of the test corpus since the simple bag-of-word model can achieve 81.67% precision@1. In terms of MAP@10, STM+BoW is better than BoW. This indicates STM+BoW brings more relevant questions up from the lower rank. The big difference in Precision@1 between BoW and BoW+STM+SEM suggests the importance of allowing fuzzy matching and relaxation of production rule matching. It echoes what we learned in Section 9.3.1, that TR and TransLM outperform LM by matching semantically similar words using their word-to-word translation probability. It would be interesting to explore the possibility of replacing WordNet-based semantic distance, $Sem(w_1, w_2)$, with similarity estimated by translation models or Wikipedia-based entity translation models.

9.4 Question Quality, Answer Quality, and User Expertise

The question retrieval models introduced in the previous sections only concern question and answer relevance. These models are effective and efficient at facilitating knowledge sharing if the question and answer (QA) pair archives in CQA sites all have high answer quality. Unfortunately, this is not always the case. Jeon et al. [319] found that about 30% of 1700 QA pairs sampled from Naver.com[15] have medium (~23%) or low (~10%) quality. Agichtein et al. [13] in Table 9.2, also found that high quality answers are not the norm

---

[14]BoW: matching stemmed words between a query and a question

[15]Naver, http://www.naver.com, is a very popular community question-answering and search engine in South Korea that had an over 70% market share in 2011.

in Yahoo! Answers. Sakai et al. [585] in Table 9.4, show that 35.3% of the Best Answers in the 1500 Japanese Yahoo! Answers test set in the NTCIR-8 Communty QA Pilot Task[16] had a grade level equal to or below L6 in a 9-level, L0 (worse) to L8 (better), scale. To ensure that users of CQA services can not only find highly relevant QA pairs but also high quality ones, it is important to incorporate quality-aware factors into question retrieval models.

Recall the query likelihood language model, LM, introduced in Section 9.3.1:

$$P(q|D) = \prod_{w \in q} P(w|D) \qquad (9.1)$$

This is a simplified version of the full ranking function below:

$$P(D, a|q) = P(D, a)P(q|D, a)/P(q) \qquad (9.41)$$

Equation 9.41 is the probability of a QA pair, (D, a), given a query q, that we use to rank QA pairs. Given a query, $P(q)$ is a constant and can be ignored for ranking. The equation is rewritten as follows:

$$\underbrace{P(D, a)}_{\text{quality}} \underbrace{P(q|D, a)}_{\text{relevance}} \qquad (9.42)$$

The right-hand side of Equation 9.41 is query dependent. It measures the relevance of a QA pair. We can plug in any retrieval models introduced in Section 9.3.1. The left-hand side is the query independent prior probability of (D, a), which can be used to model the quality of (D, a). Equation 9.42 is a quality-aware relevance ranking measure in which a QA pair of high quality, $P(D, a)$, and high relevance, $P(q|D, a)$, will have a higher value. The challenge is how to estimate $P(D, a)$. In general, we can replace $P(D, a)$ with any quality estimation function that positively correlates to the quality of (D, a). We then rewrite Equation 9.42 to:

$$\underbrace{Q(D, a)}_{\text{quality}} \underbrace{P(q|D, a)}_{\text{relevance}} \qquad (9.43)$$

We discuss the definitions of quality and expertise, quality indicators, and how to model quality using these indicators in the rest of this section.

9.4.1 Defining Quality and Expertise

We have referred to "quality" and "expertise" many times in the previous section and tried to emphasize their importance in providing high performance question search in CQA. However, we have not explicitly defined what we mean by "quality" or "expertise." In fact, researchers in CQA are not very precise in defining what they mean by "quality" and "expertise."

---

[16] http://research.nii.ac.jp/ntcir/ntcir-ws8/yahoo/index-en.html

Given a query, Liu et al. [416] defined an "expert" as a person who has answered questions similar to the query in the past. Similarity is computed using the query likelihood language model between the query and user profiles. A user profile can be created from different combinations of previously answered question and answer pairs by the user. "Expertise" is defined as relevance of a user profile to a query.

Jeon et al. [319] asked annotators[17] to rate answers of 1700 QA pairs from Naver.com according to three levels: Bad, Medium, and Good. A good answer should be *relevant*, *informative*, *objective*, *sincere*, and *readable*.

To discover authorities in a CQA community, Jurczyk and Agichtein [326] used three "gold standards" that reflect expertise to evaluate their expertise estimation algorithm: 1. *Votes*, the difference in positive and negative votes over positive votes an answerer received averaged over all answers attempted; 2. *%Best*, the ratio of best answers received over all answers attempted; 3. *Ratings*, the average number of stars an answerer received over all the best answers received.

Zhang et al. [764] categorized the users of Java Forum into five expertise levels: Level 5, a *top Java expert* who deeply understands the core Java theory and related advanced topics; Level 4, a *Java professional* who can answer all or most java concept questions and also knows one or several subtopics very well; Level 3, a *Java user* who knows advanced Java concepts and can program relatively well; Level 2, a *Java learner* who knows basic concepts and can program, but is not good at advanced topics of Java; Level 1, a *Newbie* who is just starting to learn Java.

Song et al. [640] defined the concept *question utility* as the likelihood that a question is asked by people. The more people that have asked a question, the more important or high quality it is. In Agichtein et al. [13], the editors sorted questions and answers for *well-formedness*, *readability*, *utility*, *interestingness*, and *correctness* into three categories: *High*, *Medium*, and *Low*. The results are shown in Table 9.2. Bian et al. [74] used regular expression patterns from the TREC QA track evaluations (1999–2006)[18] to label answers for factoid QA retrieval evaluations. Bian et al. [75] took the "*top contributors*" from Yahoo! Answers as users with high expertise and the "*best answers*" as high quality answers. Suryanto et al. [653] determined answer quality by the content of an answer and the expertise of the answerer.

Ishikawa et al. [307] in an NTCIR-8 Community QA Pilot task asked annotators to rate answers in three grades (see Section 9.2) and created the 9 levels of graded answer quality shown in Table 9.3. Liu et al. [412] defined the relative expertise between users by assuming: (1) an answerer who provides the best answer, a best answerer, has higher expertise than the asker; and (2) a best answerer has higher expertise than all other answerers participating in the same question threads. Li et al. [398] created a 4-level ground truth for the

---

[17]The number of annotators is not reported in their paper.
[18]http://trec.nist.gov/data/qa.html

evaluation of question quality based on: 1. NT, the number of tag-of-interests; 2. NA, the number of answers; 3. RM, the reciprocal of the minutes for getting the best answer.

In summary, no commonly agreed upon definitions of question quality, answer quality, and expertise exist in CQA research. Each research team created its own standard to suit its own research needs, which mostly relied on laborious manual annotations or circumstantial evidence derived from user interaction data of CQA sites. Despite the lack of common definitions, researchers have made good progress in modeling quality and expertise. In the next section, we discuss what indicators researchers have used to model them.

9.4.2 Indicators of Quality and Expertise

In the CQA services shown in Figure 9.5, users do not only ask and answer questions but also evaluate questions and answers. For example, Yahoo! Answers has a Points and Levels[19] system to encourage good user behavior and incentivize high quality questions and answers. A Yahoo! Answers user starts with 100 points. It costs 5 points to ask a question. A user earns points back by answering questions, 2 points per answer, 10 points per best answer, and 1 point per "thumbs-up" rating on a best answer. A user also obtains 1 point by voting for answers. A daily limit of user actions, that is, asking and answering a question, commenting and voting answers, and starring a question, is enforced according to the user level (1–7). Users can rate as many answers as they want. These mechanisms are designed to solicit good quality questions and answers and entice user participation. Along with hundreds of millions of question answer (QA) threads accumulated over time, rich interactions among users, questions, and answers are also recorded that can be used to infer question quality, answer quality, and user expertise.

Table 9.13 summarizes quality and expertise indicators or features used by Jeon et al. [319], Agichtein et al. [13], and Bian et al. [75]. These features were used to learn the quality of question, quality of answer, and expertise. We follow Agichtein et al. [13] in labeling each indicator with its type tag, U, Q, and A. Tags U, Q, and A mark indicators related to users, questions, and answers, respectively. Indicators marked with a single Q or A type tag are intrinsic features of questions or answers. Indicators marked with a U tag and other tags are features involving user interaction. For example, "best answer ratio" is related to users and their answers so it is assigned a UA type tag; "ratio of thumbs up vote" is related to an answerer (U) and an evaluator (U) so it is tagged as UU. In Jeon et al. [319], they reported that "length of answer," "total # of questions and answers (user activity level), and "total # of question answered in query category" are the three most effective indicators or features in estimating answer quality. Agichtein et al. [13] conducted an in-depth study of question and answer quality in Yahoo! Answers. They reported

---

[19]http://answers.yahoo.com/info/scoring_system

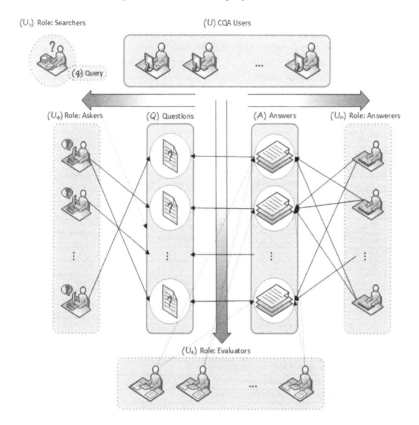

FIGURE 9.5: User roles, asker, answerer, evaluator, in CQA and interactions between questions and answers. **(See color insert.)**

the 20 most significant features for question and answer quality. Only the top 5 are listed in Table 9.13. For answer quality, the single feature "answer length" is the most effective. Harper et al. [271] also separately confirmed that *"answers with high quality ratings were long and contained many links."* However, answer length is one of the statistical features used by Bian et al. [74] that does not have a significant impact on factoid question retrieval. This is not a surprise since factoid questions ask for simple facts in which length is not a discriminative feature of quality. In the next section, we summarize a few retrieval models utilizing such quality indicators and the interaction between questions, answers, and different roles of users to improve question retrieval performance.

TABLE 9.13: Question Quality, Answer Quality, and Expertise Indicators Used by Jeon et al. [319] (J) in Naver (N) and Bian et al. [75] (B) in Yahoo! Answers (Y) (The top 5 most significant indicators (or features) for question quality (AQ) and answer quality (AA) as reported by Agichtein et al. [13] in Yahoo! Answers. U: indicators related to user, Q: indicators related to question, A: indicators related to answer.)

Type	Indicator/Feature	Site	Ref
UA	best answer ratio	N	J
A	*1 length of answer	N	J
UA	stars given to answer by its asker	N	J
UQA	*2 total # of questions and answers (user activity level)	N	J
UQ	*3 total # of question answered in query category	N	J
AU	# of times answer printed	N	J
AU	# of times answer copied to blog	N	J
AU	# of times the answer is recommended by other users	N	J
AU	# of times the answer is recommended by editors	N	J
AU	answer by the category sponsor	N	J
AU	# of times the answer is clicked	N	J
AU	# of times the answer is dis-recommended by other users	N	J
Q	# of words of question title	Y	B
Q	# of words of question detail	Y	B
Q	date and time a question posted	Y	B
QU	# of stars of a question	Y	B
QA	# of answers received of a question	Y	B
AQ	answer and question word shared	Y	B
AU	# of comments added by other participants	Y	B
AU	# of thumbs up votes for an answer	Y	B
AU	# of thumbs down votes for an answer	Y	B
U	total points earned so far	Y	B
UQ	# of questions asked	Y	B
UQ	# of questions resolved	Y	B
UA	total # of answers	Y	B
UA	total # of best answers	Y	B
UQ	total # of stars	Y	B
UU	ratio of thumbs up vote	Y	B
UU	ratio of thumbs down vote	Y	B
UU	# of other users whose questions are answered by the user	Y	B
UU	# of other users who answer questions posted by the user	Y	B
UU	hub score computed by HITS	Y	B
UU	authority score computed by HITS	Y	B
Q	the punctuation density in the question's title	Y	AQ
QU	the question's category assigned by the asker	Y	AQ
Q	normalized clickthrough in its category	Y	AQ
UU	average # of thumbs up of the answers received by the asker	Y	AQ
Q	# of words per sentence	Y	AQ
A	answer length	Y	AA
A	# of words in the answer with corpus frequency larger than c	Y	AA
AU	difference in thumbs up and thumbs down divided by thumbs up	Y	AA
A	the entropy of the trigram character-level model of the answer	Y	AA
UU	best answer ratio	Y	AA

9.4.3 Modeling Quality and Expertise

We start with a discussion of quality-aware question retrieval models that utilize question quality, answer quality, and expertise individually. We then describe models that take advantage of combinations of quality and expertise.

9.4.3.1 Question Utility-Aware Retrieval Model

Song et al. [640] introduced a concept called "Question Utility" as a proxy of question quality. The more a question is repeatedly asked by the community the more useful it is, that is, high utility and high quality. They proposed three ways to model question utility: (1) a length normalized n-gram language model with Katz smoothing [332] (LM-QU), (2) LexRank [207], and (3) LM-QU and LexRank combined. The LM-QU approach uses an n-gram language model to measure popularity. To avoid being biased in favor of short questions, a normalized version is used as shown in Equation 9.44.

$$
\begin{aligned}
Q(D, a) &= P_{norm}(D) \\
&\propto \exp\left[\frac{\log P(D)}{\log(m+\alpha)}\right] \qquad m\text{: length of } D, \alpha = 0.1 \text{ for smoothing}
\end{aligned}
$$

$$
\begin{aligned}
P(D) &= P(w_1, w_2, ..., w_m) \\
&= \prod_{i=1}^{m} P(w_i | w_{i-n+1}^{i-1})
\end{aligned}
$$

$$(9.44)$$

The LexRank approach uses the centrality of a question among all similar questions in a QA collection. Similarity is measured by cosine similarity and centrality, $c(D)$ is computed using LexRank on a question similarity graph (see Erkan and Rader [207] for more information):

$$
\begin{aligned}
Q(D, a) &= c(D) \\
&= \lambda/N + (1-\lambda) \sum_{d \in adj[D]} \frac{c(d)}{deg(d)}
\end{aligned}
\qquad (9.45)
$$

λ is a damping factor and d is a question adjacent to question D in the similarity graph, $c(d)$ is the centrality of d, and $deg(d)$ is the degree of node d. LexRank can be combined with LM-QU as shown in Equation 9.46:

$$
\begin{aligned}
Q(D, a) &= c(D) \\
&= \lambda p(D) + (1-\lambda) \sum_{d \in adj[D]} \frac{c(d)}{deg(d)}
\end{aligned}
\qquad (9.46)
$$

where LM-QU, $p(D)$, substitutes $1/N$ in Equation 9.45, so a question with higher LM-QU will have a higher combined score. Song et al. [321] reported that a baseline LM model in Equation 9.1 can achieve a MAP score of 48.9%. Adding question utility to the baseline model, the MAP of LexRank is 49.4%, LM-QU is 50.9%, and LM-QU combing with LexRank is 51.2%. These results show that the popularity of n-gram sequences and similarity among questions are effective quality proxies.

9.4.3.2 Answer Quality-Aware Retrieval Model

Jeon et al. [319] proposed a maximum entropy-based framework to estimate answer quality. They used a set of 13 answer quality indicators as shown in Table 9.13 (Ref = J) and applied kernel density estimation (KDE) [302] to convert nonmonotonic feature into monotonic. There were 894 training answers and quality label pairs, $\{(a_i, y_i)\}$, from Naver.com that were labeled by human annotators and used for maximum entropy training. The quality of a QA pair, $Q_{nt}(D, a)$ ($Q(D, a)$ in Equation 9.43, can be computed as follows:

$$
\begin{aligned}
Q_{nt}(D, a) &= p(y|a) \\
&= \frac{1}{Z(a)} \exp\left[\sum_{i=1}^{13} \lambda_i f_i(a, y)\right]
\end{aligned}
$$

$$
f_i(a, y) = \begin{cases} kde(a_{f_i}) & \text{if } i\text{th feature is nonmonotonic} \\ a_{f_i} & \text{otherwise} \end{cases}
$$

(9.47)

where $p(y|a)$ is the probability of whether an answer a is *good* or *bad*, where $y \in \{good, bad\}$, $Z(a)$ is a normalization factor, λ_i is a model parameter, $f_i(a, y)$ is the ith predicate, $kde(\cdot)$ is a kernel density function, and a_{f_i} is the raw value of the ith feature. Their experimental results on 1700 Naver.com test questions showed that a quality-aware question retrieval model (MAP: 29%) significantly (P-value = 2.96E-11) outperformed a quality-agnostic model (MAP: 22.2%).

9.4.3.3 Expertise-Aware Retrieval Model

Expertise estimation or expert finding is a major research topic in CQA or UGC research. Intuitively, a user with high-domain expertise should contribute high quality answers. Liu et al. [416] compared three different language models for expert finding by using questions or answers as user profiles for language modeling. Jurczyk and Agichtein [326] applied an HITS algorithm on an asker and answerer graph to compute the authority and hub scores of a user. The authority score is used as expertise. Zhang et al. [764] compared Number of Answers, Indegree, Z-Score, HITS Authority, and their own PageRank-like ExpertiseRank and found they reflected user expertise equally well. Bouguessa et al. [88] modeled user expertise as a mixture of gamma distributions. However, these studies mainly rely on link analysis to estimate expertise or authority.

Yang et al. [743] analyzed the bidding and win-loss interactions in a Chinese task market site, Taskcn.com. They described structural prestige [704] in users and tasks where the winners of a bidding event have expert prestige over the losers and a task lost by a bidder has a higher task prestige over a task won by the bidder. They proposed five different metrics to measure prestige: (1) WinRate, (2) Indegree, (3) Closeness, (4) Betweenness, and (5) PageRank. Among them, WinRate was equal to the best answer ratio of a user. The remaining four metrics are related network structures and none

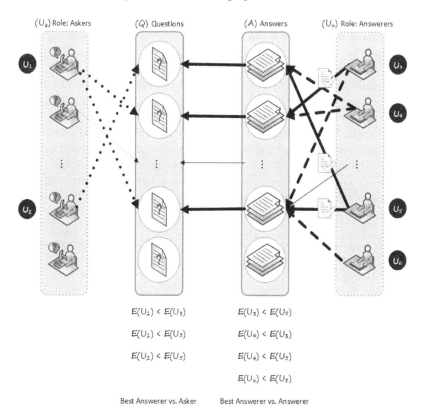

FIGURE 9.6: Competition-based expertise score estimation, Liu et al. [412]: (1) Expertise of a best answerer (solid line) is greater than its asker (dotted line); (2) Expertise of a best answerer (solid line) is greater than other answerers (dashed line). $E(U_i)$ is the expertise score of user U_i. (**See color insert.**)

of them directly measure expertise. Liu et al. [412] proposed a competition-based approach that directly models expertise and evaluated the quality of their estimation against graded answer quality. As shown in Figure 9.6, given a question thread, they made two assumptions:

1. The best answerer, U_{ba}, has greater expertise than the asker, U_q, has: $E(U_q) \prec E(U_{ba})$.

2. The best answerer has greater expertise than any other answerer, U_i, has: $E(U_{i \neq ba}) \prec E(U_{ba})$.

where $E(\cdot)$ is an expertise function. Given a question thread of n answers, n such comparisons can be generated where 1 from the best answerer and the asker and $n - 1$ from the best answerer and the other answerers. Each comparison is then casted as a two-player competition with the same outcome, that is, the best answerer always wins the game. A set of win-loss results can then be generated for a QA collection and the relative expertise of users are learned by applying TrueSkill [282], a Bayesian skill rating system or SVM [121]. They found that SVM-based relative expertise learning achieved a significantly better nDCG@1 (88.7%) than the HITS-based method (82.7%) and PageRank-based method (82.7%) on a set of selected 975 NTCIR-9 CQA Pilot Task questions with graded-relevance levels shown in Table 9.3. However, they also found that WinRate or best answer ratio (BAR) had an nDCG@1 of 87.7%. Their results show that expertise can be a proxy of answer quality and it would be useful to include it in a question retrieval model alongside question and answer quality. A straightforward application of answerer expertise to question retrieval is to approximate the quality of a QA pair by the expertise of its answerer as follows:

$$Q(D, a) = E(U_a) \tag{9.48}$$

where U_a is the answerer who provides answer a of question D and $E(U_a)$ is the expertise of U_a.

9.4.3.4   Quality and Expertise-Aware Retrieval Model

So far, we have described methods that model quality and expertise individually. In this section, models combining quality and expertise are discussed. Suryanto et al. [653] compared LM (Equation 9.1), LM with Jeon el al.'s [319] answer quality model (Q_{nt}, Equation 9.47) using nine features, and four other models, EXHITS, EXHITS_QD, EX_QD, and EX_QD', as shown in Table 9.14. EXHITS in Equation 9.49 computes the asking expertise E_q of a user U_i from the sum of the answering expertise of all the answerers who answer questions from U_i. This corresponds to the hub score of the HITS algorithm. EXHITS computes the answering expertise E_a of a user U_i by adding all asking expertise E_q of the users who ask the questions that U_i answers. This is the authority score of the HITS algorithm. The final quality score, $Q(D, a)$, is a linear combination of E_q and E_a. Equations 9.50, 9.51, 9.52, and 9.53 are query dependent models. The rationale behind these models is the intuition that expertise should be query or topic dependent. Given a query q, the query likelihood language model LM is used to find relevant questions d or d_j in a QA collection. Liu et al. [416] used LM to estimate user expertise. The answer quality of relevant questions was estimated using Q_{nt}. EXHITS_QD is a straightforward extension of EXHITS that has added LM and Q_{nt} as weighting factors. A user U_i has a high asking expertise $E_q(U_i, q)$ given a query q, if he or she asks more relevant questions that have high quality answers given by people with high answering expertise. Similarly, a user has a high answering expertise $E_a(U_i, q)$, if he or she gives many high quality answers to many relevant questions asked by people with high asking expertise. EX_QD removes the mutual reinforcement between asking expertise and answering expertise by computing $E_q(U_i, q)$ and $E_a(U_i, q)$ independently. EX_QD' drops the answer quality weighting factor from computing asking expertise.

From the experimental results of over 50 Yahoo! Answers questions, we have found that adding EXHITS to the LM question retrieval model with Q_{nt} for answer quality (NT model) does not outperform the NT model alone. Only a query dependent extension of EXHITS, that is, EXHITS_QD, EX_QD, and EX_QD', consistently performs better than NT. EX_QD and EX_QD' achieved similar performance levels but both are better than EXHITS_QD. Examining the query dependent models in Table 9.14, the weighting factors LM and Q_{nt} are also computed by the NT question retrieval model. The only thing that EXHITS_QD, EX_QD, and EX_QD' adds is the reranking answers of NT model by boosting answers provided by users who:

1. Contribute answers of high quality to relevant questions, and

2. Ask high quality, relevant questions.

Suryanto et al.[653] noted that setting λ to 0.2 obtained better results than setting it to 0, which implies the benefit of considering asking (or questioning) expertise.

Bian et al. [75] proposed a coupled mutual reinforcement model CQA-MR to learn question quality, y_q, answer quality y_a, asking or questioning expertise (question reputation) of a user y_u^q and answering expertise (answer reputation) or a user y_u^a. The connection between users ($\mathcal{U}$), questions ($\mathcal{Q}$), and answers ($\mathcal{A}$) are represented as three matrices: $M_{\mathcal{U}\mathcal{A}}$, $M_{\mathcal{U}\mathcal{Q}}$, and $M_{\mathcal{Q}\mathcal{A}}$, where their element $m_{ij} = 1$ if a user i provides an answer j, a user i asks a question j, or a question i has an answer j, otherwise $m_{ij} = 0$. By using vector and matrix representation, Bian et al. summarized their coupled mutual reinforcement model as follows:

$$\mathbf{y}_u^a = M_{\mathcal{U}\mathcal{A}}' \mathbf{y}_a \tag{9.54}$$

$$\mathbf{y}_a = \alpha M_{\mathcal{U}\mathcal{A}}^T \mathbf{y}_u^a + (1 - \alpha) M_{\mathcal{Q}\mathcal{A}}^T \mathbf{y}_q \tag{9.55}$$

$$\mathbf{y}_u^q = M_{\mathcal{U}\mathcal{Q}}' \mathbf{y}_q \tag{9.56}$$

$$\mathbf{y}_q = \gamma M_{\mathcal{U}\mathcal{Q}}^T \mathbf{y}_u^q + (1 - \gamma) M_{\mathcal{Q}\mathcal{A}} \mathbf{y}_a \tag{9.57}$$

where M^T is the transpose of M, $M_{\mathcal{U}\mathcal{A}}'$ and $M_{\mathcal{U}\mathcal{Q}}'$ are derived from $M_{\mathcal{U}\mathcal{A}}$ and $M_{\mathcal{U}\mathcal{Q}}$, $m_{ij}' = \frac{m_{ij}}{\sum_{j=1}^{|\mathcal{A}|} m_{ij}}$ if $m_{ij}' \in M_{\mathcal{U}\mathcal{A}}'$, and $m_{ij}' = \frac{m_{ij}}{\sum_{j=1}^{|\mathcal{Q}|} m_{ij}}$ if $m_{ij}' \in M_{\mathcal{U}\mathcal{Q}}'$. Equation 9.54 indicates the answering expertise of users, $\mathbf{y}_u^a$, is the sum of the answer quality, $\mathbf{y}_a$, of all their answers. Equation 9.55 says the quality of answers, $\mathbf{y}_a$, is the linear combination of the answering expertise of their answerers, $\mathbf{y}_u^a$, and the quality of their questions, $\mathbf{y}_q$. Similarly, Equation 9.56 says the asking expertise of users, $\mathbf{y}_u^q$, is the sum of the question quality, $\mathbf{y}_q$, of all their questions. Equation 9.57 says the quality of questions, $\mathbf{y}_q$, is the linear combination of the asking expertise of their askers, $\mathbf{y}_u^q$, and the quality of their answers, $\mathbf{y}_a$. Based on these equations, Bian et al. designed an iterative algorithm, CQA-MR, to learn the probability of a answerer being a good answerer, an answer being a good answer, an asker being a good asker, and

TABLE 9.14: Quality Models Consider Expertise of Askers and Answerers (EXHITS: Asker (hub) and Answerer (Authority) Expertise Model Based on HITS, EXHITS_QD: Question Dependent EXHITS, EX_QD: Question Dependent Asker Expertise and Answerer Expertise Modeled Separately, and EX_QD': The Asker Expertise in EX_QD Is Not Answer Quality Dependent [653] (λ: the linear combination parameter between 0 and 1, q: input query, E_q: asker expertise, E_a: answerer expertise, LM: the query likelihood language model in Equation 9.1, Q_{nt}: answer quality based on Jeon et al. [319], $\mathfrak{I}_a(a)$: answerer index who gives answer a, $\mathfrak{I}_a(d)$: indexes of all answerers answer d, $\mathcal{A}(U_i)$: all answers given by U_i, $\mathcal{D}(U_i)$: all questions asked by U_i, $\mathfrak{I}_d(a)$: user index of the asker who ask the question with answer a, $\mathcal{A}(U_j, d)$: the answer given by answerer U_j for question d, and $\mathcal{D}(U_j, a)$: the question asked by answerer U_j with answer a.)

EXHITS

$$
\begin{aligned}
Q(D, a) &= \lambda E_q(U_{i=\mathfrak{I}_a(a)}) + (1 - \lambda) E_a(U_{i=\mathfrak{I}_a(a)}) \\
E_q(U_i) &= \sum_{d \in \mathcal{D}(U_i)} \sum_{U_j \in \mathfrak{I}_a(d)} E_a(U_j) \\
E_a(U_i) &= \sum_{a \in \mathcal{A}(U_i)} \sum_{U_j \in \mathfrak{I}_d(a)} E_q(U_j)
\end{aligned}
\tag{9.49}
$$

EXHITS_QD

$$
Q(D, a) = \lambda E_q(U_{i=\mathfrak{I}_a(a)}, q) + (1 - \lambda) E_a(U_{i=\mathfrak{I}_a(a)}, q) \tag{9.50}
$$

$$
\begin{aligned}
E_q(U_i, q) &= \sum_{d \in \mathcal{D}(U_i)} LM(q, d) \sum_{\substack{U_j \in \mathfrak{I}_a(d) \\ a_j = \mathcal{A}(U_j, d)}} Q_{nt}(d, a_j) E_a(U_j, d) \\
E_a(U_i, q) &= \sum_{a \in \mathcal{A}(U_i)} \sum_{\substack{U_j \in \mathfrak{I}_d(a) \\ d_j = \mathcal{D}(U_j, a)}} LM(q, d_j) Q_{nt}(d_j, a) E_q(U_j, d_j)
\end{aligned}
$$

$$\tag{9.51}$$

EX_QD

$$
\begin{aligned}
E_q(U_i, q) &= \sum_{d \in \mathcal{D}(U_i)} LM(q, d) \sum_{\substack{U_j \in \mathfrak{I}_a(d) \\ a_j = \mathcal{A}(U_j, d)}} Q_{nt}(d, a_j) \\
E_a(U_i, q) &= \sum_{a \in \mathcal{A}(U_i)} \sum_{\substack{U_j \in \mathfrak{I}_d(a) \\ d_j = \mathcal{D}(U_j, a)}} LM(q, d_j) Q_{nt}(d_j, a)
\end{aligned}
\tag{9.52}
$$

EX_QD'

$$
\begin{aligned}
E_q(U_i, q) &= \sum_{d \in \mathcal{D}(U_i)} LM(q, d) \\
E_a(U_i, q) &= \sum_{a \in \mathcal{A}(U_i)} \sum_{\substack{U_j \in \mathfrak{I}_d(a) \\ d_j = \mathcal{D}(U_j, a)}} LM(q, d_j) Q_{nt}(d_j, a)
\end{aligned}
\tag{9.53}
$$

---

a question being a good question. The features that they used in training are listed in Table 9.13, Ref=B. They reported that CQA-MR learned answering expertise (answer reputation) significantly better than HITS and SVM when trained on the same set of data. It also outperformed SVM in learning question quality. When applying the learned question quality, answer quality, answering expertise, and questioning expertise to a factoid QA retrieval task, CQA-MR enhanced ranking function GBRank-MR performed better than its quality-agnostic counterpart GBRank [74].

9.5   Conclusion

In this chapter, we summarized recent research activities in question-answering of UGC. We first introduced quality-agnostic retrieval models and then described quality-aware retrieval models. How to estimate the quality of questions and answers and user expertise were also included. Specifically, we focused our discussion on community question-answering due to the ready availability of CQA archives and rich metadata that record interactions between users, and between users and data associated with CQA archives. Question-answering in CQA is cast as a question search problem. A simple query likelihood model, LM (Equation 9.1), was introduced as the baseline question retrieval system. Translation model TR (Equation 9.4) and its variants TransLM (Equation 9.6), TransLM+QL (Equation 9.8), and ETLM^{wiki} (Equation 9.24) are models designed to address the paraphrase problem. We have shown how statistical machine translation technologies are used to learn word-to-word translation probability. In addition to these models, Zhou et al. [776] described a phrase-based translation model for question search. Recent advances in statistical machine translation should benefit question search of UGC. Please refer to Koehn [356] for more in-depth information.

The simple LM model can be expanded to take advantage of CQA topic categories as shown in LM-C (Equation 9.14), LM-QC (Equation 9.19), and LM-LQC (Equation 9.21). Structural information within questions can be utilized to pinpoint matching units within questions and prioritize matching order and weighting schemes as illustrated in topic-focus mixture model (Equations 9.22 and 9.23), entity-based translation models, ETLM^{wiki}, or syntactic tree matching models (Equations 9.40 and 9.39). However, these models have yet to take advantage of traditional question-answering research in question classification [401], question analysis [383], and question and answer typology [297]. For example, similar to Duan et al. [185] and Cao et al. [114], Lally et al. [383] pointed out the four major components in IBM Watson's question analysis module: question focus, lexical answer type (LAT), question classification (QClass), and question sections (QSection). Question focus is what a question asks, LAT is the type of answer, QClass is the class of a question, and

QSection is a question fragment requiring special handling. For an example Jeopardy![20] question:

> [CHARACTERS IN PLAYS] This woman wished to be taken to "Bucknam Pellis ... don't you know where it is? In the Green Park, where the king lives." [21]

The question focus is "this woman," the LAT is "woman," its QClass is "category-relation," and QSection is the span "Bucknam Pellis ... don't you know where it is? In the Green Park, where the king lives," which needs to be recognized to find the play in question. Lessons learned in developing Watson might be applied to analyzing question focus, answer type, question category, and special question format in UGC.

Models related to the query likelihood language model were the main theme throughout this chapter. However, Lavrenko and Croft [390] have shown relevance-based language models are more effective in document retrieval than simple query likelihood language models. It would be interesting to see how question-answering in UGC can take advantage of such relevance-based models in the future. In addition, supervised learning to rank methods [413] have been proposed to rank answers. Bian et al. [74] proposed GBrank and their subsequent work, GBrank-MR, mentioned in Section 9.4.3.4, are evaluated on factoid questions and are good representative methods. For a nonfactoid learning to rank method, please see Surdeanu et al. [652] for an example.

Due to the nature of UGC, high quality content cannot always be guaranteed. Relevant question retrieval models need to be coupled with quality models to ensure high quality and relevant questions and answers are retrieved. Several effective methods to estimate question quality, answer quality, and user expertise were described in Section 9.4. Agichtein et al. [13] proposed a general classification framework for identifying high quality items in UGC. However, the framework and many other quality estimation methods require large training data. How to obtain high quality training data with minimum cost is a challenging issue. Fortunately, the rich interaction data recorded by UGC sites might be leveraged to address this data requirement. For example, the competition-based expertise estimation model introduced by Liu et al. [412] (see also Section 9.4.3.3) utilizing Best Answer selections are available in all CQA sites. Bian et al. [74] used user thumbs up and thumbs down votes to capture user preference over a pair of answers. Sun et al. [651] designed a majority-based perception algorithm that leverages unlabeled question data for question recommendation. The issue of how to calibrate votes across users was discussed in Chen et al. [130]. We expect more researchers will start taking advantage of this rich metadata in the future.

One major roadblock to advancing state-of-the-art question-answering of CQA or UGC is the lack of standard test collections. Almost all research efforts covered in this chapter used their own proprietary test collections, mostly

---

[20] Please see J! Archive for more examples, http://www.j-archive.com

[21] Answer: Eliza Doolittle

from a single source, that is, Yahoo! Answers. This lack of standard evaluation corpora hinders objective comparison of existing methods and knowledge sharing. The only exception is the NTCIR-8 Pilot QA Task that created a set of 1500 Japanese QA thread collections with graded relevance judgment.

In addition to standard test collections, we should also branch out to different UGC sites such as StackExchange[22] and MathOverflow,[23] and online forums such as Java Forum in Zhang et al. [764] or TripAdvisor,[24] where users share more domain-specific knowledge. Tausczik and Pennebaker [663] investigated the relationship between online and offline reputations of contributors in MathOverflow. Cong et al. [145] and Ding et al. [172] proposed methods to detect questions, extract question contexts, and get answers from forums.

Question-answering of UGC should not be limited to question retrieval or quality and expertise estimation. Answer summarization technologies as proposed by Liu et al. [417] and Tamasoni and Huang [670] are a great way to increase the usability of CQA archives and user satisfaction of CQA services. Cross-lingual and multi-lingual document retrieval or question-answering methods [389, 354] can facilitate access of CQA services in different languages. When time-sensitive solutions are needed and when no obvious answers can be found, question routing to potential answers becomes a natural solution. Li and King [399] tracked 3000 newly posted questions in Yahoo! Answers and Baidu Zhidao for 48 hours. They found that 17.6% of questions in Yahoo! Answers and 22.7% of questions in Baidu Zhidao received satisfactory results. Twenty percent of unresolved questions in Yahoo! Answers and 42.8% of unresolved questions in Baidu Zhidao received no answers at all. Horowitz and Kamvar [292] described a social search engine, Aardvark,[25] which routes user questions to their extended social network. A recent experiment reported by Shtok et al. [629] showed that three automatic answering robots Alice, Jane, and Lilly, deployed on Yahoo! Answers achieved between 12.6–28.8% of Best Answer precision over three Yahoo! Answers categories when the Best Answers were selected by askers. This performance is much higher than a typical Yahoo! Answers user whose Best Answer precision is between 5.3% to 7.4%. Alice, Jane, and Lilly even have their own fans. With these encouraging results, we are looking forward to more exciting research to come in question-answering of UGC.

---

[22] http://stackexchange.com
[23] http://mathoverflow.net
[24] http://www.tripadvisor.com
[25] Aardvark was acquired by Google in February 2010 and closed in September 2011

Chapter 10

Summarization of UGC

Dominic Rout

University of Sheffield

Kalina Bontcheva

University of Sheffield

10.1 Introduction

The phenomenal growth of the social Web 2.0 and user generated content (UGC), such as blogs and online social networks, is driven by tapping into the social nature of human interactions, making it possible for people to gain a wider audience for their opinions, become part of a virtual community, and collaborate remotely. At the same time, the unprecedented volume and velocity of incoming UGC has resulted in individuals starting to experience information overload, perceived by users as "seeing a tiny subset of what was going on" [178]. In the context of Internet use, previous research on information overload has shown already that high levels of information can lead to ineffectiveness, as "a person cannot process all communication and informational inputs" [57].

Information access to UGC is an emerging research area, combining methods from many fields, for example, speech and language processing, social science, machine learning, personalization, and Web science. Traditional search methods are no longer able to address the more complex information seeking behavior in UGC, which has evolved toward sense-making, learning and investigation, and social search [539].

In the context of news and longer Web content, automatic text summarization has been proposed as an effective way of addressing information overload. At the same time, research on text summarization of UGC is still in its infancy, especially with respect to aiding information interpretation. Unlike carefully authored news text or scientific articles, UGC poses a number of new challenges for summary generation (see Section 10.3) due to its large-scale, noisy, irregular, and social nature.

Potential applications of summarization for UGC include the ability to easily manage information from user timelines, tools to assist in the discovery and exploration of aggregate trends online, and the display of overall and specific sentiments from social media Web sites, in response to current events.

We start by providing a brief overview of automatic text summarization, as originally developed for well-formed, long textual documents, such as news articles and scientific papers. The chapter then surveys the state-of-the-art in UGC summarization, including research on text-based UGC summaries (Section 10.4), structured, sentiment-based summarization (Section 10.5), keyword- and topic-based summarization (Section 10.6), and summary-based visualizations (Section 10.7). Section 10.8 discusses evaluation challenges and methods, followed by a concluding discussion on outstanding challenges (Section 10.9).

10.2   Automatic Text Summarization: A Brief Overview

Textual summaries are extremely common in online and printed media. Table 10.1 lists some examples of types of summaries which are commonly encountered. These classes have been described as either critical, informative, or indicative, where critical summaries attempt to appraise and evaluate a work in some way, informative summaries try to capture the content of the original document, and indicative summaries aim to enable a reader to decide whether or not to read the whole document [442, 493].

Researchers have developed methods for summarizing single and multiple documents, either by combining sentences and phrases extracted from the

TABLE 10.1: Example
Classes of Summary

Summary	Purpose
Journal abstract	Indicative
News report	Informative
Movie review	Critical
Novel blurb	Indicative
Football highlights	Informative

original texts (called *extractive summarization*, e.g., [584, 55]) or by using Natural Language Generation (NLG) to create *abstractive*, interpretative summaries (also called concept-to-text generation) (e.g., [86, 752]). The former type of summary, the extract, is composed entirely from text which can be found in the original document(s). Overall, extractive summarization is arguably easier to explain and implement, however, the resulting summaries reflect strongly the original document(s), which could be problematic on short texts, such as tweets.

Extractive summaries are generally produced according to two steps.

1. Score textual units (sentences, phrases, paragraphs, etc.) according to some representation of the document or document set.

2. Generate summaries by selecting high scoring textual units until some desired compression ratio has been achieved.

The textual unit to be included in a summary could be a word, phrase, sentence, or whole paragraph depending on the application. Different methods for scoring textual units have been developed, including word frequencies (*tf-idf*), sentence position in the document [424], and centroid-based methods [561].

On the other hand, abstractive summarization algorithms tend to be much more complex. The advantage of the abstractive approaches is that they enable succinct summaries of the content, independent of its original presentation in the source document collection [115], as well as the generation of different (personalized) summaries from the same formal input [86].

In addition to being described by their form (abstractive or extractive) and their purpose (critical, informative, or indicative) summaries can also be classified by whether they are derived from single or from multiple documents. The two types are considered somewhat separate, because multidocument summarization must address different challenges to single document summarization such as repeated text between documents, order of publishing, and inter-document references.

Summaries may be topic-centric (generic), user-focused (i.e., personalized), or query focused. The former class of summary is meant simply to summarize the content with no bias as to whom can benefit from it. Query focused summarization, on the other hand, involves building a summary to meet a specified information need; in this sense it is related to the task of question-answering. User focused or personalized summarization must model in some way the information needs and interests of a specific user, arranging a summary containing details which they alone may find salient.

10.3   Why Is User Generated Content a Challenge?

State-of-the-art automatic text summarization algorithms have been developed primarily on news articles and other carefully written, long documents [442, 493]. In contrast, user generated content tends to be very different: often short, strongly grounded in context, temporal, noisy, and full of slang.

In more detail, a study comparing Twitter and *New York Times* (NYT) news [769] has identified three kinds of topics: event-oriented, entity-oriented, and long-standing topics. Topics are also classified into categories, based on their subject area. Nine of the categories are those used by NYT (e.g., arts, world, business) plus two Twitter-specific ones (Family&Life and Twitter). Family&Life is the most predominant category on Twitter (called "me now" by Naaman et al. [484]), both in terms of number of tweets and number of users. Automatic topic-based comparison showed that tweets abound with entity-oriented topics, which are much less dominant in traditional news media.

With respect to message content, Naaman et al. [484] found that over 40% of their sample of tweets were "me now" messages, that is, posts by a user describing what they are currently doing. Next most common were statements and random thoughts, opinions and complaints, and information sharing such as links, each taking over 20% of the total. Less common tweet themes were self-promotion, questions to followers, presence maintenance for example, "I'm back!" anecdotes about oneself and anecdotes about others. Messages posted from mobile devices are more likely to be "me now" messages (51%). Females post more "me now" messages than males. A relatively small number of people undertake information sharing as a major activity; users can be grouped into *informers* and *meformers*, where meformers mostly share information about themselves. Informers and meformers differ in various ways. Informers tend to be more conversational and have more contacts.

These idiosyncratic characteristics of user generated content are also opportunities for the development of new text summarization approaches, which are better suited to media streams:

Short messages (microtexts): Twitter and most Facebook messages are very short (140 characters for tweets). Text summarization methods could supplement these with extra information and context coming from embedded URLs and hashtags.[1]

Noisy content: Social media content often has unusual spelling (e.g., 2moro), irregular capitalization (e.g., all capital or all lowercase letters), emoticons (e.g., :-P), and idiosyncratic abbreviations (e.g., ROFL, ZOMG). Spelling and capitalization normalization methods have been developed [262], coupled with studies of location-based linguistic variations in shortening styles in microtexts [246].

Temporal: In addition to linguistic analysis, user generated content lends itself to summarization along temporal lines, which is a relatively under-researched problem. Addressing the temporal dimension of UGC is a prerequisite for summaries of conflicting and consensual information as well as changes in opinions over time.

Social context: Social context is crucial for the correct interpretation of UGC. Summarization methods could make use of social context (e.g., who is the user connected to, how frequently they interact), in order to tailor the content of summaries accordingly, for example, make more prominent content from users of specific interest, for example, highly authoritative users, groups of similar users.

User generated: Unlike traditional Web content, UGC is a rich source of explicit and implicit information about the user, e.g., demographics (gender, location, age, etc.), interests, opinions. This enables new kinds of summaries, e.g., location-based, by age groups.

Multilingual: UGC is strongly multilingual. For instance, less than 50% of tweets are in English, with Japanese, Spanish, Portuguese, and German also featuring prominently [120]. Unfortunately, text summarization methods have so far mostly focused on English, while low-overhead adaptation to new languages still remains an open issue. Automatic language identification [120, 44] is an important first step, allowing applications to first separate social media in language clusters, which can then be processed using different algorithms.

In our experience, among all kinds of user generated content, tweets and similar short status update messages pose the biggest challenge. This is due to the fact that state-of-the-art text summarization methods tend to make certain assumptions, which clearly do not hold for the short, interconnected, and noisy messages typically found on Twitter, Facebook, and other similar sites:

---

[1]A recent study of 1.1 million tweets has found that 26% of English tweets contain a URL, 16.6%–a hashtag, and 54.8% contain a user name mention [120].

- Frequency-based methods, such as *tf-idf*, must necessarily make the assumption that salient terms will be repeated within a document. However, individual UGC messages, for example, tweets, are unlikely to contain any repeated terms, so term frequency (*tf*) must be defined in some other scope—usually by broadening the definition of a "Document" to include many posts. Additionally, the inverse document frequency (*idf*) for infrequent and out-of-vocabulary words is usually very high, and such terms are very common within microposts.

- Position is difficult to extract from a set of microposts since messages are generally only ordered temporally, it is not necessarily clear whether or not the ordering within a stream of messages is due to some conscious effort by the author. The assumption that a series of "documents" extracted from microposts will contain some common structure is somewhat difficult to defend.

- Deeper parsing and discourse analysis methods generally assume that the necessary tools have been developed for a domain. However, parsing tweets has been shown to be somewhat more difficult than parsing many other kinds of text [572].

Consequently, the appropriateness of using a method developed for traditional text summarization, without adaptation specific to microposts in particular, is deeply questionable for a number of reasons.

First, we dispute that a single tweet (or a similar micropost) is in any way comparable to a single document as used in the classical document-based summarization setting. Though short units of text have been summarized in the past, such as single paragraphs in isolation, short messages, such as tweets, are almost unique in their conversational nature, diversity, and length. Additionally, tweets are often far more context-dependent than longer documents. While larger texts may reference one another, references between tweets are often implicit and difficult to identify.

An alternative to defining a document as a single tweet is to form some collection of them and treat that as a single document for summarization. There are also problems with this approach; the collection will carry far less coherence than a longer document composed by a single author. If automatically collected, the tweets are unlikely to all cover the same specific topic, creating an additional summarization challenge.

Aside from defining the granularity of a document when summarizing tweets, it is also unclear how large a textual unit should be. In some sense, a single tweet might be analogous to a sentence, since their shortness makes messages containing multiple sentences uncommon, but this cannot always be assumed. However, while individual tweets are less self-contained than documents, they are more so than sentences. They do not always "make sense" when viewed alone, but a collection of tweets embodies less narrative than a paragraph of sentences.

Depending on the source of messages used, Twitter can be informationally efficient or contain lots of redundancy. Tweets can involve lots of co-reference or none at all. Sometimes order matters and sometimes it does not. The problem of defining what summarization for Twitter actually requires, or what form summary takes, is still very much under-explored. However, the sheer quantity of information nevertheless motivates work in this area.

The rest of this chapter provides an overview of the state-of-the-art in summarization of different kinds of user generated content and then concludes with open issues and future work.

10.4   Text Summarization of UGC

Research on text-based summarization of user generated content has predominantly focused on three kinds of UGC: online reviews, blogs, and short status updates (mostly Twitter messages). Both online reviews and blog posts tend to be longer, which makes "traditional" text summarization techniques easier to apply, including single document and multidocument summarization methods. In contrast, the summarization of short status updates has proven much more challenging for state-of-the-art text-based methods. Now let us examine these in more detail.

10.4.1   Summarizing Online Reviews

Summarizing product reviews is one of the most researched text-based UGC summarization topics. Sentiment-based quantitative summaries, for example, the percentage of positive versus negative or star ratings, are covered in Section 10.5. With respect to text-based review summaries, there has been work on aspect-based summarization [669, 115], comparative summaries of contradictory opinions, and ultra-concise summaries.

In terms of approaches, abstractive summarization is much more common than extractive approaches, largely due to the specifics of product reviews. In particular, Carenini and Cheung [115] have argued that the abstractive summarization paradigm achieves better results on product reviews than extractive summarization techniques.

One kind of product review summarization that has been studied is *aspect-based summaries*. This kind of summaries consist of a number of aspects or product features (e.g., food, price for a restaurant), a numeric value for the overall aspect rating from the reviews, and a set of textual snippets highlighting opinions on each of the aspects (e.g., "great price," "awful waiter"). As discussed by Titov and McDonald [669], aspect-based summarization needs to solve two problems: *aspect mention extraction* (e.g., service from the phrase "awful waiter") and *sentiment classification* (e.g., awful as being negative). Sentiment is also aggregated for each aspect, in order to produce a numeric value for the overall sentiment across all product reviews (e.g., service 1 star) (see Section 10.5 for details). For example, Hu and Liu [298] use association mining to identify frequently mentioned product features, coupled with using opinion words as context for identifying infrequent ones. More recently, Titov and McDonald [669] studied the problem of identifying all mentions of product aspects (i.e., features) at a phrase level and using these textual snippets in the aspect summaries. This abstractive summarization method, called multiaspect sentiment model, assigns words from the reviews to aspects using a topic model, coupled with aspect-specific maximum entropy classifiers, which predict the sentiment rating toward each aspect. Carenini and Cheung [115] instead propose an approach based on Natural Language Generation (NLG) techniques, which produce more qualitative aspect summaries of opinions (e.g., "Customers had mixed opinions about the Apex AD2600"). In addition, they define a *controversiality* measure for a set of opinions and demonstrate that NLG-based abstractive summaries are better than extractive ones, especially on highly controversial topics.

Another UGC summarization problem is that of *contrastive opinion summarization*, where the aim is to extract contrastive pairs of sentences, which contain contradictory opinions. Kim and Zhai [344] argue that such summaries are helpful for people wanting to digest mixed product reviews, for example, some reviews may rate iPhone battery life highly, while others might criticize it. Kim and Zhai [344] formulate the problem as an extractive summarization task, where positive and negative sentences are chosen based on two criteria. The first is representativeness, that is, a similar positive/negative opinion must be expressed in many reviews, and the second is contrastiveness, that is, the contradictory opinions must be on the same aspect or feature of the product. More recently, Paul et al. [526] investigated summarization of contrastive viewpoints of political opinions, for example, points raised by people for and against a new health care reform. The algorithm has two stages. First, it clusters opinionated texts by viewpoint based on a topic model—a step called macro viewpoint summarization. Then a micro viewpoint summary is generated, containing multiple sets of contrastive sentences.

Going below the sentence level, researchers have studied the problem of generating *very concise summaries*. Glaser and Schütze [240] present an unsupervised approach, which given a product review (tested on reviews longer than 5 sentences) selects a single *supporting sentence* which best captures the overall sentiment of that review. Another kind is the pros and cons product summary, which aims to convey the sentiment expressed by the majority of product reviews. Branavan et al. [91] develop a model that assigns key phrases to product reviews and generates a pros and cons list of these phrases, which tend to be indicative of product properties. The Opinosis system [227] goes one step further by generating text-based pros and cons summaries, using a graph-based method for abstractive summarization. The method utilizes the highly redundant nature of product reviews, in order to extract the most representative phrases. The most recent abstractive approach [228] focuses on micro opinion review summaries, which in addition to product properties, also include sentiment-bearing adjectives (e.g., very short battery life, big screen).

Representative phrases are chosen using point-wise mutual information and scored for readability using the Microsoft *n*-gram service.[2] The method improves on the results of Opinosis and is evaluated on user-generated reviews for 330 products from CNET. The ROUGE evaluation metric [407] is used for quantitative evaluation, while human assessors also assigned qualitative scores for grammaticality, nonredundancy, and informativeness. Although the method has only been evaluated on product reviews, it should generalize to summarizing other types of short UGC, for example, tweets and comments.

10.4.2 Blog Summarization

Unlike product reviews, blog post summarization has been approached mostly through extractive summarization techniques and modelled as the problem of selecting the most representative sentences from one or more blog posts (i.e., single-document versus multidocument summarization).

In order to determine which sentences need to be kept in the blog summary, Zhou and Hovy [777] made use of the content of news articles linked from the blog post. In other words, only sentences in the blog post, which are similar to the linked articles, were retained. This approach was, however, only tried on political blogs and it remains unclear whether it would generalize to other kinds of links to external Web content. The authors raise the question of evaluating the quality of blog post summaries and propose, but do not carry out, extrinsic, task-based evaluation instead.

One of the first papers on *opinion-based blog summarization* is by Ku et al. [372], who distinguish between negative and positive documents for a given topic, based on the topics and sentiment expressed in the individual sentences. A brief positive/negative summary of these two sets of documents is generated based on the document headlines. The detailed positive/negative summaries consist of representative sentences with the required polarity, that is, an extractive summarization approach.

Further research on this topic has been driven by the TAC 2008 opinion summarization task,[3] which built a gold standard dataset of summaries of opinions expressed in a given set of blog posts about a given target (i.e., a multidocument summarization problem). For instance, Schilder et al. [610] approached the TAC 2008 opinion-based blog summarization task by extending the FastSum extractive multidocument summarization system with a lexicon-based sentiment tagging module and blog-specific preprocessing. In a follow-up work [147], FastSum is applied to legal blogs and made less dependent on the TAC 2008 task specifics. In more detail, following the blog preprocessing step, the method filters out sentences from the blog posts, which do not match the given opinion target (a named entity in TAC 2008 and a noun phrase in the legal blogs). The remaining sentences are sentiment tagged, based on a

---

[2]http://web-ngram.research.microsoft.com
[3]http://www.nist.gov/tac/2008/summarization/op.summ.08.guidelines.html

lexicon of positive and negative words. An SVM classifier is trained to rank the sentences for inclusion in the opinion summaries based on various word frequency features, as well as sentence length and position features.

Using the TAC 2008 corpus, Mithun and Kosseim [477] carry out an error analysis of opinion-based blog summarization in comparison to news summarization and note that the latter is an easier task, where automated methods score higher. This is attributed to the differences between the two genres, with blogs containing much more pronounced opinions, being noisier, and not having a stereotypical structure (e.g., sentence position in news articles is a very important feature). A finer-grained analysis showed that errors in the summaries related to topic irrelevancy, incoherent discourse, presence of irrelevant information, and syntactic and lexical mistakes are much more frequent in blogs than in news.

Hu et al. [299] address the problem of *comments-oriented blog summarization*, that is, selecting representative sentences from a blog post by leveraging the topics covered in the associated comments. Sentence selection is based on the representativeness scores of the contained words, normalized for sentence length. Comment-based word representativeness scores are computed in four ways: binary (whether a word appears in a comment); comment frequency (number of comments containing the word); term frequency; and the best performing ReQuT (Reader, Quotation, and Topic) model. The reader measure is based on how often a user mentions other users in the comments; quotation captures comments quoting other comments; whereas comments topics are discovered via clustering and scored for importance via cosine similarity to the cluster centroid. Even though the ReQuT model was defined originally for blog summarization, it could be applied also to the problem of summarizing a set of tweets, due to the fact that tweets have similar user mention networks, can quote or reply to other tweets, and can be clustered around common topics (e.g., [562]).

Song et al. [639] addressed the problem of *summarizing the blog network* by finding the most influential blogs and the opinions they contain. Given a search query (e.g., YouTube), a network of relevant blogs is constructed, where nodes correspond to blogs and edges correspond to links between blog posts in the respective blogs. The method ranks blogs for importance to other blogs and the novelty of the information contained in the posts. Hassan et al. [273] investigate a different graph-based approach which uses lexical centrality and is based on the LexRank [208] extractive summarization algorithm.

10.4.3   Summarizing Very Short UGC

As discussed in Section 10.3, summarizing tweets and other kinds of short UGC (e.g., comments on a news or a video site) is a particularly challenging problem. Table 10.2 provides a high-level overview of state-of-the-art summarization of short UGC. This section will discuss methods that cast short message summarization as an extractive summarization problem, where the

TABLE 10.2: Overview of Summarization Approaches on Short UGC

	Domain	Method	Output produced
Inouye et al. [306]	Trending topics	Hybrid *tf-idf*	Top k tweets
Becker et al. [59]	Events	Centroid, LexRank	Top 5 tweets
Khabiri et al. [339]	YouTube comments	*tf-idf*, MEAD, LexRank	Top k comments
Harabagiu et al. [270]	Events	Retweet and User Model	Top k tweets ($<$ 250 words)
Yan et al. [740]	Any	Graph co-ranking	Top k tweets
Zubiaga et al. [784]	Events	Kullback-Leibler divergence	Subevents and repres. tweets
Wu et al. [728]	User Timelines	*tf-idf*, TextRank	Keywords
Xin et al. [734]	Curated topics	PageRank (modified), LDA	Key phrases
Sharifi et al. [624]	Trending topics	Phrase Re-enforcement	Key phrases
Judd et al. [310]	Trending topics	Phrase Re-enforcement	Key phrases
Pak et al. [517]	Tweets	Unigram, Bigram, POS	Aggregate Sentiment
Go et al. [241]	Tweets	Unigram, Bigram, POS	Aggregate Aggregate
Lai [382]	Political Tweets	Lexicon	Aggregate Sentiment
Diakopoulos [169]	Political Tweets	Lexicon Lexicon	Sentiment over time

goal is to select the most representative subset of posts, up to a given number k or a set word limit. Other ways to summarize short UGC are to produce high-level overviews based on keyphrases and topics (see Section 10.6) or sentiment (see Section 10.5).

First, looking at Twitter, Inouye and Kalita [306] have compared several summarization algorithms on producing multipost summaries of tweets, where the four most informative tweets are selected as the summary. A Hybrid *tf-idf* algorithm is defined, where term frequencies are computed by regarding all tweets as a single document, but IDF computation considers each tweet as a separate document. This is motivated by the shortness of tweets (and status updates in general), which makes it very unlikely that a word appears more than once in a tweet. The authors collect tweets containing a trending hashtag and observe that even though there is a common overall topic, the posts often tend to cluster around several aspects or subtopics. Therefore, they also propose a clustering-based approach, which first applies k-means clustering (with k set to 4) and then for each cluster of tweets, their Hybrid *tf-idf* algorithm selects the best tweet. Inouye and Kalita [306] compared a number of summarization algorithms, including a random baseline; a baseline selecting the most recent tweets; the MEAD multidocument summarizer [560]; LexRank [208]; and their own cluster-based and Hybrid *tf-idf* algorithms.

The results (both quantitative and human-produced scores) showed that the frequency-based extractive summarization algorithms, such as their Hybrid *tf-idf*, did best, whereas centroid and graph-based algorithms did not perform well, most likely due to tweets being stand-alone and short.

A similar problem is summarizing user comments on news sites, YouTube, and other social Web sites. Khabiri et al. [339], in particular, studied extractive comment summarization on YouTube and formulated the problem as selecting the most representative top k comments, that is, the same as Inouye and Kalita [306] did for tweet summaries. Khabiri et al. [339] also first cluster the user comments, then apply a precedence-based ranking to select the most representative comments for each of the clusters. Two clustering approaches were tried—k-means (used also by Inouye and Khabiri [306] above) and LDA-based topic clustering—with the latter producing better results. Different comment selection methods were tried: *tf-idf*, mutual information, MEAD [560], and LexRank [208]. Mutual information outperformed *tf-idf* and again, MEAD and LexRank did not perform as well.

One particular kind of short message (or microblog) summarization is event-based summarization, where the structure of real-world events can be used to help with the selection and ordering of the most relevant microblog content. For summarization of such short UGC sets, Becker et al. [59] selected tweets based on their textual quality (e.g., no spelling mistakes), relevance to the event, and usefulness for conveying details about the event. The top five short posts are selected on that basis, using methods based on centroid similarity, degree centrality, and LexRank [208]. Their findings indicate that the centroid method is significantly better than the other two on the relevance and usefulness criteria, with no significant difference between degree centrality and LexRank. Again, similar to the methods discussed above, only tweet content is used as input, in a bag of words fashion.

However, as discussed in Section 10.3, microblogs and social network updates in particular contain a wealth of implicit semantics which could be used to improve the performance of purely text-based summarization methods. In particular, information propagation metadata in tweets can be used as an additional source of relevance and importance. More specifically, Harabagiu and Hickl [270] focus on retweets, responses (a user responds to another user's post), and quote chains (where a post quotes from another). The method also makes use of richer semantic knowledge from the microposts themselves, namely named entities, event mentions, temporal information, and inter-event relationships (identity and temporal precedence). The resulting summary consists of the top ranked unique tweets in chronological order, not exceeding a limit of 250 words.

In addition to exploring the graph-like relationships between tweets (e.g., retweets, replies, mentions), researchers have also started to exploit information from the social user networks. For instance, Yan et al. [740] propose a graph co-ranking method which makes use of the following relations in Twitter to form a user network graph; a micropost network based on content similarity and relationships between posts; and a bi-partite graph which connects the two kinds of networks. The co-ranking approach is motivated by the connection between the content of a post, who posted it, and what is their standing in the social network (e.g., celebrities have millions of followers on Twitter).

Returning to the problem of event-based summarization, researchers have also studied ways to generate useful thematic/topical descriptors for automatically discovered subevents. For example, in the context of subevents of football games (e.g., red card, goal), Zubiaga et al. [784] select one most representative tweet per subevent. They compare a term frequency count in tweets occurring in the minute of the subevent against the Kullback-Leibler divergence metric, which not only captures frequency within a subevent, but also takes into account the overall frequency in the entire event-related set of tweets, up until the new subevent occurred. The latter method was shown to produce consistently better results, also evaluated across three languages: English, Spanish, and Portuguese. By making an algorithm sensitive to the originating location, it is possible to see what people from a given location are saying about an event (e.g., those in the United States), as well as how this differs from tweets elsewhere (e.g., those from India). Similarly, the temporal information results in different text descriptors being extracted on different days, as the event unfolds.

10.5 Structured, Sentiment-Based Summarization of UGC

The focus of this section is on methods for generating structured summaries based on quantitatively aggregated sentiment from UGC. Naturally, the first step of such methods is *sentiment detection*, followed by a *quantitative summarization* step.

Recently, techniques for sentiment detection and aggregation have begun to focus on UGC, combined with a trend toward its application as a proactive rather than a reactive mechanism. Understanding public opinion can have important consequences for the prediction of future events.

It is beyond the scope of this chapter to provide an in-depth review of automatic sentiment detection techniques, instead we refer the reader to Pang and Lee [520]. In general, sentiment detection techniques can be roughly divided into *lexicon-based methods* [e.g., 543, 596, 656] and machine learning methods [e.g., 677, 80, 517, 241]. Lexicon-based methods rely on a sentiment lexicon, a collection of known and precompiled sentiment terms. Machine learning approaches make use of syntactic and/or linguistic features [517, 241], and hybrid approaches are very common, with sentiment lexicons playing a key role in the majority of methods [e.g., 169].

With respect to quantitative aggregation of sentiment and opinions, especially coupled with monitoring over time, methods can vary greatly in their degree of sophistication. The simplest approach is to produce overall statistics of positive versus negative opinion, for example, in a given set of documents or toward a given entity, such as a famous politician [382] or a product [298]. A slightly more complex approach is to calculate quantitative statistics within specific time intervals, for example, daily, weekly. In some applications, more detailed approaches are needed, such as modeling the opinion holders and strength of conflicting opinions and how they change over time.

A number of methods are surveyed next, grouped according to the type of user generated content they focus on.

Starting with product reviews, Hu and Liu [298] propose a semistructured, aspect-based summarization approach to quantitative sentiment summarization. For each sentence in a product review, the method discovers which feature is talked about, then categorizes the sentences into positive versus negative, and increments the aggregated sentiment for this feature. The result, for example, on a set of digital camera reviews would be: picture quality (positive 253; negative 6); size (positive 134; negative 10).

Sentiment detection and aggregation research has also gone beyond the basic positive versus negative sentiment, toward assigning multipoint ratings to the entire review [522] or at aspect level (called *rated aspect summaries* [409]) [e.g., 409, 254, 420]. These ratings can be viewed as stars (e.g., one to five stars) or discrete values and aggregated across multiple reviews for the same product or shown on a review by review basis.

Similar methods have also been studied on Twitter data. Pak and Paroubek [517] classify arbitrary tweets on the basis of positive, negative, and neutral sentiment and then aggregate the overall sentiment. They construct a binary classifier which used n-gram and POS features, and train it on instances, which had been annotated according to the existence of positive (':)') and negative (':(') emoticons. Their approach has a lot in common with an earlier sentiment classifier constructed by Go et al. [241], which also used unigrams, bigrams, and POS tags, though the former demonstrated through analysis that the distribution of certain POS tags varies between positive and negative posts.

Lai [382] tackles a somewhat different sentiment analysis and aggregation task. Tweets relating to President Obama are analyzed and a daily overall "strong sentiment" is calculated. This figure is given as the ratio of the count of strongly positive tweets over the strongly negative ones. The strength and polarity of tweets in the dataset is calculated according to learned lexicons, which are lists of keywords which in general correspond to either positive or negative sentiment.

Diakopoulos et al. [169] also made use of a sentiment lexicon to annotate and aggregate positive and negative sentiment in tweets related to political events. They performed supervised learning with manually annotated examples to train a binary classifier of political opinion, using this second classifier when the former failed to make a classification. They only report the overall sentiment from a collection of tweets during a specific time window, and their system will refrain from reporting sentiment when no consensus appears to be reached for that period.

There also exists a plethora of commercial search-based tools for performing quantitatively aggregated sentiment analysis of tweets. Generally, the user enters a search term and gets back all the positive and negative (and sometimes neutral) tweets that contain the term, along with some graphics such as pie charts or graphs. Typical basic tools are Twitter Sentiment,[4] Twends, and Twitrratr.[5] Slightly more sophisticated tools such as SocialMention[6] allow search in a variety of social networks and produce other statistics such as percentages of Strength, Passion, and Reach, while others allow the user to correct erroneous analyses. On the surface, many of these appear quite impressive, and have the advantage of being simple to use and providing attractive quantitative summaries with copious information about trends. However, such tools mostly aim at finding public opinion about famous people, sports events, products, movies, and so on, but do not lend themselves easily to more complex kinds of opinion or to more abstract kinds of searches. Furthermore, their analysis tends to be fairly rudimentary, performance can be quite low, and many of them do not reveal the sources of their information or enable any kind of evaluation of their success: if they claim that 75% of tweets about Whitney Houston are positive, or that people on Facebook overwhelmingly believe that Greece should exit the Eurozone, we have no proof as to how accurate this really is.

10.6 Keyword-Based Summarization of UGC

While textual summarization typically attempts to address not only the content of a summary but also its properties as a single piece of text, such as its coherence and cohesiveness, there is a specific formulation of the task of summarization in which these issues are avoided altogether. In keyword extraction, a summary is simply a list of terms which can be considered salient.

Automatically selected keywords are useful in representing the topic of a document or collection of documents, and less effective in delivering arguments or full statements contained therein. It is therefore necessary to consider keyword extraction as a form of indicative summarization, allowing the reader to decide whether or not to view the full text. Keywords can also be used in the context of information retrieval, as a means of dimensionality reduction, and allowing systems to deal with smaller sets of important terms rather than whole documents.

In early summarization, terms with high frequency within a document were assumed to be important and sentences which contained these terms were

---

[4]http://twittersentiment.appspot.com/
[5]http://twitrratr.com/
[6]http://socialmention.com/

favored for inclusion in a summary [423]. Additionally, Brandow et al. [92] used *tf-idf* to characterize important terms in a document. Both these approaches share the property that they rely on models of term significance.

Later approaches to keyword extraction exploited term co-occurrence; forming a graph of terms with edges derived from the distance between occurrences of a pair of terms and assigning weights to vertices [462]. This class of keyword extraction was found to perform favorably on Twitter data compared to methods which relied on text models [728].

These graph-based approaches to extracting keywords from Twitter perhaps perform well because the domain contains a great deal of redundancy [762]. While this property of Twitter is somewhat beneficial when producing keyword summaries, another less helpful trait is the sheer variety of topics discussed on the service. When it is not known that a document discusses a single topic, it can be more difficult to extract a coherent and faithful set of keywords from it.

While Wu et al. [728] used TextRank on the whole of a user's stream, they did not attempt to model or address topic variation, unlike Xin et al. [734], who incorporated topic modeling into their approach to keyword extraction. Likewise, Ramage et al. [562] discovered topic models for Twitter data, though they did not make use of these for summarization.

Other work has focused on keyword generation for tweets that have already been clustered by topic. Becker et al. [59] evaluated for such tweet sets several different methods based on centroid, degree centrality, and LexRank, and found that centroid works the best in some cases; however, they did not manage to demonstrate a statistically significant difference, and the methods all performed poorly. Sharifi et al. [624] extracted key phrases for trending topics by exploiting textual redundancy and selecting common sequences of words, using an algorithm that they label "phrase re-enforcement." The short phrases produced are pithy and eminently readable, though they can be ungrammatical—an issue that has been addressed by other recent work [310].

10.7   Visual Summarization of UGC

Twitter data can be summarized visually as well as textually. These "visual summaries" can take many forms, including graphs and charts, maps, and timelines. In this section, we will briefly discuss the forms which nontextual summaries of UGC can take in existing systems.

One of the simplest and widely used summary visualizations is word clouds. These generally use single word terms, which can be somewhat difficult to interpret without extra context. Word clouds have been used to assist users in browsing social media streams, including blog content [46] and tweets [621, 485]. For instance, Phelan et al. [536] use word clouds to present the results

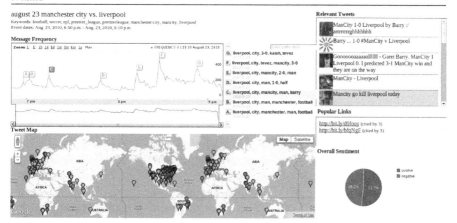

FIGURE 10.1: TwitInfo tracks a football game (http://twitinfo.csail.mit. edu/). **(See color insert.)**

of a Twitter based recommendation system. The Eddi system [69] uses topic clouds, showing higher-level themes in the user's tweet stream. These are combined with topic lists, which show who tweeted on which topic, as well as a set of interesting tweets for the highest ranked topics. The Twitris system (see Figure 10.3) derives even more detailed, contextualized phrases by using 3-grams instead of uni-grams [485].

The main drawback of cloud-based visualizations is their static nature. Therefore, they are often combined with timelines showing keyword/topic frequencies over time [9, 69, 301, 710], as well as methods for discovery of unusual popularity bursts [46]. Diakopoulos et al. [169] use a timeline which is synchronized with a transcript of a political broadcast, allowing navigation to key points in a video of the event, and displaying tweets from that time period. Overall sentiment is shown on a timeline at each point in the video, using simple color segments. Similarly, TwitInfo (see Figure 10.1 [444]) uses a timeline to display tweet activity during a real-world event (e.g., a football game), coupled with some example tweets, color-coded for sentiment. Some of these visualizations are dynamic, are updated as new content comes in (e.g., topic streams [176], falling keyword bars [301], and dynamic information landscapes [301]).

In addition, some visualizations try to capture the semantic relatedness between topics in the media streams. For instance, BlogScope [46] calculates keyword correlations by approximating mutual information for a pair of keywords using a random sample of documents. Another example is the information landscape visualization, which convey topic similarity through spatial proximity [301] (see Figure 10.2). Topic-document relationships can be shown also through force-directed, graph-based visualizations [196]. Last,

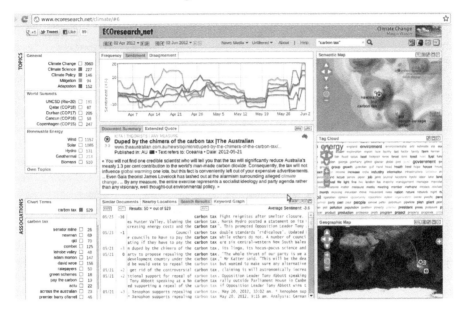

FIGURE 10.2: Media watch on climate change portal (http://www. ecoresearch.net/climate). **(See color insert.)**

Archambault et al. [30] propose multilevel tag clouds, in order to capture hierarchical relations.

Another important dimension of user generated content is its place of origin. For instance, some tweets are geo-tagged with latitude/longitude information, while many user profiles on Facebook, Twitter, and blogs specify a user location. Consequently, map-based visualizations of topics have also been explored [460, 444, 301, 485] (see also Figures 10.2 and 10.1). For instance, Twitris [485] allows users to select a particular state from the Google map and it shows the topics discussed in social media from this state only. Figure 10.3 shows the Twitris US 2012 presidential elections monitor, where we have chosen to see the related topics discussed in social media originating from California. Clicking on the topic "female democratic senators" displays the relevant tweets, news, and Wikipedia articles.

Opinions and sentiment also feature frequently in UGC summarization interfaces. For instance, Media Watch (Figure 10.2 [301]) combines word clouds with aggregated sentiment polarity, where each word is colored in a shade of red (predominantly negative sentiment), green (predominantly positive), or black (neutral/no sentiment). Search results snippets and faceted browsing terms are also sentiment colored. Others have combined sentiment-based color coding with event timelines [9], lists of tweets (Figure 10.1 [444]), and mood maps [9]. Aggregated sentiment is typically presented using pie charts [710]

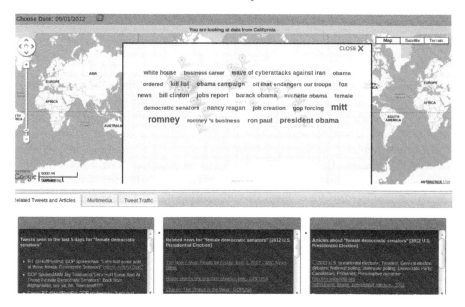

FIGURE 10.3: The Twitris social media event monitoring portal (http://twitris.knoesis.org). **(See color insert.)**

and, in the case of TwitInfo, the overall statistics are normalized for recall (Figure 10.1 [444]).

Researchers have also investigated specifically the problem of summarizing visually social media conversations about real-world events, for example, broadcast events [621], football games (Figure 10.1 [444]), conferences [176], and news events [460, 9]. A key element here is the ability to identify subevents and combine these with timelines, maps, and topic-based visualizations.

Last, given the user-generated and social nature of the media streams, some visualizations have been designed to exploit this information. For instance, the PeopleSpiral visualization [176] plots Twitter users who have contributed to a topic (e.g., posted using a given hashtag) on a spiral, starting with the most active and 'original' users first. User originality is measured as the ratio between the number of tweets authored by the user versus re-tweets made. OpinionSpace [212] instead clusters and visualizes users in a two-dimensional space, based on the opinions they have expressed on a given set of topics. Each point in the visualization shows a user and their comment, so the closer two points are, the more similar the users and opinions are. However, the purely point-based visualization was found hard to interpret by some users, since they could not see the textual content until they clicked on a point. ThemeCrowds [30] instead derives hierarchical clusters of Twitter users through agglomerative clustering and provides a summary of the tweets, generated by this user cluster, through multilevel tag clouds (inspired by treemap visualization). Tweet volumes over time are shown in a timeline-like view, which also allows the selection of a time period.

10.8   Evaluating UGC Summaries

In any domain, the task of summarization can be a difficult one to evaluate. Summaries can take many different forms, and even for the common case of textual summarization it is difficult to automatically compare summaries to a gold standard. Issues arise from the ability to validly represent a compressed form of a document in any of a number of ways. The problem can be even more acute on short UGC, such as tweets, where summaries may take the form of lists, or visual representations of tweet volume or other types of timeline.

Additionally, since it is generally impossible to read all of the short messages for a corpus to be summarized, gold-standard human generated summaries can be very incomplete or may miss information which should have been included.

The difficulty of evaluating visual summaries of UGC is so acute that many choose not to address it at all [710, 621, 485, 146]. Visual summaries typically contain information other than raw text, for example, they may display information from tweets on a map or include timelines of topics and tweet volume. They may include less local information, like news stories or video. The variability of such summaries makes them very difficult to evaluate using a single standard method. Addressing this very issue, Diakopoulos et al. [169] carry out a user study of their system, performing extrinsic testing by having journalists attempt to use the summarizer to form ideas about possible articles. The 18 journalists taking part were asked to complete surveys about the experience, and the stories they produced were assigned individual types. Though the authors admit that evaluation on such a small set of users is not enough to truly test the efficacy of their summarizer, they argue that the experiment has allowed them to see the ways in which it could be used, and they believe that testing on a larger set of users could lead to more significant results.

For truly textual UGC summaries on relatively small test corpora, authors can reasonably hope to use the standard DUC evaluation measures on their systems. For instance, Sharifi et al. [624] gather 100 tweets per topic for 50 trending topics on Twitter, and then ask volunteers to generate summaries which they feel best describe each collection. The automatic summaries produced by their algorithm are then tested using a manual content annotation method, testing that the same content is available as in the gold standard, and automatically using Rouge-1. Harabagiu and Hickl [270] again make use of model summaries, though they eschew Rouge in favor of the Pyramid method [494].

Another class of evaluation treats summarization as a document retrieval problem. Chakrabarti and Punera [125] use knowledge about the significant plays in a sports match to build a gold standard for what must be discussed in a summary. After simplifying the problem somewhat by assuming that the search process is perfect and manually validating the input to their system, they calculate recall based on the events from the game, before asking users to subjectively classify the content of tweets in the summaries. Tweets with a certain content type are said to be irrelevant, providing a measure of precision.

Becker et al. [59] similarly have users score the quality, relevance, and usefulness of the selected tweet summary, though they do not attempt to address the problem of calculating recall.

10.8.1 Training Data, Evaluation, and Crowdsourcing

The evaluation of summaries can be very data-intensive, and human input is generally required both to develop such data sets and to evaluate the quality of generated summaries. The Pyramid method, for example, demands that the researchers initially construct a series of gold standard summaries before manually comparing generated candidates to the gold standard. Since neither gold standards for tweet summarization, nor the methodologies to carry out human evaluation exist at this point, one potential solution to both problems is the use of crowdsourced summaries developed through services, such as Mechanical Turk.

When humans are asked to create a text summary for one or more given documents, this is effectively a content generation problem. Gathering these through crowdsourcing has been shown to be particularly challenging, since naive task definitions produce low-quality corpora [760, 492]. Consequently, the design and quality control of the summary collection crowdsourcing tasks is nontrivia. Crowd workers generate multiple diverse answers, all of which could be correct, that is, different, good summaries can be provided for the same UGC content. For instance, El-Haj et al. [199] create a corpus of extractive summaries for Arabic texts collecting three summaries per text where summaries consist of a subset of representative sentences from the article. They use majority voting to determine which sentences need to be kept in the summary, that is, at least two of the workers need to agree.

The issue of cheating must also be considered, whereby users attempt to falsely gain the financial reward for completing a task without actually attempting it. Researchers are reporting mixed experiences with crowdsourcing so far, for instance, Gillick and Liu [238] have found that nonexpert evaluation of summarization systems produces noisier results thus requiring more redundancy to achieve statistical significance and that MTurk workers cannot produce score rankings that agree with expert ranking. The authors suggest that redesigning the AMT task definition according to other summarization evaluation approaches could improve results.

A key challenge in using MTurk for summary evaluation is to transform a complex expert-based evaluation protocol (which typically relies on detailed instructions) into smaller, simpler tasks that can be explained to nonexperts [451]. One such task was designed by Inouye and Kalita [306] for evaluation of tweet summaries. Inouye and Kalita asked the MTurk workers to indicate on a five-point scale how much of the information from the human produced summary is contained in the automatically produced summary.

Another simplistic task design that has achieved successful results on MTurk is pair-wise ranking [240]. The summarization task in this case is to identify the most informative sentence from a product review. In this case, the crowd-workers are asked to indicate whether a sentence chosen by the baseline system is more informative than a sentence chosen by the author's method. Sentence order is randomized and it is also possible to indicate that none of these sentences are a good summary.

Overall, even though crowdsourcing is increasingly playing a role in summarization research, using it successfully still requires significant expertise. Further research is required in making the process scalable, repeatable, and capable of producing high quality summaries and evaluation results.

The next step forward would be to make freely available reusable task definitions and crowdsourcing work-flow patterns, as well as providing more details in the research papers on the exact methodology that was followed.

10.9   Outstanding Challenges

Within the scope of this chapter, we have discussed the current strands of research into summarizing user generated content. Many of the methods discussed here have not traditionally been considered types of summarization, for example, the creation of keyword-based and visual summaries of UGC.

We believe that summarization for Twitter and similar online social networks is a problem of the utmost practical relevance. While users post an enormous wealth of extremely useful UGC with frightening regularity, it is simply impossible to filter and manually process all but the smallest data stream. Where the task of summarization might once have been to find the salient points in a document collection, it is now required to find the salient points to a particular user, on a particular topic, in the entire of the Twitter-verse.

This need for compression and summarization—the requirement for users to be shown what is relevant to them and little else, has driven our interpretation of many existing strands of work in the light of UGC summarization. In the remainder of this chapter we will discuss several major outstanding research challenges.

10.9.1   Spatio-Temporal Summaries

Even though UGC is strongly grounded in the spatio-temporal context, this additional semantic information has so far mostly been neglected in UGC summarization. For instance, where visualization is concerned, it is mostly limited to map-based and topic-based timeline visualizations (see Section 10.7). Additional summarization dimensions can be users' age, gender, political views, interests, and other such latent characteristics (see Section 10.9.4 below). In addition, UGC summarization methods based on social networks (e.g., hubs and authorities) could be combined with the currently prevailing topic- and content-centric approaches.

The main sources of user location information are GPS coordinates attached to a message and self-disclosed location information in user profiles. However, Cheng [135] found that only around 36% of users actually provide a valid location in their profiles. Furthermore, when we analyzed a dataset of over 30,000 tweets discussing the 2011 London Riots, less than 1% of microposts contained any GPS information.

Therefore, an important prerequisite for location-based summarization is the automatic geolocation of users of social networks, based on publicly available data, for example, their profile, posts, and social network. Broadly speaking, existing methods fall into two different categories: content-based (i.e., using the textual posts of a given user) and network-based (i.e., using the social network).

Content-based methods ("you are where you write about") typically gather the textual content produced by the user and infer their location based on features, such as mentions of local place names [219] and use of local dialect. In the work of Eisenstein [197] and Cheng [135], region-specific terms and language that might be relevant to the geolocation of users were discovered automatically. A classification approach is devised in Mahmud et al. [436] that also incorporates specific mentions of places near to the user. One obvious disadvantage to this method is the fact that someone might be writing about a popular global event, which is of no relevance to his actual location. Another is that users might take deliberate steps to hide their true location by alternating the style of their posts or not referencing local landmarks.

In contrast, network-based geolocation methods ("you are where your friends are") aim to use the user's social network to infer their location. To the best of our knowledge, the only existing method of this kind (i.e., relying on the user's social network alone) is the work of Backstrom et al. [37], who first created a model for the distribution of distance between pairs of friends, before using this to find the most likely location for a given user. The influence of distance in social network ties is demonstrated by the earlier work of Liben-Nowell et al. [405]. Two limitations of this approach are that it assumes all users globally have the same distribution of friends in terms of distance and fails to account for the density of people in an area. In conclusion, automatic user geolocation is still a relatively underexplored problem, but nevertheless, where known, location information could usefully be incorporated in UGC summaries.

One example application, needing spatio-temporal summaries, is monitoring political elections and the popularity of political parties and politicians over time. These not only vary on a local, regional, and national level, but also change over time. As part of the TrendMiner[7] project, we are currently developing methods for spatio-temporal summarization of Twitter streams.

10.9.2   Exploiting Implicit UGC Semantics

Although inroads have been made already, current methods for UGC summarization have many limitations. First, most methods address the more shallow problems of keyword and topic extraction, while frequency-based extractive summarization techniques do not reach the significantly better performance obtained by more sophisticated methods on longer text documents.

Second, the majority make very few or no adaptations to better model the specifics of user generated content. UGC abounds with implicit semantic information, which is very different from the discourse and positional features in traditional text documents. More specifically, UGC summarization methods need to tap better into the knowledge from the user social networks (who is connected to who), information diffusion networks (who re-tweeted, replied, and mentioned who), the user's own produced UGC, temporal information (e.g., recency), and user demographics. For instance, one could envisage a new kind of opinion-based summaries, which summarize opinions according to influential groups, demographics and geographical, and social cliques.

10.9.3   Multilinguality

With fewer than 50% of tweets in English [120], another related major challenge is multilinguality. Most of the methods surveyed here were developed and tested on English content, with some exceptions, for example, Zubiaga et al. [784], who also considered Spanish and Portuguese for event-based summarization.

Multilingual summarization is a challenge even in the context of standard, well-formed documents. As recently as 2011, the Text Analysis Conference (TAC) ran the MultiLing pilot competition,[8] specifically with the aim to promote the development of multilingual algorithms for summarization. The task was to create short summaries of around 240 words of 10 news texts on a given topic. Seven languages were covered and each system had to produce summaries in at least two languages. The best performing system [645] used a summarization algorithm based on latent semantic analysis, in order to determine the highest scoring sentences for the summaries. The only language-specific resources were stop word lists. The question of how well such an approach would cope with user generated content and the different kinds of UGC summaries that could be produced requires further experimentation.

---

[7]http://www.trendminer-project.eu
[8]http://users.iit.demokritos.gr/ ggianna/TAC2011/MultiLing2011.html

10.9.4   Personalization

The fourth major challenge is the generation of personalized summaries of UGC. As discussed in Section 10.9.1, the user's profile and the content they contribute online to the various social networking sites can be a useful source for deriving information about the user and using that to personalize the summaries.

For instance, Yan et al. [740] have recently proposed a way to inject a topic-based model of user interests in their tweet recommendation system. There have also been efforts to discover user demographics information, when it is not available already. Burger et al. [106] classify users as male or female based on the text of their tweets, their description fields, and their names. They report better-than-human accuracy, compared to a set of annotators on Mechanical Turk. Pennacchiotti and Popescu [531] present a general framework for user classification that can learn to automatically discover political alignment, ethnicity, and fans of a particular business.

With respect to capturing user interests from tweets, further work is required on distinguishing globally interesting topics (e.g., trending news) from interests specific to the given user (e.g., work-related, hobby, gossip from a friend, etc.).

What is interesting to a user also ties in with user behavior roles. In the case of online forums, the following user behavior roles have been identified [127]: *elitist*, *grunt*, *joining conversationalist*, *popular initiator*, *popular participant*, *supporter*, *taciturn*, and *ignored*. In Twitter, the most common role distinction is between *meformers* (80% of users) and *informers* (20% of users) [484].

In turn, this requires more sophisticated methods for the automatic assignment of user roles, based on the semantics of posts and user interaction patterns, as well as the successful integration of these features into the UGC summarization algorithms.

10.9.5   Evaluation

As discussed in Section 10.8, there are a number of key challenges to consider when evaluating summarization for user generated content:

- There are few preexisting corpora.

- Data sets can be difficult to reproduce and share, due to the terms of service of many social networks.

- For certain domains, the relevant content can be difficult to obtain.

- Where messages are short, a large number of them would typically need to be annotated.

- When crowdsourcing data, tasks must be defined in as simple a way as possible.

- Summaries vary dramatically in terms of form, content, or purpose. It is not yet well understood what evaluation techniques are appropriate in which circumstances.

We have now started to address some of these issues, specifically gold standard collection and evaluation of personalized summaries of Twitter timelines [577].

10.10 Conclusion

This chapter introduced the task of UGC summarization, discussing its potential usefulness and relevance as an information filtering technique to address UGC information overload. In addition, work in this area is extremely well motivated by a myriad of potential applications, from content management to data mining.

Our introduction to textual summarization serves to provide the basis for a reader unfamiliar with the state-of-the-art in this area. The challenges of summarization in UGC are also discussed, justifying the development of new approaches specifically created for social media.

We introduced state-of-the-art research in online-review summarization, and blog summarization, before advancing to summarization of very short UGC. An exciting problem area was discussed—that of automated summarization of global events. By producing summaries of events based on UGC, we allow the collective hive-mind of the Internet to perform a task that is traditionally the reserve of a few (arguably biased) journalists—that of distilling and representing current events for easy consumption.

To similar ends, we discussed work in sentiment extraction, and structured summaries of those sentiments. Though it may seem that identifying sentiment automatically from such content is enough, the ability to accurately and succinctly represent that sentiment is of great importance given the thousands of product and service reviews that are being continuously created.

Keyword-based extraction is where the differences between traditional summarization and summarization for UGC become less pronounced. Here the problem is one of content ranking, albeit with the content generally not recombined into coherent summaries afterward. Some of the unique properties of online social networks are relevant here—they contain a large amount of redundancy, and the posts themselves are often short.

Visual and multimodal summarization can provide interesting new ways to present content in aggregate to users. Sentiment and geographical information can both be incorporated into such displays. It is perhaps appropriate that this novel domain for summarization should be met with novel interfaces for displaying and browsing through summaries.

Last, we discuss evaluation and other issues in summarization of UGC. Many of these problems remain open, though the field is still nascent and many of them provide interesting or relevant challenges to which researchers will almost certainly rise in the following years.

Throughout this chapter, the intention has to provide a fast paced, general overview of an equally fast moving field. We have refrained from delving into technical details of promising methods and approaches which may nontheless be forgotten in the years to come. This chapter contains nearly a hundred references, and there is much secondary reading available for students and researchers who wish to go further in-depth. It is our sincere hope that this work can provide a useful reference point, and enthuse others to explore the problem of summarization for user generated content.

10.11 Acknowledgments

This work was supported by funding from the Engineering and Physical Sciences Research Council (Grant EP/I004327/1).

Chapter 11

Recommender Systems

Claudio Lucchese

Istituto di Scienza e Tecnologie della Informazione, Italy

Cristina Ioana Muntean

Istituto di Scienza e Tecnologie della Informazione, Italy

Raffaele Perego

Istituto di Scienza e Tecnologie della Informazione, Italy

Fabrizio Silvestri

Istituto di Scienza e Tecnologie della Informazione, Italy

Hossein Vahabi

Istituto di Scienza e Tecnologie della Informazione, Italy

Rossano Venturini

Istituto di Scienza e Tecnologie della Informazione, Italy

The explosive growth of the Web due to user generated content has enabled a huge and heterogeneous repository of sources of information and documents. Users may be overwhelmed by the volume of available information. Let us consider, for instance, the social network context. Users may face interaction overload due to the high number of messages generated by their friends, or due to the large number of voters or commenters on a particular Web page, and they may face information overload due to the vast quantity of social media available such as shared photos, video, bookmarks, and so on [249, 418]. To overcome these problems, several methods have been proposed in different but related fields such as Information Retrieval, Information Filtering, and Recommender Systems.

Information Retrieval (IR) is a process through which users' information needs are converted into a set of useful references [38, 480]. Although traditionally IR refers to the extraction of relevant documents from textual corpora, nowadays it copes with the retrieval of information from collections of any kind of data such as videos, images, audios, and so on.

Information Filtering (IF) is a method for delivering relevant information to people who need it [267, 63, 211]. While the retrieval process focuses on finding relevant data in a stream, the main goal of the filtering process is the removal of uninteresting data from an incoming stream. IF is designed to work with large amounts of semistructured or unstructured data and the filtering process is typically based on user profiles, that is, demographic information, user interests, and so on.

Recommender Systems (RSs) [565] are another method to solve the overload of information and interaction that users face. RSs assist the natural process of everyday life where a user relies on recommendations from other people in order to decide based on absent or limited personal information. Their goal is suggesting items based on user profiles and item contents, in order to direct users to the items that best meet their preferences and tastes. Even if RSs have their origin in the IF field, their objectives differ: RSs *find* and *add* interesting items to the stream of information, while IF systems *identify* and *remove* uninteresting items from a stream.

In many cases, especially when dealing with the information overload problem, the borders among the disciplines of IR, IF, and RS are fuzzy, and interdisciplinary approaches are successful most often. All of the techniques designed in these fields aim at exploiting any available source of knowledge to match the user with the required bit of information. Such information sources, of course, include the description of an item in the given collection, for example, the text of a document, the text surrounding an image, or the number of comments of a video. In fact, user generated content (UGC) is an invaluable source of information. By UGC we signify not only items, such as documents, that the user is willing to search through, but more importantly a vast amount of side information that can be exploited, for example, to profile a user according to his past actions or to enrich the description of an item by the manual annotations provided by users. To this end, several techniques for mining UGC and to apply the extracted knowledge have been developed. It is possible to find the most interesting examples in the area of RSs, where a combination of IR, IF, and mining of UGC is mandatory to provide a satisfactory interaction with the user.

UGC helps widen the information of more classical recommendation systems by adding different facets. The wisdom of the crowd contributes with information from social networks, uploaded and shared content (multimedia or text), check-ins and map locations, social bookmarks, folksonomies, blog posts, comments, reviews, rates, and tags to make more efficient recommendations. Recommender systems based on data from social networks use social relationships between users like friendships, communities, and groups to infer the degree of similarity or dissimilarity between users. Moreover, they explicitly express preferences, opinions (through votes, likes, clicks, or sharing) and annotate UGC with tags, locations, categories, and descriptions. Through user generated data and its annotations, recommender systems can harness implicit and explicit information and offer diversified, serendipitous personalized or long-tail suggestions. Various inferences on the available metadata can be found and integrated as new features in UGC recommendation systems, so the possibilities are practically innumerable/countless/inexhaustible/manifold. Sections 11.2, 11.3, and 11.4 describe in detail how this kind of data can be exploited for recommendations.

This chapter presents an overview of the general recommendation techniques used in modern recommender systems and describes how these systems can exploit the knowledge mined from, or applied to, a variety of different classes of user generated content (UGC). In Section 11.1 we will describe the fundamental recommendation techniques: *Collaborative Filtering recommenders* (Section 11.1.1), *Demographic recommenders* (Section 11.1.2), *Content-Based recommenders* (Section 11.1.3), *Knowledge-Based recommenders* (Section 11.1.4), and *Hybrid recommenders* (Section 11.1.5). The aim of the subsequent sections (Sections 11.2, 11.3, and 11.4) is that of presenting three case studies exemplifying the use of UGC for different sources of information to offer personalized recommendations in different contexts.

11.1 Recommendation Techniques

RSs are tools aimed at *guiding the user in a personalized way to interesting or useful items in a large space of possible options* [566, 366, 108, 109]. In recent years they have proven to allow users to effectively cope with the information overload in popular e-commerce and online environments. Movies, images, videos, and friends are classical examples of objects commonly managed by

RSs, even if we could also have more complex kinds of items such as travels, jobs, financial investments, and so on [479]. The users may have different characteristics and expectations. Modeling user profiles and understanding their interests is a complex task that also depends on the type of items to suggest.

Formally, an RS [11] is composed of a set of users U, a set of items I, and a utility function $f : U \times I \to R$, where R is a totally ordered set. Given a user $u \in U$, we would like to choose the item $i \in I$ which maximizes the user's utility:

$$i = \arg\max_{i' \in I} f(u, i').$$

The value of $f(u, i)$ depends both on the profile of user u (e.g., age, gender, interests, context, and so on) and on the set of features of item i (e.g., price or color of a product, keywords, valuation of other users, and so on). The content of each user profile, the set of features of interest for each item, and the definition of the utility function depend on the particular recommendation technique. The following sections will briefly describe the traditional recommendation approaches.

11.1.1   Collaborative Filtering-Based Recommendations

Collaborative filtering is probably one of the most popular and widely implemented recommendation techniques. Collaborative filtering tries to automate the process of word of mouth by aggregating user ratings on items by trying to find a set of similar users based on their ratings, and, finally, by recommending items based on user similarities [108, 623]. In other variants of this technique, users' rates may be replaced by clicks, purchases or other explicit or implicit signals that allow the users' interest in a particular item to be established. In contrast to other recommendation techniques (i.e., content-based recommenders), collaborative filtering systems do not consider item contents: characteristics that render them particularly useful for complex items such as movies, videos, music, and so on.

Formally, given a user u and an item i that has not been rated by u, a collaborative filtering system tries to predict a rating on item i for user u. This prediction process is composed of two steps: first, a set of users U_u having similar tastes to u is selected on the basis of previously rated items, and then, ratings assigned to item i by the users in U_u are aggregated [564]. A speculative approach consists of considering the items similar to i instead of considering users similar to u, and on aggregating ratings assigned by u to those items [594].

Table 11.1 shows a depiction of a user-item rating matrix for a movie dataset. Rows represent users and columns represent movies. The empty spaces indicate that the user has not yet rated the corresponding movie. Collaborative filtering tries to predict the values of these empty cells.

Before going deeper into the description of the collaborative filtering method, it is useful to emphasize the *main advantages and drawbacks* of this approach. Collaborative filtering is a simple, effective, and generic technique

TABLE 11.1: A Depiction of a User-Items Rating Matrix for a Movie DataSet of 5 Users and 4 Items (Values in each row are ratings by the corresponding user to a particular item.)

	Movie a	Movie b	Movie c	Movie d
User A	-	1	-	5
User B	2	-	4	-
User C	3	-	5	1
User D	3	-	5	-
User E	3	3	-	4

that can deal with any type of items (also complex ones) because there is no need to consider the content of each item. Moreover, collaborative filtering does not suffer from overspecialization, in contrast to content-based RSs that may risk to suggest items too similar to the user's profile.

On the other hand, recommendations for new users or for new items are problematic due to the fact that the information regarding them is missing or is too poor to provide interesting suggestions. This is a well-studied issue known in literature as the *cold-start recommendation problem* [608, 387, 235]. In general, any RS that exploits the historical rating information has this problem whenever it has not yet gathered sufficient information about a particular user or item.

In the following, we present a brief description of two of the most important types of collaborative filtering algorithms: *memory-based* and *model-based*.

Memory-based collaborative filtering is a method based on the entire user-items rating matrix. Given a user u and an item i, the first step of recommendation is the selection of the set $U_u^{(k)}$ of the k closest neighbors of u. The distance between users is established by defining an appropriate *user similarity function*. The second step of recommendation is the aggregation of ratings on item i over the set $U_u^{(k)}$. For this step, it is required to define an appropriate rating aggregation function.

Possible rating aggregation functions are the mean arithmetic rate or the weighted majority voting over $U_u^{(k)}$. Garcin et al. [231] compare the accuracy of three different aggregation functions: mean, median, and mode. Results show that median can significantly improve recommendation accuracy and robustness w.r.t. mean.

One of the main issues of the memory-based collaborative filtering system is the *sparsity* of user-items matrix: in large-scale systems users usually rate only a small fraction of available items and thus, the number of items in common between two given users is usually small. Data sparsity results in a poor prediction of user ratings. Many solutions are proposed in literature in order to solve this problem. For example, *default voting* [129] extends each user's rating history with the clique's averages, while *effective missing data prediction* [429] combines user's information and items information.

Model-based collaborative filtering constructs a predictive model based on historical training data. In contrast with memory-based collaborative filtering, model-based collaborative filtering techniques do not need to store the whole user-items rating matrix, but use the historical user-items information only during the learning phase. The learned model is then used to make predictions on test data. Bayesian models collaborative filtering, clustering models collaborative filtering, and dependency networks collaborative filtering are examples of model-based collaborative algorithms that have been proposed.

Collaborative filtering successfully employs UGC for improving recommendations, a classical example is by Resnick et al. [564]. Usenet news is a platform offering a big quantity of news personalized according to each user's explicit preferences. GroupLens is a collaborative system designed for Usenet news. The UGC consists of pieces of articles written by users and the ratings provided for them.

Accordingly, if previously predictions were made based on content filters, GroupLens is set to improve the service. The basic assumption is that people with similar tastes (based on their rating history) will tend to agree also in the future. The system previously explained functions in two steps: searches for user ratings similar to each other and predicts the rating for a new item based on ratings from similar users.

11.1.2   Demographic Recommendations

Demographic recommender systems aim to categorize users based on personal demographic attributes, and to recommend items based on the demographic profile (age, country, language, level of instruction, etc.) of users [108, 109, 566]. The assumption is that users within the same demographic class have similar interests. An example of demographic RS is the book recommendation system presented by Rich [567]. The author gathered personal information and matched it against manually created classes of users. Another example of demographic RS is the classifier based on demographic data presented by Pazzani [527] that resorts to user features extracted from users' home pages. However, there are *advantages and disadvantages* to this technique. One of the main advantages of demographic RSs is that they partially solve the cold-start recommendation problem. However, these systems have to deal with the difficulty of collecting users' demographic data, which can be sensitive and thus subject to security and privacy regulations.

An example of how demographic data can be used to offer recommendations can be found in Weber and Castillo [706]. The main goal of the paper is to identify how different demographic segments differ in their Web search behavior. The authors use three sources of information: a subset of Yahoo! U.S. query log, profile information (birth year, gender, and ZIP code) provided by users, both user generated data, and U.S.-census information including demographic information for U.S. zip codes. They also point out the difference between grouping users on demographic features like age or income and make personalized recommendations, meaning learning a model for each individual user. The advantages lie in having to train less data, protecting user privacy, and having a simpler interpretation.

11.1.3   Content-Based Recommendations

Content-based recommender systems have been studied in the past with the purpose of identifying interesting Web sites or articles and recommending them based on their content. Content-based RSs process the content of the items and recommend them based on a user's profile. Different from CF systems, in content-based RSs the user profiles are constructed on the basis of the content of the items that users previously liked or disliked. The representation of items through a set of relevant attributes extracted from their content is far from being a trivial task, and strongly depends on the kind of items at hand.

An effective way of representing the content of items is the Vector Space Model [587], where an item is represented as a weighted vector of features. A typical weighting representation for items having a textual description is the *tf-idf* weighting, defined as:

$$w(t, i) = tf_{t,i} \times idf_t,$$

where t is a term or attribute value, i is an item or document, $tf_{t,i}$ is the frequency of t in i, and idf_t is the inverse document frequency of term t in the whole collection of items.

Content-based RSs need a model to represent the profiles of users to be defined. User preferences on items can be asked explicitly or can be extracted from implicit information. An example of explicit data collection are Web forms that allow users to select among a set of known attributes values (for instance, the genre of a book). An example of implicit data are the collection of user-clicks on a Web site. The hypothesis is that if a user clicks on a item she is interested on its content even if not explicitly stated. Obviously, explicit profiles are generally less noisy than implicit ones but collecting them is often not feasible.

The choice of the representation of user profiles may depend on the training phase used by content-based RS with the aim of learning to rank items with respect to the user's profile. The training phase may make use of a learning classification algorithm based on the features of items rated by the user. For example, decision tree learners are used to predict the user interest for a given item on the basis of the values of several attributes [557]. The decision tree is built for each user that describes her preferences on the basis of the values of the attributes for a set of labeled examples. Figure 11.1 shows a toy example of a decision tree for a user u. By using this decision tree, we could infer that u would consider positively a new low cost Mexican restaurant.

Regarding *advantages and disadvantages*, the main strong points of content-based RSs are the possibility of explaining intuitively the reason why

294

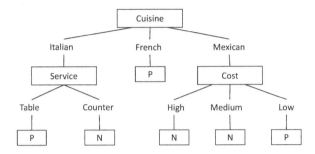

FIGURE 11.1: Restaurant decision tree based on the profile of a user.

an item has been suggested on the basis of its features, and the fact that this technique does not suffer from the cold-start problem affecting recommenders using collaborative filtering. On the other hand, content-based RSs may be over-specialized, and always recommend very similar items [25]. Moreover, the analysis of item content could be difficult in the case of complex items or due to privacy issues [566].

A tag recommender system for photos on Flickr is described by Sigurbjörnsson and van Zwol [631]. It is based on the UGC from the photo sharing service, namely tags already attached to photos. Users manually annotate their photos with tags that they find relevant, enriching the context and the semantical information of the photos. The idea of the recommender is to aid the user with his tagging. Recommendations are based on the co-occurrence of tags in various photos.

Given a photo and a few user-defined tags, the system generates a wide list of candidate tags for each of the existing photo tags, obtained by exploiting their co-occurrence. The recommender produces a number of ranked results, obtained from the aggregation of all co-occurrence lists, which is finally presented to the user. In order to obtain reasonable values of co-occurrence, a large quantity of supporting data is necessary. This data can be easily obtained from a huge UGC platform like Flickr. The dataset used for experimentation consists of 52 million publicly available Flickr photos with annotations. They contain 188 million tags, from which 3.7 million are unique.

11.1.4 Knowledge-Based Recommendations

Knowledge-based recommender systems are based on rules, patterns, and on some kind of functional knowledge regarding how a given item meets a specific user in the particular application domain [108, 419]. As an example, a knowledge-based recommender system can exploit an ontology built over the categories of items available from an e-commerce site in order to generate suggestions that better meet users' preferences. The technique offers some *advantages and disadvantages* as well. The availability of domain

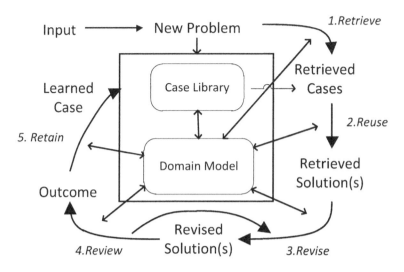

FIGURE 11.2: Case-based reasoning problem solving cycle [18].

knowledge allows knowledge-based recommenders to mitigate the effect of the cold-start problem [608, 387], and usually the recommended items are intuitively explainable. There are also two drawbacks: the first is the suggestion ability, which is static [108], and the second is the pruning techniques errors in the knowledge extraction process. In the rest of this section, we will describe *case-based* recommenders as a notable example of knowledge-based systems.

Case-based recommendations are computational reasoning models that try to solve problems based on the experience collected with past problem solutions [363, 2, 364]. When a new problem is presented, the system tries to find similar problems that have already been solved in the knowledge base. The solution of the retrieved problem is possibly adapted to the new problem, and also the new case is stored for future usage. A case model is an entry in the knowledge base, with problem and solution descriptions. Figure 11.2 shows a depiction of the problem solving cycle of case-based reasoning systems. Case-based reasoning is a cyclic process, composed by five steps: retrieve, reuse, revise, review, and retain. Revise and review steps are also called adaptation phase steps [419]. The goal of the revise step is to adapt the solution of an old problem to a new problem. The adapted solution is than evaluated by the review step of the case-based reasoning systems problem solving cycle. The retrieving step goal consists in finding, given a new problem, a similar problem that has been solved in the past. Once the new problem is solved, the adaptation of the original solution and the new problem are stored for future usage. The case model is one of the most important issues in case-based reasoning systems. It requires an appropriate representation language, and an appropriate choice of the attributes to store. Comparison-based retrieval [452], compromise-driven retrieval [454], and order-based retrieval [95] are typical methodologies for case-based reasoning RS.

In O'Sullivan et al. [508] propose using collaborative filtering data in case-based recommendations. The two methods were seen as both complementary and contrasting. Case-based relies on rich feature representation and complex similarity metrics, while collaborative filtering relies on simple correlation based similarity between users.

However, the intention is to employ user ratings-based profiles directly as cases. They refer to PTV, a recommender for TV listings, for applying their finding and offer improvement. They address the problem of sparsity in recommender system and explain how it can be tackled in CBR through mining similarity knowledge. The mining process is based on association rules, characterized by confidence and support. They treat user profiles as transactions and rated programs as itemsets and use the Apriori algorithm to derive programme-programme similarity rules with associated confidence levels. The created knowledge serves in the process of making recommendations, composed of two steps: (1) the target profile is compared with every profile case and a top k are retrieved, and (2) the items in the selected cases, which are not contained in the initial profile, are ranked according to relevance and top r are offered as recommendations.

11.1.5 Hybrid Methods

Hybrid methods combine multiple recommendation techniques to compensate for limitations of single recommendation techniques. Burke [108] proposed a taxonomy for hybrid RSs classifying them into seven categories: *weighted, mixed, switching, feature combination, feature augmentation, cascade,* and *metalevel*.

1. In a *weighted* recommender, the score of each item is computed from the results of each recommendation technique in the system. For instance, the final score of an item can be a linear combination of the scores computed by each different recommendation technique. In order to build a weighted RS, it is necessary to follow three steps: (1) selection of multiple recommendation techniques; (2) generation of a set of candidates by using the recommendation techniques; (3) scoring of the candidates with the weighted combination of individual scores. Computing the final score as a combination of scores of each recommendation technique can be implemented very easily. However, it might be possible that a specific recommendation technique has different strength in different parts of the item space. For instance, a collaborative filtering recommender cannot recommend items that have not been rated yet. A solution to this problem is to use the switching hybridization technique.

2. In a *switching* recommender, the system uses some criterion to switch from one recommendation technique to another based on the current context. For instance, it might select a specific recommendation technique based on the users' profiles. In order to build a switching RS, it is necessary to deploy a three-steps process: (1) selection of the recommendation technique on the basis of the switching criteria; (2) generation of the candidates using the selected recommendation technique; and (3) rating of the candidates on the basis of the chosen technique.

3. In a *mixed* recommender, the system simultaneously returns the items suggested by different techniques. The main issue to solve in order to build a mixed RS is homogenizing and normalizing the scoring functions used by the different techniques.

4. In a *feature combination* recommender, the system uses a single technique in order to compute recommendations. However, the output from other recommendation techniques are used to enrich the set of features associated with items or the user. For instance, the output of a collaborative filtering recommender may be injected as input to a content-based recommender.

5. A *feature augmentation* recommender is composed by two components: *contributing recommender* and *actual recommender*. It is similar to a feature combination recommender, with two main differences: (i) for each step two components instead of one are used; (ii) the input of each step is used only by the *contributing recommender* component. In order to build a feature augmentation RS, it is necessary to follow three steps: (1) the training data is used by the *contributing recommender* and the output (augmented training data) is used as input to the *actual recommender*; (2) the user profile is used by the *contributing recommender*, and the output (augmented profile) is used as input to the *actual recommender*; (3) the candidates are used by the *contributing recommender*, and the output (augmented candidate representation) is used as input to the *actual recommender* to obtain the overall score of the candidates.

6. A *cascade* recommender requires a hierarchical hybridization. A cascade recommender is composed at each step by a *primary* and a *secondary* recommender. In order to build a cascade RS, it is necessary to follow three steps: (1) the training data is used as input by both components; (2) the *primary recommender* generates the candidates based on the user profile; (3) for each candidate the *primary recommender* generates a score, the *secondary recommender* uses this score and the candidate to compute the overall score of the candidates.

7. A *metalevel* recommender uses a model learned from one recommender component as input for another component. A metalevel recommender has two components: *contributing recommender*, and *actual recommender*. In order to build the RS, it is necessary to follow three steps:

(1) the *contributing recommender* uses the training data to generate a learned model that is used by the *actual recommender* in the training phase; (2) the *contributing recommender* uses the user profile to generate a learned model that is used by the *actual recommender* in the candidate generation phase; (3) for each candidate the *actual recommender* (alone) generates a score.

Wetzker et al. [712] describe a hybrid approach for recommending items from tagging communities, folksonomies, where users can annotate interesting items with tags. Folksonomies can be described as a tripartite graph, whose vertices consist of three disjoint sets: users, tags, and items. This model is simplified into a collaborative filtering model IU between items and users (based on co-occurrences) and an annotation-based model IT, from the co-occurrence of items and tags.

As a dataset they collect user generated data from the Delicious bookmarking service, a corpus composed of 142 million bookmarks. From the dataset they exclude the top 10% of users with the highest URLs per domain in order to limit the impact of spam. The resulting dataset contains 109 million bookmarks.

The proposed model is, from an algorithmic perspective, a fusion of collaborative and content based models, using probabilistic latent semantic analysis. The goal is to recommend interesting new item to a user, by taking into account his history.

The authors find that the hybrid model outperforms a baseline model when both methods are taken into account and at the same time offers a low dimensional data representation, thus decreasing recommendation time.

11.2 Exploiting Query Logs for Recommending Related Queries

Giving suggestions to users of Web search engines is a common practice aimed at enhancing the quality of experience by helping users to rapidly satisfy their information needs. Suggestions are normally provided as queries related to those recently submitted by the user. Suggestion generation often exploits the expertise of skilled users to help inexperienced ones. The knowledge mined for making this possible is contained in the query logs, which store the past interactions of users with the search system [633]. Since a query log stores the information about the usage of the system by its users, it can be considered a particular kind of user generated content. The more content, in terms of records generated by users who satisfied their past information needs, the more effective the recommendation model.

In this section, first, the valuable information recorded in the query logs of Web search engines is described and then some interesting approaches to exploit these important sources of information are reviewed. Finally, an in-depth view over a recent and effective technique for the effective and efficient generation of query suggestions is presented [85].

It is important to remark that generating effective suggestions for user queries which are rare or have never been seen in the past is an open issue poorly addressed by state-of-the-art query suggestion techniques. As it was pointed out by Downey et al. [179] through an analysis on search behavior, rare queries are very important, and their effective satisfaction is very challenging for search engines. Therefore, it is even more important to provide good recommendations for long-tail queries. The query suggestion technique surveyed in this section is specifically tailored to address this issue.

11.2.1 Query Logs as Sources of Information

The analysis of the query logs collected by Web search engines has increasingly gained interest across the Web mining research community [633]. Query logs record detailed information about the interactions of users with the search system and they are a precious source of user-generated information for understanding how and why people search the Web. Each record of a query log comprises the query issued by a user and other information such as a anonymized userID, the time stamp, the URLs of clicked results if any, and so on. By grouping these records by user and time, the long-term history of all the interaction of users with the search engine can be obtained. Each per-user list of queries constitutes a *long-term user session*, which in turn can be split into a series of *logical sessions*. Since users tend to issue bursts of queries for relatively short periods of time, which are usually followed by longer periods of inactivity, the time gap between queries plays a significant role in detecting logical session boundaries [632].

User sessions are very useful for studying search intents, the query formulation process, and for predicting usage patterns. As can be seen in more detail in the following, models mined from user sessions are routinely exploited to generate suggestions for related queries that may help the user in better satisfying her information need. As a matter of fact, there are many other important tasks that exploit the knowledge drawn out of query log data. The ranking subsystem, for instance, uses click-through information as a source of implicit relevance feedback. Historical queries can be used to depict user profiles, to classify new users, and to supply a more personalized service to them (e.g., by re-ranking pages according to their personal preferences). Finally, search systems use historical information to also speed-up query processing operations by exploiting specialized caching techniques or smart partitioning of the huge indexes.

11.2.2   A Graph-Based Model for Query Suggestion

The query suggestion technique discussed here for exemplification purpose is based on a graph-model called TQ-Graph (*Term-Query Graph*). A TQ-Graph is a digraph $G = (V, E)$ with vertices V and edges E defined as follows. Let T be the set of all the distinct terms appearing in queries of Q. V contains a node for each term $t \in T$ and for each query $q \in Q$. In particular, let V_T be the set of *Term* nodes and V_Q be the set of *Query* nodes, then $V = V_T \cup V_Q$. Likewise, E is the union of two different sets of edges E_Q and E_{TQ}. Edges in E_Q are defined as in QFG [81] and connect only nodes in V_Q. E_{TQ} contains edges (t, q) where $t \in T$ is a term contained in query $q \in Q$. Finally, let $w : E \to [0..1]$ be a weighting function assigning to each edge $(u, v) \in E$ a value $w(u, v)$ defined as follows. For edges $(t, q) \in E_{TQ}$, $\frac{w(t,q)=1}{d}$ where d is the number of distinct queries in which the t occurs, that is, the number of outlinks of t. For edges $(q, q') \in E_Q$, the QFG weighting scheme is applied. In the original QFG paper, the authors describe two distinct weighting schemes, namely the *chaining probability* and *relative frequencies*. In the case of edge weighting, it has been shown that the *chaining probability* is the most effective scheme. To estimate such chaining probability, a set of features is extracted for each edge $(q, q') \in E_Q$. Such features are aggregated over all sessions in which queries q and q' appear consecutively and in this order. Finally, the chaining probability is computed by using logistic regression. Noisy edges, that is, edges having a probability of being traversed lower than a minimum threshold value, are removed. In other words, query reformulations that are not likely to be made are not considered.

Further details regarding the features used and the QFG and TQ-Graph models can be found in Boldi et al. [81] and in Bonchi et al. [85], respectively.

Given a TQ-Graph G, the query suggestions for an incoming query q composed of terms $\{t_1, \ldots t_m\} \subseteq T$ are generated from G by extracting the center-piece subgraph [671] starting from the m term nodes corresponding to terms $t_1, \ldots, t_m$. Given a directed graph and m of its nodes, the center-piece subgraph is informally defined as a small subgraph that best captures the connections between the m nodes. In our case, the center-piece subgraph represents the set of queries that better represent terms of the original query q.

The center-piece subgraph for a query q composed by m terms is obtained by performing a Random Walk with Restart (RWR) from *each one* of the m term nodes corresponding to terms in q. The resulting m stationary distributions are then multiplied component-wise. More formally, given an incoming query $q = \{t_1, \ldots, t_m\}$, m RWRs are computed from the m query-terms of q to obtain m vectors of stationary distribution $\mathbf{r}_{t_1}, \ldots, \mathbf{r}_{t_m}$. Then, the *Hadamard* (i.e., component-wise) product of the m vectors $\mathbf{r}_{t_1} \circ \mathbf{r}_{t_2} \circ \ldots \circ \mathbf{r}_{t_m}$ is computed to obtain the final scoring vector $\mathbf{r}_q$. Following the definition of Hadamard product, the i-th component of $\mathbf{r}_q$, that is, $\mathbf{r}_q(i)$, is given by

$$\mathbf{r}_q(i) = \prod_{j=1}^{m} \mathbf{r}_{t_j}(i).$$ Since each dimension of $\mathbf{r}$ corresponds to a query in Q,

TABLE 11.2: Suggestions for Rare Queries with the MSN TQ-Graph (Top) and for a Rare Query and a Frequent One with the Yahoo! TQ-Graph (Bottom)

Suggestions for query: lower heart rate	Suggestions for query: dog heat
things to lower heart rate	heat cycle dog pads
lower heart rate through exercise	what happens when female dog
	is in heat and a male dog is around
accelerated heart rate and pregnant	boxer dog in heat
Web md	dog in heat symptoms
heart problems	behavior of a male dog around
	a female dog in heat
Sugg. for query: social katz index	**Sugg. for query:** bill clinton
katz index of activities of daily living	president bill clinton speeches
modified barthel index	famous bill clinton quotes
barthel index score	monica lewinsky and bill clinton scandal
modified barthel index score	bill clinton foundation website
youtube	former president bill clinton biography

the TQ-Graph recommendation algorithm suggests the k queries having the k highest scores, where k is a parameter determining the maximum number of recommendations shown for each query. The reason for resorting to the product of the entries (namely, *Center-piece*) instead of their sum (namely, *Personalized PageRank*) is the aim to discover queries that are *"strongly"* related to *"most of the terms"* in the starting query instead of queries that are highly related even to just a few of them.

The above technique was experimented by Bonchi et al. [85] on two different very large query logs, namely Yahoo! and MSN (Table 11.2). The Yahoo! query log consists of approximately 581 millions of anonymized queries sampled from Yahoo! USA, queries submitted within a short period of time in the spring of 2010. The TQ-Graph built on the Yahoo! log consists of 6, 261, 105 term nodes and 28, 763, 637 query nodes. The number of term-query edges is 83, 808, 761, whereas the number of edges between query nodes is 56, 250, 874. The MSN Query Log, released in the context of the 2009 Workshop on Web Search Click Data[1], contains approximately 15 million queries from the USA search volume. The TQ-Graph built on this log consists of 2, 014, 547 term nodes and 6, 488, 713 query nodes, 19, 740, 312 term-query edges, and 5, 051, 843 query-query edges.

Before discussing recommendation effectiveness, query coverage is first addressed. As already mentioned, one of the advantages of the above recommendation technique over the state of the art is the capability of providing useful recommendations even for "difficult" queries (i.e., rare or never-seen-before). Accordingly, in order to produce recommendations for a given query, the method needs all the query terms to belong to the TQ-Graph. Fortunately, while unique queries are quite frequent, unique terms are not. For instance, out of the 581 million of queries contained in the Yahoo! query log about 162.2 million of them are unique. In the same log the number of unique terms is, instead, 5.1 million. Therefore, on this query log the coverage of the model

---

[1]http://research.microsoft.com/en-us/um/people/nickcr/wscd09/

is more than 99%, while the maximum coverage of QFG is 73% (i.e., the percentage of queries occurring more than once).

The reader interested in the evaluation of the quality of the recommendations produced by using the TQ-Graph models built with the two query logs can refer to Bonchi et al. [85], where a proposal for the efficient computation on approximate center-piece subgraphs by means of an inverted index data structure is also detailed. Some anecdotal examples of query recommendations produced with the TQ-Graph are further presented. The exemplary queries considered belong to the set of 50 queries of the standard TREC Web diversification track testbed.[2] The query *"lower heart rate"* is one among the eight from the TREC testbed that do not appear at all in the MSN query log. Below, the top 5 recommendations generated by using the TQ-Graph model are reported. It can be seen that all the top 5 suggestions can be considered pertinent to the initial topic. Moreover, they present some *diversity*: the first two are *how-to* queries, while the last three are queries related to finding information w.r.t. possible problems (with one very specific for pregnant women). An interesting recommendation is *"Web md,"* which makes perfect sense (WebMD.com is a Web site devoted to provide health and medical news and information), and has a large edit distance from the original query. The next query, *"dog heat,"* is rare since it appears only twice in the MSN query log. As in the previous example, the top 5 suggestions are qualitatively good and present some diversity. Let the Yahoo! testbed and the query *"social katz index"* be considered. The first four suggested queries are highly related with the input query. Both *"katz index"* and *"barthel index"* are indeed indexes used to measure performance in basic activities of daily living. The last query suggested is not related with the query. However, its score is $4.3\ e^{-19}$, that is, five orders of magnitude smaller than the one of the fourth result suggested ($8.8\ e^{-14}$). This high difference in the score indicates that the last suggestion generated is not of high-quality and should be discarded, thus witnessing the robustness of the scoring metrics used.

Obviously, the method should also perform well for frequent queries. To evaluate this, the same table shows the first five results obtained by querying for *"bill clinton."* Even if this query is not in the long tail, and there is a query node `bill clinton` in V_Q, it is interesting to observe that by splitting the query in terms, computing the random walks, and then combining the results, there is no loss in precision. In fact, it is noticeable that all the top 5 queries are very related to the input query. Moreover, the results are diversified, namely "clinton's speeches," "scandal," "foundation and biography."

---

[2]http://trec.nist.gov/data/web09.html

11.3 Exploiting Photo Sharing and Wikipedia for Touristic Recommendations

Designing an application for travel itinerary planning is a complex task, which requires to identify the so-called Points of Interest (PoIs), to select a few of them according to user tastes and potential constraints (e.g., time), and finally to set them in a meaningful visiting order. Skilled and curious travelers typically consult several sources of information such as travel books, travel blogs, photo sharing sites, and many others. The number of possible choices easily blows up, making it difficult to find the right blend of PoIs that best fits the interests of a particular user.

Online photo sharing services, such as Flickr and Picasa,[3] allow users to upload and share their collections of photos. Often these collections document touristic experiences: tourists publish the photos of interesting locations or monuments visited, and they can also share comments, annotations, and even the GPS traces of their visits. By analyzing such User Generated Content, it is possible to turn colorful photos into metadata-rich trajectories through the points of interest present in a city with the ultimate goal of designing tools that help tourists in planning their visits of a city.

The following section first describes the precious touristic information that can be automatically gathered from sites like Flickr and Wikipedia. The subsequent section revises many interesting approaches to exploit these important sources of information in a touristic scenario. Finally, a more in-depth description of a recent and effective recommender system for tourism [421], supporting interactive and personalized travel planning, is presented.

11.3.1 Flickr and Wikipedia as Sources of Information

The easiness and attractiveness of producing and sharing multimedia content through these sites motivates the exponential growth of the number of their users. Tourists are a typical example: while visiting a city, they take pictures of the most interesting places. These pictures are associated with a time stamp, often with geographic coordinates, and sometimes enriched with user-provided textual tags. A photo album can thus be considered evidence of the route taken by a tourist while visiting a city. These data may, however, be very noisy. User-provided tags, when present, can be too general to identify a specific PoI (e.g., "Europe Tour 2011," "New York"), or irrelevant (e.g., "Me and Laura"), incorrect, or misspelled. The same holds true for the geographic coordinates, since they can be missing or have different precision if provided by a GPS device or by the users, or they cannot help to discriminate between two very close PoIs.

---

[3]http://www.flickr.com and http://picasa.google.com

The task of recognizing the PoIs of a city given such set of photos is not trivial, since it requires to determine the landmarks depicted in any given image. In Lucchese et al. [421], it is suggested to use Wikipedia as a trustable and complete source to solve the problem of PoI identification. Indeed, Wikipedia has geo-referenced articles describing the most interesting PoIs within a given city. Thus, we can identify the PoIs by collecting all the geo-referenced Wikipedia articles that fall within the smallest region that encloses the city and by considering the title of each articles as a PoI's name. The advantage of using Wikipedia to determine the set of PoIs is twofold: (1) it identifies a large number of PoIs in every city, even the less popular ones; (2) it provides additional structured information about the PoI, such as a subdivision in categories and subcategories.

Once the set of PoIs has been identified, Flickr is queried in order to find the photos whose tags contain exactly the name of a PoI. For a given region, the number of results obtained with these queries is fewer with respect to other types of queries, for example, spatial queries. False positives are rare, however, since it is unlikely that a user adopted a very specific tag by chance or mistake. If an image is tagged with a Wikipedia article title, then it is very likely that the image renders the corresponding PoI. For each retrieved image, the user ID, the image time stamp, and the corresponding PoI are sufficient to reconstruct the trajectories of the tourists within the city.

11.3.2 From Flickr and Wikipedia to Touristic Recommendations via Center-Piece Computation

After having identified the set of PoIs and mapped each user image to a single PoI, the temporal sequence of images taken by each distinct user can be trivially translated into a trajectory.

In Lucchese et al. [421], a so-called *Itinerary Graph* is used to model the identified PoIs and to represent a measure of their pairwise relatedness. An Itinerary Graph $G = (V, E, w)$ is an undirected weighted graph where each node in V corresponds to a PoI of a given region or city, and edge $e = (u, v)$ connects two PoIs if they are likely to belong to the same touristic itinerary, and $w(u, v)$ weights such probability. Thus, an edge $e = (u, v)$ is added if there is at least one user that visited both u and v. The time stamp of each photo is not considered, since the main objective here is that of establishing relations of mutual interest between PoIs independently of the time of their visits. The weight $w(e)$, $e = (u, v)$, is set equal to the number of different users that have the two PoIs u and v in their albums. The graph G is used to estimate the probability that a user having visited a PoI u is also interested in visiting the PoI v. The graph G is further enriched by exploiting Wikipedia categorization. Categories, indeed, provide strong signals about a more semantical correlation between PoIs. PoIs may belong to the same class in some classification, or share the same architect or building period and so on. Thus, we obtain a new set of edges from Wikipedia, where the weight of each edge is given by the number

TABLE 11.3: Statistics Regarding the Two Datasets Used in Our Experiments

	Florence	San Francisco
Number of PoIs	1, 022	550
Images gathered from Flickr	124, 223	937, 389
Number of distinct albums (at least two photos)	2, 919	4, 411
Average distinct PoIs per album	3.71	3.61
Number of edges	131, 238	39, 372
Edges from Flickr	22, 164	26, 752
Edges from Wikipedia's categories	111, 778	16, 038
Maximum (out)degree	415	263
Average (out)degree	121.86	71.59

of categories shared by two PoIs. Then, the two sets of edges are merged by equally weighting the Flickr-based and the Wikipedia-based contributions.

The recommendation algorithm uses information in G to provide suggestions starting from an initial set of PoIs $U \subset V$ that the tourist has already visited, or that she has already showed interest in. The set U is used as a sort of user profile to personalize the generated recommendations. Thus, the goal of the algorithm is that of ranking the remaining PoIs in V with respect to the ones in U. Ranking *all* the remaining PoIs is useful for various postprocessing phases. For example, if the tourist is at her desk and she is planning a visit to the city, the system can simply show the top k PoIs in the computed ranking, and support her in the interactive *selection and recommendation* of PoIs. On the other hand, if she is currently visiting the city, the ranked PoIs could be filtered by removing all the PoIs that are too far from her current position.

The ranking of PoIs V with respect to U is obtained by resorting to the center-piece computation with a strategy similar to the one presented in Section 11.2. We compute a Random Walks with Restart (RWR) on G by starting from each node in U in order to obtain the steady state distribution r_z for each node z in U. Then, we obtain the vector r_U, which assigns a score to each PoI in V by computing the Hadamard product of all these steady state distributions. Once r_U is computed, the recommender system suggests the k PoIs having the highest probabilities in r_U. As anticipated, the actual suggestion could be preceded by a preprocessing phase that filters out some of the PoIs (e.g., PoIs that are too far from the current position of the tourist), or that rearrange them in order to provide a suitable visiting path.

In order to argue the effectiveness of the above approach, we present some experimental results for the cities of Florence and San Francisco. Table 11.3 reports some statistics regarding the datasets, that is, the PoIs and the graphs obtained for the cities of Florence and San Francisco. Figure 11.3 instead, shows a list of the top 10 PoIs in each of the considered towns along with their normalized frequency in the datasets.

We conclude by briefly discussing some examples of suggestions computed by the recommender system. In the first example, the set of starting PoIs U contains two of the most important PoIs of Florence: *Palazzo Vecchio* and *Piazza della Signoria*. The top 10 PoIs ranked by the recommender are shown

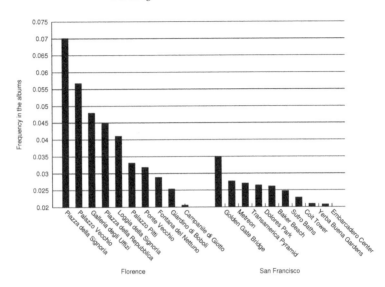

FIGURE 11.3: Normalized frequency of the top 10 most frequent PoIs in the Flickr photo albums for the cities of Florence and San Francisco.

in Table 11.4(a). Without any doubt these 10 PoIs are among the most important PoIs in Florence. In the presence of very popular PoIs in U, the system responds by producing a ranking that has other very famous PoIs on its top. These are conditions where the edges gathered from Flickr come into play. Most of the tourists perform, in fact, tours of the city by mainly visiting its most important PoIs. Thus, since many albums in Flickr contains all these PoIs together, our graph has a large component that connects all of them. This component tends to increase the ranking probabilities of these PoIs when some of them belong to U.

For the second example we selected the following, less famous, four PoIs: *La Specola, Museum of Prehistory, Museo Horne*, and *Bargello*. These are museums in Florence. The top 10 PoIs ranked by our recommender are reported in Table 11.4(b). We observe that the top 10 ranked PoIs can be classified as museums. This kind of response is mainly due to the structure gathered from Wikipedia. As we already pointed out, the system is able to relate together PoIs that are semantically similar by exploiting categories of Wikipedia. We also observe that these museums are presented in an order that reflects their relative importance. For example, *Uffizi* is probably the most important museum in Florence. This second effect is again a consequence of the edges extracted from Flickr.

The last example is for the city of San Francisco. We start from the two PoIs: *Golden Gate Theatre* and *San Francisco Conservatory of Music*. The top-10 PoIs ranked by the recommender are shown in Table 11.4(c). Also, in

TABLE 11.4: Examples of PoI Recommendations in Florence and San Francisco

PoIs in U	PoIs in U	PoIs in U
Palazzo Vecchio	La Specola	Golden Gate Theatre
Piazza della Signoria	Museum of Prehistory	Conservatory of Music
	Museo Horne	
	Bargello	
Top-10 ranked PoIs	**Top-10 ranked PoIs**	**Top-10 ranked PoIs**
Ponte Vecchio	Uffizi	War Memorial Opera House
Piazzale Michelangelo	Giotto's Campanile	Dolores Park
Palazzo Pitti	Palazzo Medici Riccardi	Castro Theatre
Giotto's Campanile	Vasari Corridor	Yerba Buena Gardens
Boboli Gardens	Medici Chapel	Embarcadero Center
Loggia dei Lanzi	Basilica of Santa Croce	Metreon
Piazza Santa Croce	San Marco's National Museum	Golden Gate Bridge
Uffizi	Dante Alighieri's House	Pacific-Union Club
Basilica of Santa Croce	Modern Art Gallery	Lake Merritt
Ponte alle Grazie	Museo Stibbert	American Conservatory Theater
(a)	(b)	(c)

this example, we have the same phenomenon observed in the previous one: PoIs related to theaters, music, and culture in general are placed among the first positions.

These examples demonstrate that the system has the intended behavior: It provides personalized suggestions by inferring the tastes of the tourist looking at the PoIs she already visited. The interested reader can consult Lucchese et al. [421] for a more detailed description of the recommender system and a more quantitative experimental evaluation.

11.4 Exploiting Twitter and Wikipedia for News Recommendations

Digital and automated information processing has worsened the *information overload* problem to unprecedented levels, transforming it into one of the crucial issues in the modern information society. This section focuses on one of the most common daily activities: news reading. Every day the press produces thousands of news articles covering a wide spectrum of topics. For a user, finding relevant and interesting information in this ocean of news is a daunting task.

Indeed, it is possible to recommend news articles to users by combining two sources of information, news streams and microblogs, and leveraging the best features of each. News streams have high *coverage* as they aggregate a very large volume of news articles obtained from many different news agencies. On the other hand, information obtained by microblogging services can be exploited to address the problems of *trend detection and personalization*, by

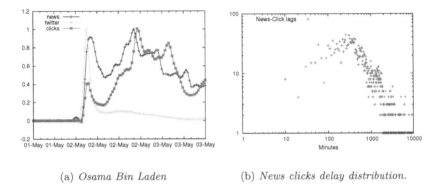

(a) *Osama Bin Laden*   (b) *News clicks delay distribution.*

FIGURE 11.4: Trends on Twitter and news streams. (**See color insert.**)

making it possible to discover emerging topics and to put users in the context of their social circles and personal interests.

11.4.1 The Blogosphere as a Source of Information

News portals like Yahoo! news and Google news often resort to recommender systems to help the user find relevant pieces of information. In recent years, the most successful recommendation paradigm has been *collaborative filtering* [12]. On the other hand, at an increasing rate, Web users access news articles via microblogging services and the so-called real-time Web. By subscribing to feeds of other users, such as friends, colleagues, domain experts, and enthusiasts, as well as to organizations of interest, they obtain timely access to relevant and personalized information.

With more than 200 million users, Twitter is currently the most popular real-time Web service. Twitter is an emerging agora where users publish short text messages, also known as tweets, and organize themselves into social networks. A small user study by Teevan et al. [665] reports that 49% of users search while looking for information related to news, or to topics gaining popularity, and in general to "to keep up with events." The analysis of a larger crawl of Twitter by Kwak et al. [380] shows that about 85% of the Twitter posts are about headlines or persistent news. Interestingly, in many cases, news have been published and commented on Twitter before any other news agency, as in the case of Osama Bin-Laden's death in 2011,[4] or Tiger Wood's car crash in 2009.[5] In fact, as shown in Figure 11.4(b), there is a significant delay between the publication of a news and its access by a user: about 60% of the clicks on a news item occur after 10 hours from the moment of its publication.

---

[4]www.bbc.co.uk/news/technology-13257940
[5]techcrunch.com/2009/11/27/internet-twitter-tiger-woods

Example. Figure 11.4(a) shows the normalized number of tweets and news articles regarding "Osama Bin Laden" during the time period between May 1st and 4th, 2011. For the news, the number of clicks in the same period are also reported. The number of relevant tweets ramps up earlier than news, meaning that the information spread through Twitter even before any press release.

In Chen et al. [132], the authors propose a URL-recommender system from URLs posted in Twitter. A user study shows that both the user content-based profile and the user social neighborhood plays a role, but the most important factor in the recommendation performance is given by the social ranking, that is, the number of times a URL is mentioned among the neighborhood of a given user. Akcora et al. [19] use Twitter to detect abrupt opinion changes. Based on an *emotion-word corpus*, the proposed algorithm detects opinion changes, which can be related to publication of some interesting news. No actual automatic linking to news is produced. The system proposed by Phelan et al. [537] is a content-based approach that uses tweets to rank news. A given set of tweets, either public or of a friend, is used to build a user profile, which is matched against the news coming from a set of user-defined RSS feeds.

Indeed, Twitter highlights in its Web interfaces the so-called *trending topics*, that is, a set of words occurring frequently in recent tweets. Asur et al. [33] crawled all the tweets containing the keywords identifying a Twitter trending topic in the 20 minutes before the topic is detected by Twitter. Authors found that the popularity of a topic can be described as a multiplicative growth process with noise. Another interesting study on a large crawl of Twitter has been conducted by Kwak et al. [380]. According to their findings, after the initial break-up, the cumulative number of tweets of a trending topic increases linearly, as suggested by Asur et al. [33], and independently of the number of users. Almost 80% of the trending topics have a single activity period, that is, they occur in a single burst, and 93% of such activity periods last less than 10 days. Finally, once a tweet is published, half of its *re-tweets* occur within an hour and 75% within one day. Also, once re-tweeted, tweets quickly spread four hops away. These studies confirm the fast information spreading occurring on Twitter.

A basic approach for building topic-based user profiles from tweets is proposed by Michelson and MacsKassy [461]. Each capitalized nonstopword is considered to be an entity. The entity is used as a query to Wikipedia and the categories of the retrieved page are used to update the list of topics of interest for the user who authored the tweet. Abel et al. [6] propose a more sophisticated user model to support news recommendation for Twitter users. They explore different ways of modeling user profiles by using hashtags, topics, or entities and conclude that entity based modeling gives the best results. They employ a simple recommender algorithm that uses cosine similarity between user profiles and tweets.

11.4.2 Using the Real-Time Web for Personalized News Recommendations

In the following, there is a description of how it is possible to harness the information present in tweets posted by users and by their social circles in order to make relevant and timely recommendation of news articles. Some notations are introduced as well as a formal definition of the problem.

Definition 22 (News stream). *Let $\mathcal{N} = \{n_0, n_1, \ldots\}$ be an unbounded stream of news arriving from a set of news sources, where news article n_i is published at time $\tau(n_i)$.*

Definition 23 (Tweet stream). *Let $\mathcal{T} = \{t_0, t_1, \ldots\}$ be an unbounded stream of tweets arriving from the set of Twitter users, where tweet t_i is published at time $\tau(t_i)$.*

It is worth noting that a tweet stream for a user is composed of tweets authored by the user and people in the social neighborhood of the user. This is an extension of the concept of "home timeline," as known in Twitter.

Problem 24 (News recommendation problem). *Given a stream of news $\mathcal{N}$, a set of users $\mathcal{U} = \{u_0, u_1, \ldots\}$ and their stream of tweets $\mathcal{T}$, find the top-k most relevant news for user $u \in \mathcal{U}$ at time τ.*

In Morales et al. [481], the authors model the relationship between tweets and news by introducing an intermediate layer between the two streams. This layer is populated by the so called *entities*. The Spectrum system [524] is used to map every single tweet to a bag of entities, each corresponding to a Wikipedia page. The same entity-extraction process is applied to the incoming stream of news, with the goal of overcoming the vocabulary mismatch problem by mapping both tweets and news in the same entity-based coordinate system. This choice could potentially allow to include additional external knowledge into the recommendation system, such as geographic position, categorization, number of recent edits by Wikipedia users, and many others.

Example. Consider the following tweet by user KimAKelly: "Miss Liberty is closed until further notice." The words "Miss Liberty" are mapped to the entity/Wikipedia page *Statue of Liberty*, which is an interesting topic, due to the just announced renovation. This allows to highly rank news regarding the Statue of Liberty, that is, "Statue of Liberty to Close for One Year after 125th Anniversary" by Fox news. Potentially, since the Wikipedia page is geo-referenced, it is possible to boost the ranking of the news for users living nearby, or being interested in the topic/entity *New York*.

Morales et al. [481] formulate the recommendation problem as a personalized news ranking problem as follows:

Definition 25 (Recommendation ranking $R_\tau(u, n)$). *Given the components Σ_τ, Γ_τ and Π_τ, resulting from a stream of news $\mathcal{N}$ and a stream of tweets $\mathcal{T}$*

TABLE 11.5: MRR, Precision, and
Coverage

Algorithm	MRR	P@1	P@5	P@10	Coverage
Recency	0.020	0.002	0.018	0.036	1.000
ClickCount	0.059	0.024	0.086	0.135	1.000
social	0.017	0.002	0.018	0.036	0.606
Content	0.107	0.029	0.171	0.286	0.158
Popularity	0.008	0.003	0.005	0.012	1.000
T.Rex	0.107	0.073	0.130	0.168	1.000
T.Rex+	0.109	0.062	0.146	0.189	1.000

authored by users $\mathcal{U}$ up to time τ, the recommendation score of a news article $n \in \mathcal{N}$ for a user $u \in \mathcal{U}$ at time τ is defined as

$$R_\tau(u, n) = \alpha \cdot \Sigma_\tau(u, n) + \beta \cdot \Gamma_\tau(u, n) + \gamma \cdot \Pi_\tau(n),$$

where α, β, and γ are coefficients that specify the relative weight of the components.

The ranking function is a linear combination of three scoring components described below.

The *social-based relatedness* Σ is a $|\mathcal{U}| \times |\mathcal{N}|$ matrix, where $\Sigma_\tau(u_i, n_j)$ is the relevance of news n_j for user u_i at time τ. This is computed on the basis of the user's social network.

The *content-based relatedness* Γ is a $|\mathcal{U}| \times |\mathcal{N}|$ matrix, where $\Gamma_\tau(u_i, n_j)$ is the relevance of news n_j for user u_i at time τ. In particular, Γ defines a news article n_j to be relevant for user u_i, if the news discusses entities that have been discussed in the past by the user in her own tweets.

The *entity-based news popularity* Π is a row-wise vector of length $|\mathcal{N}|$, where $\Pi_\tau(j)$ measures the popularity of the news article n_j at time τ. The popularity of a news item is given by the popularity of the entities it discusses, and the popularity of the entities is measured both on news stream $\mathcal{N}$ and on the tweet stream $\mathcal{T}$. An important aspect in updating the popularity counts is to take into account recency: new entities of interest should dominate the popularity counts of older entities. Therefore, popularity counts are updated using an exponential decay rule.

At any given time, the recommender system produces a set of news recommendations by ranking a set of candidate news, that is, the most recent ones, according to the ranking function R. Similarities with popular recommendation techniques can be noted. When $\beta = \gamma = 0$, the ranking function R resembles collaborative filtering, where user similarity is computed on the basis of their social circles. When $\alpha = \gamma = 0$, the function R implements a content-based recommender system, where a user is profiled by the bag-of-entities occurring in the tweets of the user. Finally, when $\alpha = \beta = 0$, the most popular items are recommended, regardless of the user profile.

The parameters α, β, and γ can be best-tuned with the use of some machine learning algorithm and exploiting real-world data, as in Morales et al. [481], where the recommendation task is reformulated into a learning-to-rank

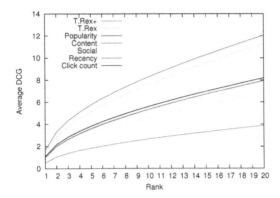

FIGURE 11.5: Average discounted cumulated gain on related entities given the top 20 ranks. **(See color insert.)**

framework [323]. The resulting algorithm is named `T.Rex`, and it is compared against a few baselines:

`Recency`: it ranks news articles by time of publication (most recent first);

`ClickCount`: it ranks news articles by click count (highest count first);

`Social`: it ranks news articles by using the algorithm with $\beta = \gamma = 0$;

`Content`: it ranks news articles by using the algorithm with $\alpha = \gamma = 0$;

`Popularity`: it ranks news articles by using the algorithm with $\alpha = \beta = 0$.

Mean Reciprocal Rank (MRR), precision, and coverage results are reported in Table 11.5. The `T.Rex+` system, which is an improvement of `T.Rex` where a number of additional features have been embedded into the learning framework, has the highest MRR. This result means that the model has a good overall performance across the dataset. `Content` also has a very high MRR. Unfortunately, the coverage level achieved by the `Content` strategy is very low. This issue is mainly caused by the sparsity of the user profiles. It is well known that most of Twitter users belong to the "silent majority."

The social strategy is affected by the same problem, albeit to a much lesser extent. The reason for this difference is that social draws from a large social neighborhood of user profiles, instead of just one. So it has more chances to provide a recommendation. The quality of the recommendation is, however, quite low, probably because the social-based profile alone is not able to catch the specific user interests.

It is worth noting that in almost 20% of the cases, `T.Rex+` was able to rank the clicked news in the top 10 results. Ranking by the `ClickCount` strategy is quite efficient despite being very simple. Interestingly, adding the `ClickCount` feature to the model does not improve the results significantly. In fact, the difference in P@10 between `T.Rex` and `T.Rex+` is only about 2%.

Figure 11.5 shows the DCG measure for the top 20 positions in the rankings. In this case, those news having some overlap with the actually clicked news in terms of discussed topics are considered partially relevant. From the figure, it appears that T.Rex and T.Rex+ are able to suggest more related news than the other strategies. This result is expected, as the system is designed to exploit the concept of entities.

11.5   Recommender Systems for Tags

Platforms designed for the publishing of user generated content also present a search feature allowing users to retrieve interesting content. Search is enabled by both full-text indexing and a particular kind of content annotation known as *tagging*. Tagging consists of adding to the content (i.e., documents, images, videos, etc.) keywords best describing the content itself. Tagging is particularly useful in the case of multimedia content, where automatic extraction of keywords struggles to deliver high quality results. Indeed, typically tags are also allowed to be added not only by the owner of the content but also by other users (different platforms implement different kinds of control policies). For this reason we usually refer to these kinds of UGC publishing services as *collaborative tagging services.*

Collaborative tagging services are one of the most distinguishing features of Web 2.0. Flickr, YouTube, Delicious, Technorati, Last.fm, or CiteULike—just to mention a few—as they allow their users to upload a photo, to publish a video, to share an interesting URL or to bookmark a scientific paper, and provide them the possibility to assign tags, that is, freely chosen keywords, to these resources. Such a collaborative content creation and annotation effort creates vast repositories of all sort of media. User-defined tags play a central role there as they are a simple yet powerful tool for organizing, searching, and exploring the resources.

11.5.1   Social Tagging Platforms as Sources of Information

An important application that is widely studied in the literature is that of *tag recommendation.* As we already stated, online photo services such as Flickr and Zooomr allow users to share their photos with family, friends, and the online community at large. In the seminal paper of Sigurbjörnsson et al. [631], the authors investigate techniques to assist users in the tagging phase. The tag recommender system is based on a two-staged approach. In the first stage, candidate tags are generated on the basis of tags already entered by a user for a resource (e.g., a picture in Flickr). In a second stage, tags are aggregated and ranked to be presented to the user for her to select the ones she retains pertinent to the resource she has to tag. Co-occurrence models, aggregation, and ranking functions are derived from a large dataset that the authors obtained from Flickr. They used a random snapshot from Flickr of 52 million publicly available photos with annotations. The photos were uploaded between February 2004 and June 2007 and each photo has at least one user-defined tag. A further refinement of the technique presented by Sigurbjörnsson et al. [631] is that of Wu et al. [727], where the authors formulate the tag recommender system as a learning problem. Given the image and one or more initial tags, the algorithm will rank and sort a list of tags previously entered by other users in the system based on the tag correlation obtained by analyzing different features such as tag co-occurrence, correlation between tag related images, the content of the target image, and so on. Each feature, then, is taken as an input feature for a weak ranker. Then Rankboost [222] is adopted to combine weak rankers and form a better ranking function. Users can click the tags on the ranking list to annotate the image. After each click, the algorithm will update the ranking function as well as the tag recommendation function. An interesting research direction is that of the *Personalized* tag recommendation, as proposed by Guan et al. [251]. In their paper, the authors have run experiments on a large-scale tagging dataset collected from Delicious. The proposed graph-based algorithm significantly outperforms algorithms that are not personalized on users' interests.

One of the major criticism of tag recommender systems is that they tend to uniform the language of tags used and to not let (lazy) users pick the right tag. This, in the long run, would reduce the *findability* of the resource itself. To overcome this issue, Wetzker et al. [713] propose a novel user-centric tag model that allows them to derive mappings between personal tag vocabularies and the corresponding folksonomies. Using these mappings, they show how to infer the meaning of user-assigned tags and to predict choices of tags a user may want to assign to new items.

Even if platforms like Flickr or Delicious are mostly known as tagging systems, another very popular social platform makes use of tags to enrich user generated content. Twitter, in fact, allows users to *hashtag* tweets (i.e., short message of 140 characters text) to allow a better findability. Yang et al. [745] investigate and quantify the effects of hashtag adoption. After designing a measure to quantify the factors affecting content tags selection, they train a machine learning model using these factors as features. The learned model can effectively predict the future adoption of hashtags that a user has never used before. Therefore, this technique can be used as a hashtag recommender technique.

Another nifty application for a social tagging system is that of tag ranking. Tags are, in fact, added almost randomly by users. Yet, when consulted, tags are more effective if they are ranked in a more reasonable order. The work of Liu et al. [410] goes exactly in this direction. They first estimate initial relevance scores for the tags based on a probability density estimation, and then perform a random walk over a tag similarity graph to refine the relevance scores.

11.5.2   Recommending Correctly Spelled Tags

Another interesting application that stems from the social tagging system is that of *tag spelling correction* [490]

All the applications shown thus far need to assume that tags are "correct." This assumption, however, is not reasonable in the real world as tags are noisy, contain typos, and many different spellings [188, 490] can be used for the same concept (e.g., the term *"hip hop"* and its variants *"hip-hop," "hiphop,"* or *"hip_hop"*). It is thus important to develop systems that help users to provide correct tags so as to improve the overall quality of annotations.

While, for example, query spelling correction in the context of Web search engines exploits the position of words within the query, in the case of tag systems words position is not meaningful, as an annotation is a set of tags and not a sequence. What is meaningful instead is the context in which a tag is used, that is, the other tags in the annotation of a resource. If we know that people tagging an object with *"apple"* are more likely to tag *"store"* instead of *"str,"* then we could suggest the former as a possible spelling correction for the latter.

Our working hypothesis is to start the spelling correction process once a tag is completely written within the tagging process. The correction process thus regards analyzing each tag while the tagging process of the user is still going on.

Model: Let R be a set of resources and let Σ be a finite alphabet. Let $T \subseteq \Sigma^*$ be a set of tags associated with each resource and let $\gamma : R \to T$ be a function mapping a resource with its associated set of tags. We define $T^* = \cup \{\gamma(r), \forall r \in R\}$ to be the union of all tags for all resources in R.

Let $G = (V, E)$ be an undirected graph. V is the set of nodes where each node represents a tag $t \in T^*$, and E is the set of edges defined as $E = V \times V$. Given two nodes, u, v, they share an edge if they are associated at least once with the same resource. More formally, $E = \{(u, v) | u, v \in V, \text{and } \exists r \in R | u, v \in \gamma(r)\}$. We denote $N(v)$ the immediate (distance 1) neighborhood of a node v, that is, $N(v) = \{t \in V | (v, t) \in E\}$.

Both edges and nodes in the graph are weighted. Let $u, v \in V$ be two tags. Let $w_e : V \times V \to \mathbb{R}$ be a weighting function for edges measuring the co-occurrence of the two tags, namely, the number of times the two tags appear together for a resource. For convenience, we assume $w_e(u, v) = 0$ when $(u, v) \notin E$. For a given node $v \in V$, $w_v : V \to \mathbb{R}$ associates a tag with its weight.

Tag and Tag context: An observation behind our model is that the user provides this set of annotations by introducing tags one by one. Following this observation, we consider as input a sequence of tags $\langle t_1, \ldots, t_{n-1}, t_n \rangle$, the order as they are introduced by the user. In this setting, t_n is the last tag introduced, which is going to be spell-checked by our model, while the set $\{t_1, \ldots, t_{n-1}\}$ refers to its context, that we denote also as $C(t_n)$. We assume that the graph does not contain misspelled tags. This can be achieved by

TABLE 11.6: Metrics Used in the Ranking Phase for a Candidate Node u, Given the Tag We Want to Correct, t_n

Metric	Unweighted Version
Pref. Attachment	$|N(u)|$
Common Neighbors	$|N(u) \cap N(t_n)|$
Jaccard of Neighbors	$\frac{|N(u) \cap N(t_n)|}{|N(u) \cup N(t_n)|}$
Metric	Weighted Version
Pref. Attachment	$\sum_{z \in N(u)} w_e(u, z)$
Common Neighbors	$\sum_{z \in N(u) \cap N(t_n)} w_e(u, z) + w_e(t_n, z)$
Jaccard of Neighbors	$\frac{\sum_{z \in N(u) \cap N(t_n)} w_e(u,z) + w_e(t_n,z)}{\sum_{z \in N(u) \cup N(t_n)} w_e(u,z) + w_e(t_n,z)}$

applying a correction technique as the one proposed by Nardini et al. [490]. We also make two assumptions: (i) The context is correct, as we correct tags one by one while they are introduced, and (ii) at the moment we process t_n, all tags in the context already belong to the graph, that is, $C(t_n) \subseteq V$.

Tag spell checking: We are given the weighted co-occurrence tag-graph G, the last introduced tag t_n, and its context $C(t_n) = \{t_1, \ldots, t_{n-1}\}$.

All tags in the context $C(t_n)$ are present in the graph. Therefore, we can define the set of candidate tags to be considered as a neighborhood of the nodes in $C(t_n)$. More formally, we define $\mathcal{N}(C(t_n)) = \bigcup_{t \in C(t_n)} N(t)$ and we consider the subgraph of G induced by $\mathcal{N}(C(t_n))$. In this induced subgraph we select the best node to be suggested as a correction. This selection is done on the basis of relatedness between a candidate tag $u \in \mathcal{N}(C(t_n))$ and the original tag t_n that we want to correct. It is important to note that the tag t_n is temporarily assumed to be linked to its context, thus it belongs to $\mathcal{N}(C(t_n))$ and, consequently, to the induced subgraph.

For defining relatedness we adopt graph neighborhood-based measures that have been successfully used, for example, for link prediction. We report the ones we used in Table 11.6.

For efficiency reasons the set of tags that we consider as candidate spell corrections are a subset of $\mathcal{N}(C(t_n))$. The selection is governed by two parameters r and δ. Starting from the subgraph induced by $\mathcal{N}(C(t_n))$, we filter it by keeping only the top-r edges with respect to their weights w_e. We then further filter the candidate nodes by keeping only nodes with edit distance[6] lower than a given threshold δ.

---

[6] We use the Damerau-Levenshtein edit distance.

11.6 Conclusion

In this chapter we presented an overview of recommender systems and different solutions to solve the information and interaction overload problems on the Web. We used three different user generated contents as sources of information: query logs, social knowledge such as Wikipedia, social photo sharing such as Flickr, and real-time microblogging such as Twitter. By exploiting these data, we have introduced several recommendation algorithms: to recommend queries, to recommend touristic points of interest, and to recommend news.

In Section 11.2, we presented an overview of query recommendation techniques. In particular, we presented a graph-based model for query suggestion that allowed us to deal with rare and unseen queries. In Section 11.3, we presented a way to harness the user generated content of social photo sharing such as Flickr and social knowledge such as Wikipedia. In particular, we presented a graph-based model for touristic points of interest suggestions. In Section 11.4, we presented a news recommender system based on real-time microblogging data such as Twitter and social knowledge such as Wikipedia.

Chapter 12

Conclusions and a Road Map for Future Developments

Marie-Francine Moens

KU Leuven, Belgium

Juanzi Li

Tsinghua University, China

Tat-Seng Chua

National University of Singapore, Singapore

12.1 Summary of the Main Findings

User generated content (UGC), available through social networking sites on the Web, offers a wealth of information about the individuals' world of living. He or she may write extensively in blogs and discussion forums, posts pictures on the Web, tweet through microblogging applications, or publish video material. The explosion of social networks has caused an explosion of UGC on the Web. What was once a privilege of the rich and famous, showing the pictures of persons and their living environment to the world, has become commonplace for everyone. As such, the Web has become a tremendously rich repository of information for current and future generations. The Web has become a mirror of life that captures in great detail opinions, thoughts, lifestyles, events at moments in time, and places worldwide. In addition, the Web has great economical and societal value. In the domains of advertisements and business intelligence there is a definite interest in processing UGC.

The events, persons, objects, and feelings that users write about or report on through photographs and video is of commercial interest as they provide the intelligence that is necessary for effective advertising and marketing. Increasingly, social, anthropological, and historical research will rely on the mining of UGC, also opening many venues of future research.

This book has shown that research on mining UGC is very current. Although some of the topics were already studied for some time, they still offer challenging research questions. One example is sentiment analysis, where topics such as recognition of refined sentiments and even personality treats, or emotional changes over time offer interesting challenges. The book also showed that mining of UGC is often an interdisciplinary endeavor, combining text mining, natural language processing, social network analysis, information retrieval, and multimedia processing. This book contains a wealth of information covering a variety of methodologies, state-of-the-art approaches, comparative evaluations, and avenues for future research, making the book a reference for mining of UGC.

The book has revealed the properties of UGC, that is, being of various types of content and of various quality, available in large amounts, and perhaps being unreliable.

The authors of the different chapters pointed to a number of challenges. A first important challenge is the lack of standard test collections for many tasks of mining UGC, where some of the collections are large enough to be called "big data." Also, how to acquire a valuable and representative set of training data is worth an investigation. We often lack high-quality annotated data where the level of bias and noise in the data is not yet well understood. The phenomena in language or other modalities in UGC often occur infrequently in the data, even in "big data" leaving many research questions on how to deal with such sparse data. Popularity biases are sometimes difficult to correctly process. We lack evaluation fora for benchmarking and comparing methodologies and approaches.

Processing of "big data" by itself might pose interesting challenges with regard to the scalability and reducing the computational complexity of the mining methods. We are confronted with ever changing UGC in a constantly evolving context, which makes it necessary for the mining and prediction algorithms to flexibly adapt to this very dynamic environment.

An interesting topic, especially in the context of "big data" is the spatio-temporal mining of information, where the mining takes into account spatial and/or temporal constraints.

UGC is characterized by its multilinguality and multimodality. Web content is written in a variety of different languages and even if the content is written in the "same" language, it might be very different across communities or Web site types. For instance, commercial Web sites might contain a language that is very different from the one used in blog or microblog posts although both languages discuss the same topics. In addition, the Web is nowadays a multimedia repository. When mining UGC we need to take into account a joint processing of these different media (text, network structure, images, videos, etc.) as their content often complements each other. In this respect, the need for advanced and scalable feature extraction approaches that easily and unambiguously link to semantic concepts is a valid study subject.

As these media often complement each other, we need advanced fusion techniques that possibly perform (uncertain) inferencing over the heterogeneous data. When and how fusion of information will yield us the most accurate results is certainly worth studying. Fusion can be done at simple feature levels, for instance, by lifted inference or by jointly training and/or predicting different dependent recognitions. When dealing with large amounts of uncertain data, scalability becomes a real issue.

Search of UGC is an understudied problem where standard information retrieval approaches such as learning to rank or relevancy modeling offer interesting points of attention. In addition, it is worth investigating ways of accurately detecting that the sought information is not available in the data.

Another important aspect regards capturing user interests by analyzing UGC in its heterogeneous context so that future systems will be able to offer personalized services for individual users or groups of users. There are many settings where personalized mining and searching are especially wanted.

Finally, this book is about mining UGC, but many findings and challenges apply to information processing in general, of which mining of UGC is just a special, more difficult case.

12.2 Road Map

In the remainder of this chapter we would like to focus on a number of what we think are important research avenues that deserve attention.

12.2.1 Processing Community Languages

It is not always easy to cope with the community languages used in UGC [52]. One important reason is that natural language processing research is often performed in ideal settings where well-formed content is processed. For instance, the text of news stories is analyzed for which highly performing syntactic parsers have been trained. Once you move this technology to a more realistic setting, for example, the language that everyday people use, the performance drops substantially. Extreme cases of everyday language are UGC, often full of spelling errors, abbreviations, phonetic writing, and grammatical mistakes. As a consequence, many different though often related languages need to be processed. Standard linguistic algorithms perform badly, as they are trained on well-formed news texts. We do not know yet how to best approach this problem. Considering the community language as a different language than its standard counterpart and learning multilingual topic models (e.g., [165]) might be an option and using the obtained representations in the classification and extraction models could be studied. Probabilistic latent class models have the advantage that they easily and in a flexible way model language variations. It would be nice to study their capabilities for modeling community languages.

12.2.2 Image and Video Processing

Beyond the analysis of pure textual information we see several additional directions for future research. An enormous amount of information is buried in the images and videos that people post on the Web. Recognition content in imagery is not easy and computer vision applications that operate on UGC need to be adapted. The photos and video shots by consumers are typically of far lower quality than their professionally generated counterparts. There are problems with motion blur, defocus, and less controlled viewpoints that render recognition of people, actions, and objects more difficult. Uploaded pictures are usually of reasonable quality, but videos are often in low resolution and/or highly compressed, with a lot of motion blur, nonsteady or fast motion, and limited editing. The audio is often particularly noisy (see below). Existing methods for people, object, or action recognition need to be robustified. A picture says more than 1000 words, which is also true for pictures taken by users of social networks. A picture or a video reveals the style and conditions of living, which also for future generations to come is of tremendous historical and anthropological importance.

Facial recognition technology has really advanced. Not only can faces easily be linked to names [534], there are lots of apps that in one way or another exploit face recognition (e.g., to quickly tag friends in pictures). Understanding the content of images or videos has been an active research topic for many years. With the advent of local feature-based methods as well as the introduction of machine learning techniques, a lot of progress has been realized, such that practical and commercial applications of object recognition more and more became a reality (see for example, Google Goggles, Picasa, Apples Iphoto, Like.com, traffic surveillance systems such as Traficon or MobilEye, to name just a few). Object, action, and event recognition have not yet been fully explored when dealing with UGC. When it comes to object recognition, computer vision is still concerned with building classifiers for well formed static images where the object takes a central position in the picture, and not so much with recognition of background objects, objects in moving pictures or video, and not at all with dealing with low quality images as often found in UGC. Action recognition remains currently a very difficult task in computer vision. However, recently we witnessed a serious interest in cross-media content recognition. More often than not the different modalities complement or disambiguate each other. Technologies inspired by statistical alignment in multilingual texts (use of Expectation Maximization algorithm enforcing the joint occurrence of a name and a face) were developed to name faces in images without any supervision of a human or any annotated examples [534]. Methods for naming faces in news broadcast videos rely on a limited number of annotated seed examples [535]. Joint processing of text and video largely improved the location recognition in broadcasted soaps [203] and the recognition of the actions performed by humans [187, 425]. Again, the content used is relatively well-formed (e.g., images with captions, videos with transcripts) and we miss studies focusing on attribute recognition. The cross-media recognition is a research topic with a large potential, the investigation of which only started recently. Current work has not yet focused on the robustness of the algorithms in a UGC context. Apart from faces, actions, and locations, many different classes of objects and their attributes are relevant to automatically recognize based on the joint processing of text and imagery.

12.2.3   Audio Processing

In Chapter 4, we have seen that music and information about music is often found as part of UGC. Apart from music, other audio signals can tell us about the living environment. We lack at this moment robust audio classifiers that recognize audio signals in video. Most of the research in this area regards the recognition of sounds captured in optimal conditions, which are different from the realistic environment in which real-world audio signals occur. We propose to train cross-modal statistical models of the semantic relations between different sounds and between sounds and textual descriptions, which has never been done before. These relations can, for instance, be used to search for related sounds in audio or multimedia archives such as YouTube videos (query-by-sound), search for sounds from a free text description (query-by-text), or search for acoustically related terms.

12.2.4   Aggregation and Linking of UGC

Whatever the purpose is for processing UGC, many of the analytics questions regard aggregating and linking bits and pieces spread over the Web. Content becomes especially valuable when it can be linked. Persons, objects, and events can be mentioned or shown at several places in the user generated media. Links in the form of hyperlinks are present in Web content, but more interestingly can be automatically generated, also across different media. Some existing techniques for linking persons can be expanded to link events, activities, and attributes and to make them more robust for realistic UGC. The information available via other media sources and social networks might help in better recognition and partly solve the problems of recognition by means of techniques of link analysis and graph-based mining. Fusion of content in text, images, videos, and social networking information has only started to emerge and often requires reasoning techniques that reason with uncertain information.

It is often necessary to link information from different sources, when the information regards equivalences or complementaries. Current research is often limited to constructing a "distributed user profile model." In the literature, entity linking and disambiguation (e.g., Web people search) [73] and event resolution, that is, detecting whether the data speak about the same event [166] are well studied. Entity resolution involves discovering the underlying entities and mapping each reference to these entities. Entities are paired often by determining their joint co-occurrence in the dataset [73, 404] including additional constraints. Event resolution is often considered as a clustering task. The linking of events by finding temporal chains of correlated events is only starting to emerge. The state-of-the-art teaches us that we need technologies to link and integrate information when dealing with multimedia, text, and social network content. Web content is increasingly becoming an active and growing dialogue. The blogging format, comments, evolving links, and referrals are examples of ways in which stories and Web pages continually develop after their initial posting. Attribute values, objects, and relations can vary over time. In many cases, this evolving content enhances the story, often opening up additional advertising opportunities. The current techniques of information fusion do not yet cope with the dynamics of environments.

The task of building intelligent agents that can reason about information from the Web has emerged as a grand challenge for artificial intelligence (AI). Seeing the Web as a knowledge base of unprecedented size, it has the potential to overcome the knowledge acquisition bottleneck that has plagued AI from the beginning. However, many fundamental obstacles are yet to be overcome. The task requires sophisticated knowledge representation techniques that are able to cope with the noisy nature of automatically extracted information and a lack of guarantees about the reliability of information sources. Any general solution needs to incorporate the fact that different sources may disagree about subjective assessments or may express the same knowledge using a different vocabulary, are uncertain about the recognitions, and needs to deal with the unavoidable incompleteness and dynamic nature of an agent's knowledge base. We really miss suitable inference techniques that reason with uncertain and incomplete information, which is typical of UGC environments. While the importance of commonsense inferences has been recognized early on in AI, at this moment, reasoning with information from the Web is mainly carried out in a deductive fashion, relying essentially on a decidable fragment of predicate logic [27, 369]. Commonsense reasoning, however, is paramount to handle at least the following three problems: (i) plausible reasoning under exceptions, (ii) dealing with conflicting sources of information, and (iii) dealing with incompleteness. The use of nonmonotonic formalisms to reason in the presence of exceptions is well understood by now. How to deal with the last two problems in an appropriate way, however, is still largely open. Since they are due to deficiencies in humanly specified knowledge, their solution should relate to our cognitive understanding of language and natural concepts. Finally, it goes without saying that proper uncertainty modeling will be key in effectively making Web reasoning work. Although much progress has been made in the area of probabilistic reasoning, it is not clear that probability theory is always suitable. When uncertainty is purely epistemic, for instance, Dempster and Shafer's theory of evidence [619], which captures both randomness and epistemic uncertainty, at the same time generalizing probability and possibility theory. How to combine different uncertainty frameworks in an effective way with symbolic reasoning is to a large extent still an open question. How to efficiently deal with often large amounts of UGC is another open research question.

When extracting information we often ignore the links between content whether they are explicit (e.g., through hyperlinking) or implicit through links automatically found. The fusion of information (and consequently resolution of ambiguous content) yields richer profiles of the ambient of a user or potential customer. Fusion of (cross-media) information in UGC is at this moment rarely studied. Intelligent fusion of information that is extracted from unstructured sources such as user generated is a difficult but very useful topic for future research, where automated cross-media content alignment, evidence fusion from content and contextual sources, and novel information fusion algorithms have a primordial place.

Information fusion cannot only teach us about inferring demographic profile information from individual users such as gender, age, relationship status, personality, number of children, location, employment, level of education, income, spending behavior, whether the user is an early adaptor of new products, and so on. It also offers the necessary building blocks for societal and business intelligence that transcend profiles of individual users, but combines the sources in the most comprehensible and relevant way to answer all kinds of research hypotheses. Again, reasoning with uncertain and incomplete information is of primordial importance, where Bayesian network technologies [159], possibility theory, and Dempster and Shafer theory could play a role. The information found in the unstructured sources need to be expanded with online knowledge repositories of ontological information, such as Freebase.com and DBPedia.org. These repositories contain semantic knowledge in a structured, machine understandable format, typically in the form of RDF-triples that encode which objects have which properties, or which relations hold between two given objects. For example, querying Freebase we can find out that "House" is a TV medical drama series produced by David Shore, together with other information about this series. To use this information when mining UGC, again demands for appropriate fusion techniques.

12.2.5 Legal Considerations

Processing UGC poses important problems with regard to privacy and intellectual property [190]. The growing integration of Web 2.0 platforms—and the personal information flows that they contain, together with the increasing power and capabilities of the technologies discussed in this book—make it possible to track user's behavior, social and intellectual activities, and lifestyles [56]. Although often driven by the need to leverage for personalized services and advertisements, less innocent usage of the collected knowledge is never excluded. We did not focus on these aspects in this book, but they are of primordial importance especially if in the future mining based on computer vision methods and aggregation of content will become mainstream methods. A lot of technological means are already out there, but are often not yet used because of privacy concerns. There is a need to know to what extent the tools used for mining can be developed in line with current data protection and International Property Rights (IPR) legislation and future legal developments, both on an international and local scale. Legal researchers need to identify legal gaps in the current legal framework that may demand changes in the current legal framework, allowing introducing new forms of mining in line with societal needs and social demands for respect of privacy. Hence, although profiling is often useful for users when providing better services for the users, profiling activities can also expose a dark side when they are used to make automatic decisions regarding users. Legal researchers should assist technical researchers to ensure the incorporation of the privacy by the legal design principles. Furthermore, legal research will probably discover gaps in the current legislation hindering the development of technologies that meet a societal need. The legal research will then provide materials for policy makers to adapt or clarify the legal framework to new developments.

In addition, the developments above will experiment with several novel forms of aggregated content coming from different sources, requiring very novel legal instruments for dealing with IPR. Information in digital form offers many possibilities previously deemed impossible. Users can upload their own blog posts, pictures, videos, and music, and view information uploaded by others. New online services, such as digital photo albums, online collaboration tools, and online video sites capitalize on the ease with which content in digital form can be exchanged. The combination of the above mentioned increases in connectivity and mobility and these evolutions on the content level has resulted in digital convergence: different kinds of content (e-mail, music, television, etc.) are available on different devices (desktop PCs, notebooks, cell phones, etc.), using different networks (wired, wireless).

Profiling and data harvesting inherently require a service provider to collect large amounts of user data in order to offer its services. Such user data is often collected surreptitiously, for example, when cookies are used to monitor a user's clickstream, or via the inclusion of Web bugs that are embedded in the invisible HTML code of a Web page. Moreover, data is preferably stored for an unlimited period of time. Such a setup obviously contrasts with the data minimization and transparency requirements laid down in the Data Protection Directive. For instance, in Europe, as the European legislation still dates from the pre-Web 2.0 area, it is not easy to apply the rules to new forms of information processing, such as personalized advertising. Legal research is necessary for identifying the legal requirements that would have an impact on the development of the technology. Based on the continuous input of the legal researchers, the technical researchers will be able to develop a personalized advertisement solution ensuring privacy compliance. Personalized advertising tools may have an impact on IPR laws. The increasing bandwidth and processing power of computers have led to the predominance of digital content. Personalized advertising tools could, for instance, by using and manipulating the digital content, enhance the advertising experience of end users. Among the legal issues associated with this trend are questions regarding the application of existing legal instruments to the new services and product development that have emerged as a result of the success of digital content. Personalized advertising making use of and manipulating the UGC is one of the activities that, if not properly managed, could be against the strict rules of the European copyright legislation. The fair use doctrine in the United States is sometimes proclaimed to offer a higher degree of flexibility in comparison with the EU copyright laws.

Current technologies that mine and give access to UGC offer many possibilities to extract personal information from the online sources and for the manipulation and fusion of the digital content. Noncompliance with legal rules on data protection and intellectual property rights may risk making technologies obsolete. Taking into account legal requirements and perhaps changing legal requirements along the development of the technologies will guarantee the development of durable solutions. Often technologies can be developed for the benefit of society, but the same technology can be misused for purposes that seriously harm the users who trust it, but we must be confident that in the long run technologies have a beneficial effect on society.

12.2.6   Information Credibility

A final very important track of research is the credibility of the information found in UGC. The mining of UGC loses its power if parts of the UGC is unreliable or even fraudulent. As mining of UGC becomes a growing trend, spamming UGC with unreliable information will only follow in even bigger volumes. The mining techniques can cope with some noise, but if nontrustable content is taking a substantial share of the data, the techniques become worthless. So current research tries to measure the credibility of Web content. The assessment of the credibility is in itself a mining task, where different sources of evidence can be used such as the content itself [379, 614], the reputation of sources, [771], interaction behavior [123] or the neighbors in the Web graph [255]. Web filtering might seem to yield well developed and performance technologies [133], mining of UGC often needs more advanced technologies, which is a difficult task as you need fine-grained semantic recognitions in text, image, or video sources and often additional inferences made over the recognitions are needed to detect contradictory or nonplausible information. The most promising research with regard to truth discovery fuse information from different sources and predicts the confidence of a fact provided by one or more data sources. Simple weighted voting is often not sufficient, more advanced optimizations possibly guided by some supervision provided through annotated examples yield promising results [747].

A relevant current project to watch is the Belgian PARIS (Personalised AdveRtisements buIlt from web Sources) project financed by the grant IWT-SBO 110067 (http://www.parisproject.be/), which runs from 2012 to 2016 and which studies several of the above proposed research tracks.

Bibliography

[1] A. Fader, S. Soderland, and O. Etzioni. Scaling Wikipedia-based named entity disambiguation to arbitrary Web text. In *Proceedings of Wiki-AI at IJCAI*, 2009.

[2] Agnar Aamodt and Enric Plaza. Case-based reasoning: Foundational issues, methodological variations, and system approaches. *AI Communications*, 7(1):39–59, March 1994.

[3] A. Abbasi, H. Chen, and A. Salem. Sentiment analysis in multiple languages: Feature selection for opinion classification in Web forums. *ACM Transactions on Information Systems*, 26(3), 2008.

[4] S. Abe, M. Eguchi, A. Sumida, A. Ohsaki, and K. Inui. Minna no keiken: Burogu kara chuushutsu shita ibento oyobi senchimento no db-ka [Everyone's experiences: Creating a database of events and sentiments extracted from blogs] (in Japanese). In *Proceedings of NLP-2009*, pages 296–299, 2009.

[5] Fabian Abel, Ilknur Celik, Geert-Jan Houben, and Patrick Siehndel. Leveraging the semantics of tweets for adaptive faceted search on twitter. In Lora Aroyo, Chris Welty, Harith Alani, Jamie Taylor, Abraham Bernstein, Lalana Kagal, Natasha Fridman Noy, and Eva Blomqvist, editors, *International Semantic Web Conference (1)*, volume 7031 of *Lecture Notes in Computer Science*, pages 1–17. Springer, 2011.

[6] Fabian Abel, Qi Gao, G. J. Houben, and Ke Tao. Analyzing user modeling on Twitter for personalized news recommendations. In *19th International Conference on User Modeling, Adaption and Personalization*, pages 1–12, 2011.

[7] Fabian Abel, Claudia Hauff, Geert-Jan Houben, Richard Stronkman, and Ke Tao. Semantics + filtering + search = twitcident. exploring information in social Web streams. In Ethan V. Munson and Markus Strohmaier, editors, *In Proceedings of HT'12*, pages 285–294. ACM, 2012.

[8] Lada A. Adamic, Jun Zhang, Eytan Bakshy, and Mark S. Ackerman. Knowledge sharing and Yahoo! Answers: Everyone knows something.

In *Proceedings of the 17th International Conference Companion on the World Wide Web, WWW'08*, pages 665–674, 2008.

[9] B. Adams, D. Phung, and S. Venkatesh. Eventscapes: Visualizing events over time with emotive facets. In *Proceedings of the 19th ACM International Conference on Multimedia*, pages 1477–1480, 2011.

[10] Eytan Adar, Matthew Hurst, Tim Finin, Natalie S. Glance, Nicolas Nicolov, and Belle L. Tseng, editors. *Proceedings of the 2nd International Conference on Weblogs and Social Media, ICWSM 2008*, Seattle, Washington, March 30–April 2, 2008. AAAI Press, 2008.

[11] Gediminas Adomavicius and Alexander Tuzhilin. Toward the next generation of recommender systems: A survey of the state-of-the-art and possible extensions. *IEEE Transactions on Knowledge and Data Engineering*, 17(6):734–749, June 2005.

[12] Gediminas Adomavicius, Bamshad Mobasher, Francesco Ricci, and Alexander Tuzhilin. Context-aware recommender systems. *AI Magazine* 32(3):67–80, 2011.

[13] Eugene Agichtein, Carlos Castillo, Debora Donato, Aristides Gionis, and Gilad Mishne. Finding high-quality content in social media. In *Proceedings of the 1st ACM International Conference on Web Search and Data Mining, WSDM'08*, pages 83–94, 2008.

[14] Eugene Agichtein and Luis Gravano. Snowball: Extracting relations from large plain-text collections. In *ACM International Conference on Digital Libraries (ACM DL)*, 2000.

[15] H. Agrawal, R. Mannila, R. Srikant, H. Toivonen, and A. I. Verkamo. Fast discovery of association rules. In *Advances in Knowledge Discovery and Data Mining*. AAAI/MIT Press, 1996.

[16] R. Agrawal, S. Rajagopalan, R. Srikant, and Y. Xu. Mining newsgroups using networks arising from social behavior. In *Proceedings of the 12th International Conference on the World Wide Web*, pages 529–535. New York, NY, ACM, 2003.

[17] R. Agrawal and R. Srikant. Mining generalised association rules. In *Proceedings of the 21st VLDB Conference*, pages 407–419, 1995.

[18] D. W. Aha. The omnipresence of case-based reasoning in science and application. *Knowledge-Based Systems*, 11(5):261–273, 1998.

[19] C. G. Akcora, M. A. Bayir, M. Demirbas, and H. Ferhatosmanoglu. Identifying breakpoints in public opinion. In *1st Workshop on Social Media Analytics*, pages 62–66, 2010.

[20] P. Alexander and P. Patrick. Text representation using dependency tree subgraphs for sentiment analysis. In *Proceedings of the International Conference on Database Systems for Advanced Applications*, pages 323–332. Springer, 2011.

[21] James Allan, Javed A. Aslam, Mark Sanderson, Cheng Xiang Zhai, and Justin Zobel, editors. *Proceedings of the 32nd Annual International ACM SIGIR Conference on Research and Development in Information Retrieval, SIGIR 2009*, Boston, MA, July 19–23. ACM, 2009.

[22] N. Alon, R. Yuster, and U. Zwick. Finding and counting given length cycles. *Algorithmica*, 17(3):209–223, 1997.

[23] S. Aman and S. Szpakowicz. Identifying expressions of emotion in text. In *Proceedings of the 10th International Conference on Text, Speech, and Dialogue (TSD-2007)*, pages 196–205, 2007.

[24] Gianni Amati. *Probability models for information retrieval based on divergence from randomness*. PhD thesis, University of Glasgow, 2003.

[25] V. Pek and A. N. Andel. Anatomy of the unsought finding. serendipity: Origin, history, domains, traditions, appearances, patterns and programmability. *The British Journal for the Philosophy of Science*, 45(2):631–648, June 1994.

[26] M. Anderson and S. L. Anderson. Robot be good. *Scientific American*, pages 72–77, October, 2010.

[27] Grigoris Antoniou and Frank van Harmelen. *A Semantic Web Primer*, 2nd Edition *(Cooperative Information Systems)*. The MIT Press, 2008.

[28] C. Antunes and A. Oliveira. Generalization of pattern-growth methods for sequential pattern mining with gap constraints. In *Machine Learning and Pattern Mining in Data Recognition*, pages 239–251. Springer-Verlag, 2003.

[29] Aozora Bunko. Project Web Site: http://www.aozora.gr.jp.

[30] D. Archambault, D. Greene, P. Cunningham, and N. J. Hurley. ThemeCrowds: Multiresolution summaries of Twitter usage. In *Workshop on Search and Mining User-Generated Contents (SMUC)*, pages 77–84, 2011.

[31] Jaime Arguello, Jonathan L. Elsas, Jamie Callan, and Jaime G. Carbonell. Document representation and query expansion models for blog recommendation. In Adar et al. [10].

[32] H. Arimura and T. Uno. An output-polynomial time algorithm for mining frequent closed attribute trees. In *Proceedings of the 15th International Conference on Inductive Logic Programming*, pages 1–19, 2005.

[33] S. Asur, B. A. Huberman, G. Szabo, and C. Wang. Trends in social media: Persistence and decay. *Proceedings of the 5th International AAAI Conference on Weblogs and Social Media*, 2011.

[34] Adrian Athique. *Digital Media and Society: An Introduction*. Polity Press, 2013.

[35] A. Aue and M. Gamon. Customizing sentiment classifiers to new domains: A case study. In *Proceedings of International Conference Recent Advances in Natural Language Processing*, 2005.

[36] Melanie Aurnhammer, Peter Hanappe, and Luc Steels. Augmenting navigation for collaborative tagging with emergent semantics. In *International Semantic Web Conference*, pages 58–71, 2006.

[37] Lars Backstrom, Eric Sun, and Cameron Marlow. Find me if you can: Improving geographical prediction with social and spatial proximity. In *Proceedings of the 19th International Conference on World Wide Web*, pages 61–70. ACM, 2010.

[38] R. Baeza-Yates and B. Ribeiro-Neto. *Modern Information Retrieval: The Concepts and Technology Behind Search*. Addison Wesley, 2011.

[39] Ricardo Baeza-Yates and Berthier Ribeiro-Neto. *Modern Information Retrieval—the Concepts and Technology behind Search*, 2nd Edition. ACM Press Books, Pearson, Harlow, England, 2011.

[40] Ricardo A. Baeza-Yates, Arjen P. de Vries, Hugo Zaragoza, Berkant Barla Cambazoglu, Vanessa Murdock, Ronny Lempel, and Fabrizio Silvestri, editors. *Advances in Information Retrieval—34th European Conference on IR Research, ECIR 2012*, Barcelona, Spain, April 1–5, 2012. *Proceedings*, volume 7224 of *Lecture Notes in Computer Science*. Springer, 2012.

[41] Amit Bagga and Breck Baldwin. Entity-based cross-document coreferencing using the Vector Space Model. In *Proceedings of the 17th International Conference on Computational Linguistics (COLING '98)*, volume 1. Association for Computational Linguistics, Stroudsburg, PA, pages 79–85, 1998.

[42] Bahman Bahmani and Ashish Goel. Partitioned multi-indexing: Bringing order to social search. In Mille et al. [464], pages 399–408.

[43] Niroshan Balasubramaniam. User-generated content business aspect of the Internet of Things. Technical report, Swiss Federal Institute of Technology Zürich, ETH, April 2007.

[44] T. Baldwin and M. Lui. Language identification: The long and the short of the matter. In *Human Language Technologies: The 2010 Annual Conference of the North American Chapter of the Association for Computational Linguistics*, pages 229–237, Los Angeles, CA, June 2010.

[45] Michele Banko, Michael J. Cafarella, Stephen Soderland, Matt Broadhead, and Oren Etzioni. Open information extraction from the Web. In *Proceedings of IJCAI*, pages 2670–2676, 2007.

[46] N. Bansal and N. Koudas. Blogscope: Spatio-temporal analysis of the blogosphere. In *Proceedings of the 16th International Conference on the World Wide Web, WWW'07*, pages 1269–1270, 2007.

[47] Shenghua Bao, Gui-Rong Xue, Xiaoyuan Wu, Yong Yu, Ben Fei, and Zhong Su. Optimizing Web search using social annotations. In *Proceedings of WWW*, pages 501–510, 2007.

[48] Shenghua Bao, Gui-Rong Xue, Xiaoyuan Wu, Yong Yu, Ben Fei, and Zhong Su. Optimizing Web search using social annotations. In Carey L. Williamson, Mary Ellen Zurko, Peter F. Patel-Schneider, and Prashant J. Shenoy, editors, *In Proceedings WWW*, pages 501–510. ACM, 2007.

[49] Shenghua Bao, Bohai Yang, Ben Fei, Shengliang Xu, Zhong Su, and Yong Yu. Social propagation: Boosting social annotations for web mining. *World Wide Web*, 12(4):399–420, 2009.

[50] A. L. Barabási, H. Jeong, Z. Néda, E. Ravasz, A. Schubert, and T. Vicsek. Evolution of the social network of scientific collaborations. *Physica A: Statistical Mechanics and Its Applications*, 311(3–4):590–614, 2002.

[51] A. L. Barabási and A. Reka. Emergence of scaling in random networks. *Science*, 286:509–512, 1999.

[52] Naomi S. Baron. Assessing the Internet's impact on language. In Mia Consalvo and Charles Ess, editors, *The Handbook of Internet Studies*, pages 117–136. Wiley-Blackwell, 2011.

[53] M. Baroni, S. Bernardini, A. Ferraresi, and E. Zanchetta. *The WaCky Wide Web: A Collection of Very Large Linguistically Processed Web-Crawled Corpora*. Kluwer Academic Publishers, 2008.

[54] M. Baroni and M. Ueyama. Building general- and special-purpose corpora by Web crawling. In *Proceedings of the 13th NIJL International Symposium on Language Corpora: Their Compilation and Application*, pages 31–40, 2006.

[55] Regina Barzilay and Kathleen R. Mckeown. Sentence fusion for multi-document news summarization. *Computational Linguistics*, 31:297–328, 2005.

[56] Nancy K. Baym. Social networks 2.0. In Mia Consalvo and Charles Ess, editors, *The Handbook of Internet Studies*, pages 117–136. Wiley-Blackwell, 2011.

[57] C. Beaudoin. Explaining the relationship between Internet use and interpersonal trust: Taking into account motivation and information overload. *Journal of Computer Mediated Communication*, 13:550–568, 2008.

[58] L. Becchetti, P. Boldi, C. Castillo, and A. Gionis. Efficient semistreaming algorithms for local triangle counting in massive graphs. In *Proceedings of ACM KDD*, 2008.

[59] H. Becker, M. Naaman, and L. Gravano. Selecting quality Twitter content for events. In *Proceedings of the 5th International Conference on Weblogs and Social Media (ICWSM)*, 2011.

[60] Dave Beckett. Semantics through the Tag. In *Proceedings of the XTech Conference*, Amsterdam, The Netherlands, 2006.

[61] Ron Bekkerman and Andrew McCallum. Disambiguating Web appearances of people in a social network. In *Proceedings COLING*, 2005.

[62] Jan De Belder and Marie-Francine Moens. Coreference clustering using column generation. In *Proceedings COLING (Posters)*, pages 245–254, 2012.

[63] Nicholas J. Belkin and W. Bruce Croft. Information filtering and information retrieval: Two sides of the same coin? *Communications of the ACM*, 35(12):29–38, December 1992.

[64] Jerome R. Bellegarda. Latent semantic mapping. *IEEE Signal Processing Magazine*, 22(5):70–80, 2005.

[65] Irad Ben-Gal, Yuval Shavitt, Ela Weinsberg, and Udi Weinsberg. Improving information retrieval in peer-to-peer networks using shared-content clustering. *Knowledge and Information Systems Journal (KAIS)*, 2013. To appear.

[66] K. P. Bennett and A. Demiriz. Semisupervised support vector machines. In *Proceedings of the 1998 Conference on Advances in Neural Information Processing Systems*, pages 368–374, 1998.

[67] Adam L. Berger, Rich Caruana, David Cohn, Dayne Freitag, and Vibhu O. Mittal. Bridging the lexical chasm: Statistical approaches to answer-finding. In *Research and Development in Information Retrieval*, pages 192–199, 2000.

[68] Delphine Bernhard and Iryna Gurevych. Combining lexical semantic resources with question and answer archives for translation-based answer

findings. In *Proceedings of the Joint Conference of the 47th Annual Meeting of the ACL and the 4th International Joint Conference on Natural Language Processing of the AFNLP: Volume 2—Volume 2, ACL'09*, pages 728–736. Stroudsburg, PA, ACL, 2009.

[69] M. S. Bernstein, B. Suh, L. Hong, J. Chen, S. Kairam, and E. H. Chi. EDDI: Interactive topic-based browsing of social status streams. In *Proceedings of the 23nd ACM Symposium on User Interface Software and Technology (UIST)*, pages 303–312, 2010.

[70] Thierry Bertin-Mahieux, Douglas Eck, François Maillet, and Paul Lamere. Autotagger: A model for predicting social tags from acoustic features on large music databases. *Journal of New Music Research*, 37(2):115–135, 2008.

[71] S. Bethard, H. Yu, A. Thornton, V. Hatzivassiloglou, and D. Jurafsky. Extracting opinion propositions and opinion holders using syntactic and lexical cues. In J. G. Shanahan, Y. Qu, and J. Wiebe, editors, *Computing Attitude and Affect in Text: Theory and Applications*, chapter 11, pages 125–141. Springer, 2006.

[72] Sudip Bhattacharjee, Ram Gopal, Kaveepan Lertwachara, and James R. Marsden. Using P2P sharing activity to improve business decision making: Proof of concept for estimating product life-cycle. *Electronic Commerce Research and Applications*, 4(1):14–20, 2005.

[73] Indrajit Bhattacharya and Lise Getoor. Collective entity resolution in relational data. *ACM Transactions on Knowledge Discovery from Data*, 1(1), 2007.

[74] Jiang Bian, Yandong Liu, Eugene Agichtein, and Hongyuan Zha. Finding the right facts in the crowd: Factoid question-answering over social media. In *Proceedings of the 17th International Conference on World Wide Web, WWW'08*, pages 467–476. New York, NY, ACM, 2008.

[75] Jiang Bian, Yandong Liu, Ding Zhou, Eugene Agichtein, and Hongyuan Zha. Learning to recognize reliable users and content in social media with coupled mutual reinforcement. In *Proceedings of the 18th International Conference on World Wide Web, WWW'09*, pages 51–60. New York, NY, ACM, 2009.

[76] Daniel M. Bikel, Scott Miller, Richard Schwartz, and Ralph Weischedel. Nymble: A high-performance learning name-finder. In *Proceedings of 5th Conference on Applied Natural Language Processing*, pages 194–201, 1997.

[77] David M. Blei, Andrew Y. Ng, and Michael I. Jordan. Latent Dirichlet allocation. *Machine Learning Research*, 3:993–1022, March 2003.

[78] K. Bloom, N. Garg, and S. Argamon. Extracting appraisal expressions. In *Proceedings of the Annual Conference of the North American Chapter of the Association for Computational Linguistics*, pages 308–315. Morristown, NJ, ACL, 2007.

[79] A. Blum and T. Mitchell. Combining labeled and unlabeled data with co-training. In *Proceedings of the 11th Annual Conference on Computational Learning Theory*, pages 92–100, 1998.

[80] E. Boiy and M.-F. Moens. A machine learning approach to sentiment analysis in multilingual Web texts. *Information Retrieval*, 12(5):526–558, 2009.

[81] Paolo Boldi, Francesco Bonchi, Carlos Castillo, Debora Donato, Aristides Gionis, and Sebastiano Vigna. The query-flow graph: Model and applications. In *Proceedings of the 17th ACM Conference on Information and Knowledge Management, CIKM'08*, pages 609–618. New York, NY, ACM, 2008.

[82] J. Bollen, H. Mao, and A. Pepe. Modeling public mood and emotion: Twitter sentiment and socio-economic phenomena. In *Proceedings of 5th International AAAI Conference on Weblogs and Social Media*, 2011.

[83] B. Bollobás. *Random Graphs*. Cambridge University Press, 2001.

[84] B. Bollobás and P. Erdős. Cliques in random graphs. In *Mathematical Proceedings of the Cambridge Philosophical Society*, volume 80, pages 419–427, 1976.

[85] F. Bonchi, R. Perego, F. Silvestri, H. Vahabi, and R. Venturini. Efficient query recommendations in the long tail via center-piece subgraphs. In *Proceedings of the 35th Annual International ACM SIGIR Conference on Research and Development in Information Retrieval, SIGIR'12*. New York, NY, ACM, 2012.

[86] K. Bontcheva and Y. Wilks. Tailoring Automatically Generated Hypertext. *User Modeling and User-Adapted Interaction*, Special issue on Language-Based Interaction, 2004.

[87] C. Borgelt. Combining ring extensions and canonical form pruning. In *Proceedings of MLG*, 2006.

[88] Mohamed Bouguessa, Benoît Dumoulin, and Shengrui Wang. Identifying authoritative actors in question-answering forums: The case of Yahoo! Answers. In *Proceedings of the 14th ACM SIGKDD International Conference on Knowledge Discovery and Data Mining, KDD'08*, pages 866–874. New York, NY, ACM, 2008.

[89] Niels Olof Bouvin. Unifying strategies for Web augmentation. In Jörg Westbomke, Uffe Kock Wiil, John J. Leggett, Klaus Tochtermann, and Jörg M. Haake, editors, *Hypertext*, pages 91–100. ACM, 1999.

[90] Danah Boyd and Nicole B. Ellison. Social network sites: Definition, history, and scholarship. *Journal of Computer-Mediated Communication*, 13(1-2):210–230, November.

[91] S. R. K. Branavan, Harr Chen, Jacob Eisenstein, and Regina Barzilay. Learning document-level semantic properties from free-text annotations. *Journal of Artificial Intelligence Research*, 34(1):569–603, April 2009.

[92] Ronald Brandow, Karl Mitze, and Lisa F. Rau. Automatic condensation of electronic publications by sentence selection. *Information Processing and Management*, 31(5):675–685, September 1995.

[93] Brants, T. and Franz, A. Web 1T 5-gram Version 1, Project Web Site: `http://googleresearch.blogspot.com/2006/08/all-our-n-gram-are-belong-to-you.html`.

[94] E. Breck, Y. Choi, and C. Cardie. Identifying expressions of opinion in context. In *Proceedings of the 20th International Joint Conference on Artificial Intelligence*, pages 2683–2688, 2007.

[95] Derek G. Bridge and Alex Ferguson. Diverse product recommendations using an expressive language for case retrieval. In *Proceedings of the 6th European Conference on Advances in Case-Based Reasoning, EC-CBR'02*, pages 43–57. London, UK, Springer-Verlag, 2002.

[96] Asa Briggs and Peter Burke. *A Social History of the Media: From Gutenberg to the Internet*. Polity Press, December 2009.

[97] B. Bringmann and S. Nijssen. What is frequent in a single graph? In *Proceedings of the 12th Pacific–Asian Conference on Knowledge Discovery and Data Mining*, pages 858–863, 2008.

[98] B. Bringmann, A. Zimmermann, L. De Raedt, and S. Nijssen. Don't be afraid of simpler patterns. In *Proceedings of the 10th European Conference on Principles and Practice of Knowledge Discovery in Databases*, pages 55–66, 2006.

[99] Christopher H. Brooks and Nancy Montanez. Improved annotation of the blogosphere via autotagging and hierarchical clustering. In *Proceedings WWW*, pages 625–632, 2006.

[100] J. Broschart. Why Tongan does it differently: Categorial distinctions in a language without nouns and verbs. *Linguistic Typology*, 1(2):123–165, 1997.

[101] Peter F. Brown, Vincent J. Della Pietra, Stephen A. Della Pietra, and Robert L. Mercer. The mathematics of statistical machine translation: Parameter estimation. *Comput. Linguist.*, 19(2):263–311, June 1993.

[102] R. Bruce and J. Wiebe. Recognizing subjectivity: A case study in manual tagging. *Natural Language Engineering*, 5:187–205, 1999.

[103] Razvan Bunescu and Marius Pasca. Using encyclopedic knowledge for named entity disambiguation. In *Proceedings EACL*, 2006.

[104] Razvan C. Bunescu and Raymond J. Mooney. Learning to extract relations from the Web using minimal supervision. In *Proceedings of the 45th Annual Meeting of the Association for Computational Linguistics (ACL'07)*, pages 576–583, June 2007.

[105] H. Bunke and G. Allermann. Inexact graph matching for structural pattern recognition. *Pattern Recognition Letters*, 1:245–253, 1983.

[106] J. Burger, J. Henderson, G. Kim, and G. Zarrella. Discriminating gender on Twitter. In *Proceedings of the Conference on Empirical Methods in Natural Language Processing, EMNLP'11*, pages 1301–1309, 2011.

[107] L. S. Buriol, G. Frahling, S. Leonardi, A. M. Spaccamela, and C. Sohler. Counting triangles in data streams. In *Proceedings of PODS*, 2006.

[108] Robin Burke. Hybrid recommender systems: Survey and experiments. *User Modeling and User-Adapted Interaction*, 12(4):331–370, November 2002.

[109] Robin Burke. *The Adaptive Web. Hybrid Web Recommender Systems*, pages 377–408. Berlin, Heidelberg, Springer-Verlag, 2007.

[110] Robin D. Burke, Kristian J. Hammond, Vladimir A. Kulyukin, Steven L. Lytinen, Noriko Tomuro, and Scott Schoenberg. Question-answering from frequently asked question files: Experiences with the FAQ Finder system. *AI Magazine*, 18:57–66, 1997.

[111] Michael Busch, Krishna Gade, Brian Larson, Patrick Lok, Samuel Luckenbill, and Jimmy Lin. Earlybird: Real-time search at Twitter. In Anastasios Kementsietsidis and Marcos Antonio Vaz Salles, editors, *Proceedings ICDE*, pages 1360–1369. IEEE Computer Society, 2012.

[112] T. Calders, J. Ramon, and D. Van Dyck. All normalized anti-monotonic overlap graph measures are bounded. *Data Mining and Knowledge Discovery*, 23:503–548, 2011.

[113] Xin Cao, Gao Cong, Bin Cui, and Christian S. Jensen. A generalized framework of exploring category information for question retrieval in community question answer archives. In *Proceedings of the 19th International Conference on World Wide Web, WWW'10*, pages 201–210, 2010.

[114] Xin Cao, Gao Cong, Bin Cui, Christian Søndergaard Jensen, and Ce Zhang. The use of categorization information in language models for question retrieval. In *Proceedings of the 18th ACM Conference on Information and Knowledge Management, CIKM'09*, pages 265–274. New York, NY, ACM, 2009.

[115] Giuseppe Carenini and Jackie Chi Kit Cheung. Extractive versus NLG-based abstractive summarization of evaluative text: The effect of corpus controversiality. In *Proceedings of the 5th International Natural Language Generation Conference, INLG'08*, pages 33–41, 2008.

[116] A. Carlson, J. Betteridge, B. Kisiel, B. Settles, E. R. Hruschka Jr., and T. M. Mitchell. Toward an architecture for never-ending language learning. In *Proceedings AAAI*, pages 109–118, 2001.

[117] A. Carlson, J. Betteridge, R. C. Wang, E. R. Hruschka Jr., and T. M. Mitchell. Coupled semisupervised learning for information extraction. In *3rd ACM International Conference on Web Search and Data Mining*, 2010.

[118] Mark James Carman, Mark Baillie, and Fabio Crestani. Tag data and personalized information retrieval. In Ian Soboroff, Eugene Agichtein, and Ravi Kumar, editors, *Proceedings SSM*, pages 27–34. ACM, 2008.

[119] Mark James Carman, Mark Baillie, Robert Gwadera, and Fabio Crestani. A statistical comparison of tag and query logs. In Allan et al. [21], pages 123–130.

[120] S. Carter, W. Weerkamp, and E. Tsagkias. Microblog language identification: Overcoming the limitations of short, unedited and idiomatic text. *Language Resources and Evaluation*, 47:195–215, 2013.

[121] Ben Carterette and Desislava Petkova. Learning a ranking from pairwise preferences. In *Proceedings of the 29th Annual International ACM SIGIR Conference on Research and Development in Information Retrieval, SIGIR'06*, pages 629–630. New York, NY, ACM, 2006.

[122] Donald O. Case. *Looking for Information: A Survey of Research on Information Seeking, Needs, and Behavior*. Emerald Group, 2012.

[123] Carlos Castillo, Marcelo Mendoza, and Barbara Poblete. Information credibility on Twitter. In *Proceedings of the 20th International Conference on World Wide Web, WWW'11*, pages 675–684. New York, NY, ACM, 2011.

[124] Òscar Celma. *Music Recommendation and Discovery—The Long Tail, Long Fail, and Long Play in the Digital Music Space*. Berlin, Heidelberg, Germany, Springer, 2010.

[125] D. Chakrabarti and K. Punera. Event summarization using tweets. In *Proceedings of the 5th International Conference on Weblogs and Social Media (ICWSM)*, 2011.

[126] Soumen Chakrabarti, Martin van den Berg, and Byron Dom. Focused crawling: A new approach to topic-specific Web resource discovery. *Computer Networks*, 31(11–16):1623–1640, 1999.

[127] J. Chan, C. Hayes, and E. Daly. Decomposing discussion forums using common user roles. In *Proceedings of WebSci10: Extending the Frontiers of Society On-Line*, 2010.

[128] E. Charniak, D. Blaheta, N. Ge, K. Hall, J. Hale, and M. Johnson. *BLLIP 1987–1989 WSJ Corpus Release 1*. Linguistic Data Consortium, 2000.

[129] Sonny Han Seng Chee, Jiawei Han, and Ke Wang. Rectree: An efficient collaborative filtering method. In *Proceedings of the 3rd International Conference on Data Warehousing and Knowledge Discovery, DaWaK'01*, pages 141–151, London, UK, Springer-Verlag, 2001.

[130] Bee-Chung Chen, Anirban Dasgupta, Xuanhui Wang, and Jie Yang. Vote calibration in community question-answering systems. In *Proceedings of the 35th International ACM SIGIR Conference on Research and Development in Information Retrieval, SIGIR'12*, pages 781–790. New York, NY, ACM, 2012.

[131] J. Chen, W. Hsu, M. Lee, and S. Ng. Nemofinder: Dissecting genome wide protein-protein interactions with repeated and unique network motifs. In *Proceedings of the 12th ACM-SIGKDD International Conference on Knowledge Discovery and Data Mining (KDD)*, pages 106–115, 2006.

[132] J. Chen, R. Nairn, L. Nelson, M. Bernstein, and E. Chi. Short and tweet: Experiments on recommending content from information streams. In *28th International Conference on Human Factors in Computing Systems*, pages 1185–1194, 2010.

[133] Thomas M. Chen and Victoria Wang. Web filtering and censoring. *IEEE Computer*, 43(3):94–97, 2010.

[134] Zheng Chen, Liu Wenyin, Feng Zhang, Mingjing Li, and Hongjiang Zhang. Web mining for Web image retrieval. *Journal of the American Society for Information Science and Technology*, 52(10):831–839, 2001.

[135] Z. Cheng. You are where you tweet: A content-based approach to geolocating Twitter users. *Proceedings of the 19th ACM Conference Information and Knowledge Management*, 2010.

[136] P. Chesley, B. Vincent, L. Xu, and R. K. Srihari. Using verbs and adjectives to automatically classify blog sentiment. In *Proceedings of AAAI-CAAW-06, the Spring Symposia on Computational Approaches to Analyzing Weblogs*, Menlo Park, CA, AAAI Press, 2006.

[137] Y. Chi, R. Muntz, S. Nijssen, and N. Kok. Frequent subtree mining—An overview. *Fundamenra Informaticae*, 66(1-2):161–198, 2005.

[138] Nancy A. Chinchor. Overview of MUC-7/MET-2. In *Proceedings of the 7th Message Understanding Conference (MUC-7/MET-2)*, 1998.

[139] Paul-Alexandru Chirita, Stefania Costache, Wolfgang Nejdl, and Siegfried Handschuh. P-tag: Large-scale automatic generation of personalized annotation tags for the Web. In *Proceedings WWW*, pages 845–854, 2007.

[140] Paul-Alexandru Chirita, Claudiu S. Firan, and Wolfgang Nejdl. Personalized query expansion for the Web. In *Proceedings SIGIR*, pages 7–14, 2007.

[141] Tat-Seng Chua, Huan-Bo Luan, Maosong Sun, and Shiqiang Yang. Next: NUS-Tsinghua center for extreme search of user-generated content. *IEEE MultiMedia*, 19(3):81–87, 2012.

[142] F. Chung. *Spectral Graph Theory*. AMS Press, 1997.

[143] Paul Clough, Colum Foley, Cathal Gurrin, Gareth J. F. Jones, Wessel Kraaij, Hyowon Lee, and Vanessa Murdock, editors. *Advances in Information Retrieval—33rd European Conference on IR Research, ECIR 2011*, Dublin, Ireland, April 18–21, 2011. *Proceedings*, volume 6611 of *Lecture Notes in Computer Science*. Springer, 2011.

[144] Michael Collins and Nigel Duffy. Convolution kernels for natural language. In *Advances in Neural Information Processing Systems 14*, pages 625–632. MIT Press, 2001.

[145] Gao Cong, Long Wang, Chin-Yew Lin, Young in Song, and Yueheng Sun. Finding question-answer pairs from online forums. In *Proceedings of the 31st Annual International ACM SIGIR Conference on Research and Development in Information Retrieval*, pages 467–474, 2008.

[146] Brendan O. Connor, Michel Krieger, and David Ahn. TweetMotif: Exploratory search and topic summarization for Twitter. In *Proceedings of the 4th AAAI Conference on Weblogs and Social Media (ICWSM)*, pages 384–385, 2010.

[147] Jack G. Conrad, Jochen L. Leidner, Frank Schilder, and Ravi Kondadadi. Query-based opinion summarization for legal blog entries. In *Proceedings of the 12th International Conference on Artificial Intelligence and Law*, pages 167–176, 2009.

[148] D. Conte, P. Foggia, C. Sansone, and M. Vento. Thirty years of graph matching in pattern recognition. *International Journal of Pattern Recognition and Artificial Intelligence*, 18(3):265–298, 2004.

[149] D. Coppersmith and S. Winograd. Matrix multiplication via arithmetic progressions. In *Proceedings of the 19th Annual ACM Conference on Theory of Computing (STOC)*, pages 1–6, 1987.

[150] L. P. Cordella, P. Foggia, C. Sansone, and M. Vento. A (sub)graph isomorphism algorithm for matching large graphs. *IEEE Transactions Pattern Analysis and Machine Intelligence*, 26(10):1367–1372, October 2004.

[151] Corpus of Spontaneous Japanese. Project Web Site: http://www.ninjal.ac.jp/products-k/katsudo/seika/corpus/public/.

[152] Frank Thomas Coulson. *The "Vulgate" Commentary on Ovid's Metamorphoses: The Creation Myth and the Story of Orpheus.* Toronto Medieval Latin Texts. Pontifical Institute of Mediaeval Studies for the Centre for Medieval Studies, 1991.

[153] Frank Thomas Coulson. *Weaving the Web.* Orion Business Books, 1999.

[154] Valter Crescenzi, Giansalvatore Mecca, and Paolo Merialdo. Roadrunner: Towards automatic data extraction from large Web sites. In *Proceedings of the 27th VLDB*, pages 109–118, 2001.

[155] Fabio Crestani and Puay Leng Lee. Searching the Web by constrained spreading activation. *Information Processing and Management*, 36(4):585–605, 2000.

[156] H. Cui, V. O. Mittal, and M. Datar. Comparative experiments on sentiment classification for online product reviews. In *Proceedings of the 21st National Conference on Artificial Intelligence*, pages 1265–1270, Menlo Park, CA, AAAI Press, 2006.

[157] A. Culotta and J. Sorensen. Dependency tree kernels for relation extraction. In *Proceedings ACL*, pages 423–429, 2004.

[158] James Curran. Rethinking Internet history. In James Curran, Natalie Fenton, and Des Freedman, editors, *Misunderstanding the Internet*, pages 34–65. Routledge, 2012.

[159] Adnan Darwiche. *Modeling and Reasoning with Bayesian Networks.* Cambridge University Press, 2009.

[160] D. Das and S. Bandyopadhyay. Labeling emotion in Bengali blog corpus—A fine-grained tagging at sentence level. In *Proceedings of the 8th Workshop on Asian Language Resources*, pages 47–55, 2010.

[161] S. Dasgupta and V. Ng. Topic-wise, sentiment-wise, or otherwise? Identifying the hidden dimension for unsupervised text classification. In *Proceedings of the 2009 Conference on Empirical Methods in Natural Language Processing*, pages 580–589, 2009.

[162] K. Dave, S. Lawrence, and D. M. Pennock. Mining the peanut gallery: Opinion extraction and semantic classification of product reviews. In *Proceedings of WWW'03: The 12th International Conference on World Wide Web*, pages 519–528. New York, NY, ACM Press, 2003.

[163] K. De Grave and F. Costa. Molecular graph augmentation with rings and functional groups. *Journal of Chemical Information and Modeling*, 50(9):1660–1668, 2010.

[164] L. De Raedt and J. Ramon. Condensed representations for inductive logic programming. In D. Dubois, C. A. Welty, and M. Williams, editors, *Proceedings of 9th International Conference on the Principles of Knowledge Representation and Reasoning*, pages 438–446. AAAI Press, 2004.

[165] Wim De Smet and Marie-Francine Moens. Cross-language linking of news stories on the Web using interlingual topic modeling. In *Proceedings of the CIKM 2009 Workshop on Social Web Search and Mining*, pages 57–64. ACM, 2009.

[166] Wim De Smet and Marie-Francine Moens. Representations for multidocument event clustering. *Data Mining and Knowledge Discovery*, 26(3):533–558, May 2013.

[167] Scott Deerwester, Susan T. Dumais, George W. Furnas, Thomas K. Landauer, and Richard Harshman. Indexing by latent semantic analysis. *Journal of the American Society for Information Science*, 41(6):391–407, 1990.

[168] A. P. Dempster, N. M. Laird, and D. B. Rubin. Maximum likelihood from incomplete data via the EM algorithm. *Journal of the Royal Statistical Society*, 39:1–38, 1977.

[169] N. Diakopoulos, M. Naaman, and F. Kivran-Swaine. Diamonds in the rough: Social media visual analytics for journalistic inquiry. In *Proceedings of the IEEE Conference on Visual Analytics Science and Technology*, pages 115–122, 2010.

[170] R. Diestel. *Graph Theory*. Springer-Verlag, 2nd Edition, 2000.

[171] R. Diestel. *Graph Theory*. Springer-Verlag, 4th Edition, 2010.

[172] Shilin Ding, Gao Cong, Chin-Yew Lin, and Xiaoyan Zhu. Using conditional random fields to extract contexts and answers of questions from

online forums. In *Meeting of the Association for Computational Linguistics*, pages 710–718, 2008.

[173] X. Ding, B. Liu, and P. S. Yu. A holistic lexicon-based approach to opinion mining. In *Proceedings of the International Conference on Web Search and Web Data Mining*, pages 231–240, 2008.

[174] Pavel A. Dmitriev, Nadav Eiron, Marcus Fontoura, and Eugene J. Shekita. Using annotations in enterprise search. In *Proceedings WWW*, pages 811–817, 2006.

[175] Marcos Aurélio Domingues, Fabien Gouyon, Alípio Mário Jorge, José Paulo Leal, João Vinagre, Luís Lemos, and Mohamed Sordo. Combining usage and content in an online music recommendation system for music in the long-tail. In *Proceedings of the 21st International Conference Companion on World Wide Web, WWW'12 Companion*, pages 925–930, 2012.

[176] M. Dork, D. Gruen, C. Williamson, and S. Carpendale. A visual backchannel for large-scale events. *IEEE Transactions on Visualization and Computer Graphics*, 16(6):1129–1138, November 2010.

[177] Zhicheng Dou, Ruihua Song, and Ji-Rong Wen. A large-scale evaluation and analysis of personalized search strategies. In *Proceedings WWW*, pages 581–590, 2007.

[178] Fred Douglis. Thanks for the fish—But I'm drowning! *IEEE Internet Computing*, 14:4–6, 2010.

[179] Doug Downey, Susan Dumais, and Eric Horvitz. Heads and tails: Studies of Web search with common and rare queries. In *Proceedings of the 30th Annual International ACM SIGIR Conference on Research and Development in Information Retrieval, SIGIR'07*, pages 847–848. New York, NY, ACM, 2007.

[180] Doug Downey, Oren Etzioni, and Stephen Soderland. A probabilistic model of redundancy in information extraction. In *IJCAI'05 Proceedings of the 19th International Joint Conference on Artificial Intelligence*, pages 1034–1041, 2005.

[181] J. Stephen Downie. The scientific evaluation of music information retrieval systems: Foundations and future. *Computer Music Journal*, 28:12–23, June 2004.

[182] Gideon Dror, Noam Koenigstein, and Yehuda Koren. Yahoo! Music recommendations: Modeling music ratings with temporal dynamics and item taxonomy. In *Proceedings of RecSys*, Chicago, IL, October 2011.

[183] Gideon Dror, Noam Koenigstein, Yehuda Koren, and Markus Weimer. The Yahoo! Music dataset and KDD-Cup'11. *Journal of Machine Learning Research*, 18:3–18, 2011.

[184] N. Du, C. Faloutsos, B. Wang, and L. Akoghi. Large human communication networks: Patterns and a utility-driven generator. In *Proceedings of 15th ACM-SIGKDD International Conference on Knowledge Discovery and Data Mining*, pages 107–115, 2009.

[185] Huizhong Duan, Yunbo Cao, Chin-Yew Lin, and Yong Yu. Searching questions by identifying question topic and question focus. In *Proceedings of 46th Annual Meeting of the Association for Computational Linguistics*, pages 156–164, 2008.

[186] Micah Dubinko, Ravi Kumar, Joseph Magnani, Jasmine Novak, Prabhakar Raghavan, and Andrew Tomkins. Visualizing tags over time. *TWEB*, 1(2), 2007.

[187] Olivier Duchenne, Ivan Laptev, Josef Sivic, Francis Bach, and Jean Ponce. Automatic annotation of human actions in video. In *Proceedings of ICCV*, pages 1491–1498, 2009.

[188] Francisco Echarte, Jose Javier Astrain, Alberto Córdoba, and Jesus Villadangos. Pattern matching techniques to identify syntactic variations of tags in folksonomies. In *Proceedings of the 1st World Summit on the Knowledge Society: Emerging Technologies and Information Systems for the Knowledge Society, WSKS'08*, pages 557–564. Berlin, Heidelberg, Springer-Verlag, 2008.

[189] Douglas Eck, Paul Lamere, Thierry Bertin-Mahieux, and Stephen Green. Automatic generation of social tags for music recommendation. In *Advances in Neural Information Processing Systems 20 (NIPS'07)*. MIT Press, 2008.

[190] Patrick Van Eecke and Maarten Truyens. *Analyzing Privacy and IPR Related Legislation on the PARIS Objectives*. Technical report, 2013.

[191] Miles Efron. Hashtag retrieval in a microblogging environment. In Fabio Crestani, Stéphane Marchand-Maillet, Hsin-Hsi Chen, Efthimis N. Efthimiadis, and Jacques Savoy, editors, *Proceedings of SIGIR*, pages 787–788. ACM, 2010.

[192] Miles Efron. Information search and retrieval in microblogs. *Journal of the American Society of Information Science and Technology*, 62(6):996–1008, June 2011.

[193] Miles Efron, Peter Organisciak, and Katrina Fenlon. Improving retrieval of short texts through document expansion. In William R. Hersh, Jamie Callan, Yoelle Maarek, and Mark Sanderson, editors, *Proceedings of SIGIR*, pages 911–920. ACM, 2012.

[194] Miles Efron, Don Turnbull, and Carlos Ovalle. University of Texas School of Information at TREC 2007. In Voorhees and Buckland [689].

[195] Einat Minkov, William W. Cohen, and Andrew Y. Ng. Contextual search and name disambiguation in e-mail using graphs. In *SIGIR'06: Proceedings of the 29th Annual International ACM SIGIR Conference on Research and Development in Information Retrieval*, 2006.

[196] J. Eisenstein, D. H. P. Chau, A. Kittur, and E. Xing. Topicviz: Semantic navigation of document collections. In *CHI Work-in-Progress Paper (Supplemental Proceedings)*, 2012.

[197] J. Eisenstein, B. O'Connor, N. A. Smith, and E. P. Xing. A latent variable model for geographic lexical variation. In *Proceedings of the 2010 Conference on Empirical Methods in Natural Language Processing*, pages 1277–1287, 2010.

[198] P. Ekman. An argument for basic emotions. *Cognition and Emotion*, 6:169–200, 1992.

[199] Mahmoud El-Haj, Udo Kruschwitz, and Chris Fox. Using mechanical Turk to create a corpus of Arabic summaries. In *Proceedings of the 7th Conference on International Language Resources and Evaluation*, 2010.

[200] Jonathan L. Elsas, Jaime Arguello, Jamie Callan, and Jaime G. Carbonell. Retrieval and feedback models for blog distillation. In Voorhees and Buckland [689].

[201] Jonathan L. Elsas, Jaime Arguello, Jamie Callan, and Jaime G. Carbonell. Retrieval and feedback models for blog feed search. In Sung-Hyon Myaeng, Douglas W. Oard, Fabrizio Sebastiani, Tat-Seng Chua, and Mun-Kew Leong, editors, *Proceedings SIGIR*, pages 347–354. ACM, 2008.

[202] Jonathan L. Elsas and Jaime G. Carbonell. It pays to be picky: An evaluation of thread retrieval in online forums. In Allan et al. [21], pages 714–715.

[203] Chris Engels, Koen Deschacht, Jan Hendrik Becker, Tinne Tuytelaars, Marie-Francine Moens, and Luc Van Gool. Automatic annotation of unique locations from video and text. In *Proceedings of 21st British Machine Vision Conference*, pages 1–11, 2010.

[204] P. Erdős and A. Rényi. On random graphs. *Publicationes Mathematicae (Debrecen)*, 6:290–297, 1959.

[205] P. Erdős and A. Rényi. On the evolution of random graphs. *Publications of the Mathematical Institute of the Hungarian Academy of Sciences*, 5:17–61, 1960.

[206] S. Erjavec, T. Erjavec, and A. Kilgarriff. A Web corpus and word sketches for Japanese. Technical report, 2008.

[207] Güneş Erkan and Dragomir R. Radev. LexPageRank: Prestige in multi-document text summarization. In *Proceedings EMNLP*, pages 365–371, 2004.

[208] Günes Erkan and Dragomir R. Radev. Lexrank: Graph-based lexical centrality as salience in text summarization. *Journal of Artificial Intelligence Research*, 22(1):457–479, 2004.

[209] A. Esuli and F. Sebastiani. Sentiwordnet: A publicly available lexical resource for opinion mining. In *Proceedings of the 5th Conference on Language Resources and Evaluation*, pages 417–422, 2006.

[210] Anthony Fader, Stephen Soderland, and Oren Etzioni. Identifying relations for open information extraction. In *Proceedings of the Conference on Empirical Methods in Natural Language Processing*, pages 1535–1545, 2011.

[211] Christos Faloutsos and Douglas W. Oard. A survey of information retrieval and filtering methods. Technical report, College Park, MD, 1995.

[212] S. Faridani, E. Bitton, K. Ryokai, and K. Goldberg. Opinion space: A scalable tool for browsing online comments. In *Proceedings of the 28th International Conference on Human Factors in Computing Systems (CHI)*, pages 1175–1184, 2010.

[213] Christiane Fellbaum, editor. *WordNet: An Electronic Lexical Database.* Cambridge, MA, MIT Press, 1998.

[214] Paul Ferguson, Neil O'Hare, James Lanagan, Owen Phelan, and Kevin McCarthy. An investigation of term weighting approaches for microblog retrieval. In Baeza-Yates et al. [40], pages 552–555.

[215] D. A. Ferrucci. Introduction to "This is Watson." *IBM Journal of Research and Development*, 56(3.4):1:1–1:15, May–June 2012.

[216] C. Fiedler and M. Borgelt. Support computation for mining frequent subgraphs in a single graph. In *Proceedings of the 5th Workshop on Mining and Learning with Graphs (MLG'07)*, 2007.

[217] Ben Fields, Kurt Jacobson, Christophe Rhodes, and Michael Casey. Social playlists and bottleneck measurements: Exploiting musician social graphs using content-based dissimilarity and pairwise maximum flow values. In *Proceedings of ISMIR*, pages 287–292, Philadelphia, PA, September 2008.

[218] Ben Fields, Kurt Jacobson, Christophe Rhodes, Mark d'Inverno, Mark Sandler, and Michael Casey. Analysis and exploitation of musician social networks for recommendation and discovery. *IEEE Transactions on Multimedia*, 13(4):674–686, August 2011.

[219] Clay Fink, Christine Piatko, James Mayfield, Tim Finin, and Justin Martineau. Geolocating blogs from their textual content. In *Working Notes of the AAAI Spring Symposium on Social Semantic Web: Where Web 2.0 Meets Web 3.0*, pages 1–2. AAAI Press, 2008.

[220] A. Finn, N. Kushmerick, and B. Smyth. Genre classification and domain transfer for information filtering. In *Proceedings ECIR Lecture Notes in Computer Science*, volume 2291, pages 349–352, 2002.

[221] Michael Ben Fleischman. Multidocument person name resolution. In *Proceedings of ACL*, 2004.

[222] Yoav Freund, Raj Iyer, Robert E. Schapire, and Yoram Singer. An efficient boosting algorithm for combining preferences. *Journal of Machine Learning Research*, 4:933–969, December 2003.

[223] M. Fürer and P. K. Shiva. Approximately counting embeddings into random graphs. In *Proceedings of the 11th International Workshop, APPROX 2008, and 12th International Workshop, RANDOM 2008 on Approximation, Randomization and Combinatorial Optimization: Algorithms and Techniques*, pages 416–429. Berlin, Heidelberg, Springer-Verlag, 2008.

[224] Evgeniy Gabrilovich and Shaul Markovitch. Computing semantic relatedness using Wikipedia-based explicit semantic analysis. In *Proceedings of the 20th International Joint Conference on Artificial Intelligence (IJCAI 2007)*, pages 1606–1611, 2007.

[225] M. Gamon. Sentiment classification on customer feedback data: Noisy data, large feature vectors, and the role of linguistic analysis. In *Proceedings of the 20th International Conference on Computational Linguistics*. Morristown, NJ, ACL, 2004.

[226] M. Gamon, A. Aue, S. Corston-Oliver, and E. Ringger. Pulse: Mining customer opinions from free text. In *Advances in Intelligent Data Analysis*, volume 3646 of *Lecture Notes in Computer Science*, pages 121–132. Springer, 2005.

[227] Kavita Ganesan, ChengXiang Zhai, and Jiawei Han. Opinosis: A graph-based approach to abstractive summarization of highly redundant opinions. In *Proceedings of the 23rd International Conference on Computational Linguistics (COLING'10)*, 2010.

[228] Kavita Ganesan, ChengXiang Zhai, and Evelyne Viegas. Micropinion generation: An unsupervised approach to generating ultra-concise summaries of opinions. In *Proceedings of the 21st International Conference on World Wide Web, WWW'12*, pages 869–878, 2012.

[229] Dehong Gao, Renxian Zhang, Wenjie Li, Raymond Yiu-Keung Lau, and Kam-Fai Wong. Learning features through feedback for blog distillation. In Wei-Ying Ma, Jian-Yun Nie, Ricardo A. Baeza-Yates, Tat-Seng Chua, and W. Bruce Croft, editors, *Proceedings SIGIR*, pages 1085–1086. ACM, 2011.

[230] Xiangzhu Gao, San Murugesan, and Bruce W. N. Lo. A simple method to extract key terms. *IJEB*, 4(3/4):221–238, 2006.

[231] Florent Garcin, Boi Faltings, Radu Jurca, and Nadine Joswig. Rating aggregation in collaborative filtering systems. In *Proceedings of the 3rd ACM Conference on Recommender Systems, RecSys'09*, pages 349–352. New York, NY, ACM, 2009.

[232] G. C. Garriga, R. Khardon, and L. De Raedt. On mining closed sets in multirelational data. In *Proceedings of the 20th International Joint Conference on Artificial Intelligence*, pages 804–809, 2007.

[233] R. Geisberger, P. Sanders, D. Schultes, and D. Delling. Contraction hierarchies: Faster and simpler hierarchical routing in road networks. In *Proceedings of the 7th Workshop on Experimental Algorithms*, pages 319–333, 2008.

[234] Gijs Geleijnse and Jan Korst. Web-based artist categorization. In *Proceedings of ISMIR*, Victoria, Canada, October 2006.

[235] Marco De Gemmis, Leo Iaquinta, Pasquale Lops, Cataldo Musto, Fedelucio Narducci, and Giovanni Semeraro. Preference learning in recommender systems. In *Preference Learning (PL-09) ECML/PKDD-09 Workshop*, Volume 41, 2009.

[236] L. Getoor and B. Taskar. *An Introduction to Statistical Relational Learning*. MIT Press, 2007.

[237] E. N. Gilbert. Random graphs. *The Annals of Mathematical Statistics*, 30(4):1141–1144, December 1959.

[238] Dan Gillick and Yang Liu. Nonexpert evaluation of summarization systems is risky. In *Proceedings of the NAACL HLT 2010 Workshop on Creating Speech and Language Data with Amazon's Mechanical Turk*, pages 148–151, 2010.

[239] K. Głowińska and A. Przepiórkowski. The design of syntactic annotation levels in the national corpus of Polish. In *Proceedings of LREC*, 2010.

[240] Andrea Glaser and Hinrich Schütze. Automatic generation of short informative sentiment summaries. In *Proceedings of the 13th Conference of the European Chapter of the Association for Computational Linguistics*, pages 276–285, Avignon, France, April 2012.

[241] A. Go, R. Bhayani, and L. Huang. Twitter sentiment classification using distant supervision. Technical report CS224N Project Report, Stanford University, 2009.

[242] S. A. Golder and M. W. Macy. Diurnal and seasonal mood vary with work, sleep and daylength across diverse cultures. *Science*, 2011.

[243] Scott A. Golder and Bernardo A. Huberman. Usage patterns of collaborative tagging systems. *Journal of Information Science*, 32(2):198–208, 2006.

[244] S. Goldman and Y. Zhou. Enhancing supervised learning with unlabeled data. In *Proceedings of the 17th International Conference on Machine Learning*, pages 327–334, 2000.

[245] G. Golub and W. Kahan. Calculating the singular values and pseudo-inverse of a matrix. *Journal of the Society for Industrial and Applied Mathematics: Series B, Numerical Analysis*, pages 205–224, 1965.

[246] S. Gouws, D. Metzler, C. Cai, and E. Hovy. Contextual bearing on linguistic variation in social media. In *Proceedings of the Workshop on Languages in Social Media, LSM'11*, pages 20–29, 2011.

[247] Sten Govaerts and Erik Duval. A Web-based approach to determine the origin of an artist. In *Proceedings of ISMIR*, Kobe, Japan, October 2009.

[248] Maarten Grachten, Markus Schedl, Tim Pohle, and Gerhard Widmer. The ISMIR cloud: A decade of ISMIR conferences at your fingertips. In *Proceedings of ISMIR*, Kobe, Japan, October 2009.

[249] B. M. Gross. *The Managing of Organizations: The Administrative Struggle*. New York, The Free Press, 1964.

[250] J. L. Gross and J. Yellen. *Handbook of Graph Theory*. CRC Press, 2004.

[251] Ziyu Guan, Jiajun Bu, Qiaozhu Mei, Chun Chen, and Can Wang. Personalized tag recommendation using graph-based ranking on multitype interrelated objects. In *Proceedings of the 32nd International ACM SIGIR Conference on Research and Development in Information Retrieval, SIGIR'09*, pages 540–547. New York, NY, ACM, 2009.

[252] R. Gugisch and C. Rucker. Unified generation of conformations, conformers and steroisomers: A discrete mathematics approach. *MATCH Communications in Mathematics and Computer Chemistry*, 61:117–148, 2009.

[253] GuoDong Zhou , Jian Su, Jie Zhang, and Min Zhang. Exploring various knowledge in relation extraction. In *ACL*, pages 427–434, 2005.

[254] Narendra Gupta, Giuseppe Di Fabbrizio, and Patrick Haffner. Capturing the stars: Predicting ratings for service and product reviews. In *Proceedings of the NAACL HLT 2010 Workshop on Semantic Search*, pages 36–43, Los Angeles, CA, June 2010.

[255] Karl Gyllstrom and Marie-Francine Moens. Wisdom of the ages: Toward delivering the children's Web with the link-based age-rank algorithm. In *Proceedings of CIKM*, pages 159–168, 2010.

[256] H. Yeye and X. C. Dong. Seisa set expansion by iterative similarity aggregation. In *Proceedings of WWW*, pages 427–436, 2011.

[257] Y. H. Zhai and B. Liu. Web data extraction based on partial tree alignment. In *Proceedings of the International World Wide Web Conference*, pages 76–85, 2005.

[258] P. Halacsy, A. Kornai, L. Nemeth, A. Rung, I. Szakadat, and V. Tron. Creating open language resources for Hungarian. In *Proceedings of LREC*, 2004.

[259] Amanda Hallay and Fiona McDonald. *The Popular History of Graffiti: From the Ancient World to the Present.* Toronto Medieval Latin Texts. Skyhorse Publishing Company, 2013.

[260] Harry Halpin, Valentin Robu, and Hana Shepherd. The complex dynamics of collaborative tagging. In *Proceedings of WWW*, pages 211–220, 2007.

[261] K. Hammond, R. Burke, C. Martin, and S. Lytinen. FAQ finder: A case-based approach to knowledge navigation. In *Conference on Artificial Intelligence Applications*, pages 80–86, 1995.

[262] B. Han and T. Baldwin. Lexical normalisation of short text messages: Makn sens a #twitter. In *Proceedings of the 49th Annual Meeting of the Association for Computational Linguistics: Human Language Technologies, HLT'11*, pages 368–378, 2011.

[263] J. Han, J. Pei, and Y. Yin. Mining frequent patterns without candidate generation. In *Proceedings of the 2000 ACM SIGMID International Conference on Management of Data*, pages 1–12, 2000.

[264] Xianpei Han, Le Sun, and Jun Zhao. Collective entity linking in Web text: A graph-based method. In *Proceedings of the 34th Annual ACM SIGIR Conference on Research and Development in Information Retrieval*, pages 765–774, 2011.

[265] Xianpei Han and Jun Zhao. Named entity disambiguation by leveraging Wikipedia semantic knowledge. In *Proceedings of CIKM*, 2009.

[266] Xianpei Han and Jun Zhao. Structural semantic relatedness: A knowledge-based method to named entity disambiguation. In *Proceedings of the 48th Annual Meeting of the Association for Computational Linguistics (ACL)*, pages 50–59, 2010.

[267] Uri Hanani, Bracha Shapira, and Peretz Shoval. Information filtering: Overview of issues, research and systems. *User Modeling and User-Adapted Interaction*, 11(3):203–259, August 2001.

[268] J. T. Hancock, C. Landrigan, and C. Silver. Expressing emotion in text-based communication. In *Proceedings of the SIGCHI Conference on Human Factors in Computing Systems*, pages 929–932. New York, NY, ACM Press, 2007.

[269] David Hannah, Craig Macdonald, Jie Peng, Ben He, and Iadh Ounis. University of Glasgow at TREC 2007: Experiments in blog and enterprise tracks with Terrier. In Voorhees and Buckland [689].

[270] Sanda Harabagiu and Andrew Hickl. Relevance modeling for microblog summarization. In *Proceedings of the 5th International Conference on Weblogs and Social Media (ICWSM)*, 2011.

[271] F. Maxwell Harper, Daphne Raban, Sheizaf Rafaeli, and Joseph A. Konstan. Predictors of answer quality in online Q&A sites. In *Proceedings of the 26th Annual SIGCHI Conference on Human Factors in Computing Systems, CHI'08*, pages 865–874. New York, NY, ACM, 2008.

[272] C. Hashimoto, S. Kurohashi, D. Kawahara, K. Shinzato, and M. Nagata. Construction of a blog corpus with syntactic, anaphoric, and sentiment annotations [in Japanese]. *Journal of Natural Language Processing*, 18(2):175–201, 2011.

[273] Ahmed Hassan, Dragomir R. Radev, Junghoo Cho, and Amruta Joshi. Content-based recommendation and summarization in the blogosphere. In *Proceedings of the 3rd International Conference on Weblogs and Social Media (ICWSM)*, 2009.

[274] V. Hatzivassiloglou and J. Wiebe. Effects of adjective orientation and gradability on sentence subjectivity. In *Proceedings of the 18th Conference on Computational Linguistics*, pages 299–305, 2000.

[275] David Hawking and Paul Thomas. Server selection methods in hybrid portal search. In Ricardo A. Baeza-Yates, Nivio Ziviani, Gary Marchionini, Alistair Moffat, and John Tait, editors, *SIGIR*, pages 75–82. ACM, 2005.

[276] Jiyin He, Wouter Weerkamp, Martha Larson, and Maarten de Rijke. An effective coherence measure to determine topical consistency in user-generated content. *International Journal on Document Analysis and Recognition*, 12(3):185–203, October 2009.

[277] Y. He and D. Zhou. Self-training from labeled features for sentiment analysis. *Information Processing and Management*, 47(4):606–616, 2011.

[278] Marti A. Hearst. Automatic acquisition of hyponyms from large text corpora. In *Proceedings of the COLING-92*, pages 539–545, 1992.

[279] A. Hearst. A hybrid approach to restricted text interpretation, *In Proceedings of AAAI Spring Symposium on Text-Based Intelligent Systems*, Stanford University, March 1990.

[280] Marti A. Hearst. A hybrid approach to restricted text interpretation, In *Proceedings of AAAI Spring Symposium on Text-Based Intelligent Systems*, Stanford University, March 1990.

[281] Monika Rauch Henzinger, Allan Heydon, Michael Mitzenmacher, and Marc Najork. Measuring index quality using random walks on the Web. *Computer Networks*, 31(11–16):1291–1303, 1999.

[282] Ralf Herbrich, Tom Minka, and Thore Graepel. TrueSkill^{TM}: A Bayesian skill rating system. In *Neural Information Processing Systems*, pages 569–576, 2006.

[283] Andrew Hickl, Kirk Roberts, Bryan Rink, Jeremy Bensley, Tobias Jungen, Ying Shi, and John Williams. Question-answering with LCC's *CHAUCER-2 at TREC 2007*. In Voorhees and Buckland [689].

[284] R. Hidderley and P. Rafferty. Democrating indexing: An approach to the retrieval of fiction. *Information Services and Use*, 17(23):101–109, 1997.

[285] I. Hiejima. *A Short Dictionary of Feelings and Emotions in English and Japanese*. Tokyodo Shuppan, 1995.

[286] H. Hofer, C. Borgelt, and M. Berthold. Large-scale mining of molecular fragments with wildcards. In *Advances in Intelligent Data Analysis V*, pages 380–389, 2003.

[287] J. Hoffart, F. M. Suchanek, K. Berberich, E. Lewis Kelham, G. Melo, and G. Weikum. Yago2: Exploring and querying world knowledge in time, space, context, and many languages. In *Proceedings of the 20th International Conference Companion on World Wide Web*, pages 229–232, 2011.

[288] Raphael Hoffmann, Congle Zhang, and Daniel S. Weld. Learning 5000 relational extractors. In *Proceedings of ACL*, 2010.

[289] Thomas Hofmann. Probabilistic latent semantic indexing. In *Proceedings of ACM SIGIR*, pages 50–57, 1999.

[290] L. E. Holzman and W. M. Pottenger. Classification of emotions in Internet chat: An application of machine learning using speech phonemes. Technical report LU-CSE-03-002, Lehigh University, 2003.

[291] P. Hopper and S. Thompson. The iconicity of the universal categories "noun" and "verbs." In *Typological Studies in Language: Iconicity and Syntax*, pages 151–183. John Benjamins Publishing Company, 1985.

[292] Damon Horowitz and Sepandar D. Kamvar. The anatomy of a large-scale social search engine. In *Proceedings of the 19th International Conference on World Wide Web, WWW'10*, pages 431–440. New York, NY, ACM, 2010.

[293] T. Horváth and J. Ramon. Efficient frequent connected subgraph mining in graphs of bounded treewidth. In *Proceedings of Principles and Practice of Knowledge Discovery in Databases 2008*, volume 5211, pages 520–535, Antwerp, Belgium, Springer-Verlag, September 2008.

[294] T. Horváth, J. Ramon, and S. Wrobel. Frequent subgraph mining in outerplanar graphs. *Knowledge Discovery and Data Mining*, 24:472–508, 2010.

[295] Tamás Horváthh and Jan Ramon. Efficient frequent connected subgraph mining in graphs of bounded tree-width. *Theoretical Computer Science*, 411:2784–2797, 2010.

[296] Andreas Hotho, Robert Jäschke, Christoph Schmitz, and Gerd Stumme. Information retrieval in folksonomies: Search and ranking. In *Proceedings of ESWC*, pages 411–426, 2006.

[297] Eduard Hovy, Laurie Gerber, Ulf Hermjakob, Chin-Yew Lin, and Deepak Ravichandran. Toward semantics-based answer pinpointing. In *Proceedings of the 1st International Conference on Human Language Technology Research, HLT'01*, pages 1–7. Stroudsburg, PA, ACL, 2001.

[298] M. Hu and B. Liu. Mining and summarizing customer reviews. In *KDD'04: Proceedings of the 10th ACM SIGKDD International Conference on Knowledge Discovery and Data Mining*, pages 168–177. New York, NY, ACM, 2004.

[299] Meishan Hu, Aixin Sun, and Ee-Peng Lim. Comments-oriented blog summarization by sentence extraction. In *Proceedings of the 16th ACM Conference on Conference on Information and Knowledge Management (CIKM)*, pages 901–904, 2007.

[300] T.-H. Hubert Chan, K. L. Chang, and R. Raman. An SDP primal-dual algorithm for approximating the Lovász-theta function. In *Proceedings ISIT*, pages 2808–2812. IEEE, 2009.

[301] A. Hubmann-Haidvogel, A. M. P. Brasoveanu, A. Scharl, M. Sabou, and S. Gindl. Visualizing contextual and dynamic features of micropost streams. In *Proceedings of the #MSM2012 Workshop, CEUR*, volume 838, 2012.

[302] Jenq-Neng Hwang, Shyh-Rong Lay, and A. Lippman. Nonparametric multivariate density estimation: A comparative study. *Transactions on Signal Processing*, 42(10):2795–2810, October 1994.

[303] Piotr Indyk and Rajeev Motwani. Approximate nearest neighbors: Towards removing the curse of dimensionality. In *Proceedings of the 30th Annual ACM Symposium on Theory of Computing*, pages 604–613. ACM, 1998.

[304] A. Inokuchi. Mining generalized substructures from a set of labeled graphs. In *ICDM*, pages 415–418. IEEE Computer Society, 2004.

[305] A. Inokuchi, Washio T., and H. Motoda. Complete mining of frequent patterns from graphs: Mining graph data. *Machine Learning*, 50(3):321–354, 2003.

[306] David Inouye and Jugal K. Kalita. Comparing Twitter summarization algorithms for multiple post summaries. In *SocialCom/PASSAT*, pages 298–306, 2011.

[307] Daisuke Ishikawa, Tetsuya Sakai, and Noriko Kando. NTCIR-8 community QA pilot task (part i): The test collection and the task. In *NTCIR-8*, pages 421–432, 2010.

[308] A. Itai and M. Rodeh. Finding a minimum circuit in a graph. *SIAM Journal on Computation*, 7(4):413–423, 1978.

[309] G. Iyengar, D. J. Phillips, and C. Stein. Approximating semidefinite packing problems. Technical report, IEOR Department, Columbia University, New York, June 2009.

[310] J. Judd and J. Kalita. Better Twitter summaries? In *Proceedings of HLT-NAACL*, 2013.

[311] J. Ulrich, G. Murray, and G. Carenini. A publicly available annotated corpus for supervised email summarization. In *AAAI08 EMAIL Workshop*, pages 77–82, 2008.

[312] Lamjed Ben Jabeur, Lynda Tamine, and Mohand Boughanem. Uprising microblogs: A Bayesian network retrieval model for tweet search. In Sascha Ossowski and Paola Lecca, editors, *Proceedings SAC*, pages 943–948. ACM, 2012.

[313] H. J. Jackson. *Marginalia*. Yale University Press, 2001.

[314] Artiles Javier, Gonzalo Julio, and Sekine Satoshi. The Semeval-2007 WePS evaluation: Establishing a benchmark for the Web people search task. In *Proceedings of the 4th International Workshop on Semantic Evaluations (SemEval 2007)*, pages 64–69, June 2007.

[315] Artiles Javier, Gonzalo Julio, and Sekine Satoshi. WePS 2 evaluation campaign: Overview of the Web people search clustering task. In *2nd Web People Search Evaluation Workshop (WePS 2009) on 18th WWW Conference*, 2009.

[316] Klaus Bruhn Jensen. New media, old methods—Internet methodologies and the online/offline divide. In Mia Consalvo and Charles Ess, editors, *The Handbook of Internet Studies*, pages 43–58. Wiley-Blackwell, 2011.

[317] Jiwoon Jeon, W. Bruce Croft, and Joon Ho Lee. Finding semantically similar questions based on their answers. In *Proceedings of the 28th Annual International ACM SIGIR Conference on Research and Development in Information Retrieval*, pages 617–618. ACM, 2005.

[318] Jiwoon Jeon, W. Bruce Croft, and Joon Ho Lee. Finding similar questions in large question and answer archives. In *Proceedings of the 14th ACM International Conference on Information and Knowledge Management, CIKM'05*, pages 84–90. New York, NY, ACM, 2005.

[319] Jiwoon Jeon, W. Bruce Croft, Joon Ho Lee, and Soyeon Park. A framework to predict the quality of answers with nontextual features. In *Proceedings of the 29th Annual International ACM SIGIR Conference on Research and Development in Information Retrieval*, pages 228–235, 2006.

[320] Valentin Jijkoun and Maarten de Rijke. Retrieving answers from frequently asked questions pages on the Web. In *International Conference on Information and Knowledge Management*, pages 76–83, 2005.

[321] Song Jin, Hongfei Lin, and Sui Su. Query expansion based on folksonomy tag co-occurrence analysis. In *Proceedings of GRC*, pages 300–305. IEEE, 2009.

[322] W. Jin, H. H. Ho, and R. K. Srihari. Opinionminer: A novel machine learning system for Web opinion mining. In *Proceedings of the 15th ACM SIGKDD International Conference on Knowledge Discovery and Data Mining*, pages 1195–1204, 2009.

[323] Thorsten Joachims. Optimizing search engines using click-through data. In *8th International Conference on Knowledge Discovery and Data Mining*, pages 133–142, 2002.

[324] D. S. Johnson, C. H. Papadimitriou, and M. Yannakakis. On generating all maximal independent sets. *Information Processing Letters*, 27(3):119–123, 1988.

[325] Joseph Hassell, Aleman-Meza Boanerges, and I. Arpinar. Ontology-driven automatic entity disambiguation in unstructured text. In *Proceedings of Semantic Web—ISWC 2006*, pages 44–57, 2006.

[326] Pawel Jurczyk and Eugene Agichtein. Discovering authorities in question answer communities by using link analysis. In *Proceedings of the 16th ACM Conference on Conference on Information and Knowledge Management, CIKM'07*, pages 919–922. New York, NY, ACM, 2007.

[327] D. Justice and A. Hero. A binary linear programming formulation of the graph edit distance. *IEEE Trans. Pattern Analysis and Machine Intelligence*, 28(8):1200–1214, August 2006.

[328] Dmitri V. Kalashnikov. A Web-querying approach to Web people search. In *SIGIR*, 2008.

[329] Toshihiro Kamishima, Masahiro Hamasaki, and Shotaro Akaho. Trbagg: A simple transfer learning method and its application to personalization in collaborative tagging. In *Proceedings of ICDM*, pages 219–228, 2009.

[330] J. Kamps, M. Marx, R. J. Mokken, and M. de Rijke. Using WordNet to measure semantic orientation of adjectives. In *Proceedings of the 4th International Conference on Language Resources and Evaluation*, pages 1115–1118, 2004.

[331] H. Kanayama and T. Nasukawa. Fully automatic lexicon expansion for domain-oriented sentiment analysis. In *Proceedings of the 2006 Conference on Empirical Methods in Natural Language Processing*, pages 355–363, 2006.

[332] Slava M. Katz. Estimation of probabilities from sparse data for the language model component of a speech recognizer. *Acoustics, Speech and Signal Processing, IEEE Transactions on*, 35(3):400–401, March 1987.

[333] Mostafa Keikha, Mark James Carman, and Fabio Crestani. Blog distillation using random walks. In Allan et al. [21], pages 638–639.

[334] Mostafa Keikha and Fabio Crestani. Effectiveness of aggregation methods in blog distillation. In Troels Andreasen, Ronald R. Yager, Henrik Bulskov, Henning Christiansen, and Henrik Legind Larsen, editors, *Proceedings of FQAS*, volume 5822 of *Lecture Notes in Computer Science*, pages 157–167. Springer, 2009.

[335] Mostafa Keikha and Fabio Crestani. Linguistic aggregation methods in blog retrieval. *Information Processing and Management*, 48(3):467–475, May 2012.

[336] Mostafa Keikha, Fabio Crestani, and Mark James Carman. Employing document dependency in blog search. *Journal of the American Society of Information Science and Technology*, 63(2):354–365, February 2012.

[337] Mostafa Keikha, Shima Gerani, and Fabio Crestani. TEMPER: A temporal relevance feedback method. In Clough et al. [143], pages 436–447.

[338] J. S. Kessler, M. Eckert, L. Clark, and N. Nicolov. The ICWSM 2010 JDPA sentiment corpus for the automotive domain. In *Proceedings of the 4th International AAAI Conference on Weblogs and Social Media Data Workshop Challenge (ICWSM-DWC)*, 2010.

[339] Elham Khabiri, James Caverlee, and Chiao-Fang Hsu. Summarizing user-contributed comments. In *Proceedings of the 5th AAAI Conference on Weblogs and Social Media*, 2011.

[340] A. M. Kibriya and J. Ramon. Nearly exact mining of frequent trees in large networks. In *Proceedings of ECML/PKDD 2012*, pages 426–440. Springer, 2012.

[341] A. Kilgarriff. Googleology is bad science. *Computational Linguistics*, 33(1), 2007.

[342] A. Kilgarriff, P. Rychly, P. Smrž, and D. Tugwell. The sketch engine. In *Proceedings EURALEX*, pages 105–116, 2004.

[343] Harksoo Kim and Jungyun Seo. High-performance FAQ retrieval using an automatic clustering method of query logs. *Information Processing and Management*, 42:650–661, 2006.

[344] Hyun Duk Kim and ChengXiang Zhai. Generating comparative summaries of contradictory opinions in text. In *Proceedings of the 18th ACM Conference on Information and Knowledge Management, CIKM'09*, pages 385–394, 2009.

[345] S.-M. Kim and E. Hovy. Determining the sentiment of opinions. In *Proceedings of the 20th International Conference on Computational Linguistics*, pages 1367–1373. Morristown, NJ, Association for Computational Linguistics, 2004.

[346] S.-M. Kim and E. Hovy. Extracting opinions, opinion holders, and topics expressed in online news media text. In *Proceedings of ACL/COLING Workshop on Sentiment and Subjectivity in Text*, pages 1–8. Morristown, NJ, Association for Computational Linguistics, 2006.

[347] Youngmoo E. Kim, Erik Schmidt, and Lloyd Emelle. Moodswings: A collaborative game for music mood label collection. In *Proceedings of ISMIR*, pages 287–292, Philadelphia, PA, September 2008.

[348] P. N. Klein and H.-I. Lu. Efficient approximation algorithms for semidefinite programs arising from MAX CUT and COLORING. Technical report CS-96-07, Department of Computer Science, Brown University, January 1996.

[349] Jon M. Kleinberg. Hubs, authorities, and communities. *ACM Computing Surveys*, 31(4es), December 1999.

[350] Alexander Klemm, Christoph Lindemann, Mary K. Vernon, and Oliver P. Waldhorst. Characterizing the query behavior in peer-to-peer file sharing systems. In *Proceedings ACM SIGCOMM IMC*, New York, NY, 2004.

[351] Peter Knees, Elias Pampalk, and Gerhard Widmer. Artist classification with Web-based data. In *Proceedings of ISMIR*, Barcelona, Spain, October 2004.

[352] Peter Knees and Markus Schedl. Towards semantic music information extraction from the Web using rule patterns and supervised learning. In *Proceedings WOMRAD*, Chicago, IL, October 2011.

[353] Peter Knees, Markus Schedl, Tim Pohle, and Gerhard Widmer. An innovative three-dimensional user interface for exploring music collections enriched with meta-information from the Web. In *Proceedings ACM Multimedia*, Santa Barbara, CA, October 2006.

[354] Jeongwoo Ko, Luo Si, Eric Nyberg, and Teruko Mitamura. Probabilistic models for answer-ranking in multilingual question-answering. *ACM Transactions on Information Systems*, 28(3):16:1–16:37, July 2010.

[355] W. Kocay and D. L. Kreher. *Graphs, Algorithms and Optimization*. Chapman & Hall, 2004.

[356] Philipp Koehn, editor. *Statistical Machine Translation*. Cambridge University Press, 2010.

[357] Noam Koenigstein, Nir Nice, Ulrich Paquet, and Nir Schleyen. The Xbox recommender system. In *Proceedings RecSys*, 2012.

[358] Noam Koenigstein and Yuval Shavitt. Song ranking based on piracy in peer-to-peer networks. In *Proceedings of ISMIR*, Kobe, Japan, October 2009.

[359] Noam Koenigstein, Yuval Shavitt, and Tomer Tankel. Spotting out emerging artists using geo-aware analysis of P2P query strings. In *Proceedings ACM KDD*, pages 937–945, Las Vegas, NV, August 2008.

[360] Noam Koenigstein, Yuval Shavitt, Tomer Tankel, Ela Weinsberg, and Udi Weinsberg. Framework for extracting musical similarities from peer-to-peer networks. In *Proceedings AdMIRe*, 2010.

[361] Noam Koenigstein, Yuval Shavitt, Ela Weinsberg, and Udi Weinsberg. Measuring the validity of peer-to-peer data for information retrieval applications. *Computer Networks*, 56(3):1092–1102, 2012.

[362] Noam Koenigstein, Yuval Shavitt, and Noa Zilberman. Predicting billboard success using data-mining in P2P networks. In *Proceedings IEEE ISM: AdMIRe*, San Diego, CA, December 2009.

[363] J. L. Kolodner. An introduction to case-based reasoning. *Artificial Intelligence Review*, 6(1):3–34, March 1992.

[364] J. L. Kolodner. *Case-Based Reasoning*. Morgan Kaufmann Series in Representation and Reasoning Series. Morgan Kaufmann Publishers, 1993.

[365] R. Komuda, M. Ptaszynski, Y. Momouchi, R. Rzepka, and K. Araki. Machine moral development: Moral reasoning agent based on wisdom of web-crowd and emotions. *International Journal of Computational Linguistics Research*, 1(3):155–163, 2010.

[366] Joseph A. Konstan and John Riedl. Recommender systems: From algorithms to user experience. *User Modeling and User-Adapted Interaction*, 22(1-2):101–123, April 2012.

[367] Yehuda Koren. Collaborative filtering with temporal dynamics. *Communications ACM*, 53(4):89–97, 2010.

[368] I. Koutis. Faster algebraic algorithms for path and packing problems. In *ICALP (1)*, volume 5125 of *Lecture Notes in Computer Science*, pages 575–586. Springer, 2008.

[369] Markus Krötzsch, Sebastian Rudolph, and Pascal Hitzler. Description logic rules. In *Proceedings of the 2008 Conference on ECAI 2008: 18th European Conference on Artificial Intelligence*, pages 80–84. Amsterdam, The Netherlands, IOS Press, 2008.

[370] G. R. Krupka and K. Hausman. IsoQuest, Inc.: Description of the NetOwl^{TM} Extractor System as used for MUC-7. In *Proceedings of the 7th Message Understanding Conference*, 1998.

[371] L.-W. Ku and H.-H. Chen. Mining opinions from the Web: Beyond relevance retrieval. *Journal of the American Society for Information Science*, 58(12):1838–1850, 2007.

[372] Lun-Wei Ku, Yu-Ting Liang, and Hsin-Hsi Chen. Opinion extraction, summarization and tracking in news and blog corpora. In *Proceedings of AAAI Spring Symposium: Computational Approaches to Analyzing Weblogs*, pages 100–107, 2006.

[373] H. Kubota, K. Yamashita, T. Fukuhara, and T. Nishida. POC caster: Broadcasting agent using conversational representation for Internet community [in Japanese]. *Transactions of the Japanese Society for Artificial Intelligence*, AI-17:313–321, 2002.

[374] T. Kudo and Y. Matsumoto. Japanese dependency analysis using cascaded chunking. In *Proceedings of the 6th Conference on Natural Language Learning 2002 (CoNLL 2002)*, pages 63–69, 2002.

[375] Kudo, T. MeCab: Yet another part-of-speech and morphological, Project Web Site: http://mecab.sourceforge.net/.

[376] Kudo, T. and Kazawa, H. Japanese Web N-gram Version 1, Project Web Site: http://www.ldc.upenn.edu/Catalog/CatalogEntry.jsp?catalogId=LDC2009T08.

[377] M. Kuramochi and G. Karypis. Finding frequent patterns in a large sparse graph. *Data Mining Knowledge Discovery*, 11(3):243–271, 2005.

[378] M. Kuramochi and G. Karypis. Discovering frequent geometric subgraphs. *Information Systems*, 32(8):1101–1120, 2007.

[379] Sadao Kurohashi, Susumu Akamine, Daisuke Kawahara, Yoshikiyo Kato, Tetsuji Nakagawa, Kentaro Inui, and Yutaka Kidawara. Information credibility analysis of Web contents. In *Proceedings ISUC*, pages 146–153, 2008.

[380] H. Kwak, C. Lee, H. Park, and S. Moon. What is Twitter, a social network or a news media? In *Proceedings of 19th International Conference on World Wide Web*, pages 591–600, 2010.

[381] John D. Lafferty, Andrew McCallum, and Fernando C. N. Pereira. Conditional random fields: Probabilistic models for segmenting and labeling sequence data. In *ICML'01 Proceedings of the 18th International Conference on Machine Learning*, pages 282–289, 2001.

[382] Patrick Lai. Extracting Strong Sentiment Trends from Twitter. http://nlp.stanford.edu/courses/cs224n/2011/reports/patlai.pdf, 2010.

[383] Adam Lally, John M. Prager, Michael C. McCord, Branimir K. Boguraev, Siddharth Patwardhan, James Fan, Paul Fodor, and Jennifer Chu-Carroll. Question analysis: How Watson reads a clue. *IBM Journal of Research and Development*, 56(3.4):2:1–2:14, 2012.

[384] Paul Lamere. Social tagging and music information retrieval. *Journal of New Music Research: Special Issue: From Genres to Tags—Music Information Retrieval in the Age of Social Tagging*, 37(2):101–114, 2008.

[385] A. S. LaPaugh and R. L. Rivest. The subgraph homeomorphism problem. In *STOC'78*, pages 40–50. New York, NY, ACM Press, 1978.

[386] J. Larrosa and G. Valiente. Constraint satisfaction algorithms for graph pattern matching. *Mathematical Structures in Computer Science*, 12(4):403–422, 2002.

[387] Yezdi Lashkari, Max Metral, and Pattie Maes. Collaborative interface agents. In *Proceedings of the 12th National Conference on Artificial Intelligence (Vol. 1), AAAI'94*, pages 444–449, Menlo Park, CA, AAAI, 1994.

[388] Cyril Laurier, Mohamed Sordo, Joan Serrà, and Perfecto Herrera. Music mood representations from social tags. In *Proceedings of ISMIR*, Kobe, Japan, October 2009.

[389] Victor Lavrenko, Martin Choquette, and W. Bruce Croft. Cross-lingual relevance models. In *Proceedings of the 25th Annual International ACM SIGIR Conference on Research and Development in Information Retrieval, SIGIR'02*, pages 175–182. New York, NY, ACM, 2002.

[390] Victor Lavrenko and W. Bruce Croft. Relevance-based language models. In *Proceedings of the 24th Annual International ACM SIGIR Conference on Research and Development in Information Retrieval, SIGIR'01*, pages 120–127. New York, NY, ACM, 2001.

[391] Edith Law, Luis von Ahn, Roger Dannenberg, and Mike Crawford. Tagatune: A game for music and sound annotation. In *Proceedings of ISMIR*, Vienna, Austria, September 2007.

[392] C. Leacock and M. Chodorow. Combining local context and WordNet similarity for word sense identification. In Christiane Fellfaum, editor, pages 265–283. Cambridge, Massachusetts, MIT Press, 1998.

[393] Wai-Lung Lee, Andreas Lommatzsch, and Christian Scheel. Feed distillation using AdaBoost and topic maps. In Voorhees and Buckland [689].

[394] Yeha Lee, Seung-Hoon Na, Jungi Kim, Sang-Hyob Nam, Hun-Young Jung, and Jong-Hyeok Lee. Kle at TREC 2008 blog track: Blog post and feed retrieval. In Voorhees and Buckland [690].

[395] B. Levin. *English Verb Classes and Alternations*. University of Chicago Press, 1993.

[396] Gina-Anne Levow. The 3rd International Chinese Language Processing Bakeoff: Word segmentation and named entity recognition. In *Proceedings of the 5th SigHAN Workshop on Chinese Language Processing*, pages 108–117, 2006.

[397] Mark Levy and Mark Sandler. Learning latent semantic models for music from social tags. *Journal of New Music Research*, 37(2):137–150, 2008.

[398] Baichuan Li, Tan Jin, Michael R. Lyu, Irwin King, and Barley Mak. Analyzing and predicting question quality in community question-answering services. In *Proceedings of the 21st International Conference Companion on World Wide Web, WWW'12*, pages 775–782. New York, NY, ACM, 2012.

[399] Baichuan Li and Irwin King. Routing questions to appropriate answerers in community question-answering services. In *Proceedings of the 19th ACM International Conference on Information and Knowledge Management, CIKM'10*, pages 1585–1588. New York, NY, ACM, 2010.

[400] Rui Li, Shenghua Bao, Yong Yu, Ben Fei, and Zhong Su. Towards effective browsing of large-scale social annotations. In *Proceedings WWW*, pages 943–952, 2007.

[401] Xin Li and Dan Roth. Learning question classifiers: The role of semantic information. *Natural Language Engineering*, 12(3):229–249, 2006.

[402] Y. Li, K. Bontcheva, and H. Cunningham. Experiments of opinion analysis on two corpora MPQA and NTCIR-6. In *Proceedings of the 6th NTCIR Workshop Meeting on Evaluation of Information Access Technologies: Information Retrieval, Question-Answering and Cross-Lingual Information Access*, pages 323–329, 2007.

[403] Feng Liang, Runwei Qiang, and Jianwu Yang. Exploiting real-time information retrieval in the microblogosphere. In Karim B. Boughida, Barrie Howard, Michael L. Nelson, Herbert Van de Sompel, and Ingeborg Sølvberg, editors, *Proceedings JCDL*, pages 267–276. ACM, 2012.

[404] David Liben-Nowell and Jon M. Kleinberg. The link-prediction problem for social networks. *Journal of the American Society for Information Science*, 58(7):1019–1031, 2007.

[405] David Liben-Nowell, Jasmine Novak, Ravi Kumar, Prabhakar Raghavan, and Andrew Tomkins. Geographic routing in social networks. *Proceedings of the National Academy of Sciences*, 102(33):11623–11628, August 2005.

[406] Cynthia C.S. Liem, Meinard Müller, Douglas Eck, George Tzanetakis, and Alan Hanjalic. The need for music information retrieval with user-centered and multimodal strategies. In *Proceedings ACM MIRUM*, pages 1–6, Scottsdale, AZ, 2011.

[407] Chin-Yew Lin. Rouge: A package for automatic evaluation of summaries. In *Text Summarization Branches Out: Proceedings of the ACL-04 Workshop*, pages 74–81, Barcelona, Spain, 2004.

[408] Chin-Yew Lin. Question-answering of UCC. In Marie-Francine Moens, Juanzi Li, and Tat-Seng Chua, editors, *Mining of User Generated Content and Its Applications, Social Media and Social Computing*, chapter 10. Taylor & Francis (CRC Press), 2013.

[409] B. Liu, M. Hu, and J. Cheng. Opinion observer: Analyzing and comparing opinions on the Web. In *Proceedings of the 14th International Conference on World Wide Web (WWW'05)*, pages 342–351. New York, NY, ACM, 2005.

[410] Dong Liu, Xian-Sheng Hua, Linjun Yang, Meng Wang, and Hong-Jiang Zhang. Tag ranking. In *Proceedings of the 18th International Conference on World Wide Web, WWW'09*, pages 351–360. New York, NY, ACM, 2009.

[411] H. Liu, H. Lieberman, and T. Selker. A model of textual affect sensing using real-world knowledge. In *Proceedings of the 8th International Conference on Intelligent User Interfaces*, pages 125–132. New York, NY, ACM Press, 2003.

[412] Jing Liu, Young-In Song, and Chin-Yew Lin. Competition-based user expertise score estimation. In *Proceedings of the 34th International ACM SIGIR Conference on Research and Development in Information Retrieval, SIGIR'11*, pages 425–434. New York, NY, ACM, 2011.

[413] Tie-Yan Liu. Learning to rank for information retrieval. *Foundations and Trends in Information Retrieval*, 3(3):225–331, March 2009.

[414] V. Liu and J. R. Curran. Web text corpus for natural language processing. In *Proceedings of the 11th Meeting of the European Chapter of the Association for Computational Linguistics (EACL)*, pages 233–240, 2006.

[415] Xiaohua Liu, Furu Wei, and Ming Zhou. QuickView: NLP-based tweet search. In *Proceedings of ACL (System Demonstrations)*, pages 13–18. ACL, 2012.

[416] Xiaoyong Liu, W. Bruce Croft, and Matthew Koll. Finding experts in community-based question-answering services. In *Proceedings of the 14th ACM International Conference on Information and Knowledge Management, CIKM'05*, pages 315–316. New York, NY, ACM, 2005.

[417] Yuanjie Liu, Shasha Li, Yunbo Cao, Chin-Yew Lin, Dingyi Han, and Yong Yu. Understanding and summarizing answers in community-based question-answering services. In *International Conference on Computational Linguistics*, pages 497–504, 2008.

[418] Fredrik Ljungberg and Carsten Sørensen. *Interaction Overload: Managing Context and Modality.* 1998.

[419] Fabiana Lorenzi and Francesco Ricci. Case-based recommender systems: A unifying view. In *Proceedings of the 2003 International Conference on Intelligent Techniques for Web Personalization, ITWP'03*, pages 89–113. Berlin, Heidelberg, Springer-Verlag, 2005.

[420] Yue Lu, ChengXiang Zhai, and Neel Sundaresan. Rated aspect summarization of short comments. In *Proceedings of the 18th International Conference on World Wide Web*, pages 131–140, 2009.

[421] Claudio Lucchese, Raffaele Perego, Fabrizio Silvestri, Hossein Vahabi, and Rossano Venturini. How random walks can help tourism. In *Proceedings of the 34th European Conference on Advances in Information Retrieval, ECIR'12*, pages 195–206. Berlin, Heidelberg, Springer-Verlag, 2012.

[422] Marika Lüders. Why and how online sociability became part and parcel of teenage life. In Mia Consalvo and Charles Ess, editors, *The Handbook of Internet Studies*, pages 452–465. Wiley-Blackwell, 2011.

[423] H. P. Luhn. A statistical approach to mechanized encoding and searching of literary information. *IBM Journal of Research and Development*, 1:309–317, 1957.

[424] H. P. Luhn. The automatic creation of literature abstracts. *IBM J. Res. Dev.*, 2(2):159–165, April 1958.

[425] Jie Luo, Barbara Caputo, and Vittorio Ferrari. Who's doing what: Joint modeling of names and verbs for simultaneous face and pose annotation. In *Proceedings of NIPS*, pages 1168–1176, 2009.

[426] M. David and H. W. Ian. Learning to link with Wikipedia. In *Proceedings of CIKM*, pages 509–518, 2008.

[427] M. De Choudhury, S. Counts, and M. Gamon. Not all moods are created equal! Exploring human emotional states in social media. In *Proceedings of the 6th International AAAI Conference on Weblogs and Social Media*, 2012.

[428] M. Dredze, P. McNamee, D. Rao, A. Gerber, and T. Finin. Entity disambiguation for knowledge base population. In *Proceedings of the 23rd International Conference on Computational Linguistics (COLING 2010)*, 2010.

[429] Hao Ma, Irwin King, and Michael R. Lyu. Effective missing data prediction for collaborative filtering. In *Proceedings of the 30th Annual International ACM SIGIR Conference on Research and Development in Information Retrieval, SIGIR'07*, pages 39–46. New York, NY, ACM, 2007.

[430] Zhongming Ma, Gautam Pant, and Olivia R. Liu Sheng. Interest-based personalized search. *ACM Transactions on Information Systems*, 25(1), 2007.

[431] A. Maayan, S. L. Jenkins, S. Neves, A. Hasseldine, E. Grace, B. Dubin-Thaler, N. J. Eungdamrong, G. Weng, P. T. Ram, J. J. Rice, A. Kershenbaum, G. A. Stolovitzky, R. D. Blitzer, and R. Iyengar. Formation of regulatory patterns during signal propagation in a mammalian cellular network. *Science*, 309(5737):1078–1083, 2005.

[432] Craig Macdonald and Iadh Ounis. Voting for candidates: Adapting data fusion techniques for an expert search task. In Philip S. Yu, Vassilis J. Tsotras, Edward A. Fox, and Bing Liu, editors, *Proceedings CIKM*, pages 387–396. ACM, 2006.

[433] Craig Macdonald and Iadh Ounis. Key blog distillation: Ranking aggregates. In Shanahan et al. [622], pages 1043–1052.

[434] Craig Macdonald, Iadh Ounis, and Ian Soboroff. Overview of the TREC 2007 blog track. In Voorhees and Buckland [689].

[435] B. Maeireizo, D. Litman, and R. Hwa. Co-training for predicting emotions with spoken dialogue data. In *Proceedings of the 42nd Annual Meeting of the Association for Computational Linguistics*, pages 203–206, 2004.

[436] Jalal Mahmud, Jeffrey Nichols, and Clemens Drews. Where is this tweet from? Inferring home locations of Twitter users. In *Proceedings of the 6th International AAAI Conference on Weblogs and Social Media*, Dublin, Ireland, 2012.

[437] Mainichi Shinbun CD. Project Web Site: http://www.nichigai.co.jp/sales/mainichi/mainichi-data.html.

[438] B. Malin. Unsupervised name disambiguation via social network similarity. In *Proceedings of SIAM*, 2005.

[439] B. Malin and E. Airoldi. A network analysis model for disambiguation of names in lists. In *Proceedings of CMOT*, 2005.

[440] R. Malouf and T. Mullen. Taking sides: User classification for informal online political discourse. *Internet Research*, 18(2):177–190, 2008.

[441] Michael I. Mandel and Daniel P.W. Ellis. A Web-based game for collecting music metadata. In *Proceedings of ISMIR*, Vienna, Austria, September 2007.

[442] Inderjeet Mani. *Automatic Summarization*. John Benjamins Publishing Company, 2001.

[443] Gideon S. Mann and David Yarowsky. Unsupervised personal name disambiguation. In *Proceedings of CoNLL*, 2003.

[444] A. Marcus, M. S. Bernstein, O. Badar, D. R. Karger, S. Madden, and R. C. Miller. TwitInfo: Aggregating and visualizing microblogs for event exploration. In *Proceedings of the 2011 Conference on Human Factors in Computing Systems (CHI)*, pages 227–236, 2011.

[445] Mitchell P. Marcus, Mary Ann Marcin-Kiewicz, and Beatrice Santorini. Building a large annotated corpus of English: The Penn treebank. *Computational Linguistics*, 19:313–330, 1993.

[446] J. R. Martin and P. R. R. White. *The Language of Evaluation: The Appraisal Framework*. New York, Palgrave Macmillan, 2005.

[447] Kamran Massoudi, Manos Tsagkias, Maarten de Rijke, and Wouter Weerkamp. Incorporating query expansion and quality indicators in searching microblog posts. In Clough et al. [143], pages 362–367.

[448] J. Matousek and R. Thomas. On the complexity of finding ISO- and other morphisms for partial k-trees. *Discrete Mathematics*, 108:343–364, 1992.

[449] K. Matsumoto, Y. Konishi, H. Sayama, and F. Ren. Analysis of Wakamono Kotoba emotion corpus and its application in emotion estimation. *International Journal of Advanced Intelligence*, 3(1):1–24, 2011.

[450] A. McCallum, K. Nigam, J. Rennie, and K. Seymore. A machine learning approach to building domain-specific search engines. In *Proceedings of the 16th International Joint Conference on Artificial Intelligence*, pages 662–667. Morgan Kaufmann, 1999.

[451] Richard McCreadie, Craig Macdonald, and Iadh Ounis. Identifying top news using crowdsourcing. *Information Retrieval*, pages 1–31, 2012. 10.1007/s10791-012-9186-z.

[452] Lorraine McGinty and Barry Smyth. On the role of diversity in conversational recommender systems. In *Proceedings of the 5th International Conference on Case-Based Reasoning: Research and Development, IC-CBR'03*, pages 276–290. Berlin, Heidelberg, Springer-Verlag, 2003.

[453] P. McNamee and H. T. Dang. Overview of the TAC 2009 knowledge base population track. In *Proceedings of TAC*, 2009.

[454] David McSherry. Similarity and compromise. In *Proceedings of the 5th International Conference on Case-Based Reasoning: Research and Development, ICCBR'03*, pages 291–305. Berlin, Heidelberg, Springer-Verlag, 2003.

[455] Alberto O. Mendelzon. Review—Authoritative sources in a hyperlinked environment. *ACM SIGMOD Digital Review*, 1, 2000.

[456] Cedric S. Mesnage, Asma Rafiq, Simon Dixon, and Romain Brixtel. Music discovery with social networks. In *Proceedings of WOMRAD*, Chicago, IL, October 2011.

[457] B. Messmer and H. Bunke. Efficient subgraph isomorphism detection: A decomposition approach. *IEEE Transactions on Knowledge and Data Engineering*, 12(2):307–323, 2000.

[458] Donald Metzler and W. Bruce Croft. Linear feature-based models for information retrieval. *Information Retrieval*, 10(3):257–274, June 2007.

[459] Donald Metzler, Congxing Cai, and Eduard H. Hovy. Structured event retrieval over microblog archives. In *HLT-NAACL*, pages 646–655. ACL, 2012.

[460] B. Meyer, K. Bryan, Y. Santos, and B. Kim. TwitterReporter: Breaking news detection and visualization through the geo-tagged Twitter network. In *Proceedings of the ISCA 26th International Conference on Computers and Their Applications*, pages 84–89, 2011.

[461] M. Michelson and S. A. Macskassy. Discovering users' topics of interest on Twitter: A first look. In *4th Workshop on Analytics for Noisy Unstructured Text Data*, pages 73–80, 2010.

[462] R. Mihalcea and P. Tarau. TextRank: Bringing order into text. In *Proceedings of the Conference on Empirical Methods in Natural Language Processing (EMNLP)*, pages 404–411, 2004.

[463] Peter Mika. Ontologies are us: A unified model of social networks and semantics. *Journal of Web Semantics*, 5(1):5–15, 2007.

[464] Alain Mille, Fabien L. Gandon, Jacques Misselis, Michael Rabinovich, and Steffen Staab, editors. *Proceedings of the 21st World Wide Web Conference 2012, WWW 2012*, Lyon, France, April 16–20, 2012. ACM, 2012.

[465] David R. Millen, Jonathan Feinberg, and Bernard Kerr. Dogear: Social bookmarking in the enterprise. In *Proceedings of CHI*, pages 111–120, 2006.

[466] G. A. Miller, R. Beckwith, C. Fellbaum, D. Gross, and K. J. Miller. Introduction to WordNet: An on-line lexical database. *International Journal of Lexicography*, 3(4):235–244, 1990.

[467] David Milne and Ian H. Witten. An effective, low-cost measure of semantic relatedness obtained from Wikipedia links. In *Proceedings of AAAI*, 2008.

[468] David Milne and Ian H. Witten. Learning to link with Wikipedia. In *Proceedings of the 17th ACM Conference on Information and Knowledge Management, CIKM'08*, pages 509–518, 2008.

[469] R. Milo, S. Shen-Orr, S. Itzkovitz, N. Kashtan, D. Chklovskii, and U. Alon. Network motifs: Simple building blocks of complex networks. *Science*, 298 (5594):824–827, 2002.

[470] J. Minato, D. B. Bracewell, F. Ren, and S. Kuroiwa. Statistical analysis of a Japanese emotion corpus for natural language processing. In *Proceedings of the 2006 International Conference on Intelligent Computing (ICIC'06): Part II*, pages 924–929, 2006.

[471] J. Minato, D. B. Bracewell, F. Ren, and S. Kuroiwa. Japanese emotion corpus analysis and its use for automatic emotion word identification. *Engineering Letters*, 16(1):172–177, 2008.

[472] Mike Mintz, Steven Bills, Rion Snow, and Dan Jurafsky. Distant supervision for relation extraction without labeled data. In *Proceedings of ACL*, 2009.

[473] G. Mishne. Experiments with mood classification in blog posts. In *Style2005: The 1st Workshop on Stylistic Analysis of Text for Information Access*, 2005.

[474] Gilad Mishne. AutoTag: A collaborative approach to automated tag assignment for Weblog posts. In Les Carr, David De Roure, Arun Iyengar, Carole A. Goble, and Michael Dahlin, editors, *Proceedings of WWW*, pages 953–954. ACM, 2006.

[475] Gilad Mishne. Using blog properties to improve retrieval. In Natalie S. Glance, Nicolas Nicolov, Eytan Adar, Matthew Hurst, Mark Liberman, and Franco Salvetti, editors, *Proceedings of ICWSM*, 2007.

[476] Gilad Mishne and Maarten de Rijke. A study of blog search. In Mounia Lalmas, Andy MacFarlane, Stefan M. Rüger, Anastasios Tombros, Theodora Tsikrika, and Alexei Yavlinsky, editors, *Proceedings of ECIR*, volume 3936 of *Lecture Notes in Computer Science*, pages 289–301. Springer, 2006.

[477] Shamima Mithun and Leila Kosseim. Summarizing blog entries versus news texts. In *Proceedings of the Workshop on Events in Emerging Text Types*, pages 1–8, Borovets, Bulgaria, September 2009.

[478] Dan I. Moldovan, Christine Clark, and Mitchell Bowden. Lymba's PowerAnswer 4 in TREC 2007. In Voorhees and Buckland [689].

[479] Miquel Montaner, Beatriz López, and Josep Lluís De La Rosa. A taxonomy of recommender agents on the Internet. *Artificial Intelligence Review*, 19(4):285–330, June 2003.

[480] Calvin N. Mooers. Zatocoding applied to mechanical organization of knowledge. *American Documentation*, 2(1):20–32, 1951.

[481] Gianmarco De Francisci Morales, Aristides Gionis, and Claudio Lucchese. From chatter to headlines: Harnessing the real-time Web for personalized news recommendation. In *Proceedings of the 5th International Conference on Web Search and Web Data Mining, WSDM 2012*, pages 153–162, Seattle, WA, February 8–12, 2012.

[482] S. Muggleton and C. D. Page. A learnability model for universal representations. In S. Wrobel, editor, *Proceedings of the 4th International Workshop on Inductive Logic Programming*, pages 139–160, Sankt Augustin, Germany, 1994. GMD.

[483] T. Mullen and N. Collier. Sentiment analysis using support vector machines with diverse information sources. In *Proceedings of the 2004 Conference on Empirical Methods in Natural Language Processing*, pages 412–418, 2004.

[484] M. Naaman, J. Boase, and C. Lai. Is it really about me? Message content in social awareness streams. In *Proceedings of the 2010 ACM Conference on Computer Supported Cooperative Work*, pages 189–192. ACM, 2010.

[485] M. Nagarajan, K. Gomadam, A. Sheth, A. Ranabahu, R. Mutharaju, and A. Jadhav. Spatio-temporal-thematic analysis of citizen sensor data: Challenges and experiences. In *Web Information Systems Engineering*, pages 539–553, 2009.

[486] A. Nakamura. *Kanjo Hyogen Jiten [Dictionary of Emotive Expressions]* (in Japanese). Tokyodo Publishing, 1993.

[487] N. Nakashole, G. Weikum, and F. Suchanek. Patty: A taxonomy of relational patterns with semantic types. In *Conference on Empirical Methods in Natural Language Processing*, 2012.

[488] Kevin Kyung Nam, Mark S. Ackerman, and Lada A. Adamic. Questions in, knowledge in? A study of Naver's question-answering community. In *Proceedings of the 27th International Conference on Human Factors*

in Computing Systems, CHI'09, pages 779–788. New York, NY, ACM, 2009.

[489] Alexandros Nanopoulos, Dimitrios Rafailidis, Panagiotis Symeonidis, and Yannis Manolopoulos. Musicbox: Personalized music recommendation based on cubic analysis of social tags. *Audio, Speech, and Language Processing, IEEE Transactions on*, 18(2):407–412, 2010.

[490] Franco Maria Nardini, Fabrizio Silvestri, Hossein Vahabi, Pedram Vahabi, and Ophir Frieder. On tag spell checking. In Edgar Chávez and Stefano Lonardi, editors, *SPIRE*, volume 6393 of *Lecture Notes in Computer Science*, pages 37–42. Springer, 2010.

[491] Gonzalo Navarro. A guided tour to approximate string matching. *ACM Computing Surveys*, 33, 2001.

[492] Matteo Negri, Luisa Bentivogli, Yashar Mehdad, Danilo Giampiccolo, and Alessandro Marchetti. Divide and conquer: Crowdsourcing the creation of cross-lingual textual entailment corpora. In *Proceedings of the Conference on Empirical Methods in Natural Language Processing*, pages 670–679, 2011.

[493] Ani Nenkova and Kathleen McKeown. Automatic summarization. *Foundations and Trends in Information Retrieval*, 5(2–3):103–233, 2011.

[494] Ani Nenkova and Rebecca Passonneau. Evaluating content selection in summarization: The pyramid method. In *Proceedings of HLT-NAACL*, pages 145–152, 2004.

[495] V. Ng, S. Dasgupta, and S. M. N. Arifin. Examining the role of linguistic knowledge sources in the automatic identification and classification of reviews. In *Proceedings of the COLING/ACL on Main Conference Poster Sessions*, pages 611–618, Morristown, NJ, 2006. ACL.

[496] S.-H. Nienhuys-Cheng and R. De Wolf. *Foundations of Inductive Logic Programming*, volume 1228 of *Lecture Notes in Computer Science and Lecture Notes in Artificial Intelligence*. New York, NY, Springer-Verlag, 1997.

[497] K. Nigam and R. Ghani. Analyzing the effectiveness and applicability of co-training. In *Proceedings of the 9th International Conference on Information and Knowledge Management*, pages 86–93, 2000.

[498] K. Nigam and M. Hurst. Towards a robust metric of opinion. In *Proceedings of the AAAI Spring Symposium on Exploring Attitude and Affect in Text*, pages 598–603, 2004.

[499] K. Nigam, A. K. McCallum, S. Thrun, and T. Mitchell. Text classification from labeled and unlabeled documents using EM. *Machine Learning*, 39(103–134), 1999.

[500] S. Nijssen and J. N. Kok. A quickstart in frequent structure mining can make a difference. In *Proceedings of the 10th ACM SIGKDD International Conference on Knowledge Discovery and Data Mining (KDD)*, pages 647–652, 2004.

[501] NIST. The ACE (2 x) 2007 (ACE07) evaluation plan: Evaluation of the detection and recognition of ace entities, values, temporal expressions, relations, and events. In *Proceedings of the 7th Message Understanding Conference*, 1998.

[502] Y. Niu, X. Zhu, J. Li, and G. Hirst. Analysis of polarity information in medical text. In *Proceedings of the American Medical Informatics Association 2005 Annual Symposium*, pages 570–574, 2005.

[503] Michael G. Noll and Christoph Meinel. Web search personalization via social bookmarking and tagging. In *ISWC/ASWC*, pages 367–380, 2007.

[504] Sérgio Nunes, Cristina Ribeiro, and Gabriel David. FEUP at TREC 2008 blog track: Using temporal evidence for ranking and feed distillation. In Voorhees and Buckland [690].

[505] O. Medelyan, I. H. Witten, and D. Milne. Topic indexing with Wikipedia. In *Proceedings of Wikipedia and AI Workshop at the AAAI-2008 Conference*, 2008.

[506] B. O'Connor, R. Balasubramanyan, B. Routedge, and N. Smith. From tweets to polls: Linking text sentiment to public opinion time series. In *Proceedings of the 4th International AAAI Conference on Weblogs and Social Media*, 2010.

[507] Etzioni Oren, Fader Anthony, Janara Christensen, Stephen Soderland, and Mausam. Open information extraction: The second generation. In *IJCAI*, pages 3–10, 2011.

[508] Derry O'Sullivan, David Wilson, and Barry Smyth. Using collaborative filtering data in case-based recommendation. In *Proceedings of the 15th International Florida Artificial Intelligence Research Society Conference*, pages 121–125. AAAI Press, 2002.

[509] I. Ounis, M. de Rijke, C. Macdonald, G. Mishne, and I. Soboroff. Overview of the TREC-2006 blog track. In *Proceedings of the 15th Text Retrieval Conference*, 2007.

[510] Iadh Ounis, Christina Lioma, Craig Macdonald, and Vassilis Plachouras. Research directions in Terrier. *Novatica/UPGRADE Special Issue on Web Information Access*, Ricardo Baeza-Yates et al., editors, Invited Paper, 2007.

[511] Iadh Ounis, Craig Macdonald, Maarten de Rijke, Gilad Mishne, and Ian Soboroff. Overview of the TREC 2006 blog track. In Voorhees and Buckland [688].

[512] Seda Ozmutlu, Amanda Spink, and Huseyin C. Ozmutlu. A day in the life of Web searching: An exploratory study. *Inf. Process. Manag.*, 40(2):319–345, March 2004.

[513] P. Marco and P. C. Patrick. Entity extraction via ensemble semantics. In *Proceedings of EMNLP*, pages 427–436.

[514] P. Marius. Weakly-supervised discovery of named entities using Web search queries. In *Proceedings of ACM 16th Conference on Information and Knowledge Management(CIKM 2007)*, pages 683–690, 2007.

[515] P. Patrick, C. Eric, B. Arkady, P. Ana-Maria, and C. Vishnu. Web-scale distributional similarity and entity set expansion. In *Proceedings of EMNLP*, pages 938–947, 2009.

[516] Lawrence Page, Sergey Brin, Rajeev Motwani, and Terry Winograd. The page-rank citation ranking: Bringing order to the Web, 1999.

[517] A. Pak and P. Paroubek. Twitter-based system: Based system—Using Twitter for disambiguating sentiment ambiguous adjectives. In *Proceedings of the 5th International Workshop on Semantic Evaluation*, pages 436–439, 2010.

[518] A. Pande, M. Gupta, and A. K. Tripathi. A decision tree approach for design patterns detection by subgraph isomorphism. In *ICT*, volume 101 of *Communications in Computer and Information Science*, pages 561–564. Springer, 2010.

[519] B. Pang and L. Lee. A sentimental education: Sentiment analysis using subjectivity summarization based on minimum cuts. In *Proceedings of the 42nd Annual Meeting on Association for Computational Linguistics*, pages 271–278. Morristown, NJ, ACL, 2004.

[520] B. Pang and L. Lee. Opinion mining and sentiment analysis. *Information Retrieval*, 2(1), 2008.

[521] B. Pang, L. Lee, and S. Vaithyanathan. Thumbs up? Sentiment classification using machine learning techniques. In *Proceedings of the 2002 Conference on EMNLP*, pages 79–86, 2002.

[522] Bo Pang and Lillian Lee. Seeing stars: Exploiting class relationships for sentiment categorization with respect to rating scales. In *Proceedings of the 43rd Annual Meeting on Association for Computational Linguistics*, pages 115–124, 2005.

[523] Ulrich Paquet, Blaise Thomson, and Ole Winther. A hierarchical model for ordinal matrix factorization. *Statistics and Computing*, 21, 2011.

[524] D. Paranjpe. Learning document aboutness from implicit user feedback and document structure. In *18th ACM Conference on Information and Knowledge Management*, pages 365–374, 2009.

[525] Marius A. Pasca and Sandra M. Harabagiu. High performance question/answering. In *Proceedings of the 24th Annual International ACM SIGIR Conference on Research and Development in Information Retrieval, SIGIR'01*, pages 366–374. New York, NY, ACM, 2001.

[526] Michael J. Paul, ChengXiang Zhai, and Roxana Girju. Summarizing contrastive viewpoints in opinionated text. In *Proceedings of the 2010 Conference on Empirical Methods in Natural Language Processing*, pages 66–76, 2010.

[527] Michael J. Pazzani. A framework for collaborative, content-based and demographic filtering. *Artificial Intelligence Review*, 13(5-6):393–408, December 1999.

[528] Ted Pedersen, Amruta Purandare, and Anagha Kulkarni. Name discrimination by clustering similar contexts. In *Proceedings of CICLING*, 2005.

[529] Jose San Pedro, Tom Yeh, and Nuria Oliver. Leveraging user comments for aesthetic aware image search reranking. In Mille et al. [464], pages 439–448.

[530] J. Pei, J. Han, H. Pinto, Q. Chen, U. Dayal, and M. C. Hsu. Prefixspan: Mining sequential patterns efficiently by prefix-projected pattern growth. In *Proceedings of the 17th International Conference on Data Engineering (ICDE)*, pages 215–224, 2001.

[531] M. Pennacchiotti and A. M. Popescu. A machine learning approach to Twitter user classification. In *Proceedings of ICWSM 2011*, pages 281–288, 2011.

[532] J. W. Pennebaker. *The Secret Life of Pronouns: What Our Words Say about Us*. Bloomsbury Press, 1st Edition. 2011.

[533] J. P. Pestian, P. Matykiewicz, M. Linn-Gust, J. Wiebe, C. K. Bretonnel, C. Brew, J. Hurdle, O. Uzuner, and B. South. Sentiment analysis of suicide notes: A shared task. *Biomedical Informatics Insights*, 5:3–16, 2012.

[534] Phi Pham The, Marie-Francine Moens, and Tinne Tuytelaars. Crossmedia alignment of names and faces. *IEEE Transactions on Multimedia*, 12(1):13–27, 2010.

[535] Phi Pham The, Tinne Tuytelaars, and Marie-Francine Moens. Naming people in news videos with label propagation. *IEEE Multimedia*, 18(3):44–55, 2011.

[536] O. Phelan, K. McCarthy, and B. Smyth. Using Twitter to recommend real-time topical news. In *Proceedings of the 2009 ACM Conference on Recommender Systems*, pages 385–388, 2009.

[537] Owen Phelan, K. McCarthy, Mike Bennett, and Barry Smyth. Terms of a feather: Content-based news recommendation and discovery using Twitter. *Advances in Information Retrieval*, 6611(07):448–459, 2011.

[538] R. W. Picard. *Affective Computing*. Cambridge, MA, MIT Press, 1997.

[539] Peter Pirolli. Powers of 10: Modeling complex information-seeking systems at multiple scales. *IEEE Computer*, 42(3):33–40, 2009.

[540] G. Plotkin. A further note on inductive generalization. In *Machine Intelligence*, volume 6, pages 101–124. Edinburgh University Press, 1971.

[541] J. Pomikálek, P. Rychlý, and A. Kilgarriff. Scaling to billion-plus word corpora. *Advances in Computational Linguistics, Research in Computing Science*, 41:3–14, 2009.

[542] Jay M. Ponte and W. Bruce Croft. A language modeling approach to information retrieval. In *Proceedings of the 21st Annual International ACL SIGIR Conference on Research and Development in Information Retrieval*, pages 275–281. ACM, 1998.

[543] A. Popescu and O. Etzioni. Extracting product features and opinions from reviews. In *Proceedings of the Conference on Empirical Methods for Natural Language Processing (EMNLP)*, pages 339–346, Vancouver, Canada, 2005.

[544] M. F. Porter. 1997. An algorithm for suffix stripping. In Karen Sparck Jones and Peter Willett, editors, *Readings in Information Retrieval*, pages 313–316. San Francisco, CA, Morgan Kaufmann, 1997.

[545] B. A. Prakash, A. Sridharan, M. Seshadri, S. Machiraju, and C. E. Faloutsos. Surprising patterns and scalable community chipping in large graphs. In *Proceedings of the 14th Pacific–Asian Conference on Knowledge Discovery and Data Mining*, volume 2, pages 435–448, 2010.

[546] M. Ptaszynski, P. Dybala, R. Rzepka, and K. Araki. Affecting corpora: Experiments with automatic affect annotation system—A case study of the 2-channel forum. In *Proceedings of the Conference of the Pacific Association for Computational Linguistics (PACLING-09)*, pages 223–228, 2009.

[547] M. Ptaszynski, P. Dybala, W. Shi, R. Rzepka, and K. Araki. A system for affect analysis of utterances in Japanese supported with Web mining. *Journal of Japan Society for Fuzzy Theory and Intelligent Informatics*, 21(2):194–213, 2009.

[548] M. Ptaszynski, P. Dybala, W. Shi, R. Rzepka, and K. Araki. Towards context aware emotional intelligence in machines: Computing contextual appropriateness of affective states. In *Proceedings of 21st International Joint Conference on Artificial Intelligence (IJCAI-09)*, pages 1469–1474, 2009.

[549] M. Ptaszynski, J. Maciejewski, P. Dybala, R. Rzepka, and K. Araki. CAO: Fully automatic emoticon analysis system. In *Proceedings of the 24th AAAI Conference on Artificial Intelligence (AAAI-10)*, pages 1026–1032, 2010.

[550] M. Ptaszynski, R. Rzepka, and K. Araki. On the need for context processing in affective computing. In *Proceedings of Fuzzy System Symposium (FSS2010), Organized Session on Emotions*, pages 920–924, 2010.

[551] M. Ptaszynski, R. Rzepka, K. Araki, and Y. Momouchi. Annotating syntactic information on 5.5 billion word corpus of Japanese blogs. In *Proceedings of the (2x) 18th Annual Meeting of the Association for Natural Language Processing (NLP-2012)*, pages 385–388, 2012.

[552] M. Ptaszynski, R. Rzepka, K. Araki, and Y. Momouchi. A robust ontology of emotion objects. In *Proceedings of the 18th Annual Meeting of the Association for Natural Language Processing (NLP-2012)*, pages 719–722, 2012.

[553] Zhenyu Qi, K. Liu, and J. Zhao. Are human-input seeds good enough for entity set expansion? Seeds rewriting by leveraging Wikipedia semantic knowledge. In *Proceedings of AIRS*, 2012.

[554] Tao Qin, Tie-Yan Liu, Xu-Dong Zhang, Zheng Chen, and Wei-Ying Ma. A study of relevance propagation for Web search. In *Proceedings SIGIR*, pages 408–415, 2005.

[555] Feng Qiu and Junghoo Cho. Automatic identification of user interest for personalized search. In *Proceedings WWW*, pages 727–736, 2006.

[556] C. Quan and F. Ren. A blog emotion corpus for emotional expression analysis in Chinese. *Computer Speech and Language*, 24(4):716–749, 2010.

[557] J. R. Quinlan. Induction of decision trees. *Machine Learning*, 1(1):81–106, March 1986.

[558] R. Quirk, S. Greenbaum, G. Leech, and J. Svartvik. *A Comprehensive Grammar of the English Language*. London: Longman, 1985.

[559] R. Mihalcea and A. Csomai. Wikify! Linking documents to encyclopedic knowledge. In *Proceedings of ACM 16th Conference on Information and Knowledge Management (CIKM 2007)*, pages 233–242, 2007.

[560] Dragomir Radev, Timothy Allison, Sasha Blair-Goldensohn, John Blitzer, Arda Çelebi, Stanko Dimitrov, Elliott Drabek, Ali Hakim, Wai Lam, Danyu Liu, Jahna Otterbacher, Hong Qi, Horacio Saggion, Simone Teufel, Michael Topper, Adam Winkel, and Zhu Zhang. MEAD—A platform for multidocument multilingual text summarization. In *Proceedings of the Conference Language Resources and Evaluation (LREC)*, Lisbon, Portugal, 2004.

[561] Dragomir R. Radev, Hongyan Jing, Malgorzata Styś, and Daniel Tam. Centroid-based summarization of multiple documents. *Information Processing and Management*, 40(6):919–938, November 2004.

[562] Daniel Ramage, Susan Dumais, and Dan Liebling. Characterizing microblogs with topic models. In *Proceedings of the 4th International Conference on Weblogs and Social Media (ICWSM)*, 2010.

[563] Tye Rattenbury, Nathaniel Good, and Mor Naaman. Towards automatic extraction of event and place semantics from Flickr tags. In *Proceedings of SIGIR*, pages 103–110, 2007.

[564] Paul Resnick, Neophytos Iacovou, Mitesh Suchak, Peter Bergstrom, and John Riedl. GroupLens: An open architecture for collaborative filtering of NetNews. In *Proceedings of the 1994 ACM Conference on Computer Supported Cooperative Work, CSCW'94*, pages 175–186. New York, NY, ACM, 1994.

[565] Paul Resnick and Hal R. Varian. Recommender systems. *Communications of ACM*, 40(3):56–58, March 1997.

[566] Francesco Ricci, Lior Rokach, Bracha Shapira, and Paul B. Kantor, editors. *Recommender Systems Handbook*. Springer, 2011.

[567] E. Rich. User modeling via stereotypes. *Cognitive Science*, 3(4):329–354, 1979.

[568] E. Riloff and R. Jones. Learning dictionaries for information extraction by multilevel bootstrapping. In *Proceedings of the 16th National Conference on Artificial Intelligence*, pages 474–479, 1999.

[569] E. Riloff and J. Wiebe. Learning extraction patterns for subjective expressions. In *Proceedings of the 2003 Conference on Empirical Methods in Natural Language Processing*, pages 105–112. Morristown, NJ, Association for Computational Linguistics, 2003.

[570] E. Riloff, J. Wiebe, and T. Wilson. Learning subjective nouns using extraction pattern bootstrapping. In *Proceedings of the 7th Conference on Natural Language Learning at HLT-NAACL 2003*, pages 25–32. Morristown, NJ, Association for Computational Linguistics, 2003.

[571] Matei Ripeanu. Peer-to-peer architecture case study: Gnutella network. In *Proceedings of the IEEE International Conference on Peer-to-Peer Computing (P2P 2001)*, Linköping, Sweden, IEEE, August 2001.

[572] A. Ritter, S. Clark, Mausam, and O. Etzioni. Named entity recognition in tweets: An experimental study. In *Proceedings of Empirical Methods for Natural Language Processing (EMNLP)*, Edinburgh, UK, 2011.

[573] Stephen E. Robertson and Steve Walker. Some simple effective approximations to the 2-Poisson model for probabilistic weighted retrieval. In W. Bruce Croft and C. J. van Rijsbergen, editors, *SIGIR*, pages 232–241. ACM/Springer, 1994.

[574] J. Rocchio. Relevance feedback in information retrieval. In G. Salton editor, *The SMART Retrieval System*, pages 313–323. Englewood Cliffs, NJ, Prentice Hall, 1971.

[575] Quillian M. Ross. Semantic memory. In M. Minsky editor, *Semantic Information Processing*, pages 227–270.

[576] R. A. Rossi, L. K. McDowell, D. W. Aha, and J. Neville. Transforming graph data for statistical relational learning. *Journal of Artificial Intelligence Research*, 45:363–441, 2012.

[577] D. Rout, K. Bontcheva, and M. Hepple. Reliably evaluating summaries of Twitter timelines. In *Proceedings of the AAAI Symposium on Analyzing Microtext*, 2013.

[578] Tom Rowlands, David Hawking, and Ramesh Sankaranarayana. New-Web search with microblog annotations. In Michael Rappa, Paul Jones, Juliana Freire, and Soumen Chakrabarti, editors, *Proceedings of WWW*, pages 1293–1296. ACM, 2010.

[579] James Rucker and Marcos J. Polanco. Siteseer: Personalized navigation for the Web. *Communications of the ACM*, 40(3):73–75, 1997.

[580] J. A. Russell. A circumplex model of affect. *Journal of Personality and Social Psychology*, 39(6):1161–1178, 1980.

[581] R. Rzepka and K. Araki. What statistics could do for ethics? The idea of commonsense processing-based safety valve. In *AAAI Fall Symposium on Machine Ethics*, Technical report FS-05-06, pages 85–87, 2005.

[582] Cucerzan S. Large-scale named entity disambiguation based on Wikipedia data. In *Proceedings of the 2007 Joint Conference on Empirical Methods in Natural Language Processing and Computational Natural Language Learning (EMNLP-CoNLL)*, pages 708–716, 2007.

[583] S. Kulkarni, A. Singh, G. Ramakrishnan, and S. Chakrabarti. Collective annotation of Wikipedia entities in Web text. In *Proceedings of 15th ACM SIGKDD International Conference on Knowledge Discovery (KDD 2009)*, pages 457–465, 2009.

[584] H. Saggion, K. Bontcheva, and H. Cunningham. Robust generic and query-based summarisation. In *Proceedings of the European Chapter of Computational Linguistics (EACL), Research Notes and Demos*, 2003.

[585] Tetsuya Sakai, Daisuke Ishikawa, Noriko Kando, Yohei Seki, Kazuko Kuriyama, and Chin-Yew Lin. Using graded-relevance metrics for evaluating community QA answer selection. In *Proceedings of the 4th ACM International Conference on Web Search and Data Mining, WSDM'11*, pages 187–196, 2011.

[586] Ruslan Salakhutdinov, Andriy Mnih, and Geoffrey Hinton. Restricted Boltzmann machines for collaborative filtering. In *Proceedings of ICML*, pages 791–798, 2007.

[587] G. Salton, A. Wong, and C. S. Yang. A vector space model for automatic indexing. *Communications of the ACM*, 18(11):613–620, November 1975.

[588] A. Sanfeliu and K. S. Fu. A distance measure between attributed relational graphs for pattern recognition. *IEEE Transactions on Systems, Men and Cybernetics*, 13:353–363, 1983.

[589] Rodrygo L. T. Santos, Craig MacDonald, Richard McCreadie, Iadh Ounis, and Ian Soboroff. Information retrieval on the blogosphere. *Foundations and Trends in Information Retrieval*, 6(1):1–125, January 2012.

[590] Sunita Sarawagi. Information extraction. In *Foundations and Trends in Databases*, pages 261–377, 2007.

[591] T. B. Sardinha, J. L. Moreira Filho, and E. Alambert. The Brazilian corpus. In *Proceedings of American Association for Corpus Linguistics*, 2009.

[592] Luís Sarmento, Fabien Gouyon, and Eugénio Oliveira. Music artist tag propagation with Wikipedia abstracts. In *Workshop on Information Retrieval over Social Networks, European Conference on Information Retrieval*, Toulouse, France, 2009.

[593] Luis Sarmento and Valentin Jijkoun. "More like these": Growing entity classes from seeds. In *Proceedings of ACM 16th Conference on Information and Knowledge Management (CIKM 2007)*, pages 959–962, 2007.

[594] Badrul Sarwar, George Karypis, Joseph Konstan, and John Riedl. Item-based collaborative filtering recommendation algorithms. In *Proceedings of the 10th International Conference on World Wide Web, WWW'01*, pages 285–295. New York, NY, ACM, 2001.

[595] Y. Sasaki, H. Isozaki, H. Taira, T. Hirao, H. Kazawa, J. Suzuki, K. Kokuryo, and E. Maeda. SAIQA: A Japanese QA system based on a large-scale corpus [in Japanese]. *IPSJ SIG Notes*, 2001(86):77–82, 2001.

[596] A. Scharl and A. Weichselbraun. An automated approach to investigating the online media coverage of U.S. presidential elections. *Journal of Information Technology and Politics*, 5(1):121–132, 2008.

[597] Markus Schedl. *Automatically Extracting, Analyzing, and Visualizing Information on Music Artists from the World Wide Web*. PhD thesis, Johannes Kepler University Linz, Linz, Austria, 2008.

[598] Markus Schedl. #nowplaying Madonna: A large-scale evaluation on estimating similarities between music artists and between movies from microblogs. *Information Retrieval*, 15:183–217, 2012.

[599] Markus Schedl and David Hauger. Mining microblogs to infer music artist similarity and cultural listening patterns. In *Proceedings of Ad-MIRe*, Lyon, France, April 2012.

[600] Markus Schedl, Peter Knees, and Gerhard Widmer. A Web-based approach to assessing artist similarity using co-occurrences. In *Proceedings of CBMI*, Riga, Latvia, June 2005.

[601] Markus Schedl, Tim Pohle, Peter Knees, and Gerhard Widmer. Exploring the music similarity space on the Web. *ACM Transactions on Information Systems*, 29(3), July 2011.

[602] Markus Schedl, Tim Pohle, Noam Koenigstein, and Peter Knees. What's hot? Estimating country-specific artist popularity. In *Proceedings of ISMIR*, Utrecht, The Netherlands, August 2010.

[603] Markus Schedl, Cornelia Schiketanz, and Klaus Seyerlehner. Country of origin determination via Web mining techniques. In *Proceedings of IEEE ICME: AdMIRe*, Singapore, July 2010.

[604] Markus Schedl, Klaus Seyerlehner, Dominik Schnitzer, Gerhard Widmer, and Cornelia Schiketanz. Three Web-based heuristics to determine a person's or institution's country of origin. In *Proceedings of ACM SIGIR*, Geneva, Switzerland, July 2010.

[605] Markus Schedl, Sebastian Stober, Emilia Gómez, Nicola Orio, and Cynthia C. S. Liem. User-aware music retrieval. In Meinard Müller, Masataka Goto, and Markus Schedl, editors, *Multimodal Music Processing*, volume 3 of *Dagstuhl Follow-Ups*, pages 135–156. Schloss Dagstuhl–Leibniz-Zentrum fuer Informatik, Dagstuhl, Germany, 2012.

[606] Markus Schedl and Gerhard Widmer. Automatically detecting members and instrumentation of music bands via Web content mining. In *Proceedings of AMR*, Paris, France, July 2007.

[607] Markus Schedl, Gerhard Widmer, Peter Knees, and Tim Pohle. A music information system automatically generated via Web content mining techniques. *Information Processing and Management*, 47, 2011.

[608] Andrew I. Schein, Alexandrin Popescul, Lyle H. Ungar, and David M. Pennock. Methods and metrics for cold-start recommendations. In *Proceedings of the 25th Annual International ACM SIGIR Conference on Research and Development in Information Retrieval, SIGIR'02*, pages 253–260. New York, NY, ACM, 2002.

[609] L. Schietgat, F. Costa, J. Ramon, and L. De Raedt. Effective feature construction by maximum common subgraph sampling. *Machine Learning*, 83(2):137–161, 2011.

[610] Frank Schilder, Ravikumar Kondadadi, Jochen L. Leidner, and Jack G. Conrad. Thomson Reuters at TAC 2008: Aggressive filtering with fast-sum for update and opinion summarization. In *Proceedings of the 1st Text Analysis Conference (TAC 2008)*, pages 396–405, 2008.

[611] Dominik Schnitzer. *Indexing Content-Based Music Similarity Models for Fast Retrieval in Massive Databases*. PhD thesis, Johannes Kepler University Linz, Linz, Austria, 2011.

[612] Dominik Schnitzer, Tim Pohle, Peter Knees, and Gerhard Widmer. One-touch access to music on mobile devices. In *Proceedings of MUM*, Oulu, Finland, December 2007.

[613] A. Schrijver. A comparison of the Delsarte and Lovász bounds. *IEEE Transactions on Information Theory*, IT-25:425–429, 1979.

[614] Julia Schwarz and Meredith Morris. Augmenting Web pages and search results to support credibility assessment. In *Proceedings of the SIGCHI Conference on Human Factors in Computing Systems, CHI'11*, pages 1245–1254. New York, NY, ACM, 2011.

[615] Kazuhiro Seki, Yoshihiro Kino, Shohei Sato, and Kuniaki Uehara. TREC 2007 blog track experiments at Kobe University. In Voorhees and Buckland [689].

[616] Y. Seki, D. K. Evans, L.-W. Ku, H.-H. Chen, N. Kando, and C.-Y. Lin. Overview of opinion analysis pilot task at NTCIR-6. In *Proceedings of the 6th NTCIR Workshop Meeting on Evaluation of Information Access Technologies: Information Retrieval, Question-Answering and Cross-Lingual Information Access*, pages 265–278, 2007.

[617] Jangwon Seo and W. Bruce Croft. Blog site search using resource selection. In Shanahan et al. [622], pages 1053–1062.

[618] Xavier Serra. Data gathering for a culture specific approach in MIR. In *Proceedings of AdMIRe*, Lyon, France, April 2012.

[619] Glenn Shafer. *A Mathematical Theory of Evidence*. Princeton University Press, 1976.

[620] Azadeh Shakery and ChengXiang Zhai. A probabilistic relevance propagation model for hypertext retrieval. In *Proceedings of CIKM*, pages 550–558, 2006.

[621] D. A. Shamma, L. Kennedy, and E. F. Churchill. Tweetgeist: Can the Twitter timeline reveal the structure of broadcast events? In *Proceedings of CSCW 2010*, 2010.

[622] James G. Shanahan, Sihem Amer-Yahia, Ioana Manolescu, Yi Zhang, David A. Evans, Aleksander Kolcz, Key-Sun Choi, and Abdur Chowdhury, editors. *Proceedings of the 17th ACM Conference on Information and Knowledge Management, CIKM 2008*, Napa Valley, CA, October 26–30, 2008. ACM.

[623] Upendra Shardanand and Pattie Maes. Social information filtering: Algorithms for automating "word of mouth." In *Proceedings of the SIGCHI Conference on Human Factors in Computing Systems, CHI'95*, pages 210–217. New York, NY, ACM Press/Addison-Wesley Publishing Co., 1995.

[624] B. Sharifi, M. A. Hutton, and J. Kalita. Summarizing microblogs automatically. In *Human Language Technologies: The 2010 Annual Conference of the North American Chapter of the Association for Computational Linguistics*, pages 685–688, Los Angeles, CA, June 2010.

[625] Yuval Shavitt, Ela Weinsberg, and Udi Weinsberg. Building recommendation systems using peer-to-peer shared content. In *Proceedings of CIKM*, 2010.

[626] Yuval Shavitt, Ela Weinsberg, and Udi Weinsberg. Estimating peer similarity using distance of shared files. In *International Workshop on Peer-to-Peer Systems (IPTPS)*, 2010.

[627] Yuval Shavitt and Udi Weinsberg. Songs clustering using peer-to-peer co-occurrences. In *Proceedings of IEEE ISM: AdMIRe*, San Diego, CA, December 2009.

[628] S. Shen-Orr, R. Milo, S. Mangan, and U. Alon. Network motifs in the transcriptional regulation network of *Escherichia coli*. *Nature Genetics*, 31(1):64–68, 2002.

[629] Anna Shtok, Gideon Dror, Yoelle Maarek, and Idan Szpektor. Learning from the past: Answering new questions with past answers. In *Proceedings of the 21st International Conference on World Wide Web, WWW'12*, pages 759–768. New York, NY, ACM, 2012.

[630] Xin Shuai, Xiaozhong Liu, and Johan Bollen. Improving news ranking by community tweets. In Alain Mille, Fabien L. Gandon, Jacques Misselis, Michael Rabinovich, and Steffen Staab, editors, *Proceedings of WWW (Companion Volume)*, pages 1227–1232. ACM, 2012.

[631] Börkur Sigurbjörnsson and Roelof van Zwol. Flickr tag recommendation based on collective knowledge. In *Proceedings of the 17th International Conference on World Wide Web, WWW'08*, pages 327–336. New York, NY, ACM, 2008.

[632] Craig Silverstein, Hannes Marais, Monika Henzinger, and Michael Moricz. Analysis of a very large Web search engine query log. *SIGIR Forum*, 33(1):6–12, 1999.

[633] Fabrizio Silvestri. Mining query logs: Turning search usage data into knowledge. *Foundations and Trends in Information Retrieval*, 4(1–2):1–174, January 2010.

[634] R. F. Simmons. Answering English questions by computer: A survey. *Communications of the ACM*, 8(1):53–70, January 1965.

[635] Amit Singh. Entity-based translation language model. In *Proceedings of the 21st International Conference Companion on World Wide Web, WWW'12 Companion*, pages 599–600. New York, NY, ACM, 2012.

[636] John R. Smith and Shih-fu Chang. An image and video search engine for the World-Wide Web. In *Proceedings of SPIE Storage and Retrieval for Image and Video Databases*, pages 84–95, 1997.

[637] Eriks Sneiders. Automated FAQ answering: Continued experience with shallow language understanding. In *AAAI Fall Symposium on Question-Answering Systems*, 1999.

[638] Ian Soboroff, Arjen P. de Vries, and Nick Craswell. Overview of the TREC 2006 Enterprise track. In Voorhees and Buckland [688].

[639] X. Song, Y. Chi, K. Hino, and B. L. Tseng. Summarization system by identifying influential blogs. In *Proceedings of ICWSM*, pages 325–326, 2007.

[640] Young-In Song, Chin-Yew Lin, Yunbo Cao, and Hae-Chang Rim. Question utility: A novel static ranking of question search. In *National Conference on Artificial Intelligence*, pages 1231–1236, 2008.

[641] Mohamed Sordo. *Semantic Annotation of Music Collections: A Computational Approach.* PhD thesis, Universitat Pompeu Fabra, Barcelona, Spain, 2012.

[642] Mohamed Sordo, Òscar Celma, Martín Blech, and Enric Guaus. The quest for musical genres: Do the experts and the wisdom of crowds agree? In *Proceedings of ISMIR*, Philadelphia, PA, September 2008.

[643] Mohamed Sordo, Fabien Gouyon, and Luís Sarmento. A method for obtaining semantic facets of music tags. In *Proceedings of WOMRAD*, Barcelona, Spain, September 2010.

[644] I. Srdanović Erjavec, T. Erjavec, and A. Kilgarriff. A Web corpus and word sketches for Japanese. *Information and Media Technologies*, 3(3):529–551, 2008.

[645] Josef Steinberger, Mijail Kabadjov, Ralf Steinberger, Hristo Tanev, Marco Turchi, and Vanni Zavarella. JRCS participation at TAC 2011: Guided and multilingual summarization tasks. In *Proceedings of the Text Analysis Conference (TAC) 2011*, 2011.

[646] David H. Stern, Ralf Herbrich, and Thore Graepel. Matchbox: Large-scale online Bayesian recommendations. In *Proceedings of WWW*, pages 111–120, 2009.

[647] Michael Strube and Simone Paolo Ponzetto. Wikirelate! computing semantic relatedness using Wikipedia. In *Proceedings of the 21st National Conference on Artificial Intelligence—Volume 2, AAAI'06*, pages 1419–1424. AAAI Press, 2006.

[648] F. M. Suchanek, G. Ifrim, and G. Weikum. Combining linguistic and statistical analysis to extract relations from Web documents. In *Proceedings of KDD*, 2006.

[649] Fabian M. Suchanek, Gjergji Kasneci, and Gerhard Weikum. YAGO: A large ontology from Wikipedia and WordNet. *Elsevier Journal of Web Semantics*, 6(3), pages 203–217, 2008.

[650] Jian-Tao Sun, Hua-Jun Zeng, Huan Liu, Yuchang Lu, and Zheng Chen. CubeSVD: A novel approach to personalized Web search. In *Proceedings of WWW*, pages 382–390, 2005.

[651] Ke Sun, Yunbo Cao, Xinying Song, Young in Song, Xiaolong Wang, and Chin-Yew Lin. Learning to recommend questions based on user ratings. In *Proceedings of the International Conference on Information and Knowledge Management*, pages 751–758, 2009.

[652] Mihai Surdeanu, Massimiliano Ciaramita, and Hugo Zaragoza. Learning to rank answers on large online QA collections. In *Proceedings of ACL-08: HLT*, pages 719–727. Columbus, OH, ACL, June 2008.

[653] Maggy Anastasia Suryanto, Ee Peng Lim, Aixin Sun, and Roger H. L. Chiang. Quality-aware collaborative question-answering: Methods and evaluation. In *Proceedings of the 2nd ACM International Conference on Web Search and Data Mining, WSDM'09*, pages 142–151. New York, NY, ACM, 2009.

[654] Panagiotis Symeonidis, Maria Ruxanda, Alexandros Nanopoulos, and Yannis Manolopoulos. Ternary semantic analysis of social tags for personalized music recommendation. In *Proceedings of ISMIR*, Philadelphia, PA, September 2008.

[655] Gabor Szabo and Bernardo A. Huberman. Predicting the popularity of online content. *Communications of the ACM*, 53(8):80–88, August 2010.

[656] M. Taboada, J. Brooke, M. Tofiloski, K. Voll, and M. Stede. Lexicon-based methods for sentiment analysis. *Computational Linguistics*, 1(September 2010):1–41, 2011.

[657] Gábor Takács and Domonkos Tikk. Alternating least squares for personalized ranking. In *Proceedings of RecSys*, pages 83–90, 2012.

[658] H. Takamura, T. Inui, and M. Okumura. Latent variable models for semantic orientations of phrases. In *Proceedings of the 11th Conference of the European Chapter of the Association for Computational Linguistics*, pages 201–208, 2006.

[659] H. Takamura, T. Inui, and M. Okumura. Extracting semantic orientations of phrases from dictionary. In *Proceedings of the Human Language Technologies: The Annual Conference of the North American Chapter of the Association for Computational Linguistics*, Morristown, NJ, 2007. ACL.

[660] P. Talukdar. Weakly supervised acquisition of labeled class instances using graph. In *Proceedings of the 2008 Conference on EMNLP*, pages 582–590, 2008.

[661] Shulong Tan, Jiajun Bu, Chun Chen, Bin Xu, Can Wang, and Xiaofei He. Using rich social media information for music recommendation via hypergraph model. *ACM Transactions on Multimedia Computing, Communications, and Applications*, 7S(1), November 2011.

[662] Ke Tao, Fabian Abel, Claudia Hauff, and Geert-Jan Houben. Twinder: A search engine for Twitter streams. In Marco Brambilla, Takehiro Tokuda, and Robert Tolksdorf, editors, *ICWE*, volume 7387 of *Lecture Notes in Computer Science*, pages 153–168. Springer, 2012.

[663] Yla R. Tausczik and James W. Pennebaker. Predicting the perceived quality of online mathematics contributions from users' reputations. In *Proceedings of the 2011 Annual Conference on Human Factors in Computing Systems, CHI'11*, pages 1885–1888. New York, NY, ACM, 2011.

[664] Jaime Teevan, Susan T. Dumais, and Eric Horvitz. Characterizing the value of personalizing search. In *Proceedings of SIGIR*, pages 757–758, 2007.

[665] Jaime Teevan, Daniel Ramage, and Merredith Ringel Morris. #twittersearch: A comparison of microblog search and Web search. In *4th International Conference on Web Search and Data Mining*, pages 35–44, 2011.

[666] N. Tetsuji, I. Kentaro, and K Sadao. Dependency tree-based sentiment classification using CRFs with hidden variables. In *Proceedings of the Human Language Technologies: The Annual Conference of the North American Chapter of the Association for Computational Linguistics*, pages 786–794. Morristown, NJ, ACL, 2010.

[667] M. Thelwall, K. Buckley, G. Paltoglou, D. Cai, and A. Kappas. Sentiment strength detection in short informal text. *Journal of the American Society for Information Science and Technology*, 61(12):2544–2558, 2010.

[668] M. Thomas, B. Pang, and L. Lee. Get out the vote: Determining support or opposition from Congressional floor-debate transcripts. In *Proceedings of 2006 Conference on Empirical Methods in Natural Language Processing (EMNLP 2006)*, pages 327–335, 2006.

[669] Ivan Titov and Ryan Mcdonald. A joint model of text and aspect ratings for sentiment summarization. In *Proceedings of ACL-08: HLT*, pages 308–316, 2008.

[670] Mattia Tomasoni and Minlie Huang. Metadata-aware measures for answer summarization in community question-answering. In *Proceedings of the 48th Annual Meeting of the Association for Computational Linguistics*, pages 760–769, 2010.

[671] Hanghang Tong and Christos Faloutsos. Center-piece subgraphs: problem definition and fast solutions. In *KDD '06: Proceedings of the 12th ACM SIGKDD International Conference on Knowledge Discovery and Data Mining*, pages 404–413. New York, NY, ACM, 2006.

[672] B. K. Y. Tsou, R. W. M. Yuen, O. Y. Kwong, T. B. Y. Lai, and W. L. Wong. Polarity classification of celebrity coverage in the Chinese press. In *Proceedings of the International Conference on Intelligence Analysis*, 2005.

[673] C. E. Tsourakakis, M. N. Kolountzakis, and G. L. Miller. Triangle sparsifiers. *Journal of Graph Algorithms and Applications*, 15:703–726, 2011.

[674] Douglas Turnbull, Luke Barrington, David Torres, and Gert Lanckriet. Semantic annotation and retrieval of music and sound effects. *IEEE Transactions on Audio, Speech and Language Processing*, 16(2):467–476, 2008.

[675] Douglas Turnbull, Luke Barrington, Mehrdad Yazdani, and Gert Lanckriet. Combining audio content and social context for semantic music discovery. In *Proceedings of SIGIR*, Boston, MA, July 2009.

[676] Douglas Turnbull, Ruoran Liu, Luke Barrington, and Gert Lanckriet. Using games to collect semantic information about music. In *Proceedings of the 8th International Conference on Music Information Retrieval (ISMIR 2007)*, Vienna, Austria, September 2007.

[677] P. D. Turney. Thumbs up or thumbs down? Semantic orientation applied to unsupervised classification of reviews. In *Proceedings of the 40th Annual Meeting on Association for Computational Linguistics (ACL'02)*, pages 417–424, Morristown, NJ, July 2002.

[678] P. D. Turney and M. L. Littman. Unsupervised learning of semantic orientation from a hundred-billion-word corpus. Technical report ERB-1094, National Research Council Canada, Institute for Information Technology, 2002.

[679] P. D. Turney and M. L. Littman. Unsupervised learning of semantic orientation from a hundred-billion-word corpus. National Research Council, Institute for Information Technology, Technical report ERB-1094, (NRC #44929), 2002.

[680] J. R. Ullmann. An algorithm for subgraph isomorphism. *Journal of the ACM*, 23(1):31–42, 1976.

[681] Julián Urbano. Information retrieval meta-evaluation: Challenges and opportunities in the music domain. In *Proceedings of the 12th International Society for Music Information Retrieval Conference (ISMIR 2011)*, Miami, FL, October 2011.

[682] M. Utiyama and H. Isahara. Reliable measures for aligning Japanese–English news articles and sentences. In *Proceedings of ACL-2003*, pages 72–79, 2003.

[683] V. Vishnu, P. Patrick, and C. Eric. Helping editors choose better seed sets for entity set. In *Proceedings of CIKM*, pages 225–234, 2009.

[684] B. van Durme and M. Pasca. Finding cars, goddesses and enzymes: Parametrizable acquisition of labeled instances for open-domain information extraction. In *Proceedings of the 23rd AAAI Conference on Artificial Intelligence*, pages 1243–1248, 2008.

[685] Roelof van Zwol, Vanessa Murdock, Lluis Garcia Pueyo, and Georgina Ramírez. Diversifying image search with user generated content. In Michael S. Lew, Alberto Del Bimbo, and Erwin M. Bakker, editors, *Multimedia Information Retrieval*, pages 67–74. ACM, 2008.

[686] N. Vanetik, S. E. Shimony, and E. Gudes. Support measures for graph data. *Data Mining and Knowledge Discovery*, 13(2):243–260, 2006.

[687] Ellen Voorhees, Donna K. Harman, National Institute of Standards, and Technology (US). *TREC: Experiment and Evaluation in Information Retrieval*, volume 63. Cambridge, MA, MIT Press, 2005.

[688] Ellen M. Voorhees and Lori P. Buckland, editors. *Proceedings of the 15th Text Retrieval Conference, TREC 2006*, Special Publication 500-272. Gaithersburg, MD, National Institute of Standards and Technology (NIST), November 14–17, 2006.

[689] Ellen M. Voorhees and Lori P. Buckland, editors. *Proceedings of the 16th Text Retrieval Conference, TREC 2007*, Special Publication 500-274. Gaithersburg, MD, National Institute of Standards and Technology (NIST), November 5–9, 2007.

[690] Ellen M. Voorhees and Lori P. Buckland, editors. *Proceedings of the 17th Text Retrieval Conference, TREC 2008*, Special Publication 500-277. Gaithersburg, MD, National Institute of Standards and Technology (NIST), November 18–21, 2008.

[691] Spyros Voulgaris, Anne-Marie Kermarrec, Laurent Massoulié, and Maarten van Steen. Exploiting semantic proximity in peer-to-peer content searching. In *Proceedings of FTDCS*, China, May 2004.

[692] V. Vyas and P. Pantel. Semiautomatic entity set refinement. In *Proceedings of CIKM*, pages 290–298, 2009.

[693] W. Zhang, J. Su, Tan Chew Lim, and W. T. Wang. Entity linking leveraging automatically generated annotation. In *Proceedings of the 23rd International Conference on Computational Linguistics (COLING 2010)*, pages 1290–1298, 2010.

[694] Dingding Wang, Tao Li, and Mitsunori Ogihara. Are tags better than audio features? The effect of joint use of tags and audio content features for artistic style clustering. In *Proceedings of ISMIR*, August 2010.

[695] Jun Wang, Arjen P. de Vries, and Marcel J. T. Reinders. Unified relevance models for rating prediction in collaborative filtering. *ACM Transactions on Information Systems*, 26(3):16:1–16:42, June 2008.

[696] Kai Wang, Zhaoyan Ming, and Tat-Seng Chua. A syntactic tree matching approach to finding similar questions in community-based QA services. In *Proceedings of the 32nd International ACM SIGIR Conference on Research and Development in Information Retrieval, SIGIR'09*, pages 187–194. New York, NY, ACM, 2009.

[697] R. C. Wang and W. W. Cohen. Character-level analysis of semisupervised document for set expansion. In *Conference on Empirical Methods in Natural Language Processing*, pages 1503–1512, 2009.

[698] Richard C. Wang and William W. Cohen. Language-independent set expansion of named entities using the Web. In *Proceedings of ICDM*, pages 342–350, 2007.

[699] Richard C. Wang and William W. Cohen. Iterative set expansion of named entities using the Web. In *Proceedings of ICDM 2008*, pages 1091–1096, 2008.

[700] Richard C. Wang and William W. Cohen. Automatic set instance extraction using the Web. In *Proceedings of World Wild Web Conference (WWW 2009)*, 2009.

[701] Richard C. Wang, Nico Schlaefer, William W. Cohen, and Eric Nyberg. Automatic set expansion for list question-answering. In *Proceedings of EMNLP*, pages 947–954, 2008.

[702] Y. Wang and J. Ramon. An efficiently computable support measure for frequent subgraph pattern mining. In *Proceedings of ECML/PKDD 2012*, pages 362–379. Springer, 2012.

[703] Y. Wang, J. Ramon, and T. Fannes. An efficiently computable and statistically motivated subgraph pattern support measure. *Data Mining and Knowledge Discovery*, 2013. DOI 10.1007/s10618-013-0318-x.

[704] Stanley Wasserman and Katherine Faust. *Social Network Analysis: Methods and Applications*. Cambridge University Press, 1994.

[705] D. J. Watts and S. H. Strogatz. Collective dynamics of small-world networks. *Nature*, 393(6684):440–442, June 1998.

[706] Ingmar Weber and Carlos Castillo. The demographics of Web search. In *Proceedings of the 33rd International ACM SIGIR Conference on Research and Development in Information Retrieval, SIGIR'10*, pages 523–530. New York, NY, ACM, 2010.

[707] Wouter Weerkamp. *Finding People and Their Utterances in Social Media*. PhD thesis, University of Amsterdam, 2011.

[708] Wouter Weerkamp, Krisztian Balog, and Maarten de Rijke. Finding key bloggers, one post at a time. In Malik Ghallab, Constantine D. Spyropoulos, Nikos Fakotakis, and Nikolaos M. Avouris, editors, *ECAI*, volume 178 of *Frontiers in Artificial Intelligence and Applications*, pages 318–322. IOS Press, 2008.

[709] Wouter Weerkamp and Maarten de Rijke. Credibility improves topical blog post retrieval. In Kathleen McKeown, Johanna D. Moore, Simone Teufel, James Allan, and Sadaoki Furui, editors, *Proceedings of ACL*, pages 923–931. ACL, 2008.

[710] J. Y. Weng, C. L. Yang, B. N. Chen, Y. K. Wang, and S. D. Lin. IMASS: An intelligent microblog analysis and summarization system. In *Proceedings of the ACL-HLT 2011 System Demonstrations*, pages 133–138, Portland, OR, 2011.

[711] D. B. West. *An Introduction to Graph Theory*. Prentice Hall, 2001.

[712] Robert Wetzker, Winfried Umbrath, and Alan Said. A hybrid approach to item recommendation in folksonomies. In *Proceedings of the WSDM'09 Workshop on Exploiting Semantic Annotations in Information Retrieval, ESAIR'09*, pages 25–29. New York, NY, ACM, 2009.

[713] Robert Wetzker, Carsten Zimmermann, Christian Bauckhage, and Sahin Albayrak. I tag, you tag: Translating tags for advanced user models. In *Proceedings of the 3rd ACM International Conference on Web Search and Data Mining, WSDM'10*, pages 71–80. New York, NY, ACM, 2010.

[714] C. Whitelaw, N. Garg, and S. Argamon. Using appraisal groups for sentiment analysis. In *Proceedings of the 14th ACM International Conference on Information and Knowledge Management*, pages 625–631, 2005.

[715] Stewart Whiting, Iraklis A. Klampanos, and Joemon M. Jose. Temporal pseudo-relevance feedback in microblog retrieval. In Baeza-Yates et al. [40], pages 522–526.

[716] Brian Whitman and Steve Lawrence. Inferring descriptions and similarity for music from community metadata. In *Proceedings of ICMC*, Göteborg, Sweden, September 2002.

[717] J. Wiebe. Learning subjective adjectives from corpora. In *Proceedings of the 17th National Conference on Artificial Intelligence*, pages 735–740. Menlo Park, CA, AAAI Press, 2000.

[718] J. Wiebe, R. Bruce, M. Bell, M. Martin, and T. Wilson. A corpus study of evaluative and speculative language. In *Proceedings of the 2nd SIGdial Workshop on Discourse and Dialogue*, pages 1–10. Morristown, NJ, ACL, 2001.

[719] J. Wiebe, T. Wilson, R. Bruce, M. Bell, and M. Martin. Learning subjective language. *Computational Linguistics*, 30(3):277–308, 2004.

[720] J. Wiebe, T. Wilson, and C. Cardie. Annotating expressions of opinions and emotions in language. *Language Resources and Evaluation*, 39(2):165–210, 2005.

[721] J. Wiebe, T. Wilson, and C. Cardie. Annotating expressions of opinions and emotions in language. *Language Resources and Evaluation*, 39(2–3):165–210, 2005.

[722] T. Wilson, D. R. Pierce, and J. Wiebe. Identifying opinionated sentences. In *Proceedings of the 2003 Conference of the North American Chapter of the Association for Computational Linguistics on Human Language Technology*, pages 33–34. Morristown, NJ, Association for Computational Linguistics, 2003.

[723] T. Wilson and J. Wiebe. Annotating attributions and private states. In *Proceedings of the ACL Workshop on Frontiers in Corpus Annotation II*, pages 53–60, 2005.

[724] T. Wilson, J. Wiebe, and R. Hwa. Just how mad are you? Finding strong and weak opinion clauses. In *Proceedings of the 19th National Conference on Artificial Intelligence*, pages 761–769. Menlo Park, CA, AAAI Press, 2004.

[725] Fei Wu and Daniel S. Weld. Automatically semantifying Wikipedia. In *Proceedings of the 16th ACM Conference on Information and Knowledge Management*, pages 41–50, 2007.

[726] Fei Wu and Daniel S. Weld. Open information extraction using Wikipedia. In *Proceedings of Annual Meeting of the Association for Computational Linguistics*, 2010.

[727] Lei Wu, Linjun Yang, Nenghai Yu, and Xian-Sheng Hua. Learning to tag. In *Proceedings of the 18th International Conference on World Wide Web, WWW'09*, pages 361–370. New York, NY, ACM, 2009.

[728] W. Wu, B. Zhang, and M. Ostendorf. Automatic generation of personalized annotation tags for Twitter users. In *Human Language Technologies: The 2010 Annual Conference of the North American Chapter of the Association for Computational Linguistics*, pages 689–692, 2010.

[729] Xian Wu, Lei Zhang, and Yong Yu. Exploring social annotations for the semantic Web. In *Proceedings of WWW*, pages 417–426, 2006.

[730] Youzheng Wu, Jun Zhao, and Bo Xu. Chinese named entity recognition combining statistical model with human knowledge. In *Proceedings of the ACL Workshop on Multilingual and Mix-Language Named Entity Recognition: Combining Statistical and Symbolic Models*, pages 65–72, 2003.

[731] Youzheng Wu, Jun Zhao, and Bo Xu. Chinese named entity recognition model based on multiple features. In *Proceedings of Human Language Technology Conference and Conference on Empirical Methods in NLP (HLT/EMNLP)*, pages 427–434, 2005.

[732] Sacha Wunsch-Vincent and Graham Vickery. Participative Web: User-created content. Technical report, Directorate for Science, Technology and Industry: Committee for Information, Computer and Communications Policy, April 2007.

[733] Jianjun Xie, Scott Leishman, Liang Tian, David Lisuk, Seongjoon Koo, and Matthias Blume. Feature engineering in user's music preference prediction. *Journal of Machine Learning Research—Proceedings Track*, 18:183–197, 2012.

[734] W. Xin, Z. Jing, J. Jing, H. Yang, S. Palakorn, W. X. Zhao, J. Jiang, J. He, Y. Song, P. Achananuparp, E. P. Lim, and X. Li. Topical key-phrase extraction from Twitter. In *Proceedings of the 49th Annual Meeting of the Association for Computational Linguistics: Human Language Technologies, HLT'11*, pages 379–388, 2011.

[735] Shengliang Xu, Shenghua Bao, Yunbo Cao, and Yong Yu. Using social annotations to improve language model for information retrieval. In *Proceedings of CIKM*, pages 1003–1006, 2007.

[736] Shengliang Xu, Shenghua Bao, Ben Fei, Zhong Su, and Yong Yu. Exploring folksonomy for personalized search. In *Proceedings of SIGIR*, pages 155–162, 2008.

[737] Xiaobing Xue, Jiwoon Jeon, and W. Bruce Croft. Retrieval models for question and answer archives. In *Proceedings of the 31st Annual International ACM SIGIR Conference on Research and Development in Information Retrieval*, pages 475–482, 2008.

[738] Y. Zhou, L. Nie, O. Rouhani-Kalleh, F. Vasile, and S. Gaffney Resolving surface forms to Wikipedia topics. In *Proceedings of the 23rd International Conference on Computational Linguistics (COLING 2010)*, pages 1335–1343, 2010.

[739] M. Yahya, K. Berberich, S. Elbassuoni, M. Ramanath, V. Tresp, and G. Weikum. Natural language questions for the Web of data. In *Empirical Methods for Natural Language Processing*, pages 379–390, 2012.

[740] Rui Yan, Mirella Lapata, and Xiaoming Li. Tweet recommendation with graph co-ranking. In *Proceedings of the 50th Annual Meeting of the Association for Computational Linguistics*, pages 516–525, Jeju Island, Korea, 2012.

[741] X. Yan and J. Han. gSpan: Graph-based substructure pattern mining. In *Proceedings of the 2002 IEEE International Conference on Data Mining (ICDM 2002)*, pages 721–724, Japan, 2002. IEEE Computer Society.

[742] C. Yang, H. Gao, and S. Chen. Emotion trend analysis using blog corpora (in Chinese). In *Proceedings of the 19th Conference on Computational Linguistics and Speech Processing*, pages 205–218, 2007.

[743] Jiang Yang, Lada A. Adamic, and Mark S. Ackerman. Competing to share expertise: The TASKCN knowledge sharing community. In Adar et al. [10].

[744] K. Yang, N. Yu, and H. Zhang. WIDIT in TREC-2007 blog track: Combining lexicon-based methods to detect opinionated blogs. In *Proceedings of the 16th Text Retrieval Conference*, 2007.

[745] Lei Yang, Tao Sun, Ming Zhang, and Qiaozhu Mei. We know what @you #tag: Does the dual role affect hashtag adoption? In *Proceedings of the 21st International Conference on World Wide Web, WWW'12*, pages 261–270. New York, NY, ACM, 2012.

[746] Wen-Yun Yang, Yunbo Cao, and Chin-Yew Lin. A structural support vector method for extracting contexts and answers of questions from online forums. In *Empirical Methods in Natural Language Processing*, pages 514–523, 2009.

[747] Xiaoxin Yin and Wenzhao Tan. Semisupervised truth discovery. In *Proceedings of the 20th International Conference on World Wide Web, WWW'11*, pages 217–226. New York, NY, ACM, 2011.

[748] Kazuyoshi Yoshii, Masataka Goto, Kazunori Komatani, Tetsuya Ogata, and Hiroshi G. Okuno. An efficient hybrid music recommender system using an incrementally trainable probabilistic generative model. *IEEE Transactions on Audio, Speech, and Language Processing*, 16:435–447, 2008.

[749] Naoki Yoshinaga and Kentaro Torisawa. Finding specification pages according to attributes. In *Proceedings of the 15th International Conference on World Wide Web (WWW 2006)*, pages 1021–1022, 2007.

[750] Naoki Yoshinaga and Kentaro Torisawa. Open-domain attribute-value acquisition from semistructured texts. In *Proceedings of the Workshop of OntoLex07—From Text to Knowledge: The Lexicon/Ontology Interface Held at the 6th International Semantic Web Conference*, pages 55–66, 2007.

[751] H. Yu and V. Hatzivassiloglou. Towards answering opinion questions: Separating facts from opinions and identifying the polarity of opinion sentences. In *Proceedings of the 2003 Conference on Empirical Methods in Natural Language Processing*, pages 129–136, 2003.

[752] Jin Yu, Ehud Reiter, Jim Hunter, and Chris Mellish. Choosing the content of textual summaries of large time-series data sets. *Natural Language Engineering*, 13(1):25–49, March 2007.

[753] N. Yu. *Semisupervised Learning for Identifying Opinions in Web Content*. PhD thesis, Indiana University, 2011.

[754] N. Yu and S. Kübler. Semisupervised learning for opinion detection. In *Proceedings of the IEEE/WIC/ACM International Conference on Web Intelligence and Intelligent Agent Technology*, volume 3, pages 249–252, 2010.

[755] N. Yu and S. Kübler. Filling the gap: Semisupervised learning for opinion detection across domains. In *Proceedings of the 15th Conference on Computational Natural Language Learning*, pages 200–209, 2011.

[756] Ning Yu. Domain adaptation for opinion classification: A self-training approach. *Journal of Information Science Theory and Practice*, 1(1):10–26, 2013.

[757] Z. Zheng, F. Li, M. Huang, and X. Zhu. Learning to link entities with knowledge base. In *Proceedings of the 2010 Annual Conference of the North American Chapter of the ACL (NAACL 2010)*, 2010.

[758] Mark Zadel and Ichiro Fujinaga. Web services for music information retrieval. In *Proceedings of ISMIR*, Barcelona, Spain, October 2004.

[759] Matei A. Zaharia, Amit Chandel, Stefan Saroiu, and Srinivasan Keshav. Finding content in file-sharing networks when you can't even spell. In *Proceedings of IPTPS*, 2007.

[760] Omar F. Zaidan and Chris Callison-Burch. Crowdsourcing translation: Professional quality from nonprofessionals. In *Proceedings of the 49th Annual Meeting of the Association for Computational Linguistics: Human Language Technologies*, pages 1220–1229, 2011.

[761] Eva Zangerle, Wolfgang Gassler, and Günther Specht. Exploiting Twitter's collective knowledge for music recommendations. In *Proceedings of #MSM2012*, pages 14–17, Lyon, France, April 2012.

[762] F. Zanzotto, M. Pennaccchiotti, and K. Tsioutsiouliklis. Linguistic redundancy in Twitter. In *Proceedings of the 2011 Conference on Empirical Methods in Natural Language Processing*, pages 659–669. Edinburgh, UK, ACL, 2011.

[763] ChengXiang Zhai and John Lafferty. A study of smoothing methods for language models applied to ad hoc information retrieval. In *Proceedings of the 24th Annual International ACM SIGIR Conference on Research and Development in Information Retrieval, SIGIR'01*, pages 334–342. New York, NY, ACM, 2001.

[764] Jun Zhang, Mark S. Ackerman, and Lada Adamic. Expertise networks in online communities: Structure and algorithms. In *Proceedings of the 16th International Conference on World Wide Web, WWW'07*, pages 221–230. New York, NY, ACM, 2007.

[765] L. Zhang, J. A. Barnden, R. J. Hendley, and A. M. Wallington. Exploitation in affect detection in open-ended improvisational text. In *Proceedings of Workshop on Sentiment and Subjectivity in Text*, pages 47–54. Morristown, NJ, ACL, 2006.

[766] M. Zhang, J. Zhang, J. Su, and G. Zhou. A composite kernel to extract relations between entities with both flat and structured features. In *Proceedings of ACL*, pages 825–832, 2006.

[767] W. Zhang and C. Yu. UIC at TREC 2007 blog track. In *Proceedings of the 16th Text Retrieval Conference*, 2007.

[768] Z. Zhang. Weakly supervised relation classification for information extraction. In *Proceedings of the 13th Conference of Information and Knowledge Management*, pages 581–588, 2004.

[769] W. X. Zhao, J. Jiang, J. Weng, J. He, E. Lim, H. Yan, and X. Li. Comparing Twitter and traditional media using topic models. In *Proceedings of the 33rd European Conference on Advances in Information Retrieval (ECIR)*, pages 338–349, 2011.

[770] Elena Zheleva, John Guiver, Eduarda Mendes Rodrigues, and Nataša Milić-Frayling. Statistical models of music-listening sessions in social media. In *Proceedings of WWW*, pages 1019–1028, 2010.

[771] Elena Zheleva, Alek Kolcz, and Lise Getoor. Trusting spam reporters: A reporter-based reputation system for e-mail filtering. *ACM Transactions on Information Systems*, 27(1), 2008.

[772] R. Zheng, J. Li, H. Chen, and Z. Huang. A framework for authorship identification of online messages: Writing-style features and classification techniques. *Journal of the American Society for Information Science and Technology*, 57(3):378–393, 2006.

[773] Ding Zhou, Jiang Bian, Shuyi Zheng, Hongyuan Zha, and C. Lee Giles. Exploring social annotations for information retrieval. In *Proceedings of WWW*, pages 715–724, 2008.

[774] Ding Zhou, Jiang Bian, Shuyi Zheng, Hongyuan Zha, and C. Lee Giles. Exploring social annotations for information retrieval. In Jinpeng Huai, Robin Chen, Hsiao-Wuen Hon, Yunhao Liu, Wei-Ying Ma, Andrew Tomkins, and Xiaodong Zhang, editors, *Proceedings of WWW*, pages 715–724. ACM, 2008.

[775] G. Zhou, H. Joshi, and C. Bayrak. Topic categorization for relevancy and opinion detection. In *Proceedings of the 16th Text Retrieval Conference*, 2007.

[776] Guangyou Zhou, Li Cai, Jun Zhao, and Kang Liu. Phrase-based translation model for question retrieval in community question answer archives. In *Proceedings of ACL*, pages 653–662, 2011.

[777] Liang Zhou and Eduard Hovy. On the summarization of dynamically introduced information: Online discussions and blogs. In *Proceedings of AAAI Symposium on Computational Approaches to Analysing Weblogs (AAAI-CAAW)*, pages 237–242, 2006.

[778] Mianwei Zhou, Shenghua Bao, Xian Wu, and Yong Yu. An unsupervised model for exploring hierarchical semantics from social annotations. In *Proceedings of ISWC/ASWC*, pages 680–693, 2007.

[779] Y. Zhou and M. Li. Semisupervised regression with co-training. In *Proceedings of the 19th International Joint Conference on Artificial Intelligence*, pages 908–913, 2005.

[780] Jun Zhu, Zaiqing Nie, Ji-Rong Wen, Bo Zhang, and Wei-Ying Ma. Simultaneous record detection and attribute labeling in Web data extraction. In *Proceedings of KDD*, pages 494–503, 2006.

[781] X. Zhu. Semisupervised learning literature survey. Technical report 1530, Department of Computer Sciences, University of Wisconsin, Madison, 2008.

[782] A. Zimmermann and L. De Raedt. Corclass: Correlated association rule mining for classification. In *Proceedings of the 7th International Conference on Discovery Science*, pages 60–72. Springer, 2004.

[783] Justin Zobel and Alistair Moffat. Inverted files for text search engines. *ACM Computing Surveys*, 38(2), July 2006.

[784] Arkaitz Zubiaga, Damiano Spina, Enrique Amigó, and Julio Gonzalo. Towards real-time summarization of scheduled events from Twitter streams. *CoRR*, abs/1204.3731, 2012.

Index

Printed and bound by CPI Group (UK) Ltd, Croydon, CR0 4YY

23/10/2024

01777700-0002